Library of
Dickinson College

Poindexter of Washington

A STUDY IN PROGRESSIVE POLITICS

By Howard W. Allen

SOUTHERN ILLINOIS UNIVERSITY PRESS
Carbondale and Edwardsville

923.2
P751a

Copyright © 1981 by
Southern Illinois University Press

All rights reserved

Printed in the United States of America

Designed by Design for Publishing

Library of Congress Cataloging in Publication Data

Allen, Howard W 1931–
Poindexter of Washington.

Includes bibliographical references and index.
1. Poindexter, Miles, 1868–1946. 2. United
States—Politics and government—1865–1933.
3. Progressivism (United States Politics)
4. Washington (State)—Politics and government—
1889–1950. 5. Legislators—United States—Biography. 6. United States. Congress. Biography.
I. Title.
E748.P68A44   1981   328.73′092′4 [B]   80-20123
ISBN 0-8093-0952-1

To my parents
Omar E. and Helen Wilson Allen

Contents

	List of Tables	ix
	Introduction	xi
1.	Early Years	1
2.	The Emergence of a Progressive Reformer	13
3.	A Hero of Insurgency	33
4.	A Senate Insurgent	59
5.	The New Freedom	85
6.	Foreign Affairs: A Progressive "Realist"	119
7.	Return to the Republican Party	142
8.	World War I: Disruption of the Progressive Coalition	170
9.	The Struggle Against Internationalism and Bolshevism	200
10.	A Harding Republican	226
11.	The Final Years	256
	Notes	271
	Index	317

List of Tables

1. House Insurgents and the Payne-Aldrich Tariff   39
2. Party Loyalty Scores in the Sixty-first Congress of Republican Members of the House   48
3. Underwood Tariff. Voting on Selected Farm and Lumber Products   89
4. Underwood Tariff. Voting on Selected Manufactured Products and Raw Materials   90
5. Vote on Selected War Measures   198
6. Fordney-McCumber Tariff. Voting on Selected Farm and Lumber Products   243
7. Fordney-McCumber Tariff. Voting on Selected Manufactured Products and Raw Materials   244

Introduction

MILES POINDEXTER from the state of Washington was one of the more outspoken and aggressive members of the progressive Republican bloc in Congress from the time of his first election to the House of Representatives in 1908 to the beginning of World War I in 1917. At the time, he received considerable attention in the press, and after his election to the Senate in 1910 he was probably as closely identified with the reform movement in Congress by the national press as any of the progressive Republicans except Robert M. LaFollette of Wisconsin. Poindexter's reputation as a leading progressive Republican among historians of the Progressive era has not of course equaled LaFollette's, and in many of the histories of the Progressive era Poindexter's name is not mentioned at all. His relative obscurity can be explained in part by the fact that he served only two terms in the Senate—he was defeated for reelection in 1922, while LaFollette, Borah of Idaho, and Norris of Nebraska served many years in Congress before and after Poindexter's defeat. At any rate, Poindexter did not serve long enough to accumulate seniority and to acquire the power and visibility which usually accompany seniority, and his role in the Congress during the Progressive era has passed by, relatively unnoticed.

xii   Introduction

   Poindexter's reputation as a prominent Senate progressive also suffered because, unlike LaFollette, Norris, and Borah, he abandoned a progressive stance after 1917 and shifted to the right during World War I and the Red Scare of 1919 and 1920. He became, indeed, even more vitriolic and intolerant in his denunciation of labor unions, Socialists, pacifists, and "Bolsheviks" after 1917 than in his attacks upon the trusts, "special interests," and their alleged defenders in the Congress in the prewar years. A shift to the right was a pattern of political behavior commonly found in the years of war and postwar adjustment during Woodrow Wilson's second term, and it is reasonable to speculate that Theodore Roosevelt, who died before his position on postwar issues was made clear, and Poindexter were both moving in the same conservative direction. In any case, Poindexter's abandonment of reform and his turn against many of his former progressive colleagues after the war, combined with his retirement from the Senate in 1923, probably served to obscure his earlier reputation as a leading Senate progressive.
   This study of Poindexter's career in Congress will attempt to describe and analyze the Washington senator's role in the United States Congress, during its most productive years prior to the early Congresses of Franklin D. Roosevelt's administration and, to the extent that evidence will permit, to explain how he became a progressive reformer and how he abandoned reform to become a conservative Harding Republican. Like most biographies, this one rests primarily upon an examination of manuscript sources. The Miles Poindexter collection, the principal manuscript source, is very rich in the years in which Poindexter was in Congress, although rather thin before 1909 and after 1923, and it is most valuable for a study of his political career. Unlike most biographies, this study attempts to support generalizations about Poindexter's base of mass support in the electorate of the state of Washington and to identify and analyze comparatively his voting record in Congress with quantitative data. The examination of county voting data in the state of Washington presented here uses only elementary methods and should be taken only as a first

step in the analysis of voting behavior in the state of Washington. The results, nonetheless, are most useful in explaining Poindexter's public stance on many important issues and his rise and fall as a senator from Washington. The quantitative analysis of the voting record in Congress is more intensive, especially for the years 1909 to 1915, and is used to identify the voting patterns in Congress and to establish Poindexter's position on the issues, relative to other members of the Congress. The combined use of quantitative and manuscript sources is intended to produce a study in the political behavior of a politician, not a personal or "humanistic" biography.

This study began as a doctoral dissertation many years ago under the direction of Thomas J. Pressly at the University of Washington. Professor Pressly's intellectual influence on my work has been profound. His willingness to devote hours of his time and energy to grapple with my early drafts, furthermore, far exceeded the normal obligations of a mentor, and his kind and thoughtful criticism and advice represent the highest form of graduate teaching. Robert E. Burke's willingness to share his encyclopedic knowledge of twentieth-century political history and his perceptive suggestions concerning this manuscript also were immensely helpful, and Walter Johnson deserves special thanks for first stimulating my interest in the study of American politics and for reading and commenting on the original manuscript. Dewey W. Grantham's comments and criticisms were most useful, and my sincere thanks as well to the anonymous readers of the original manuscript. Over the years I have learned much about the study of politics, and many other things, from my good friend and collaborator Jerome M. Clubb, and long conversations with Michael Batinski have clarified my thinking on this and other projects. I wish to acknowledge financial support for the completion of this study from the American Philosophical Society and the Office of Research Development and Administration at Southern Illinois University; computer time and consultation were provided by the Office of Academic Computing, Southern Illinois University. My greatest debt, however, is to my wife, Kay Warren Allen, who has contributed to this study as critic, research assistant, proofreader, and typist, while at the same time shouldering more than her share of caring for Mark, Robin, and Laura. The shortcomings of my work, of course, are my own responsibility.

Howard W. Allen

Southern Illinois University
Carbondale
June 16, 1980

Poindexter of Washington

1.

Early Years

MILES POINDEXTER spent most of his life before he was twenty-three years old near Lexington, Virginia, but he was born in Tennessee in 1868. He was always very proud of his family ties to Virginia, and he believed he could trace his father's descendants back to "an ancient and gentle line in the Island of Jersey."[1] His first Poindexter descendant in Virginia was George Poindexter who immigrated to America, the family thought, in the mid-seventeenth century, and Miles apparently shared his brother's belief that the family descended "from a line of blue-blooded ancestry down here in Virginia as long as the James River."[2]

Miles's father, William B. Poindexter, the son of George B. and Frances Hubbard Bowyer Poindexter, was born in 1835. William B. Poindexter attended Judge Brockenbrough's Lexington Law School, later to become Washington and Lee University Law School, periodically from 1855 to 1860, but probably he did not complete the course of study and there is no indication that he ever practiced law. On April 18, 1861, just six days after the firing on Fort Sumter, William B. enlisted in the Confederate Army at the rank of corporal to serve in Company C, 1st Virginia Cavalry. He apparently participated in the Battle of Bull Run, and later in 1861 he was wounded while on picket duty. According to his son Fielding's account, William participated in many other military engagements toward the end of the Civil War and was captured at the war's end. When hostilities ceased in 1865 William B. was twenty-nine years old and penniless, his property destroyed by the war.[3] After the war he sold insurance in Arkansas and later recalled that he had worked as "a general agent for Southern Life Ins. Co." and had "a tremendous business."[4]

William Poindexter returned to Virginia in 1867 to marry Josephine Anderson, daughter of Judge Francis T. and Mary A. Anderson; she accompanied him back to Arkansas. Miles, their first son, was born on April 22, 1868 in Memphis, Tennessee. In 1871 William returned with his family to Virginia where they settled down to a life of farming in a new home built by his father-in-law in the Shenandoah valley on "Glenwood," his wife's family estate. Judge Anderson apparently gave the property to the young Poindexters as a wedding gift, and they lived there the remainder of their lives. To this marriage were born five sons, Miles, George Fauntleroy, Fielding, Ernest, and William, and one daughter, Mary.[5]

It was apparent that William B. Poindexter lived under the shadow of the more successful Anderson family. The land he farmed had been given to him and his wife by her father, and his wife's brother, William A. Anderson, managed "Glenwood." William Poindexter did not provide the money to send Miles to college; this, too, came from his wife's inheritance and was administered by her brother. Miles's father apparently dabbled in politics, and in 1901 he ran unsuccessfully for the state legislature, but from all indications his living was eked from the land. He seemed content to bask in the glory of the military exploits of his youth. He told one of his sons in 1902 that he "had rather be a soldier than anything else"; and in 1907 he wrote enthusiastically of viewing the unveiling of a statue of General J. E. B. Stuart whom, William said, "I followed from the beginning of hostilities to the time of his death."[6] William loved the outdoors and riding, hunting, and fishing, and in 1899 he informed Fielding that "there will be plenty of birds to shoot this fall." Fielding observed in 1899 that his father "is 64, but he thinks this does not make any difference when it comes to riding fine horses." William's reference in 1905 to the years after the war when he sold insurance in Arkansas as a time when "everyone looked up to me" suggested that he was aware of his inferior status in the family. Miles may have had his own father in mind when he wrote in 1915 that "many" of the Virginia Poindexters "became wealthy planters and influential people in that state," but others, he said, "have been subject to the vicissitudes of war and the existence of fortune and the weaknesses of human nature, which have affected them like all families."[7]

Miles Poindexter's maternal grandfather, Francis T. Anderson, was a man of high distinction in his community. He was educated at Washington College, later Washington and Lee University, and admitted to the Virginia bar in 1830. He became a prominent lawyer in Lexington, served as a member of the Virginia House of Delegates, was a member of the Electoral College in 1861, and from 1870 to 1872 served as judge of the Supreme Court of Appeals of Virginia. Judge Anderson was an elder in the Presbyterian church and for many years served as rector of Washington and Lee University. His brother, General Joseph Reid Anderson (1813-92), was a brigadier general in the Confederate army and the founder and president of the famous Tredegar Iron Works of Richmond, Virginia.[8]

Little is known about Miles's mother, Josephine Anderson Poindexter. She was born on November 5, 1838, and in 1912 her husband William described her as "not demonstrative." In an essay written in memory of his mother, Fielding Poindexter stated that she was "a great reader . . . and a talented musician," and he remembered that she frequently looked to her father and her brother "as examples for her own sons; and to their influence she doubtless attributed in some degree the success and distinction achieved by her eldest son, Miles."[9]

Josephine Poindexter's brother, William A. Anderson, known as "Uncle Willie" to Miles and his brothers, was the most imposing man in Miles's early life. Anderson served in the Confederate infantry at the beginning of the Civil War; but after receiving a serious wound at the first Battle of

Bull Run, he left the army and attended Washington College. He took a degree in law from the University of Virginia in 1866 and served as a member of the Virginia state legislature and as attorney general of the state of Virginia from 1902 to 1910. In 1885 he became a trustee of Washington and Lee University and its rector in 1914. A county historian who interviewed him after World War I called him "a Virginia gentleman of the old school."[10]

William A. Anderson's successful career contrasted sharply with William B. Poindexter's very modest achievements, and Anderson did not hesitate on occasion to criticize his brother-in-law's family. "Uncle Willie" complained to Miles in 1899 that seven years before he had provided Miles's father with a plot of ground to farm which "with fairly good management could be made to yield a profit of from $60 to $120 per year," in addition to a forty-dollar monthly rent from a house on the property. If "it had been properly cultivated and managed," he declared, it would have provided "for the whole family." But, he concluded in disgust, two of Miles's brothers "actually tore down part of the . . . house. They did it they said to build an ice house. . . . The ice house was a failure." Miles's brother Fielding recognized the contrast between his father and "Uncle Willie" in a letter to Miles in 1908. Fielding recalled some words of advice that Miles had given him, and added half in jest, "Uncle Willie would have said: 'Fielding's just like his father. He sits up till 12 o'clock because he's too lazy to go to bed.' In the enclosing [sic] sentence of your letter you encourage me to take advantage of opportunities for healthful outdoor sports. Uncle Willie would say: All they think about is pleasure. Their father before them spent his life seeking pleasure. No wonder he failed."[11]

From his father Miles probably acquired his enthusiasm for hunting and outdoor sports and, perhaps, his appreciation of the natural beauty of Virginia. It was an area where a boy could easily experience the exhilaration of dropping a bobwhite with the family shotgun or the excitement of catching a bass in nearby Elk Creek, and Poindexter sometimes dreamed of returning to Virginia to stay, long after he moved to the state of Washington. He confided to his brother Fauntleroy's wife in 1902 that he had "always regarded youall as especially fortunate in having a comfortable house in such a beautiful and healthful country, the most attractive place in the world to me." He added, "It is certainly worth something to anyone to be able to remain in the house of his father." He still held, he wrote, "a vague hope that someday I might settle down comfortably on a farm in Rockbridge [County] at Glenwood and do my work there."[12] And, indeed, after Poindexter retired he returned to Glenwood where he lived the last years of his life.

On the other hand, Miles seemed to have acquired most of his personal traits from his mother's family. He displayed the ambition, energy, and seriousness of his uncle, William A. Anderson, and except for the time spent hunting and fishing, Poindexter had little time for frivolous amusements. He had a puritanical dedication to hard work, no sense of humor, and he was intensely aggressive, even combative, as if he were driven to overcome his father's lack of success and to match the notable achievements of the Andersons and the greatness of his Poindexter ancestors. One boyhood chum recalled in 1912, "You have been a wonder to me since when I was nine years old, you showed me that you could catch more mud-cats from Wood's Creek in five minutes than I could in an hour." Another old friend remembered when "you spit on my floor, and we scrapped over it."[13] As time would tell, Poindexter was a scrapper. His public career was stormy, characterized by fierce moralistic onslaughts upon the forces of evil, and he assailed his public enemies with the zest of one convinced of his own righteousness.

Miles, in fact, spent a large part of his early life living with his grandfather Anderson in Lexington, Virginia, near his "Uncle Willie," where he attended Fancy Hill Academy, a private school, and later, in the family tradition, Washington and Lee University. He first enrolled at Washington and Lee on September 20, 1883 at the age of fifteen. Miles stayed in college for two years, until 1885, took a traditional nineteenth-century curriculum, and distinguished himself in English and Rhetoric.

He dropped out of school for five years but later returned to Washington and Lee to complete the law degree in 1891. His law school grades were above average, and he was honored for achievement in several fields of law and awarded the orator's medal for the class of 1891.[14]

Upon graduation from law school, Poindexter, at the age of twenty-three, left Virginia for the West. He located first in Walla Walla, Washington. No explanation for his choice of location is found in his papers, but his son believed that Miles's mother had insisted that he go to Portland, Oregon, since she had relatives living there. On the way Miles stopped off at Walla Walla to work in the wheat harvest to replenish his exhausted finances; he liked Walla Walla and decided to stay. While reasons for his choice of location remain uncertain, Poindexter's actions, once he settled there, leave little doubt that he had moved to the West to seek a career in politics. Less than one year after arriving, on August 6, 1892, the twenty-four-year-old lawyer delivered a speech at a Democratic rally, and a week later he was nominated by the Walla Walla County Democratic convention for the office of County Prosecutor. Eighteen ninety-two was a year of Populist protest in eastern Washington politics and a good year for Democrats, and Poindexter defeated the Republican candidate with a vote of 1,449 to 1,281. Two years later Poindexter ran for reelection as a Democrat and lost, and he evidently did not run for a political office again during the years he lived in Walla Walla.[15]

Poindexter found the Pacific Northwest a most suitable spot to hunt and fish, and he spent the limited leisure time he allowed himself in the nearby wilderness of southeastern Washington. Apparently while he was still in Walla Walla in the early 1890s he tried unsuccessfully to publish an article in *Forest and Stream* about bass fishing in Elk Creek near the family home in Virginia, and he also tried to publish an historical novel written in the tradition of Sir Walter Scott. The young Virginian also seems to have enjoyed a social life in Walla Walla, because it was here that he met his wife, Elizabeth Page, a descendant of an early Northwest pioneer, Joseph Gale. Her father was

Thomas Page of Walla Walla. Elizabeth had attended St. Paul's Episcopal School for Girls and was a member of the Episcopal church. Miles and Elizabeth were married in June 1892, and their only child, Gale Aylette Poindexter was born on June 16, 1894.[16]

At the time of Poindexter's arrival in Washington most of the state's population was concentrated on Puget Sound where lumber production, coal mining, railroad building, and great expectations had attracted 42,837 people to Seattle and 36,006 to Tacoma by 1890. The communities on Puget Sound were separated from their hinterland by the Cascade Mountains that ranged south from Canada to Oregon forming a formidable barrier to transportation between the Sound and eastern Washington that was not overcome until the Northern Pacific broke through the Cascades and terminated its line at Tacoma in the early 1880s.[17] That portion of Washington east of the Cascades remained largely undeveloped until after the coming of the transcontinental railroads, but the region developed a vigorous mining and agricultural economy as quickly as rail transportation became available. The eastern half of Washington was well suited to the production of wheat, particularly the southeastern counties where Adams, Columbia, Lincoln, Spokane, Walla Walla, and Whitman counties each produced over one million bushels of wheat in 1899. Whitman County, just south of Spokane, alone produced over six million bushels of wheat in 1899, and in 1909 it was said to be one of the richest farm counties in the United States.[18]

During Poindexter's years in Walla Walla, Washington and the nation were in the grip of the depression of the 1890s. Eastern Washington farmers, seriously hurt by low wheat prices and the generally disastrous impact of the depression, joined many other farmers in the West and South to support the People's or Populist party. The Populists favored the federal ownership of railroads, warehouses, and grain elevators, postal savings banks, a graduated income tax, the direct election of United States senators and other political reforms, and an inflationary scheme, the free coinage of silver. Even though Washington, in its brief history as a state, was "normally" Republican, Populist sentiment was strong there throughout the 1890s.

In the presidential election of 1892 the Republican Benjamin Harrison carried Washington, but James B. Weaver, the Populist nominee, polled almost 22 percent of the popular vote and finished second in the balloting in six of the thirty-five Washington counties.[19]

The strength of Populism in Washington reflected serious economic difficulties in the state. In 1890 it was the sixth most heavily mortgaged farm state in the nation—26.8 percent of all farms in the state were mortgaged, and the import price of wheat at Liverpool, where most of the Northwest's crop was sold, declined even more disastrously between 1891 and 1894. Washington farmers and businessmen, moreover, were deeply dissatisfied with the monopolistic power which the railroads enjoyed and especially with railroad rates which to them seemed too high, and they were unhappy that some of the most valuable land in the state had been granted to the railroads by the federal government.[20] Farm discontent in Washington gained momentum after the election of 1892, and in 1896 at a convention in Ellensburg, Washington Populists, Democrats, and some Republicans (who were attracted to Bryan because he advocated the free coinage of silver) agreed upon a fusion ticket endorsing Bryan's nomination and the nomination of J. R. Rogers as the fusionist candidate for governor. Although he was defeated nationally by the Republican William McKinley, Bryan carried Washington with 57 percent of the total vote; and Rogers was elected governor.[21]

The heaviest majorities for Bryan in Washington came from Poindexter's section, the eastern counties, particularly the wheat counties and Stevens County, the center of the state's silver and gold mining located directly north of Spokane. Bryan's lowest percentages were cast in the southwestern part of the state, along the Columbia River and the Pacific Coast, and he carried the central counties including King (Seattle) and Pierce (Tacoma) with moderate-sized majorities. This sectional pattern—the eastern Washington counties firmly in support of the reform candidate, the southwestern counties as firmly opposed to the reform candidate, and the heavily populated central counties somewhere in the middle—was a voting pattern to appear many times after 1896 in Washington's elections, and it was a political phenomenon which would figure heavily in the political career of Miles Poindexter.

Within a year after the election of 1896, Poindexter had made two major changes in his life. He left Walla Walla to move to Spokane, and at about the same time he joined the Republican party. His move to Spokane reflected in part a recognition of the emerging significance of Spokane to the area east of the Cascades. Spokane had been a town of only 350 people in 1880 when the first Northern Pacific train arrived, but by 1900 the town had mushroomed into a community of 36,848. Spokane's growth was closely related to the direct connection which the railroads gave it to Puget Sound and to the East, but its growth was also stimulated by the construction of branch lines from Spokane to such towns as Pullman in Whitman County and to Moscow and Lewiston, Idaho. These taproots into the hinterland brought to Spokane wheat and cattle from the west and south and silver, lead, and other mining products from Stevens County to the north and from the Coeur d'Alene country of the Idaho panhandle. Over the same routes from Spokane flowed tools, equipment, and the comforts of life to the wheat farmers and the miners. Spokane provided the economic, social, and cultural activities for the area; and it frequently provided the most talented and attractive political leadership. It was this latter service that Miles Poindexter aspired to provide his new neighbors.[22]

Poindexter was probably encouraged to move to Spokane by his wife's brother-in-law, Robert Lewis Rutter, who was by 1896 a prominent young banker in Spokane. Rutter had graduated from the University of Pennsylvania in 1886 with a degree in mechanical engineering, and, after leaving college, he worked first in his father's business in Pennsylvania and then moved West. For a short time he lived in Walla Walla where he married Elizabeth Poindexter's sister, Isabel Page, and later he moved to Spokane where he opened a bank. Soon afterward he was invited to join the Spokane and Eastern Trust Company which had been founded in 1890; in 1916 he became president of that bank, and he held that position until his retirement in 1931. Rutter was a leader in the organization of the Western Union Life Insurance Company, incorporated in 1906, and served as its first president. In 1928 he sold his control of this firm for almost three million dollars. Rutter became one of Poindexter's few lifelong friends, and in 1896 he was in a position to assure Poindexter of legal business with the Spokane and Eastern Trust Company and to introduce the young Virginian to influential Spokane businessmen, politicians, and leading citizens.[23]

Poindexter's decision to become a Republican was made at the same time he moved to Spokane. Less than a year after his arrival in Spokane, on July 25, 1898, he announced his candidacy as a Republican for the office of County Prosecutor, the same position he had held in 1893-94 in Walla Walla. Poindexter later (in 1910) explained his decision to change parties in 1896 as a move motivated by his aversion to William Jennings Bryan and the Populist-dominated Democratic party in Washington: "I think . . . if you had been here in 1896 when the old democracy was swallowed up in populism, free silver, single tax and fusion, you would have probably been one [a Republican] yourself. At any rate I supported Wm. McKinley, and in the issues since . . . have found my alignment consistent with my former beliefs."[24] This explanation offered many years afterward is supported indirectly by a letter to Poindexter from his brother, Ernest, written in 1898. In the late 1890s Ernest practiced law in Walla Walla, and apparently he supported Republican candidates in this period. Probably he reflected his elder brother's views when he wrote Miles on November 25, 1898 of the election campaign just concluded. "After my trip east," he said, "I saw a great deal to be lost by this fusionist element." He claimed that he had helped to bring "the best element of the old Democratic party with us over to the Republicans," and in doing so, wrote Ernest, "I took the stand for what I believed was just and right."[25] Poindexter's critics were to charge in later years that he had become a Republican in order to succeed in politics in a Republican state. This charge probably had some truth to it, for certainly Poindexter was politically ambitious, and a change of parties must have seemed essential to him.

Democrats had not done well in Washington until 1896, and though Spokane supported Bryan in that year, it had done so through Republican leadership.

Poindexter's conversion to Republicanism, like his decision to relocate in Spokane, may also have been influenced by R. L. Rutter who was a Republican. In 1896 when Poindexter recalled that he left the Democratic party to avoid supporting the Populists and Bryan, ironically, Rutter actually played a major role in carrying Spokane County for Bryan. Rutter was a prominent figure in the Spokane Businessmen's Bimetallic Club for Bryan, a group dominated by Republicans, which joined enthusiastically with the neighboring wheat farmers in the crusade for Bryan. The prospect of a boom promised by Bryan's crusade for the free coinage of silver was too alluring to resist in the frontier, boomtown atmosphere that seemed to characterize Spokane in the late 1890s. The Businessmen's Bimetallic Club campaign for Bryan was supported warmly by the town's major newspaper, the *Spokesman-Review*, owned and edited by W. H. Cowles, and it worked for Bryan and the free coinage of silver throughout the campaign.[26]

The *Spokesman-Review* and most Spokane businessmen were also in complete accord with Bryan, the Democrats, and the Populists on the issue of railroad regulation. Business interests in Spokane had been involved since the early 1890s in a dispute with the transcontinental railroads especially over freight rate policy. The railroads charged Tacoma and Seattle on Puget Sound lower rates than Spokane to compete with cheap water transportation at these points. As a result, according to the *Review*, Seattle and Tacoma businessmen imported goods from Chicago at a rate sufficiently lower than the Spokane-to-Chicago rate to enable them to return the goods to eastern Washington and undersell Spokane businessmen. In March 1896, Cowles's editorials in the *Review* complained of this situation by pointing out that the Trail Creek mining district, which had been a Spokane market, was now dominated by Seattle merchants. "How the coast jobbers can ship goods 400 miles further, right through Spokane and into territory right at Spokane's doors and undersell the jobbers of that place seems impossible." The "abuses" of the railroads "have been . . . grave, and the need of relief . . . pressing," was the judgment of the *Review*. The election of 1896 brought no end to the dissatisfaction with railroads, however, and it was the railroad rate issue more than any other which seemed throughout the early years of the twentieth century to stimulate in Spokane and eastern Washington a continuous demand for federal regulation of the "trusts."[27]

The nomination for county prosecutor which Poindexter sought in 1898 from the Spokane Republican party went to another candidate, Judge J. Z. Moore, who was elected, but there must have been an understanding between Moore and Poindexter. After Moore's election, he appointed Poindexter to his staff as deputy prosecuting attorney. Thus just before the twentieth century began, Miles Poindexter at the age of thirty successfully established himself as an officeholder in the majority party in the commercial and transportation center of eastern Washington. His relationship with his brother-in-law R. L. Rutter was almost certainly instrumental in this rather impressive achievement, and Poindexter was, for the first time since his arrival in Washington almost ten years before, in a strong position to launch a successful political career.

2.

The Emergence of a Progressive Reformer

THE PERSONAL and political activities of Miles Poindexter in the years between 1898 when he took up his first position as a Republican officeholder in Spokane and 1908 when he was elected to the House of Representatives by the voters of eastern Washington provide important clues which help explain how Poindexter emerged as a leader of the insurgent Republican movement in eastern Washington. In these years he developed important personal and political friends; he became a member of the Spokane business and professional "establishment"; and he accumulated modest but yet substantial financial assets. In his first decade as a resident of Spokane, in short, Poindexter achieved social status and recognition as a community leader within the governing elite that dominated the town of Spokane.

Poindexter's appointment as deputy prosecutor was a major step in the advancement of his political career, and in this position he developed friendships and associations that would be of major assistance to him in the years to come. Most important among these new friends was Horace Kimball. Judge Moore appointed Kimball to serve along with Poindexter as deputy prosecuting attorney in 1898. Kimball was born in Indiana, but he had been educated at the University of Virginia and had come to Spokane in 1892 from Arkansas where he had been in law practice with his father. Kimball had practiced law and had worked in the Spokane Republican party for several years before he met Poindexter, and in 1898 he became secretary of the Republican county committee. Like Poindexter, Kimball was an ardent fisherman and hunter, and in later years he would share Poindexter's deep admiration of Theodore Roosevelt. The two lawyers, in short, had much in common, and they soon became trusted friends, business, and, above all else, political associates.[1]

After working together two years in the county attorney's office, Poindexter and Kimball were nominated for county office in 1900 by the Republican county convention. Poindexter was selected to run for judge of the Superior Court of Spokane and Stevens counties and Kimball to replace Judge Moore as county attorney.[2] The election of 1900 in Washington indicated that the state had returned to the Republican column, though by a very narrow margin. McKinley carried the state with almost 52 percent of the vote, and the entire Republican slate was elected in Spokane County. Poindexter, however, lost Stevens County and hence his election. In Stevens County the Populist influence apparently still predominated, and the entire Democratic slate there was elected by a heavy majority.[3]

As the prosecuting attorney after 1900, Kimball kept Poindexter on as a deputy prosecuting attorney. The work was demanding; the financial rewards slight Poindexter complained in 1902 that the job "has largely cut off . . . side business and compelled me to get along on the small salary of the office itself," and on many occasions in letters to friends and clients he apologized for neglecting to write because of "press of business" or because "I have been in court constantly for some time." But, if the job was demanding and paid very little, it had its rewards. Poindexter, himself, admitted in 1902 that "it has given me an extensive acquaintance in the county," and "I am getting pretty firmly established."[4] Such was the prerequisite to future political success.

A second political ally who contributed in a very crucial way to Poindexter's early success was W. H. Cowles, the powerful editor of the *Spokesman-Review*. Cowles had become editor of the *Spokesman-Review* in 1893 and immediately had inaugurated a vigorous crusade, typical of urban "middle-class" progressive reform elsewhere, to drive graft, dishonesty, and immorality from Spokane. Under Cowles's personal leadership, the *Review* had "joined hands with the law-abiding element" to rid Spokane of the "frontier-type of amusement resorts" to make it a "clean" town. In this "clean" city crusade the *Review* claimed the support of the local ministers "and the city's business and professional men generally," and it aimed to close the saloons on Sunday and to stop the practice then commonly found in the local saloons and the "variety theaters" of maintaining "wine rooms and private boxes" with couches for the use of the customers.[5] Although a Republican, Cowles and his paper vigorously supported the local businessmen in their effort to elect Bryan in 1896. He was an enthusiastic advocate of the war against Spain in 1898, and in the pages of the *Review* he supported the annexation of the Philippine Islands. In the election of 1900 his *Review* abandoned Bryan to endorse William McKinley, Theodore Roosevelt, and the Republican party.[6]

Poindexter's political activities in 1901 and 1902 were confined to personal contacts and party work; and although he did not run for office himself, he took an active part in the 1902 campaign. He was thanked for his efforts by the Republican county chairman, D. T. Ham, who noted, "Many fine compliments have been sent me in your behalf." There are other indications that his political star was on the rise after 1900. Congressman Francis W. Cushman of Seattle took considerable pains—including two trips to the White House—to get one of Poindexter's brothers, Fielding, a commission in the army. Ernest Poindexter was informed, when he applied to Senator A. G. Foster of Washington for a position on the Federal Board of Pensions, that all letters of recommendation he could get from Washington would be useful "and particularly letters from the friends of your brother who is prominent in Republican ranks and works in Spokane." The number of requests for Poindexter's endorsements for political appointments seemed more frequent after 1900.[7]

Encouraged by his rapid acceptance in Republican circles in Spokane, Poindexter rashly announced his candidacy for governor of the state in the fall of

1903! The move seemed premature, perhaps even unwise. Poindexter was still unknown outside Spokane and probably not that well established even in his own county. He claimed at one point that he and his supporters would "have the county convention our way without trouble."[8] But his efforts to win the endorsement of major state politicians, including two political leaders usually identified as "pro-railroad" Republicans, U.S. Senator Levi Ankeny and Samuel Piles, a Seattle railroad attorney who was later elected to the Senate, failed. The hopelessness of this effort became apparent fairly soon, and Poindexter withdrew his candidacy for governor to accept instead the Republican nomination for the office of judge of the Superior Court of Spokane and Stevens counties, the same position he had run for unsuccessfully in 1900. The year 1904, however, was a good time to run on the Republican ticket, for Theodore Roosevelt was the party's nominee for the presidency, and he swept Washington and the nation in a landslide victory. Poindexter carried Stevens County as well as Spokane and was elected. His victory was not so overwhelming as Roosevelt's but satisfying nonetheless.[9]

Poindexter's first decade in Spokane also brought him financial security and status in the community. R. L. Rutter and the Spokane and Eastern Trust Company figured considerably in Poindexter's quick success in Spokane. As early as January 28, 1898, only a few months after he had arrived in Spokane, he was asked by an acquaintance if a position could be obtained "through your connection with the Spokane and Eastern Trust Company." Two letters from Rutter to Poindexter written early in 1899 indicate more positively that Rutter was channeling the bank's legal business to Poindexter. He pointed out that the legal fee the bank paid per mortgage foreclosure was twenty-five dollars, and he continued, "We have given you all our mortgages since we put the Williams Note and Mortgage in your hands. . . . We do not want to be understood as being bound to give you all our foreclosures but as long as we do give you all foreclosures we will expect the same rate to prevail." Rutter evidently passed other business Poindexter's way, for in April 1899 Poindexter received a request to handle the local affairs of the Banker's Commercial League which used "attorneys recommended very highly by local banks." Rutter gave Poindexter a year's subscription to *Success* magazine for Christmas in 1901 and observed, "It must be gratifying to you to look back upon the ten years within the borders of this state and to note how you have grown in strength of mind and finance. . . . Thinking that 'Birds of a feather flock together' is my excuse for sending you the Success Magazine."[10]

Aside from his legal activities, Poindexter also dabbled in a variety of business ventures in which he evidently did well. While Ernest Poindexter was in Walla Walla the two brothers invested in a mining company called the Columbia River Gold, Silver and Lead Mining Company. It was incorporated in 1898 with Ernest as president and Miles as legal counsel. This venture did not prosper, for Ernest left Walla Walla soon afterward, and Miles found investments in real estate more attractive. He retained ownership of a house in Walla Walla, for example, until 1902 when he tried to sell it, and as late as March 1902 he owned two additional lots in Walla Walla.[11]

After his move from Walla Walla Poindexter purchased a modest little home at 924 Indiana Avenue and a "ranch" north of town on the Little Spokane River which apparently produced an income, and he kept a cow in Spokane which was milked by banker Rutter for several weeks in 1899 while Poindexter represented the county in a case before the United States Supreme Court. Then in 1905 he began to lay plans for the construction of a building in the downtown area, which when completed was valued at $9,000 by the architect.[12]

Indications of Poindexter's rise in status and influence in his community are abundant. His election to the superior court is one, and there are others. For a time he served as a member of the board of trustees of St. Agnes' Mission; and he was a leader in the Episcopal church in Spokane, a member of the board of education for Houston School, and a member of the Spokane Country Club. He was one of the principal speakers at an important Republican meeting, the Scandinavian-Republican Club's banquet in October 1906. He was requested, in February 1907, by the debating council of the University of Idaho to serve as a judge during a debate between the University of Idaho and the University of Oregon, and in that same month he was asked to judge a debate between two high schools in eastern Washington. Poindexter was one of a few city leaders asked by W. H. Cowles in November 1907, to write a short Thanksgiving essay for the *Review*, and he was elected president of the Spokane Southern Society in 1908 and shortly thereafter was asked to speak at the annual banquet of the Dairymen's Association.[13]

Hard work and ambition consumed most of Poindexter's energies as he endeavored to establish himself in Spokane. He often worked late and arrived home for the evening meal at irregular hours. Life around him was always a bustle of activity. Sunday dinners in Spokane were often taken with the Rutters, and even on Sunday when the two were together business frequently intervened. Seldom was a meal eaten when the phone did not ring at least once for either Rutter or Poindexter.[14]

Poindexter was not demonstrative in expressing his personal feelings, and his letters are almost totally devoid of self-description, criticism, or any form of introspection. Self-doubt, insecurity, affection, or disappointment were rarely, if ever, revealed in a lifetime of voluminous correspondence. Miles's wife, Elizabeth, on occasion expressed concern over her husband's inattentiveness. "Lizzie," as she was called, wrote of how "we miss you very much indeed" and added, "while you are never very talkative at night, without you this house seems very lonely indeed." She frequently chided him for his negligence in writing and once while vacationing at a resort in 1903 "Lizzie" sarcastically thanked him for having written. "I was anxious to know how you were getting on and then too all the women asked me each morning if I did not hear from my husband." In 1905 she prodded him to write with a letter of exaggerated formality, addressing him a "My Dear 'Judge,'" and in another letter in 1907 she declared, after waiting much too long for news from him, "I thought possibly you had forgotten you had a family."[15]

Though Elizabeth Poindexter sometimes worried at his strenuous activity, Poindexter could hardly have lived any other way. He had a great joy for the game of politics; he enjoyed the backslapping, the speech making, and the negotiating. At the drop of a hat he was ready to give a speech, and while living in Spokane he was called upon annually to give "patriotic" orations at Fourth of July celebrations. Poindexter's son recalled that his father was a popular and effective orator, and an observer in 1919 agreed: "Poindexter is a good campaigner. . . . He does not possess any graces of oratory, but he hammers away with great earnestness at whatever subject he tackles." He made up for his "personal magnetism" with "his downright methods of attack."[16]

In physical appearance Poindexter was over six feet tall and "slender—painfully slender." Early in life he developed a receding hairline, but later his gray hair combined with his fashionable and meticulous dress helped contribute to a dignified, senatorial image. His sober, staid appearance was only natural to "a serious man" who was "little given to jest and a poor hand at subtlety." His voice was noticeably loud, and "He can make himself heard in any hall in the United States." This voice and a loud, booming laugh, often characteristic of persons ill at ease in small groups, and formal and quiet around the house, became his trademark.[17]

The family in Virginia, as well as his wife and son, demanded help and attention, and Poindexter responded with exceptional generosity and patience. He obviously harbored unusually strong feelings of responsibility for the Virginia Poindexters. Before 1900 three of his brothers, Ernest, Fielding, and Willie, came to Walla Walla to find success under the guidance of their eldest brother; and evidently they cost him considerable anxiety and expenditure of time and money at a time of economic depression and when Miles was straining himself to the utmost to acquire property and establish himself in politics.

Willie stayed in Washington only a short time and Fielding, with Miles's congratulations, joined the Oregon volunteers when the Spanish-American War broke out in 1898. Ernest, also a lawyer, stayed on for some time in Walla Walla. He was not successful, and Miles tried to help by giving him a commission to manage the property in Walla Walla.[18] As Miles indicated to Ernest, he gave willingly and often to the family in Virginia. His father and his brothers seemed in frequent financial difficulty in those years, and they apparently depended heavily upon the financial aid of "Uncle Willie" Anderson and Miles. "Uncle Willie" did not hesitate to criticize his brother-in-law's family, but Miles usually reacted with extraordinary patience and tolerance to his family's problems and failures, and at some personal sacrifice. For many years he sent money when it was needed and in general evidenced a strong sense of responsibility for his father's family.[19]

The first decade Poindexter lived in Spokane coincided with the early years of the Progressive era. In these years diverse urban, state, and national reform groups, in response to the rapid industrial and social change which transformed the United States into an industrial nation in the late nineteenth and early twentieth centuries, proposed an array of reforms intended to solve some of the problems of industrialization. Some reform groups seemed most concerned with eradicating alleged corruption and special privilege from government by promoting such measures as the secret ballot, voter registration laws, and the popular election of United States senators, and others stressed the need for state and federal regulation of big business and the national banking system. In major urban areas some political leaders and social workers sought to find solutions to problems created by immigration, rapid population growth, and the factory system. The objectives and values of these groups differed sharply, but probably most could have agreed that President Theodore Roosevelt was their national leader. Roosevelt joined the fight to promote federal regulation of the railroads in 1902 by instituting an antitrust suit against the Northern Securities Company; in 1905 and 1906 he was active in the passage of the Hepburn Act which increased the Interstate Commerce Commission's power to regulate railroads; and during 1907 and 1908 his administration instituted antitrust suits against the "Sugar Trust," the American Tobacco Company, and Standard Oil. Roosevelt also voiced his approval of such measures as the income tax, a postal savings bank, and a pure-food law; and he was especially outspoken in his opposition to corruption and special favors in government.[20] Most Republicans in Congress, however, reacted with little enthusiasm or with outright opposition to Roosevelt's proposals. In the House of Representatives many of Roosevelt's proposals were blocked by the Speaker, Joseph Cannon of Illinois. Cannon used the rules of the House to dominate that body, and toward the end of Roosevelt's second term the Speaker's obstructive tactics stimulated a growing resentment among progressive Republicans against his leadership.[21]

In the state of Washington there seemed to be little difference between the reform efforts of the Populists of the early 1890s and the work of the progressives after 1896, and the geographical or sectional pattern of support for reform candidates in Washington remained consistent throughout Poindexter's years in politics. The strongest popular support for Populist and fusionist candidates and for the Democratic presidential nominee William Jennings Bryan in 1896 was in Spokane County and the agrarian, wheat producing counties of eastern Washington. The eastern Washington counties remained somewhat more Democratic than the rest of the state for many years after the Populist era, and the voters of the eastern counties also showed a somewhat stronger inclination to support reform candidates, although the majority of voters in the state over the years of Poindexter's career usually supported reform candidates too. But the support for reform in eastern Washington was stronger, and in the years between the 1890s and the 1920s those counties usually led the state in support of reformers of a variety of political labels: Populists, fusionists, Democrats, Republicans, and Progressives.

The persistence of this sectional pattern in the county election returns in Washington will be discussed again later in this study, but illustration of the pattern can be seen by examining the distribution of the county election data cast in 1900 and 1904. In the presidential elections of 1900 and 1904 the Democrats were strongest in eastern Washington counties where Bryan and the fusionist candidate for governor in 1896 had been strongest.

Bryan was the Democratic nominee again in 1900, although he failed to carry the state by a narrow margin; but in 1904 Bryan was replaced by Alton B. Parker and the sectional distribution remained essentially the same, but weaker since Parker lost Washington badly. Theodore Roosevelt, the Republican nominee in 1904, was a very attractive candidate to the voters of Washington, and he carried every county in the state. His margin of victory in the eastern Washington counties, however, was less than in the counties west of the mountains. In the gubernatorial race in 1904 the sectional pattern emerged more starkly. The Democratic nominee, George Turner, a former silver Republican and fusionist, lost to the Republican Albert Mead but only by a very slim margin, and Turner ran strongest in the counties of eastern Washington where Bryan had been strongest in 1896 and 1900. Most eastern Washington counties thus cast their majorities in 1904 for reform candidates, for a "trust-busting" Republican for president and a Democratic candidate who apparently symbolized the Populist tradition for governor. There is no evidence to show that Poindexter consciously recognized the significance of this pattern of voting in eastern Washington, but not long after the election of 1904 he became for the first time publicly identified with progressive reform causes.[22]

During the years immediately following the election of 1904, as Poindexter sat on the bench of the superior court, the sentiment in favor of progressive reform in Washington began to achieve results. The state legislature established a railroad regulatory commission, a tax commission, and a juvenile court, and it passed a child labor bill, and a measure designed to prohibit the granting of free railroad passes to public officials. A Direct Primary League was organized in 1906 in Seattle; and in 1907 the League, supported by the *Seattle Post-Intelligencer*, the American Federation of Labor, and the Washington State Grange helped persuade the legislature to enact a direct primary law and a law which apportioned the state into congressional districts. A bill providing for the initiative and referendum passed the lower house only to meet defeat in the senate, but still it seemed as if the entire state had absorbed the reforming zeal of Spokane and eastern Washington.[23]

In the same years that President Roosevelt took up the cause of progressive reform and the state legislature in Washington enacted a package of progressive legislation, Poindexter began to participate in campaigns for reform in Spokane. In the summer of 1905, in his capacity as judge of the superior court, he convened a grand jury to investigate corruption in local politics. Shortly thereafter he became a member of the 150,000 Club, which was associated with the Spokane Chamber of Commerce. This group proposed to attract to Spokane a population of 150,000 by 1910 by aiding the city in its fight against the railroads and by promoting general civic improvements. In addition, Poindexter became one of the Spokane advocates of a juvenile court modeled on the work of the well-known Judge Ben Lindsey of Denver, Colorado.

The first indication that Judge Poindexter would convene a grand jury to investigate charges of corruption in local government appeared in the *Review* in early June 1905, just a few months after the judge had taken up his duties. No doubt Poindexter had consulted privately on the matter with editor Cowles, for the *Spokesman-Review* provided both ample publicity and enthusiastic support of Poindexter's investigation. The *Review* predicted that the jury would be called "to investigate alleged crookedness and grafting in city and county affairs," charges that had been made about the use of free passes by the railroad to influence the Board of County Commissioners, alleged graft in the purchase of property by the city, and alleged bribery of city councilmen by companies seeking street car franchises. Poindexter's call for a grand jury became official on June 11; it was summoned to convene on July 10.[24]

As time for the meeting of the grand jury approached, noted the *Review*, "Some nervousness is . . . manifest." Slot machines were being "turned to the wall," and many feared an inquiry into the practice of assessing county employees for campaign expenses. The *Review*'s advanced information was reliable, for in July during a sweltering heat wave the county assessor, the county treasurer, the sheriff, and other local officials appeared before Poindexter's grand jury to answer questions about campaign assessments and special favors given to business by county officials. Personal tax records were subpoenaed and examined, reported the *Review*, particularly those from "wealthy men . . . who are under suspicion of having made a false return."[25] When the hearings ended in August, the *Review* gave Judge Poindexter's charge to the jury considerable attention. Both the jurors and the crowd in the courtroom, declared the *Review*, were "profoundly impressed." The grand jury eventually brought indictments against the county clerk and county treasurer, and the hearings ended.[26] Poindexter had brought political graft to the bar of justice and achieved a very favorable rating by the *Review*.

Poindexter's participation in the activities of the 150,000 Club was another illustration of his association with a reform effort led by the *Review* and leading businessmen, and it also indicated his acceptance by the business elite of Spokane. The club was essentially an effort to foster Spokane's economic progress, but it also intended to reform Spokane in a manner not unlike campaigns which could be observed at the same time in some eastern cities. It proposed to secure a population of 150,000 by 1910 through "systematic advertising of the city to attract manufacturers, investors, businessmen, and the development of our suburban territory." Dues were one dollar per year, and Poindexter probably first became a member in September 1905. One of the first campaigns of the club was to cooperate with the Chamber of Commerce to organize a "City Beautiful" committee. R. L. Rutter participated in this effort and so did Poindexter.[27] In November 1906 the club brought a nationally known Republican progressive, Senator Robert LaFollette of Wisconsin, to Spokane to speak. LaFollette spoke to an overflow crowd at the Spokane theater where he discussed his efforts in the Senate to strengthen the Hepburn Act, President Roosevelt's railroad bill—an issue of no small significance to the members of the 150,000 Club.[28]

Poindexter's association with the juvenile court idea developed out of his judicial duties, and again he was apparently encouraged in his efforts by W. H. Cowles and the *Spokesman-Review*. The juvenile court idea became popular during the Progressive era as an attempt to treat the problem of juvenile delinquency and was identified nationally with the work of Judge Lindsey. In January 1905 the *Review* pointed to the need for a juvenile court in Washington and maintained that young offenders should be treated separately from adult criminals because "evil associations corrupt good morals." Not long afterward the state legislature provided for the establishment of such a court, and it was put into operation as a responsibility of the superior court in June 1905.29 Poindexter was not responsible for the new court until 1907, when he became the director of juvenile court in Spokane County and became identified with a local effort to establish a parental school to cope with youthful offenders of the law. He joined a committee formed by the Board of Education, the 150,000 Club, and Associated Charities "to urge the necessity of . . . a Parental School upon the County Board of Commissioners." In April 1908 Poindexter was invited to attend a lecture by Judge Lindsey, who had been brought to Spokane by the 150,000 Club, and in all probability he attended. Several months before, however, he had announced his intention to run for eastern Washington's seat in the House of Representatives and had severed his connection with the juvenile court.30

The time was ripe to act, for in late 1907 it became known that the popular Congressman Wesley F. Jones of Yakima intended to vacate his seat in the House of Representatives to contend for Levi Ankeny's seat in the United States Senate. The situation was even more attractive to Poindexter since the state legislature had recently assigned Jones's seat to the newly created third congressional district in eastern Washington. Spokane, with its large population, was in a position to elect one of its citizens to Jones's place if it could unite on a single candidate. The Republican nominee would not be selected by a party convention, as in years past, because of the new direct primary law; and a victory in the Republican primary was tantamount to election. Soon several candidates were in the fray.31

Poindexter set the tone for his campaign at a "mass meeting" of the Spokane County Republican League which met at the Masonic Temple in early

January 1908. He "raised applause," according to the *Review*, when he affirmed his conviction that the Republican convention would select a presidential candidate who would "carry out the Roosevelt policies," and he discussed at length the need for greater efforts to reduce freight rates and to stimulate irrigation. Later that same month at a public meeting in Spokane called by a "citizens'" committee to consider the problem of securing more street crossings from the Northern Pacific railroad, Poindexter, although not a scheduled speaker, joined in the discussion from the floor. He generated, according to the *Review*, "marked enthusiasm." A few days later he published a long letter on the railroad problem in the *Review*. "The city has control of the entire situation," he declared, "by means of its undoubted right to make reasonable regulations of railroad operation in the city"; and he placed himself squarely in opposition "to any plan . . . which contemplates an enlargement of heavy railroad traffic through the heart of the business district of the city." Poindexter did not publicly announce his candidacy for the House, however, until early April when the *Review* reported that a Poindexter Club had been formed at a meeting in Horace Kimball's office. It was announced that this group was to be the nucleus of a much larger group which would canvass the city and the entire congressional district on Poindexter's behalf. Those present included Kimball, R. L. Rutter, O. C. Moore, a friend of Poindexter's and a lawyer, Judge J. Z. Moore, and probably W. H. Cowles. Rufus Woods, editor of the *Wenatchee World*, also was an early member of Poindexter's organization, although it is not clear exactly when Woods became Poindexter's friend and supporter. In any case Woods, who was one of the first promoters of the construction of Grand Coulee Dam, was an enthusiastic progressive and, in the years to come, one of the most influential Poindexter boosters in central Washington. Through the members of this group, said the *Review*, efforts were to be made to win the support of the legal and business community of Spokane and eastern Washington.[32]

Poindexter's close relationship to the business community was emphasized in a letter which went out from his headquarters on April 20. It claimed that

The Emergence of a Progressive Reformer 27

Poindexter "is being supported by a great many of the [illegible] business houses in Spokane, and a great many of the oldest and strongest businessmen who feal [sic] that it is necessary to elect men . . . who will further the interests of the Inland Empire in every way possible." The letter went on to say that Poindexter "has pledged himself to fight first, last and all the time for fair and just freight rates for the Inland Empire" and, that "he is free from all connections with Trusts and Monopolies."[33] Other appeals for support also laid heavy emphasis upon Poindexter's independence from "Trusts and Monopolies." One pointed out that "Judge Poindexter is not tied up by any corporation interests nor by other interests, except the interest and welfare of our people at large." Another asserted that "heretofore we have never had a man in Congress who represents the interests of the farmer and the country merchant of Eastern Washington, and we certainly feel in Judge Poindexter we will have a man that will represent all the citizens in all the interests of the Inland Empire, and not the railroad interests."[34]

The primary election took place on September 8. Poindexter won the nomination against a field of six candidates with 29 percent of the first-choice votes. (At this time the primary law in Washington provided that each voter indicate his first and second choice.) He carried Spokane and five other counties while his leading opponent, State Representative Lee Johnson, carried nine counties but received only 23 percent of the vote. Poindexter's large plurality in Spokane was obviously a critical factor in his victory.[35]

After a short rest in September, Poindexter began his campaign for the November election by emphasizing his identification with the progressive policies of Theodore Roosevelt. He informed a reporter from the *Review* that during the October campaign he would "give considerable attention to the question of the Roosevelt policies and the manner in which they can best be perpetuated." In his opinion, "the big contest in this campaign is between the progressives and the reactionaries." and he charged that the reactionaries were in "secret league with Standard Oil and other gigantic combinations of capital" who seek to thwart the completion of Roosevelt's reform program.[36]

As a progressive Republican candidate in 1908 Poindexter did not advocate far-reaching or fundamental changes in the status quo, for, after all, he was a member of the respectable, prosperous, property owning, middle-class elite of Spokane. He attacked a Democratic senator who, scoffing at Republican talk about "trust busting," had asked to be shown where "the dead trusts, killed by the Republicans, be buried." Poindexter retorted, "The Republican party is not seeking to kill or destroy the great enterprises of the land, thereby bringing disaster upon millions, but it is seeking to make them obey the law." He asked only that the rules of society be obeyed, to enable small businessmen and small towns and cities to compete for survival; and he maintained that he was not an enemy of the railroads, "these great necessary adjuncts of our civilization." On the contrary, he felt that "their rates should be sufficiently high to enable them to pay good wages to their employees, to furnish good freight and passenger service to the public and pay a reasonable interest upon the money invested in their properties." He supported federal regulation only to prevent the railroads from eliminating "competition regardless of the interests of the people."[37]

An even more precise definition of Poindexter's progressivism emerges from his response to the proposal to establish a federal parcel post system. The Washington State Grange supported the parcel post bill wholeheartedly, but local merchants, fearing the competition of the large eastern mail-order houses, opposed it, because, as a letter to Poindexter from the Inland Empire Implement and Hardware Association pointed out, the parcel post law would be "a 'body-blow' to the retail merchants in all lines all over the entire U.S." Poindexter was requested to explain his position to the Association and to keep in mind that it would distribute his answer to its more than three-hundred members.[38] The issue posed a serious dilemma for Poindexter, since the Grange, primarily a spokesman for the wheat farmers, and small businessmen constituted two of the most important interest groups in eastern

Washington. The Grange and presumably most farmers wanted parcel post; small businessmen feared it.

Poindexter's answer appeared in the newspaper a few weeks later, and his views were precisely those that could be expected from a lawyer closely associated with Spokane businessmen. "The principal advocates" of the parcel post law, he stated, "are the large mail order houses and in that connection I am opposed to government aid to such houses at the expense of local concerns; or to any measure which would extend the principle of centralization of government subsidy to private business." A proposal which threatened local business, threatened the whole community, Poindexter concluded, because, "The welfare of the local merchant is intensely connected with the welfare of the entire community." Forced to choose between local businessmen and farmers, Poindexter lined up solidly with the businessmen.[39]

Both local businessmen and farm spokesmen probably did agree, on the other hand, that the interests of the people of eastern Washington were being thwarted by Speaker of the House of Representatives, Joe Cannon, who generally opposed the "Roosevelt policies." Queries as to how Poindexter stood on the reelection of Cannon as Speaker arose as soon as the October campaign opened, and he was warned by a friend that "you will be called on to state what you will do with regard to 'Uncle Joe.'" The friend added, "there is no strong sentiment in this district in his favor, and . . . should you feel constrained to declare yourself on this subject it would . . . be better to be against Cannon."[40]

In private Poindexter readily identified Cannon as a "reactionary" and one of "those who are opposed to the policies of the present republican administration of strictly enforcing the law against the special interests and trusts." He refrained from committing himself to vote against Cannon for Speaker of the House, however, since "it can not be foreseen at this time what situation will be developed . . . and no definite line of action . . . could be laid down." But, he continued, if a "formidable opposition to Mr. Cannon with reasonable prospect of success could be organized . . . I would be inclined to favor it."[41] Not until a few days before the election, in a speech at Rosalia, it appears, did Poindexter first publicly criticize Cannon, though again he declined to say categorically that he would vote against Cannon for Speaker. But he came very close to saying that. "I am opposed to the reactionaries and in favor of the present administration," he declared, "and consequently I am opposed to Mr. Cannon as speaker of the house of representatives."[42]

In the same speech, Poindexter presented a somewhat more specific program to the voters than he had in earlier speeches, by announcing his support for the income tax and the establishment of a federal postal savings bank. By the end of the campaign, therefore, Poindexter had placed himself solidly behind the Roosevelt administration; he had endorsed a few specific reform measures, and he had proclaimed his hostility to Joe Cannon, the Speaker of the House, who had apparently become a symbol of the political opposition in Congress to measures and programs favored by important groups in eastern Washington. The voters who listened to Poindexter's words could have had little doubt that they were being asked to vote for a progressive reformer who would go to Washington to battle against Joe Cannon and for the Roosevelt policies.[43]

Poindexter's Democratic opponent was William Goodyear, a manager of a printing company in Colfax.[44] Goodyear announced that he too favored the "Roosevelt policies," but, as a Democrat, he claimed that he would be in a better political position to help put them into law. Said Goodyear, "If elected, Judge Poindexter would be handicapped in his support of these reforms by the opposition of his party." Goodyear repeated the charges first made in the Republican primary that Poindexter was a late convert to the support of railroad regulation and he criticized Poindexter's opposition to the parcel post law, a measure he said was supported by Theodore Roosevelt. He endorsed many other reform measures, and he pledged to oppose the reelection of Cannon as Speaker of the House.[45]

Both candidates, in short, endorsed a progressive reform program, but the voters of eastern Washington selected the Republican reformer. Poindexter received a sizable majority, 61 percent of the vote.

It was another Republican year in Washington, and Theodore Roosevelt's successor, William H. Taft, carried eastern Washington handily and the entire state with almost 58 percent of the vote. As in earlier elections, the sectional pattern of 1896 was discernible, although weaker than before, and the Democratic vote in eastern Washington was heavier than in the western and southwestern counties.[46]

Poindexter's seemingly sudden and overwhelming conversion to progressive reform between 1904 and 1908 led his critics to charge that he was an "opportunist"—that he became a progressive reformer because it was politically expedient to do so. Personal ambition, or even opportunism, probably figures in the behavior of most men and women, and Poindexter was by no means free from it, but other factors help to explain his behavior. One factor certainly was his personality. A review of Poindexter's career turns up several such sudden reversals. His decision to run for governor in the 1904 election, for instance, seemed very precipitous, and so did the turn away from reform after 1917. But the reversal in 1917 was not popular in Washington; it contributed heavily to his defeat in 1922; and it cannot be seen as having been motivated primarily by ambition. These dramatic shifts probably were more a reflection of the man's temperament than of political ambition. Once convinced of the righteousness of a cause, Poindexter characteristically rushed into the fray headlong. He made his decisions quickly in the heat of battle and acted instinctively. Furthermore, Poindexter was a member of the business-professional elite of Spokane, a property owner, and a brother-in-law of a prominent banker; and it does not seem startling that, after he moved to Spokane, he came to share the interests, views, and objectives of the Spokane Chamber of Commerce. His own interests and values had become intertwined with those of his community and his friends. As Richard Hofstadter has observed, "That impecunious young or small-town lawyers or practitioners associated with small business . . . should often have approached the problems of law and society from a standpoint critical of the great corporations is not too astonishing."[47]

Finally, Poindexter was motivated apparently by the same impersonal forces which affected many other Americans of his social-economic status in other parts of the nation. Most of the leaders of the Progressive era were, as was he, native-born, protestant Americans with a college education; a large number of them, particularly in the West, were lawyers; and most of them lived in northern cities. Poindexter, one can conclude, must have been stimulated to support progressive reforms by the same factors that affected most progressive leaders.

Poindexter's sudden conversion to reform was similar in some important respects to the reversal in position that has been noted in the careers of other progressives. Theodore Roosevelt, for example, campaigned against Bryan and the Democratic platform in 1896 as if they represented the work of the devil himself. Yet by 1904 Roosevelt was hailed by the *Spokesman-Review* as the national champion of the fight against the transcontinental railroads. Such prominent progressives as Robert M. LaFollette of Wisconsin, Tom Johnson of Cleveland, Albert J. Beveridge of Indiana, William Allen White of Kansas, and Woodrow Wilson of New Jersey opposed Bryan in 1896 but before 1910 had joined the national surge toward reform. In fact, George E. Mowry's conclusion, after examining a sample of over four-hundred progressive reformers, that "the overwhelming number of this group . . . had been conservatives in the nineties" and had voted for William McKinley in 1896, applies very well to Miles Poindexter.[48] It appears, in sum, that several complex factors combined to lead Miles Poindexter into the ring against the "special interests": his impulsive personality, his compulsion to excel in politics, his identification with the welfare and special interests of his Spokane neighbors and friends, and the more impersonal national forces which drove many solid members of the American middle class in the same progressive direction.

3.

A Hero of Insurgency

THE REELECTION of Joseph G. Cannon of Illinois as Speaker of the House of Representatives became a dominant issue at the close of Poindexter's campaign in eastern Washington in 1908, and in fact the hostility to the Speaker's reelection was apparently widespread. Efforts to reduce his power in the House had occurred in previous years, and in 1908 and 1909, according to one authority, there was a "strong anti-Cannon tide of opinion" discernible in the national press.[1] Cannon had been Speaker since 1903, and his authoritarian role in the House had antagonized many congressmen, none more so than those from the Great Plains and the West, the areas by and large where the Populists and Bryan had run well in the 1890s. Cannon led the opposition to the Newlands Reclamation bill, a conservation measure of obvious importance to westerners, enacted in 1902, and he antagonized people in most sections of the West because he used his power to stifle what he called "class and local legislation." Cannon was also criticized for utilizing his powers to discourage efforts to reform the tariff, which many in the West and South thought discriminated against the producers of agricultural products and raw materials and served as a stimulus to the growth of trusts. As could be seen in Poindexter's 1908 campaign, Cannon had become a symbol of standpat opposition to legislative measures designed to encourage the economic development of Poindexter's section of the country and to efforts by western and southern progressive reformers to achieve relief from eastern "colonialism" through effective federal regulation of big business.[2]

Speaker Cannon antagonized some easterners as well. President Taft, for example, had been irritated in 1908 by Cannon's opposition to a plank in the Republican platform favoring tariff reduction and limitations on the use of court injunctions in labor disputes. However, Taft abandoned his plan to oppose the reelection of Cannon as Speaker because Roosevelt, Elihu Root, and other Republican party leaders argued that Cannon could not be defeated.

Undaunted by the reluctance of Republican leaders to oppose Cannon's reelection, a group of Republican Insurgents in the House, most of them from Wisconsin and the northern Great Plains states, met in the office of Congressman Hepburn of Iowa on December 11, 1908, under the leadership of George W. Norris of Nebraska, Henry A. Cooper of Wisconsin, Victor Murdock of Kansas, and Charles A. Lindbergh of Minnesota. The group adopted a list of reforms to be made in the rules of the House in the next Congress and forwarded the list to President-elect Taft. The list included three major objectives: 1) abolish the power of the Speaker to recognize members on the floor arbitrarily; 2) remove the Speaker's power to appoint the members of the powerful Rules Committee and provide instead that the members be elected by the House; and 3) adopt a compulsory and regular calling of committee hearings.[3]

Poindexter, as has been seen, had indicated an unfriendliness toward Cannon and a support of progressive reforms during the final days of the congressional campaign, but he had not specified how far he would go in cooperating with the Insurgents. Only a few days after the election, he received several letters from people in the East inquiring whether he intended to join the Insurgents.[4] Poindexter's responses show how closely he agreed with Cannon's critics. He said that he favored Burton of Ohio for Speaker, the same man whom President-elect Taft had considered supporting, and added that he would support "a revision of the rules of the House so that the arrogant dictatorship which has characterized the conduct of its business at certain times will be impossible." He opposed Cannon because "Popular opinion has been aroused in this district to the desirability of the reforms generally outlined in your letter," and he listed a number of measures important to the West which Cannon opposed, including appropriations for the Panama Canal, "the improvement of waterways generally," conservation, reforestation, and "irrigation, which we . . . regard as the greatest event in the course of our material development." The Congress, Poindexter concluded, should elect a Speaker who was "more in harmony with . . . the dominant and progressive elements of the party, and with the great spirit of reform which is prevading the entire country." He promised to meet with the Insurgents as soon as he reached Washington, D.C., and to support "any measures necessary to the success of this movement." True to his word, on March 11, 1909 Poindexter attended the Insurgent caucus and two days later informed a constituent that he would vote against Cannon and support "a substantial amendment to the rules."[5]

Poindexter's resolution was to be speedily put to the test, for on March 15, when the first and special session of the Sixty-first Congress convened, the election of the Speaker was the initial order of business. The Republicans, acting on the authority of the party caucus, nominated Cannon; the Democrats nominated Champ Clark of Missouri; and Cannon was easily reelected by the Republican majority. Poindexter along with eleven additional Republican congressmen voted for other Republicans. Consideration of the House rules of procedure was the second order of business, and in a series of votes Poindexter aligned himself with a group of over twenty-five Republicans in favor of reform of the House rules. A resolution proposed by Clark of Missouri, similar to the demands of the Insurgents—to deprive the Speaker of the power to appoint committees and to enlarge the Rules Committee—was defeated, although nearly thirty Republicans, including Poindexter, joined with most Democrats to support it. A compromise resolution with the Speaker's power left basically intact then passed.

Poindexter along with a handful of Republicans voted with most Democrats against the compromise. "We did not accomplish the vital reforms that we were seeking," he admitted afterward, but "a compromise was forced upon the Cannon crowd which contains substantial reforms and paves the way for more later on."[6]

After the adoption of the rules, the House proceeded to consider tariff reduction. For several years there had been a strong sentiment in the West and Midwest for such action, and both the Populist and Democratic platforms of 1892 and 1896 had called for lower rates. Even President McKinley in 1901 had come to believe that the tariff needed some reductions, and President Roosevelt, too, favored revision. Roosevelt, however, had been frequently reminded of the political difficulties which threaten a president who tampers with the tariff by Speaker Cannon and conservative Senator Nelson Aldrich of Rhode Island, the Senate majority leader, and Roosevelt had never made a specific proposal to Congress that it should take up reform of the tariff. It was largely at Taft's insistence, therefore, that the Republican party platform of 1908 pledged to revise the tariff; but because of the opposition to reduction from Republicans such as Speaker Cannon and Senator Aldrich, the Republican platform did not specify what sort of revision there would be. Nonetheless, Taft had taken the platform to be a pledge for a tariff reduction and had campaigned on that basis.

The tariff question had been discussed little by Poindexter during his campaign. After his election, however, he stated privately that "if the Republican party had declared in favor of increasing the tariff it would have been overwhelmingly defeated." His first public commitment on the tariff was made as he prepared to leave Spokane for the East, when he assured the mayor of Spokane and an official of the 150,000 Club that he would favor the repeal of the tariff on Canadian coal, because "I am convinced [it] is an unjust and unnecessary burden upon our community." But not many days later in a public speech to the Spokane 150,000 Club he defended the tariff on lumber by declaring, "I . . . would be untrue to the wishes of my constituents were I to vote for the removal of the tariff from a product that has made Washington the greatest lumber-producing state in the nation."[7] While in principle Poindexter endorsed tariff reduction, in practice he was equally concerned with the economic needs of Spokane and eastern Washington.

The revision of the tariff was to be the objective of this special session of the Sixty-first Congress. Early in the proceedings, Congressman Payne of the House Ways and Means Committee introduced a tariff bill which at the insistence of President Taft placed lumber, coal, and hides on the free list and substantially reduced the rates on many other items. During the debate Poindexter played a very minor role—his only contribution was a speech on behalf of repeal of the tariff on jute bags—but he did declare that "there are a great many other general provisions in the bill that I am opposed to."[8]

After debate over the Payne bill ended, on April 5 the House adopted a special rule from the Rules Committee to limit amendments. This order, probably designed by Cannon to embarrass the Insurgents who for the most part represented states which produced raw materials and agricultural products, opened to amendment only the rates on lumber, oil, barley, malt, tea, and coffee. Many Insurgents voted with most Democrats against the special order, for it not only prevented them from attempting to reduce schedules on eastern products, it also represented the sort of arbitrary "undemocratic" action by the Republican leadership which they had pledged themselves to oppose. The rule was adopted, however, and changes were proposed on those schedules open to amendment. Roll-call votes were recorded on lumber, hides, barley, oil, and on all products imported from the Western hemisphere. Poindexter supported the high tariff position on all but one of these recorded votes, the amendment to place oil on the free list, and on the final vote he joined with the Republican majority in support of the Payne bill. "Generally speaking," he concluded, the bill "is a good one. . . . where it raises one article it reduces three."[9]

Poindexter's voting record on these specific amendments was similar to that of many of the Insurgents.

An examination of the votes on lumber, hides, barley, and the products from the Western hemisphere reveals that all twenty-seven Insurgents voted at least twice in the eight votes recorded for higher schedules. Victor Murdock of Kansas and George Norris of Nebraska supported the tariff on hides and on barley; Cary of Wisconsin supported a higher duty on barley and on all products imported from the Western hemisphere; and other Insurgents had similar records. While these Republicans as a group indicated little enthusiasm for protection of lumber and petroleum, they were much more consistent in supporting higher duties on barley, hides, and products from the Western hemisphere (see table 1).[10]

Poindexter was committed to support reductions in the tariff. "Undoubtedly the Republican party pledged itself in the last campaign . . . to a lowering of tariff duties," he had written in 1909. But in practice this pledge meant reduced tariffs only on articles produced outside his own state. The same rule seemed to be adhered to by other Insurgents, for they supported tariffs on products when it seemed in their interest to do so. This observation was made at the time by Speaker Cannon who sarcastically noted that the Insurgents "voted with the Republicans on schedules that protected the property of their constituents and with the Democrats on schedules that protected the property of other sections of the country." Senator Wesley Jones, a Republican from Washington and a defender of the Taft administration, expressed similar views. During the campaign of 1910 he singled out Poindexter's voting record on the tariff bill for special criticism by informing a Poindexter supporter, "I voted for a tariff of $1.25 a thousand on lumber" and "our friend Poindexter voted against this and maintained for $2.00 a thousand on lumber." Jones concluded, "This would seem to be a case where my vote was for the interest of the people, . . . and, according to your contention, his vote was in the interest of the 'interests.'"[11]

Though there was justice in the Insurgent conviction that protection for western products was neglected by the Cannon-Aldrich organization, it is not accurate to conclude that the Insurgents were dominated by a desire to reduce costs for the

TABLE 1

HOUSE INSURGENTS AND THE PAYNE-ALDRICH TARIFF

X - Vote for higher duty
O - Vote for lower duty

	Timber	Lumber	Products of Western Hemisphere	Lumber	Lumber	Barley	Hides	Petroleum	Totals X	O
Cary, Wisconsin	O	O	X	X	O	X	O	O	3	5
Cooper, Wisconsin	O	O	X	X	O	X	O	O	3	5
Davidson, Wisconsin	O	O	X	O	O	X	O	O	2	6
Davis, Minnesota	O	O	X	O	O	X	X	O	3	5
Fowler, New Jersey	X	X	X	X	X	X	O	O	6	2
Garner, Massachusetts	X	X	X	X	X	X	O	O	6	2
Good, Iowa	O	O	X	O	O	X	X	O	3	5
Gronna, North Dakota	O	O	X	O	O	X	X	O	3	5
Haugen, Iowa	O	O	X	O	O	X	X	O	3	5
Hayes, California	X	X	X	X	X	X	O	X	7	1
Hinshaw, Nebraska	O	O	O	O	O	X	X	O	2	6
Hubbard, Iowa	O	O	X	X	O	X	X	O	4	4
Kendall, Iowa	O	O	X	X	O	X	X	O	4	4
Kopp, Wisconsin	O	O	X	O	X	X	X	O	4	4
Kinkaid, Nebraska	O	O	O	O	O	X	X	O	2	6
Lenroot, Wisconsin	O	O	X	X	O	X	X	O	4	4
Lindbergh, Minnesota	O	O	X	X	O	X	X	O	4	4
Madison, Kansas	O	O	O	O	O	X	X	O	2	6
Morse, Wisconsin	X	X	X	X	X	X	O	O	6	2
Murdock, Kansas	O	O	O	O	O	X	X	O	2	6
Pickett, Iowa	O	O	X	X	O	X	X	O	4	4
Poindexter, Washington	X	X	X	X	X	X	X	O	7	1
Nelson, Wisconsin	O	O	X	X	O	X	O	O	3	5
Norris, Nebraska	O	O	O	O	O	X	X	O	2	6
Steenerson, Minnesota	O	O	X	O	O	X	X	O	3	5
Volstead, Minnesota	O	O	X	O	O	X	X	O	3	5
Woods, Iowa	O	O	X	X	O	X	X	O	4	4
Totals for higher duty	5	5	22	15	5	27	19	1		

consumer. A strong element of sectional self-interest lay at the core of Poindexter's and the Insurgents' fight for "the people," and despite Poindexter's attacks on "special interests," he himself represented "interests," eastern Washington interests. He voted for a tariff on lumber for local lumber companies and lumber towns, and he supported protection for barley and hides for eastern Washington farmers. He opposed a duty on coal because Spokane imported it from Canada; he voted against a tariff on oil, for oil was consumed, not produced in Washington; and he favored a removal of protection on jute bags because they were imported by eastern Washington wheat farmers. The central point is that in general, like most Republicans, Poindexter was a tariff protectionist who merely sought minor alterations in the interests of his constituents.

That the Insurgent Republicans in the House generally supported protective tariffs when it seemed in the interest of their constituents to do so has sometimes been overlooked. The classic study of insurgency maintained that "the Insurgents were not fighting for greater consideration for any one group, but for a better balance in the entire protective system." This generalization was based upon an examination of the letters and speeches of the Insurgents.[12] The voting record on the Payne tariff bill suggested that the statements made by the Insurgents were not always consistent with their voting.

Upon its passage in the House, the Payne bill was submitted to the Senate where, as the *New York Sun* aptly observed, "things really happen to a tariff bill." The chairman of the Senate Finance Committee, Senator Nelson Aldrich of Rhode Island, revised the rates of the Payne bill upward to the extent that it became unacceptable to the tariff reformers in the Senate. Aldrich's changes created the greatest opposition among Republican senators who, like their counterparts in the House, represented farm states largely from west of the Mississippi River. Despite their angry efforts to lower schedules, the Senate passed the Aldrich bill in July 1909.[13]

When the House-Senate conference committee met to seek a compromise between the Payne and Aldrich bills, Taft succeeded in persuading the committee to reduce rates on hides, lumber, coal, glass, and iron ore. The reduction of the rates on hides and lumber, together with the general increase in rates on eastern products, offered persuasive evidence to the Insurgents that the tariff had been written for eastern interests and that it had taken little consideration of the interests of the western and midwestern sections of the nation. In the House, when the conference report was voted on, about two-thirds of the Insurgents (eighteen on one vote and fifteen on the second) voted against it. By these votes Insurgents opposed not only the Republican congressional organization but the wishes of President Taft who was now convinced that the bill in general was a victory for tariff reductions.[14]

Poindexter voted against the conference report on both occasions, thus establishing his steadfast opposition to the new tariff. The reasons he offered to his constituents and friends to explain why he opposed the tariff so tenaciously can be divided into two categories: 1) sectional or economic reasons and 2) democratic or political reasons. The economic advantages of the tariff, in his view, were claimed by the eastern interests. "New England is jubilant," he exclaimed, "because the only rates lowered were those on western products, while the rates on New England products were either not changed or raised." The Insurgents were convinced, he maintained, that the new tariff "failed to deal fairly with Western interests . . . we were of the opinion that it was entirely unjust to put hides upon the free list and fail to lower the tariff upon the products of hides, such as suit cases and other articles of that kind."[15]

The fight against the tariff was closely associated in Poindexter's statements with the struggle for free, democratic government, and he frequently linked his opposition to Speaker Cannon, Senator Aldrich, and the "reactionaries" with his opposition to the Payne-Aldrich tariff. He presented the tariff fight as part of the great moral crusade against "the interests." The congressmen from the East who supported the new tariff were not democratically elected and did not represent "the people," he reasoned; for, "There are too many 'rotten boroughs' in such states as Rhode Island, New Jersey, Pennsylvania and especially such cities as New York, Pittsburgh, Philadelphia, etc. These people know nothing about the interest of the people of the West and care nothing about the interests of the people. They are merely representatives of the great interests who pay their campaign expenses and look after their political existence." The result, said Poindexter, is that "dishonest profits . . . wrung from the American people have made so many sudden millionaires in Pittsburgh that the whole city reeks with scandal and corruption." Though he admitted that some supporters of free lumber were Insurgents from the "middle West," he emphasized the fact that "the fight upon that issue was led by [Congressman] Tawney of Minnesota, a rank Cannonite and reactionary." Furthermore, it was "the reactionary element . . . which was led by Senator Aldrich" that "put hides upon the free list."[16]

After the passage of the tariff bill, Congress adjourned and Poindexter returned to Spokane. He had been "very much gratified" by his first taste of national politics. He probably had obtained more publicity than most congressmen could hope to receive in their first term in Congress: he was now becoming well known in Seattle, as well as in Spokane, and he had achieved a bit of national prominence. In the March 27 issue of *Collier's Weekly*, which had championed "the people's" fight against Cannon and the House rules, Poindexter's picture was published alongside the eleven other Insurgents who had voted against Cannon for Speaker. "Twelve Men of Courage" they were called.[17]

By the end of the special session in July 1909, the breach between the Insurgents and the Republican congressional organization was serious, and a misunderstanding had developed between President Taft and the Insurgents as well. Taft apparently shared the Insurgents' opposition to the reelection of Cannon as Speaker, but on the advice of Roosevelt and others he had decided not to oppose Cannon. Probably he expected the Insurgents to follow his lead. The Insurgents, on the other hand, could not understand why Taft did not join in what they thought was the president's battle. Undoubtedly Taft's insistence that the duties on hides and lumber be dropped from the tariff irritated some

Insurgents as much as it did Poindexter and it made Taft seem partial to eastern interests. In addition, there was indication during the early months of his administration that Taft found the standpat members of the Republican Senate, especially Senator Aldrich, much more to his liking than the rebels from the Midwest and West, particularly after these progressives voted against the Payne-Aldrich bill. This association appeared even more ominous to congressmen from the West when President Taft declared in a speech at Winona, Minnesota, that the Payne-Aldrich bill was one of the best tariff bills ever passed.

Less than a month after Taft's Winona statement Poindexter informed the Economic Club in Spokane that President Taft had failed to oppose the efforts of Senator Aldrich and "the despotic dictatorship" of Joe Cannon. "From the night that Theodore Roosevelt stepped out of the presidential chair we . . . have been going backward!" he exclaimed.[18]

As the resentment against the eastern, standpat Republicans and the Payne-Aldrich tariff reached its climax during the autumn of 1909, a new controversy developed to aggravate the split in the Republican party and further widen the breach between the president and the Insurgents. This was the Ballinger-Pinchot controversy which involved Gifford Pinchot, a champion of the conservation of natural resources and head of the Forestry Bureau in the Department of Agriculture since the beginning of Theodore Roosevelt's administration, and Taft's Secretary of Interior, Richard A. Ballinger from Seattle, Washington. Essentially the controversy involved a difference in opinion over how the national conservation program should be administered and a personality conflict between Pinchot and Ballinger.

Alarmed by Ballinger's policies, Pinchot readily accepted charges brought to him by an investigator in the Interior Department, Louis R. Glavis, that Secretary Ballinger had improperly assisted a group of Seattle land speculators in league with the "Morgan-Guggenheim Syndicate" to procure important coal deposits in Alaska. Pinchot presented these charges to the president who examined Glavis's charges, concluded they were groundless, and allowed Ballinger to discharge Glavis. Pinchot then forced Taft to fire him by making a public attack upon Ballinger.

When Poindexter returned to Washington, D.C., in early December 1909 for the second session of the Sixty-first Congress, the demand for an investigation of Pinchot's and Glavis's charges against Ballinger were widespread. Poindexter characteristically rushed into the fray immediately in support of Pinchot. "The admitted facts and bare history of the Interior Department and of Secretary Ballinger," he commented to Norman Hapgood, editor of *Collier's*, "ought to be sufficient to condemn to say nothing of what may be discovered should a complete investigation of the secret history of the department be possible."[19]

Poindexter's willingness to back Pinchot placed him even more completely in opposition to President Taft's administration. As a consequence, he was one of those referred to in the administration's announcement on January 5, 1910 that it would henceforth treat supporters of Glavis and Pinchot as political enemies and no longer honor their wishes in patronage matters. Undaunted, Poindexter's position became more extreme: "There is . . . increasing evidence that as during the fight over the tariff and the reorganization of the House, the administration is being gradually pulled in, hoodwinked by Aldrich and Cannon, and proposed legislation is either emasculated or side tracked. This is evident now and will become obvious a little later on."[20]

Congress quickly passed a resolution to investigate Glavis's and Pinchot's charges, and later in 1910 an investigating committee exonerated Ballinger of all charges of wrongdoing. Poindexter's conduct continued to seem intentionally defiant of the party leadership and Taft. On one vote, for example, he was the only Republican to vote with the Democrats in favor of a motion to investigate only Ballinger's Interior department, rather than both his and Pinchot's Forestry Service as had been provided in the Republican resolution. Poindexter somehow interpreted the conflict as a matter of the highest principle. He declared "that the line of division between the Tories and the progressives is more clearly marked over this Pinchot affair than any other." It demonstrated, he told his friend O. C. Moore, that the Taft "administration is reactionary and . . . has betrayed the people."[21]

While the congressional investigation which would finally clear Ballinger proceeded during the early months of 1910, the fight against Speaker Cannon's control of the House of Representatives flared up again in early March 1910, when Norris of Nebraska found an opportunity to take the floor and offer the more thorough rules reforms that had been rejected in 1909. After a thirty-six-hour session, the House adopted the Norris amendments,[22] and Cannon, observing that the House was now controlled by a Democratic-Insurgent coalition, asked for a motion to declare his position vacant. Poindexter and eight other Republicans voted with the Democrats to oust Cannon, but the motion failed, 155 to 192. Poindexter thus maintained his record of extremism or independence (as he would have described it) throughout the struggle to reform the rules of the House.[23]

Even as the fight against Cannon progressed, differences over the issue of railroad regulation contributed to the increasing hostility between President Taft and the Insurgents. During the fall of 1909 the Taft administration prepared a bill to revise and strengthen the Hepburn Act of 1906. The new bill, to be known as the Mann-Elkins Act, granted increased powers to the Interstate Commerce Commission to regulate railroad securities and rates and provided for the establishment of a Commerce Court to review and enforce decisions of the ICC. The bill partially set aside the Sherman Act by permitting railroad mergers under certain conditions, and it did not include a provision promoted by Senator LaFollette of Wisconsin to provide for a physical evaluation of railroads in order to determine a "scientific" basis for rate making.

Though the Democrats and the Insurgent Republicans in the House and Senate desired more effective regulation of railroads, they were critical of the administration's railroad bill. They were suspicious of the new powers given the Commerce Court; they opposed all railroad mergers; and they protested against the ommision of the physical evaluation scheme. In the Senate the Democrats, supported frequently by LaFollette, Cummins, and other Senate Insurgents, opened fire on the administration's railroad bill. Some of their proposals to strengthen the bill were accepted, and on the final vote most Insurgents supported their party's bill while the Democrats, declaring the bill too weak, voted against it.

The House Insurgents, too, displayed much dissatisfaction with the administration's bill. Poindexter singled out the proposed Commerce Court because he thought it reduced the power of the Interstate Commerce Commission and gave too much personal power to the Attorney General. He presented an amendment to strike out the clause which increased the authority of the Attorney General in handling the litigation of the Interstate Commerce Commission. "I am opposed," he announced, "to the Attorney-General superseding in any degree the powers of the Interstate Commerce Commission in the conduct of these suits." It was his view "that progressive legislation along these lines would be to increase rather than curtail the powers of the Interstate Commerce Commission." After several days of debate, the House Insurgents and the Democrats tried to strike out the Commerce Court section of the House bill and failed. Then Poindexter and eleven other Insurgents joined the Democratic minority to vote for a motion to recommit the entire bill to committee. When the motion to recommit was rejected, Poindexter and the other Insurgents voted with the Republican majority to pass the bill,[24] as the Senate Insurgents had done.

Poindexter's speeches and correspondence during the Sixty-first Congress leave no doubt that he was a member of the Insurgent Republican bloc, but these textual sources are of only limited help in assessing Poindexter's behavior in comparison to other Insurgents and to the members of the Republican party in the House more generally. To fully assess his place in the Insurgent revolt it is necessary to examine Poindexter's behavior in relation to that of other congressmen. It seems especially useful to know precisely who the other Insurgent Republicans were, what sections of the nation they represented, and where Poindexter stood on the major issues of the Sixty-first Congress in comparison to other Insurgents. These questions can be answered by an examination of the voting record of the House of Representatives. A list of the

A Hero of Insurgency   47

congressmen who made up the Insurgent coalition has been compiled by the author from an examination of the roll-call votes in the House on the attack on Speaker Cannon; the Payne-Aldrich tariff; the Mann-Elkins railroad bill; and the Ballinger-Pinchot controversy. Sixteen roll-call votes on these issues selected by the author produce a list of twenty-seven Republicans who voted "Insurgent" at least ten times. Most of the twenty-seven were from the wheat-producing states of the Great Plains: seven represented congressional districts in Wisconsin, six in Iowa, four in Minnesota, three in Nebraska, two in Kansas, and one each in California, Massachusetts, New Jersey, North Dakota, and Washington.[25] Most of the Insurgents by this definition, in other words, represented districts from the same part of the nation as did Poindexter, with an economic base very similar to that of eastern Washington.

Using a somewhat different selection of roll-call votes as well as other indicators of support for progressive reform, John D. Baker argued that the Insurgents divided into two distinct groups, the "progressive Insurgents" and "nonprogressive Insurgents." In Baker's analysis only a small number, sixteen, including Poindexter, qualified as "progressive Insurgents." Every one of the sixteen, however, represented Wisconsin or a state west of the Mississippi River.[26] Both Baker's and the author's analysis are subject to the same obvious weakness—the evidence was selected arbitrarily in terms of the researcher's own subjective standards. A way to avoid bias introduced by the roll-call selection process is to test for party regularity, using all the votes cast in the Sixty-first Congress, irrespective of substantive meaning. This procedure involves computing a party loyalty score for each member of the Sixty-first Congress; it is simply the percentage of times each congressman voted with the simple majority of his own party. The results of this analysis suggest (table 2), in the first place, that the Insurgent revolt in the House, as in the Senate, involved only a few individuals and that Republican voting solidarity did not appear to be seriously shaken. In the Sixty-first Congress the average Republican congressman voted with his party 86.1 percent of the times he voted, and the Republicans did not seem much more divided than the Democrats, whose average party loyalty score was 90.1 percent. Compared to the average party loyalty scores of both Republicans and Democrats in the Senate in the Sixty-first, Sixty-second, and Sixty-third Congresses, moreover, House Republican party loyalty scores in the Sixty-first Congress seemed relatively high.[27]

TABLE 2

PARTY LOYALTY SCORES IN THE SIXTY-FIRST CONGRESS OF REPUBLICAN MEMBERS OF THE HOUSE OF REPRESENTATIVES WHO VOTED WITH THE REPUBLICAN MAJORITY ON LESS THAN 50 PERCENT OF THE TOTAL VOTES CAST

NAME AND STATE	PARTY LOYALTY SCORE	NAME AND STATE	PARTY LOYALTY SCORE
Volstead, Minn.	69.9	Cooper, Wis.	56.5
Kopp, Wis.	69.3	Haugen, Iowa	53.2
Pickett, Iowa	67.8	Murdock, Kans.	51.8
Kinkaid, Neb.	66.7	Poindexter, Wash.	51.7
Kendall, Iowa	64.2	Norris, Neb.	51.5
Madison, Kans.	63.9	Davis, Minn.	49.4
Morse, Wis.	60.8	Nelson, Wis.	49.1
Lenroot, Wis.	60.2	Cary, Wis.	49.0
Woods, Iowa	59.5	Lindbergh, Minn.	47.1
Hinshaw, Neb.	59.4	Gronna, N.Dak.	44.1
Hubbard, Iowa	58.9		

In the second place, an analysis of party loyalty scores shows that only a very few Republican congressmen actually voted consistently against the party majority. Only twenty-one Republicans had party loyalty scores of less than 70 percent, and only five less than 50 percent. Every House Republican whose party loyalty score fell below 70 percent represented Wisconsin, Washington, and the states of the Great Plains. This list of the most disloyal Republicans in the House is nearly identical to the list produced in the author's analysis, and it is also very similar to Baker's list; the eleven Republicans with the lowest party loyalty scores in the Sixty-first Congress were on Baker's list of thirteen "progressive Insurgents." In this instance different methods of analysis present only trivial difference in results, and the main point is clear: the House Insurgent Republicans represented Wisconsin and states west of the Mississippi River, areas like eastern Washington that were heavily dependent upon commercial agriculture.[28] All three efforts to identify the Insurgents, finally identify Poindexter as one of the most active members of the Insurgent faction.

Having passed the Mann-Elkins Act, the Sixty-first Congress quickly adjourned. It was an election year, and Poindexter anxiously anticipated the campaign, for in November 1909 he had announced his candidacy for election to the Senate to replace Senator Piles who had declined to run for reelection. Many formidable obstacles had to be overcome by Poindexter to win a seat in the Senate. Tradition in Washington called for the election of one senator from each side of the mountains, and the other Washington senator, Wesley L. Jones, was from Yakima, an eastern Washington town. Thus Poindexter could look for opposition from the populous west side cities, Seattle and Tacoma, as well as from Jones, who, if a Spokane man were elected in 1910, could expect the east-west tradition to hinder his reelection in 1914. A second obstacle to Poindexter's election to the Senate lay in the fact that, as one of the most outspoken of the House Insurgents, he had aroused the antagonism of President Taft and most regular Republicans. He was, in Taft's opinion, "a blatant demagogue and a Democrat," and, said a friendly editor, he "more than any insurgent . . . incurred the wrath and enmity of Joe Cannon."[29] On the other hand, there were three compelling reasons to run: Poindexter was convinced that a majority of "the people" was behind him, he thought he perceived an opportunity to divide his opposition, and he had no doubt that righteousness was on his side.

If Poindexter had the majority of the voters behind him, it was possible that he could be elected without the support of the Republican organization, for Washington's 1908 primary law required that the party nominees for the Senate be selected in a primary election. The Republican and Democratic members of the state legislature were expected to support the victorious candidates in their respective party primaries. Thus, if Poindexter's insurgency was popular with "the people," he could overcome the opposition of the party organization. Further encouragement was found in the fact that the Republican state organization was not united in support of a single, strong candidate. Two prominent Republicans from Seattle were in the race, John L. Wilson and Judge Thomas Burke; both were regular Republicans who supported President Taft. There were, in addition, several other candidates, none of whom was well known, and all in all, the prospects for a Poindexter victory in the Republican primary seemed excellent.[30]

Once Poindexter determined to run, he recruited an eastern journalist, Rufus Rockwell Wilson, to manage the campaign and to edit the *Malden* (Washington) *Herald*. To assist Wilson, there were the prominent businessmen and lawyers of Spokane who had supported Poindexter in 1908 and were still behind him. He still enjoyed the backing of W. H. Cowles and the powerful *Spokesman-Review*. Horace Kimball, Rufus Woods, editor of the *Wenatchee Daily World*, O. C. Moore, Postmaster W. P. Edris, and R. L. Rutter of the Spokane and Eastern Trust Company were some of his most active supporters. As in 1908, Poindexter opened his primary campaign in mid-October by inviting eastern Washington newspaper editors to Spokane to hear Senator LaFollette speak. LaFollette endorsed Poindexter's record and that night sat up talking over the campaign with him until 2:00 A.M. After LaFollette's address, the Republican Progressive League was formed; the policies of Theodore Roosevelt were acclaimed; the actions of the Insurgents during the recent session of Congress were heartily endorsed; and the new League pledged itself to arouse the state against "Cannonism and Aldrichism" and to "uphold the hands of Congressman Miles Poindexter." Approximately one month later at a luncheon in Seattle, Poindexter formally announced his intention to run.[31]

The news of Poindexter's decision to run for the Senate added considerably to the consternation about him in the Taft Republican camp. The chairman of the Spokane County Republican Committee, D. T. Ham, who was close to Senator Jones, immediately notified Jones that he was ready to lead the Spokane opposition against Poindexter. Senator Jones was alarmed: "Mr. Poindexter's election would mean my elimination at the end of my term." Another active Poindexter opponent was M. T. Hartson, a leading Jones supporter and a collector of internal revenue. Hartson noted as early as November 23, 1909 that "Poindexter is rapidly reading himself out of the party," and he warned Jones, "Poindexter is going down the line displacing Postmasters with good records and putting in such people as Rufus Woods of Wenatchee." Hartson added that "every office so appointed would be part of his personal political machine" and "adverse to the interest of the entire Republican party." No doubt Hartson was being intentionally sarcastic, for he well knew that "machine politics" was one of Poindexter's chief objects of attack. Hartson did not feel that Poindexter could win, but he was impressed by the optimism and confidence which the Insurgent displayed. Poindexter, reported Hartson, "is taking himself seriously," and he warned Jones, "should the Aldrich-Cannon matter continue to be so much in the public eye as it now seems to be, and should LaFollette aid Poindexter . . . there might be more to his candidacy than there now seems to be." He closed his letter by urging Senator Jones to see to it that Rufus Woods did not get the postmastership at Wenatchee.[32]

To stop Poindexter's campaign and to bring him and other Insurgents into line, President Taft in January 1910 denied them Post Office patronage. Senator Jones informed M. T. Hartson that Poindexter no longer would receive any consideration from the administration and that "the President spoke very postively [sic] regarding the matter." But the withdrawal of patronage from Poindexter, as Rufus Wilson noted, seemed to be "making us new friends on every hand." Taft's patronage policy merely gave Poindexter another opportunity to dramatize himself as a spokesman of "the people" against the "machine."[33]

As the summer of 1910 approached, it became increasingly clear to the Taft Republicans that Poindexter indeed was a formidable candidate. Senator

Jones was informed by a supporter near Yakima that farmers there "seemed all to be for Poindexter right off the bat." The state Republican committeeman from Douglas County in eastern Washington warned that Poindexter "would carry eastern Washington like wild fire," and Senator Jones, himself, privately admitted that Poindexter and the Insurgents would probably win.[34]

Poindexter's candidacy received a major boost at the end of June when Theodore Roosevelt invited him to come to Oyster Bay. Roosevelt had recently returned to the United States from a hunting trip in Africa and a triumphal tour of Europe, and the entire nation expectantly waited to see how he would react to the split in the party which had developed during his absence. Poindexter and many of the Insurgents loudly claimed to represent the views of Roosevelt, and they hoped to receive Roosevelt's endorsement. In late June Roosevelt saw Pinchot, LaFollette, and other Insurgents, including Poindexter. On June 28 Poindexter informed A. E. Griffiths, "I . . . have been urged to stop over and see Colonel Roosevelt for a few hours and may do so." The *Spokesman-Review* reported that Gifford Pinchot had secured Poindexter's appointment with Roosevelt.[35]

After Poindexter's visit to Oyster Bay, headlines in the *New York Times* reported that Roosevelt had promised to support Poindexter. As the *Portland Oregonian* saw it, "Theodore Roosevelt today, not by direct statement, but by implication so strong that it admits of no misinterpretation, said that he will support Miles Poindexter." The day following, Roosevelt's office denied the report, but many interpreted the meeting as an endorsement nonetheless.[36] Certainly President Taft viewed the proceedings as an effort by Roosevelt to promote Poindexter's candidacy. "You may have noted," he wrote to Secretary Ballinger, "that there are a good many interviews being held at Oyster Bay with the insurgents and others, and that sometimes authentic statements are made that are not authentic—or at least statements made one day are denied the next." Poindexter, said Taft, "is one of the most bitter political opponents and always has been. Mr. Roosevelt's support of him seems most gratuitous and unnecessary."[37]

Poindexter, too, treated the interview as if it were an endorsement. The evening he stepped from the train at Spokane in early July he told reporters that his talk with Roosevelt "was of the most friendly character and satisfactory to me." A few days later in Seattle when commenting on the interview, he claimed, "I found that so far as politics are concerned he and I are in entire harmony." He did not exaggerate the importance of his interview, moreover, for, as the *Seattle Times* admitted, "there can be no honest denial of the fact that the Washington Insurgent was a welcome visitor, and that the conference which ensued gave him great comfort in his Senatorial aspirations."[38]

Soon after his interview with Roosevelt, Poindexter campaigned in Seattle and western Washington where his opposition seemed strongest. As the Republican state convention prepared to meet in Tacoma in August, he emphasized his departure from "machine politics": "I am not negotiating for the office of the United States Senator. . . . I do not expect to get it by making terms with politicians or political leaders." As he had anticipated, he received no consideration from the "machine politicians" gathered in Tacoma. The proceedings were completely dominated by administration Republicans who praised President Taft, endorsed a program of "sensible" conservation, expressed confidence in Richard A. Ballinger, and approved the record of every Republican congressman from Washington except Poindexter's. He was ignored. "It was," concluded the *Spokesman-Review*, "a typical old line, machine-made, boss-ruled, party-loyal political convention."[39]

On the day following the Tacoma convention, Poindexter had his own triumph in Seattle. There at a political rally he, Senator Jones, Senator Piles, and other Republicans were scheduled to speak, but the crowd almost rioted in its desire to do him honor. Senator Piles could not be heard, and the crowd cheered at every mention of Poindexter's name. Cheering and applause interrupted Poindexter's speech frequently; and when he finished, the crowd attempted to break up the meeting.[40]

Despairing that Poindexter would win, President Taft telegraphed Senator Jones shortly after the

Tacoma convention to urge Jones to try to reduce the number of candidates from Seattle by persuading either Burke or Wilson to withdraw. "Everyone in Washington last winter knew," Taft later explained, "that Poindexter opposed the administration more bitterly than any Democrat." A few days later Taft wrote to Ballinger, declaring "that Burke and Wilson ought to get together and have patriotism enough to save the country from the disaster of Poindexter," and finally, scarcely two weeks before the primary, Wilson withdrew. Taft immediately telegraphed his thanks to Wilson, but he refused to oppose Poindexter openly. He had concluded, he said, that his best strategy was "to saw wood and keep quiet."[41]

Poindexter's campaign speeches expressed the ideas that he had used since he had gone to Congress. He represented his fight as one of honesty and principle against an organized system of political "bossism" and "special interest." His speeches sometimes seemed to resurrect the ghost of Populism: "Tammany Hall in New York, the Quay crowd in Pennsylvania, the Guggenheim-Weyerhaeuser crowd in this state and the Cannon-Aldrich combine in Congress," he declared, were "all financed by the same money and all devoted to the same interests." Regarding the rumor that President Taft interceded to have John L. Wilson withdraw, Poindexter declared, "It was not the president who withdrew Mr. Wilson from the contest; it was Jim Hill." Poindexter presented himself as the protector of the people. "The thing that counts" is whether the candidate is "the representative of the people or the special interests," he declared. "The issue today is whether the people of the United States shall take charge of their own business or whether the interests shall continue to run the government."[42]

Although Poindexter had been an outspoken Insurgent in Congress and had once proclaimed that the progressive movement had "reached the dimensions of a revolution," his economic views seemed no more radical in 1910 than during his 1908 campaign for Congress. He called for no radical economic or social reforms, and he continued to express a high regard for property rights. In fact, he insisted that he was not a radical: "I do not think that any man can ever show from anything that I have ever said that I have been violent as to any person or radical or extreme to any measure. . . . I know that essentially I am conservative rather than radical."[43]

As the primary election approached, it was apparent that Poindexter had satisfied almost all important factions in the state except the opponents of reform and the friends of President Taft. His Insurgent record pleased eastern Washington farmers who in past elections had shown a decided preference for reform candidates. C. B. Kegley, head of the Grange, praised Poindexter's "strong, unwavering stand on public questions and his refusal to be dominated by any motive but the people's interests." Samuel Gompers of the AFL gave Poindexter an enthusiastic endorsement; *LaFollette's Weekly* endorsed him as "a leader among the Insurgents" and "a fighting, militant Progressive"; and the Inland Empire Retail Dealers Association "heartily endorsed" his record because "on all occasions" he worked "in the interests of the people and against special privilege." The latter was one of Poindexter's strongest endorsements, but it was no wonder. He wrote it himself.[44]

Letters of support came from almost every nationally known Insurgent including Governor Hiram Johnson of California, and Senators LaFollette, Beveridge, and Cummins. Beveridge sent telegrams calling Poindexter "one of the ablest, bravest, and cleanest of present day public men" to Poindexter's Spokane headquarters, to the *Seattle Star*, and to the University of Washington *Daily*. A copy was also sent by Beveridge to Mark Sullivan, who was giving Poindexter national publicity in his column in *Collier's*, with the comment, "I hope they will do Poindexter good." Congressman Victor Murdock of Kansas came to Washington to campaign for Poindexter. "I am here," he told his Spokane audience, "in behalf of a young man whose heart beats true to the cause of the people."[45]

On primary election day in September the Republican voters of Washington endorsed Poindexter's insurgent-progressive record in dramatic fashion. Running against a field of seven opponents (John L. Wilson's name remained on the ballot although he had withdrawn in favor of Burke), Poindexter amassed 67,714 votes, 58 percent of the total vote cast. His triumph was a direct rebuke to President Taft, and it was part of a national trend. In the general election in November 1910 across the nation Democrats and Insurgent or progressive candidates swept the field, and forty-one incumbent Republican representatives, including Speaker Cannon, were defeated. Poindexter accurately described the election results for Theodore Roosevelt: "Our victory here was almost unprecedented in its overwhelming character, but was only a consistent part of the national movement of the people to preserve self government."46

The primary election results show that Poindexter received his greatest majorities in the eastern Washington counties where William Jennings Bryan had been strongest in 1896 and in 1900, and where in 1904 George Turner, the anti-railroad Democrat, had been most successful in his campaign for governor. Like Bryan in 1896, Poindexter carried the urban belt of Puget Sound counties, but with slightly reduced majorities, and like Bryan in 1896 and 1900, and Turner in 1904, Poindexter lost most of the "lumber" counties in the southwest. This sectional pattern, it can be inferred, reflected an underlying set of political attitudes in Washington which Poindexter tapped in his dramatic sweep of the state in the 1910 primary. While he was not a Democrat, he nonetheless seemed to invoke symbols of the Populist-Democratic campaigns of the past and to identify himself, both in the counties that opposed him and in the counties that supported him, with, for lack of a better term, the reform tradition of Washington.47

The results of the senatorial contest in Washington in November were anticlimactic, for the major struggle had occurred in the Republican primary. There was initially some concern in the Poindexter camp that regular Republicans elected to the Washington state legislature might ignore the results of the primary and vote for another Republican, but this fear proved to be without foundation. The Democratic senatorial nominee, George F. Cotterill, had admitted publicly in July that he expected most Democrats to vote in the Republican primary for Poindexter, and it seemed, according to the *Seattle Times* in early November, that there was no popular interest in the Senate election. In Washington, the *Times* pointed out, the Republican nomination "in most cases is equivalent to an election," and that observation proved accurate in 1910. The Republicans elected a majority to the state legislature which in turn honored the primary results and elected Poindexter to the United States Senate.[48]

The election of 1910 presents an opportunity to examine the relationship between the Populist and Bryan campaigns in the 1890s and the Poindexter campaign. In Washington there was continuity between the two campaigns in the sense that most counties which in the 1890s supported Bryan and Populist candidates voted for Poindexter in 1910; and this continuity was noted by several contemporaries. A Republican state committeeman from Douglas County stated, "I know the disposition and temper of the east side farmers. They are still innoculated with the old populist virus. By education they are against corporations and corporate interest good or bad." Similarly, Senator Jones in April 1910 compared Poindexter's campaign to the campaign of 1896 when he predicted, "Our party may go down to defeat as it did in '96." Later in the campaign, the editor of the *Portland Oregonian* was reported as thinking that "under Poindexter's banner the populists, socialists, greenbackers, silverites, cranks, kickers and discontented souls . . . are enlisted," and in August 1910, the editor of the *Yakima Republic* lamented, "The old state has gone Populist."[49]

These continuities between Bryanism and progressivism in the state of Washington seemed reflected to some extent in Poindexter himself. In some of his speeches and letters he echoed the rhetoric of Bryan, and he supported many of the reforms which had first been brought to the fore in his state during the 1890s: the regulation of railroads and other trusts, the direct election of senators, and the elimination of corruption and "special favor" in politics. On the other hand, Poindexter manifested important differences between Populism and progressivism. He had not been a Populist or sympathetic to Bryanism in the 1890s and had not been converted to support reform until after 1904. By his own testimony Poindexter had voted for McKinley in 1896, and he maintained that there was a difference between his own program in 1910 and the Bryan program of 1896. It was, indeed, just after his overwhelming victory in September 1910 when Poindexter explained that he had left the Democratic party in 1896 because "the old democracy was swallowed up in populism, free silver, single tax and fusion." Poindexter was one of the many among the "middle classes," to quote Richard Hofstadter, who "joined the trend toward protest" which had been under way since the 1890s and "took over its leadership."[50]

Examination of the issues, the political rhetoric, and the county election data of the senatorial election of 1910, and the campaign of insurgency in Washington provides convincing evidence to support Samuel P. Hays's conclusion that national politics in the Progressive era was characterized by a pattern of "colonialism" in which leaders from the South and West labored under "a common colonial economic position" relative to the industrial and urban Northeast.[51] The evidence presented in this study bears primarily upon a single western state, of course, but the hostility toward eastern railroads and trusts, cities, and political leaders abounds in Poindexter's speeches and letters, in the correspondence from his supporters, and in the local newspapers, especially the *Spokane Spokesman-Review*. The hostility to the Northeast, furthermore, was by no means limited to farmers and their spokesmen. While the leader of the Washington State Grange supported Poindexter and while he carried most eastern Washington farm counties in the Republican primary, Poindexter's most solid backing centered in the middle-class, business-legal establishment in Spokane. His popular vote in Spokane County exceeded 70 percent of the vote cast, and he seemed, from the point of view of Spokane and eastern Washington businessmen, to be carrying on in a conflict against eastern "colonialism" which had originated much earlier in the 1890s.

4.

A Senate Insurgent

THE SIXTY-SECOND Congress (1911-13) was Poindexter's first in the Senate, and he deserved some credit for making the first session of that Congress, according to one Taft Republican, "the most annoying, pestiferous, aggravating session I've ever attended." Poindexter behaved, as an admiring editor put it, as if "he would rather fight than eat." Hostility between the regular Republicans and the progressives surfaced almost immediately over the election of a new majority leader—Aldrich of Rhode Island had retired—and over committee assignments. Republicans still held a majority in the Senate, but the success of the Democrats in the election of 1910 had reduced the Republican advantage considerably. This meant that the votes of the progressives were essential to maintain Republican control, and that circumstance may have contributed to the adoption of a compromise arrangement. At first LaFollette, Poindexter, and six other progressives refused to attend the Republican caucus and to support Gallinger of New Hampshire, another easterner of course, who was the choice of most Republicans to replace Aldrich. LaFollette demanded that the progressives be given one-fourth of the committee assignments, but that proposal failed to carry in the Republican committee on committees. After some negotiation the progressives agreed to vote for Gallinger with other Republicans, to guarantee Republican control of the Senate in exchange for suitable committee assignments. As a result of the bargaining Poindexter, despite his unpopularity with the regulars, received desirable assignments: the Committee on Naval Affairs, which, next to the Committee on Foreign Relations, was the post he desired most, and the Committee on Mines and Mining.[1]

Just as in the House in the Sixty-first Congress, Poindexter's speeches and writings identify him as an outspoken critic of Republican party leadership and an advocate of progressive reform legislation, but, to repeat a point made in the previous chapter, Poindexter's place in the Senate during the Progressive era can be more precisely determined by comparing his voting behavior with the voting record of other members of the Senate. Voting in the Senate on progressive reform issues indicated that Poindexter voted consistently for reform issues along with a bloc of Republican senators who represented Wisconsin and states west of the Mississippi River. These were senators who represented essentially the same region as did the Insurgent Republicans in the House in the previous Congress and who spoke for states with economic and sectional interests very similar to the state of Washington.[2] Although doubts concerning the validity of these conclusions, published in an earlier study, were expressed by Barton J. Bernstein and Franklin A Leib, additional research on the Sixty-first, Sixty-second, and Sixty-third Congresses using both party loyalty scores and Guttman scaling analysis, indicates that these conclusions were based on a valid, though rough approximation of the positions taken by Republican senators on reform issues.[3] Party loyalty scores, in fact, yield very similar results. In the Sixty-second Congress in these terms the most disloyal Republicans were by and large the same senators who previously were identified as leading supporters of progressive reform legislation. All of the nineteen Republicans, except Robert M. LaFollette of Wisconsin, who voted with their party less than 80 percent of the time represented states west of the Mississippi River. LaFollette, the most disloyal Republican in the Sixty-second Congress, voted with the Republican majority 52 percent of the time, Clapp of Minnesota 58 percent, Gronna of North Dakota and Kenyon of Iowa 59 percent, and Poindexter 60 percent. In the Sixty-second Congress, in other words, Poindexter was the fifth most disloyal Republican, and more importantly, he voted on most issues with the western Republicans. It should be noted, however, that even LaFollette voted with the Republican majority more than half of the time and that even during these years of intense intraparty strife the Senate Republican party, while more divided than the Democrats, was more united—or at least the Republicans voted together more consistently—than in the 1890s, or in the late 1920s and early 1930s.[4] Whether measured in terms of arbitrarily selected votes on progressive issues or by a measure of general partisan loyalty, the Senate voting record demonstrated that, comparatively speaking, Poindexter was one of the most extreme of the Insurgents. Defined either by arbitrarily selected votes or by all votes cast in the Sixty-second Congress, furthermore, the Insurgent group in the Senate was a western voting bloc which included even some vigorous supporters of President Taft, such as Poindexter's colleague from Washington, Senator Wesley Jones. Both textual and quantitative sources suggest, in sum, that a sectional effort to free the West from the "colonial" domination of the Northeast, to use Samuel P. Hays's term, was a prime ingredient in the provocation of the Insurgent revolt against Republican party leadership.

The first major legislation taken up by the Senate in 1911 was a reciprocal trade agreement which President Taft had negotiated with Canada. This arrangement, which in essence provided that Canada and the United States mutually reduce tariff duties, dramatized once again the sectional, East-West split in the Republican party. Taft promoted the agreement vigorously to offset some of the criticisms of the Payne-Aldrich tariff, to avoid a trade war with Canada, and to provide American manufacturers with cheap Canadian raw materials. The president was convinced that since American farmers produced more than could be consumed domestically, the price of agricultural products was determined by the world market. Hence, the reduction of the tariff on Canadian wheat and other farm commodities would not depress American farm prices. Such arguments had little effect on western representatives in Congress, however, and it was soon apparent that most of the progressive Republicans from the West would oppose the agreement on the grounds that Taft and the party leaders again had sacrificed the interests of their constituents on behalf of eastern interests.[5]

The Canadian reciprocity agreement had been introduced into the Congress at the close of the Sixty-first Congress, but it had failed to pass and was taken up again early in the Sixty-second Congress. Thus Poindexter participated in the deliberations on that issue twice, first in the House and later in the Senate. In both instances he did not stand consistently with the progressive bloc on Canadian reciprocity. In the House he spoke vigorously for the principle of tariff reform; but only reluctantly, he said, would he support the Taft proposal, "not for what it is, but for what it may and should lead to." The agreement was barely acceptable to him because it "gives a market in the United States to the agricultural products of Canada and retains the great consuming market of Canada for the manufacturers of Great Britain." In contrast to "politicians" who would vote on the agreement for "private benefit" and "for purely local and private advantages," Poindexter declared he would vote for reciprocity, although, "I desire to do so . . . with this distinct understanding, that . . . we will never rest nor cease our efforts until we have gained . . . reduction of tariffs" and relief from "an exaggerated and exorbitant tariff [that] now compels us to buy from tariff-made monopolies of the Eastern States."[6]

Poindexter's voting record indicates that despite his ringing speech endorsing tariff reform, his position on Canadian reciprocity was ambiguous, and in fact he voted for it only once, on the final vote, after it became certain that the House would pass the bill no matter how he voted. The majority, a combination of Taft Republicans and Democrats passed a special order prohibiting amendments, but twenty Insurgents, including Poindexter, voted in the negative. Then Norris of Nebraska moved to

recommit the entire bill to committee. This seemed
the critical vote, and it was defeated, with
Poindexter and eighteen of the Insurgents voting
with Norris in an effort to kill the bill. On final
passage of the bill, the Insurgents divided.
Poindexter and six others voted for passage with
the Republican majority, while sixteen voted
against passage. Before the Senate acted, however,
the Sixty-first Congress adjourned, and the president, in spite of warnings that he would split the
party, immediately called for a special session of
the Sixty-second Congress to consider his Canadian
trade agreement.[7]

Before the beginning of the Sixty-second Congress,
Poindexter returned briefly to Spokane where he
discovered he had handled reciprocity satisfactorily so far as most of his constituents were concerned, even though the two key elements in his
coalition, small businessmen and eastern Washington
farmers, were diametrically opposed on the matter.
C. B. Kegley, head of the state Grange, praised the
speech Poindexter had given in the House because
Poindexter had criticized the Taft agreement. Exclaimed Kegley, "You have hit the key note and I
want you to go back with a determination to fight
it to a finish. We will not protest if the manufactured goods as well as all farm produce are
placed on the free list." But in an open letter to
all Washington members of Congress, Kegley made it
explicit that "as it stands" the Canadian reciprocity bill "is not honest reciprocity. It is
plain unadulterated free trade for the farmer on
all he produces, and high protection on all he has
to buy." Although Poindexter had voted for reciprocity on the final vote, his speech in defense of
local agricultural intersts and his vote to return
the bill to committee obviously pleased Kegley.[8]

In direct contrast to the position of the head of
the Grange, many small businessmen in Washington
seemed to favor reciprocity because it promised
more profitable trade with Canada. The owners of
the William Sumner Silk Importers Company, for example, declared in a letter to Poindexter that reciprocity "will be a boon to every importer and jobber in the border states." A Seattle dealer in wool
wrote that he favored the adoption of the treaty

because, "We have a very extensive business throughout British Columbia and Alberta and have had for years." Although one owner of a lumber company objected strenuously to reciprocity, another, the owner of the Washington Manufacturing Company of Tacoma, wrote that he did not object. "As it is today, we ship considerable stock into Canadian territory, and are necessarily handicapped because of this 25% duty," he explained. The senator managed to keep this group happy because he voted for the reciprocity measure on final passage. When his friend Arthur Cory of the Chehalis National Bank exclaimed, "we want the Canadian reciprocity treaty passed," Poindexter could respond more or less honestly, "I voted for it in the House and expect to do so again in the Senate as I am in favor generally of reciprocity and we have got to begin somewhere."[9]

Business interests were not alone in support of reciprocity. Fruit growers, too, were very much for it. The Grandview District Fruit Growers Association urged the Washington delegation in Congress to support it and a correspondent from Wenatchee, where the apple orchards were plentiful, pointed out that there reciprocity was most popular, and he added, "it is simply a case of local selfishness, opening a small market for our fruit." The *Spokane Spokesman-Review* also endorsed the treaty because "it will lead to general free trade with Canada," and on March 24, 1911 the editor of the *Walla Walla Evening Bulletin* likewise urged Poindexter to support the agreement.[10] Evidence of substantial support for reciprocity in Washington encouraged Poindexter to take a more decided stand, and when a Spokane manufacturer of farm machinery asked him if the treaty would be a good thing for the farm machinery business, Poindexter answered emphatically: "I am certain that liberal trade relations with Canada, or even free trade with Canada, would on the whole prove very greatly to the advantage of the United States."[11]

The Canadian reciprocity agreement was the first legislative proposal taken up by the Sixty-second Congress when it met in April 1911. The Senate began to vote on amendments to the measure on July 10, and passed it July 22. Analysis of the voting record demonstrates that the opponents of this kind of tariff reform were the Insurgent or progressive Republicans from Wisconsin and states of the West. The list of opponents to tariff reciprocity with Canada included LaFollette, Cummins of Iowa, and Borah of Idaho. Three Democrats voted with the progressives, but most remained true to the Democratic free trade tradition and voted for tariff reform along with the regular Republicans. It was a pattern of voting rarely seen in the Congresses of the Progressive era.

Although the opponents of this particular kind of tariff reform were largely the progressive Republicans, Poindexter voted for reciprocity. He supported Taft's measure on every vote, despite the fact that he had received letters from C. B. Kegley and several local chapters of the Washington Grange in opposition to the bill, and a telegram from the National Lumber Manufacturer's Association urging him to support the amendment protecting lumber.[12] Admitting that the Taft measure "is about as unsatisfactory as any which could be framed," Poindexter defended his support of reciprocity by pointing to the need for "liberal trade" with Canada. He repeated the argument that Washington farmers could not be injured by reciprocity since their wheat "will continue to be shipped to Liverpool as formerly," and he emphasized the advantages to eastern Washington which would result from the treaty—"In the Spokane country, at least, the demand of the country immediately to the north for horses and stock of various kinds should be of benefit to our country."[13]

By supporting reciprocity Poindexter cast his lot with Washington's small businessmen, because reciprocity seemed to him profitable to local business, with no real threat to farm prosperity. It was testimony to his courage that he disregarded the views of the state Grange on this issue and testimony to his political ability that he was able to do so without arousing C. B. Kegley's hostility. But Kegley and the Grange had the victory after all, as the reciprocity agreement was not destined to become law. On September 21, 1911 the Laurier government in Canada, which had negotiated the agreement, was defeated at the polls, and Taft's hopes for tariff reform were lost. Most of the members of the Insurgent or progressive band had come down solidly for protection for their products and, in this instance, against tariff reform. A western Senate Republican who on occasion voted with the progressives, McCumber of North Dakota, summarized the progressive position very well in 1912 to Elihu Root of New York: "the farming element . . . may be infested by this microbe of insurgency," he observed "but they are nonetheless protectionists."[14]

A second issue of major importance to Poindexter in the Sixty-second Congress involved the Industrial Workers of the World and a textile workers' strike in Lawrence, Massachusetts. The IWW had been organized in Chicago in 1905 by radical labor leaders who had become convinced that existing unions were not making satisfactory progress in alleviating working conditions. The new union demanded industrial unionism and the abolition of the wage system, and it emphasized the organization of unskilled and migratory workers. During the years after 1905, the "Wobblies," who were especially strong in the mining and lumbering camps of Washington, adopted the practice of entering towns in large numbers to make radical speeches, knowing that the local authorities would put them in jail and thereby incur heavy expenses for their maintenance. Such "free-speech" fights occurred in Poindexter's hometown, Spokane, in 1909, and in Wenatchee and Walla Walla in 1910, but the IWW gained its national reputation as a radical labor organization by supporting the Lawrence strike. The strike involved an estimated fourteen thousand textile workers who were resisting a reduction in wages. Though the IWW had only a small membership in Lawrence when the strike began, it recruited vigorously and became publicly identified with the strike. Many of the strikers were immigrants—the *New York Times* claimed that forty-five languages and fifty-two nationalities were represented. Violence quickly erupted, and Massachusetts authorities employed the state militia before the strike was broken and order restored.[15]

It is not clear precisely how Poindexter became involved in the Lawrence strike, and there is no evidence that he was concerned with labor conditions before 1912. He was in all likelihood encouraged to take up the issue by some of his progressive associates in the East even though the IWW was a labor group that probably had antagonized most members of the business-legal elite in Spokane. It is known that a friend of Louis Brandeis encouraged Poindexter to go to Lawrence to investigate the strike, and Brandeis, who had been Pinchot's and Glavis's counsel during the congressional investigation in 1910, probably cooperated with Poindexter on this issue. Furthermore, the election of 1912 was on the immediate horizon and Poindexter's passion for reform causes was high. In that spirit he took a position he probably would not have taken before 1910 and certainly would not take after 1917.[16]

In any case, Poindexter did go to Lawrence, and upon his return to the Capitol he launched an attack upon the millowners and "the miserable condition of mill employees in the country." The situation in the textile industry, he said, "is simply an example of the exploitation of human beings for the crudest and coarsest kind of greed." He declared that he had visited a tenement house in Lawrence where fifty-four people lived. The average wage there, he said, was $6.60 a week or $2.75 for each person who lived in the building, and he severely criticized the millowners for these conditions: "I do not think I have ever seen a more prejudiced or unfeeling set of people than they are!" Conditions at Lawrence, he declared, are "but a symptom of a far-reaching social and political danger which, if aggravated by such action as that of the authorities at Lawrence, may at any time assume alarming proportions."[17]

Poindexter then introduced a resolution which requested the Department of Commerce and Labor to investigate working conditions in Lawrence and to report to the Senate information about wages, working conditions, the percentage of foreign born involved in the strike, and the nature of the action taken by the local authorities. The resolution was immediately challenged by Gallinger of New Hampshire, Lodge of Massachusetts, and Root of New York, "the advocates of . . . mill owners," Poindexter called them. They protested against his resolution and defended the employers and the Massachusetts authorities. Democrats Bailey of Texas and Bacon of Georgia joined in to argue that the issue was a matter for the state to handle.[18]

In response to the argument that the strike was a states' rights matter, Poindexter asserted that "anything that degrades these people, anything that grinds them down to a condition of absolute penury . . . degrades the average citizenship of the United States. It is a circumstance in which everyone is interested." When Senator Lodge remarked that the IWW had been "treated with some severity" in Spokane, Poindexter admitted that IWW members had not been permitted to enter Spokane and that the police had broken up their meetings, but he insisted "There was considerable opposition to that action of the police by the people of the city." There had never been, in Spokane or elsewhere in the United States, he exclaimed, "such unprecedented, extraordinary procedure as has taken place in the city of Lawrence."[19] Poindexter's efforts to aid the mill workers in Lawrence were postponed repeatedly by the Senate until May 1912, after the strike had been crushed, when the resolution was taken up and passed, too late of course to help the strikers.[20]

Poindexter's spirited defense of the Lawrence strike is the most puzzling episode in his political career. There was ample evidence that many of his business and legal friends in Spokane feared and detested the IWW, and certainly the senator had shown no sympathy for the workingman or the immigrant nor even an awareness of the problems faced by the urban poor in industrial America prior to the Lawrence strike. His attitude toward organized labor and especially the IWW after 1917, moreover, could only be described as extremely, almost hysterically, hostile. Perhaps he had been in Washington, D.C., long enough to lose touch with the attitudes of his supporters and friends in Spokane, and perhaps he was influenced by advanced social liberals like Brandeis. His personal inclination, furthermore, was to take the most extreme, partisan position, and the Lawrence strike provided him a good opportunity to attack the "enemy," eastern senators like Lodge and Root, and eastern corporations. But however his actions are explained, and none of these suggestions seem entirely satisfactory, the fact remains that Poindexter did speak against working and living conditions of the urban poor and in sympathy with their hopeless fight against the forces of law and order in Lawrence, Massachusetts.

The defense of the Lawrence strikers identified Poindexter as one of the most advanced of the progressives in the Senate, for in defending immigrant laborers and the IWW he endorsed groups who rarely found a sympathetic hearing in the Congress in the Progressive era. The reform issues which received the greatest attention from the progressives, such matters as tariff reform, railroad, banking, and business regulation, and political reform, offered little benefit to the immigrant, urban populations of the eastern cities, and no major effort was made in the Progressive era by Congress to enact meaningful social and labor legislation. There were of course some exceptions to this generalization, such as the LaFollette Seamen's Act and the Child Labor Act, but members of the progressive coalition in Congress, both Democrats and Republicans, focused basically upon problems which concerned their own constituencies which were, by and large, the agricultural South and West. Poindexter's efforts to help the striking textile workers in Lawrence, therefore, was out of character, even "abnormal" in terms of the political context of progressivism in Congress, and it seemed even more unusual in view of the hostility toward the IWW which must have existed in middle-class groups in Spokane and eastern Washington.

While the Lawrence strike was a more exciting issue and perhaps, from Poindexter's perspective in the Senate, more important, another matter, the parcel post bill, was probably more critical to his Washington constituents. It will be recalled that during Poindexter's campaign for Congress in 1908 he had opposed parcel post legislation because it aided mail-order houses at the expense of local merchants. At that time there seemed to be no question in his mind about parcel post, and, largely because of his position on this issue, he had received the endorsement of the Inland Empire Retail

Dealers Association in 1908 and 1910. However, by the summer of 1910 Poindexter showed signs of wavering in his opposition to this issue. In July 1910 he admitted that "there are some special interests" opposed to parcel post, but he added, "the only opposition which has any weight with me . . . is that of our country retail merchants." Of course, the country merchants did not seem to Poindexter to be "special interests." They had, he thought, legitimate reasons for opposing this reform measure: "it will take the money from the country communities to the large cities."[21]

Shortly after the primary election of 1910 he changed his position rather substantially. "Undoubtedly there must be something in regard to parcels post," he wrote to one constituent. However, he continued, "the only embarrassment I am suffering from in this connection is the apparent unanimous opposition of the country retail merchants." The pressure on Poindexter to support the parcel post bill came primarily from the leader of the Washington State Grange, C. B. Kegley, who presumably spoke for many of Washington's farmers. There is indirect, but rather persuasive evidence to suspect that during the primary campaign in 1910 Poindexter privately assured Kegley that at the proper time he would change his position and support parcel post. In a letter from an associate of Gifford Pinchot's, Kegley was advised that Poindexter actually supported a parcel post law, but he could not openly support it without alienating business groups in Washington. Kegley was told to take a "friendly word on the quiet" and keep the parcel post issue "as much as possible in the background."[22] The parcel post issue, in fact, played no role in the 1910 campaign, and two years later, in August 1912, the Senate without controversy passed a parcel post law as an amendment to a general post-office appropriations bill. The vote for it was almost unanimous, and Poindexter voted for it. He received some complaints from small businessmen in Washington because of this vote, but he defended the measure by arguing that after all it was not such a bad thing for small business since it would lead to a "lowering of railroad rates."[23]

It appears that in Poindexter's perspective the parcel post bill and the Canadian reciprocity agreement were closely related, for the two measures offered him an opportunity to balance off the economic interests of the progressive coalition in Washington. On both issues the line was rather clearly drawn between small businessmen and farmers (assuming that the Grange indeed did represent what farmers wanted): the farmers opposed reciprocity and favored parcel post and the businessmen wanted reciprocity but not parcel post. The senator's solution to the problem was a compromise. He yielded to small business on reciprocity but came around to the demands of the Grange on parcel post. In this way, Poindexter was able to keep the two important groups in the progressive coalition in Washington behind him.

The issues which Poindexter emphasized in the Sixty-second Congress, Canadian reciprocity, the Lawrence strike, and the parcel post bill, were by no means the only progressive reform measures he supported. He voted consistently with the progressive coalition in favor of a number of political reforms including the popular election of United States senators and woman suffrage, and he assumed an advanced position on a second labor issue, the Republican Railroad Workman's Compensation bill of 1912.[24]

Poindexter's activities on behalf of progressive reform legislation in the Sixty-second Congress served to point up two distinct themes present in his early congressional career—his sensitivity to the economic welfare of his constituents and his proclivity to take advanced positions (compared to other Republicans in the Senate) on reform questions. His support of Canadian reciprocity and, in another way, his vote for the parcel post law demonstrated very well this sensitivity to the interests of his constituents. The information available to him convinced him that Washington businessmen and some other groups as well wanted a more liberal trade policy with Canada; so he supported the Taft administration's proposal, and in so doing he split off from his fellow progressive Republicans and voted with the party regulars. He defended his position on reciprocity with ringing pronouncements in favor of tariff reform, but the good will and continued political support of the businessmen in Washington probably help more to explain his position than his dedication to tariff reform. The interests of the farm belt likewise apparently convinced most in the progressive Republican bloc to oppose Taft's second effort at tariff reform, and in voting against the Insurgents Poindexter was in a sense behaving like them. In yielding to local businessmen on reciprocity Poindexter rejected the demands of the Grange, but on the parcel post issue he ultimately went along with the most vocal farm organization in Washington and against some local businessmen. Though Poindexter probably identified instinctively with local businessmen, since he was one of them, he knew it was critical to maintain the political support of both farm and business groups, and in balancing off reciprocity and parcel post he seems to have avoided alienating either of the two sometimes conflicting major elements in his progressive political base.

Poindexter's defense of the IWW and the strikers in Lawrence, plus his voting record on the Railroad Workman's Compensation bill, revealed a reaction to the labor issue somewhat in advance of most progressive Republicans. In defending the Lawrence strikers, in fact, he was alone; no one in the Senate rose to back him in his assault upon the millowners in Massachusetts. Issues that would develop later, particularly in foreign affairs, would reveal more clearly that Poindexter's point of view about a number of national issues was rather different from the view of most of his fellow progressives from the West.

Even as Poindexter and his Senate colleagues grappled with the parcel post bill and other legislative issues before the Sixty-second Congress, many found much of their time and interest gradually absorbed by the 1912 campaign for the presidency. The inept Taft by the end of 1911 had thoroughly alienated the progressive element in the Republican party, and it was virtually certain that the progressives would challenge his claim to renomination. Poindexter favored nominating Theodore Roosevelt, as did several other well-known progressives, but Roosevelt at first refused to run and officially claimed to be neutral. He did, however, provide some support for Poindexter's senatorial candidacy in 1910, as well as for some other progressives, and he had heartened his followers with a speech at Osawatomie, Kansas, in 1910, in which he advocated a greater use of federal powers and a reconsideration of the traditional rights of property to achieve social justice in America. He would not permit his name to be put forward as a challenger to Taft, nonetheless, and many progressives who would have preferred him turned to Senator LaFollette of Wisconsin.

Poindexter attended meetings of progressive senators in 1911 and early 1912 where it was decided that LaFollette would run against Taft with progressive backing. In June 1911 Poindexter endorsed LaFollette, but his statements were halfhearted. He was waiting to see what Roosevelt would do. In answer to a query from a group of Minnesota progressives, Poindexter stated that the progressives in Congress "would be delighted to see Senator LaFollette nominated," and a day later he publicly announced that he "would like to see" LaFollette become president. Others displayed Poindexter's lack of enthusiasm. Senator Cummins, for example, held the view that LaFollette could not "get more than 200 votes in the convention. Bourne is the only man who is optimistic about his chances." Thomas R. Shipp, a friend and colleague of Gifford Pinchot's, seconded Cummins's view: "The LaFollette boom has been making little headway . . . [and] great difficulty has been experienced in lining up Senate Progressives in his behalf."[25]

Enthusiasm for LaFollette's candidacy, however, soon appeared in Poindexter's correspondence from home. C. B. Kegley, for example, reported that the Grange was "solid" in its support for LaFollette, but W. H. Cowles was still for Taft, and he was worried that the progressive faction was disorganized. Poindexter's presence seemed needed in Washington, and when Congress recessed he traveled west with Gifford Pinchot to inspect coal deposits in Alaska and then back to Spokane where he tried to ready his progressive faction for the coming election and, in particular, the Republican state convention. "The people," he wrote to one supporter, must "take an interest in the matter and get control of the convention."[26]

In Spokane Poindexter communicated with C. B. Kegley and conferred with W. H. Cowles. He fulfilled speaking engagements; and he talked with his constituents. He seemed so busy that one observer noted in jest that "Mrs. Poindexter even managed to get a glimpse of him once or twice." The same observer noticed that Poindexter's office was filled "with the every-day sort of people" who "looked exactly like ranchers and workingmen" and that they all were received with untiring patience by the good senator. That reporter felt that Poindexter seemed almost unchanged from the days he had spent on the Spokane County Superior Court bench except that his hair was slightly thinner and he was even "more serious" than he used to be. Cartoons accompanying this article showed lines of anxious, crowded citizens standing in line to talk with Senator Poindexter, the "people's" representative, who had come home to renew his contacts with the "grass roots."[27]

The senator also managed to find a moment to write his son Gale who was studying at Annapolis. He sent Gale tickets for the Army-Navy game and urged him to be "duly economical," and he complained of his crowded schedule: "You can imagine the accumulation of correspondents, interviews, engagements, etc., which I have to deal with here and my limited time before having to go East."[28]

While Poindexter endeavored to put the Washington progressive campaign in order, the contest between President Taft and Senator LaFollette for the Republican nomination was complicated by none other than Theodore Roosevelt who began to show unmistakable signs that he would run after all. Roosevelt ceased asking supporters not to work for him in late 1911, and by early January 1912 he was definitely in the race. Poindexter was not long in boarding the Roosevelt bandwagon, but his position was delicate because LaFollette was popular in Washington. A switch to Roosevelt threatened to split the progressives in Washington, and Poindexte was anxious to avoid that catastrophe. To Lorenzo Dow of Tacoma, Poindexter pointed out that there were many LaFollette supporters in Washington who would not accept Roosevelt, and he urged Dow at all costs to avoid a split between the Roosevelt and LaFollette progressives. "If LaFollette cannot get the nomination still he ought to have as many delegates as can be secured for him," Poindexter suggested. "Then," he added, "the delegates when elected can vote for LaFollette and nominate him, if possible; if not, they will be in a position to vote for Roosevelt."29

The justification which Poindexter and others needed to dump LaFollette came on February 2, 1912 when, at a meeting of publishers in Philadelphia, LaFollette, near exhaustion, delivered a confused and long harangue. Poindexter was in attendance and the next day wrote his friend O. C. Moore that LaFollette seemed "to be completely broken down physically and mentally—I mean simply exhausted from his campaign." Poindexter made essentially the same point to Horace Kimball and then described a meeting he had attended of LaFollette's "closest advisors at which, however, he [LaFollette] was not present." They decided, reported Poindexter "that it was hopeless to undertake further to nominate him. Many who had been supporting him then turned to Roosevelt." Poindexter of course included himself in the latter group, and he added, "long before that time it had become very apparent that LaFollette could not defeat Taft. . . . The only hope in that regard was Roosevelt."30 So Poindexter, along with Gifford Pinchot and others, scurried aboard the Roosevelt bandwagon.

LaFollette and his followers, however, did not willingly yield to Roosevelt the claim to the leadership of the progressive Republicans, and in Washington Poindexter made a desperate effort to prevent the progressive faction from being "split to pieces as between LaFollette and Roosevelt." Attempting to placate LaFollette's supporters, Poindexter argued that the primary objective of progressives should be to defeat Taft and that was more significant than "the personal merits or fortunes of any individual." Poindexter reminded LaFollette men that he had supported LaFollette until the Philadelphia speech, but at that time "his closest advisors" agreed that he could not win. Thus, "the only alternative with any possibility of defeating Taft was Roosevelt."31

During most of the presidential campaign Poindexter was required to be at work in the Senate, and he left the work of trying to unify the Washington progressive Republicans and to organize control of the state Republican convention in the hands of two trusted lieutenants, Tom Murphine in Seattle and Horace Kimball in Spokane. They assured him as the meeting of the state Republican convention approached that, despite poor organization, ambition, and bickering, the progressives would control the meeting, and Poindexter in turn predicted to Gifford Pinchot that "the State of Washington now seems assured of a progressive delegation secured under rather adverse circumstances."[32]

Such, however, was not to be the case. The Republican state central committee had shown itself to be dominated by Taft Republicans as early as February 1912, when it had defeated an effort by Spokane progressive committeemen to hold the convention in Spokane. The committee had voted to hold the convention at Aberdeen, on the Pacific coast, instead. It was well known that Spokane was the core of Insurgent sentiment in the state and certainly not a place to hold a convention which Taft supporters hoped to control.[33] The critical struggle for congrol of the state convention was over before it convened. Taft men dominated the state central committee, and it seated the Taft delegates from all contested counties except two. Fearing a split in the state organization, Republican Governor Hay called a meeting of leaders of both factions to attempt a compromise, but before the conference could act, the progressives rejected all compromise and formed a new convention which proceeded to elect a Roosevelt delegation to the national Republican convention. The Taft-dominated convention responded by electing its own national delegation pledged to the president.[34]

When the news of the outcome of the Washington Republican convention reached Poindexter, he was furious: "throwing out the King county and other delegations was utterly without color of right and cannot be recognized," he wrote to one supporter. To another in Seattle he exclaimed, "Our Washington delegation could only be refused seats in the [national] Convention by absolute lawlessness and defiance of all principles of government. If that course should be pursued by any party in this country ahd [sic] they should gain power on the strength of it, it would lead inevitably to revolution."35

The Taft faction did control the Republican National Convention, and there was a "revolution," if the Roosevelt bolt in 1912 may be so described. The seating of the delegation from Washington, as well as the seating of most of the 254 contested delegates from other states, was settled by decisions of the National Republican Committee, which, like the state Republican committee in Washington, was dominated by Taft supporters. And, as in Washington, the resulting victory of Taft forces seemed, on the basis of the primary elections before the convention and the November election which followed, not in conformity with the wishes of the majority of Republicans. It should be pointed out, however, in fairness to Taft and his supporters, that the works and actions of the progressive faction in Washington were not above reproach. In Seattle Tom Murphine's actions, the statements made by him, and the statements made by Poindexter and other progressives suggest that the Poindexter faction manipulated the rules to their advantage at times too, but they were not in a position to manipulate effectively. The Taft Republicans controlled the party machinery.

Poindexter appeared in Chicago at the head of the Washington Roosevelt delegation, and he participated in the debate before the credentials committee. His efforts were in vain, however, and Washington's Taft delegates were seated. Altogether the committee awarded only 19 of the 254 contested delegates to Roosevelt. The refusal to seat his delegates led the enraged Roosevelt to decide to lead his faction out of the Republican party. He was promised financial support by George Perkins of the Morgan banking firm and by Frank Munsey, the publisher, and after an all-night conference on June 20, which Poindexter evidently did not attend, the die was cast. Roosevelt announced that he would accept the nomination from a new party based upon progressive principles. Roosevelt attempted to justify his decision and to persuade Poindexter to lead his state into the new third party. "There are irreconcilable elements in the old parties and," he told Poindexter "it is nonsense to try to keep these elements together in the old organization."[36]

Roosevelt's decision to leave the Republican party was very bad news indeed to Poindexter and to most progressive Republicans who held public office. On July 1, "In view of the present political situation," Senator Cummins of Iowa invited Poindexter, LaFollette, Bourne of Oregon, Borah of Idaho, Brown of Nebraska, Clapp of Minnesota, Dixon of Montana, Bristow of Kansas, Crawford and Gronna of North Dakota, Kenyon of Iowa, and Works of California to his office for "a free, frank conference, not to take concerted action or to bind any of us to a proposed course, but to exchange our opinions." Nothing remains in Poindexter's files to indicate what transpired at this meeting, but it is clear that the majority of the group was solidly opposed to joining Roosevelt's new party. Only Poindexter, Bristow, Clapp, and Dixon actually joined the Progressive party, and, as will be seen, Poindexter did so only under extreme pressure from his followers in Washington. Such reluctance was most disturbing to Roosevelt. "What a miserable showing some of the so-called Progressives have made!" he exclaimed. "They represent nothing but mere sound and fury."[37]

Meanwhile, at the end of June the Democratic convention convened in Baltimore. The split in the Republican party only a few days earlier made it seem very probable that the Democratic nominee would be the next president, and there was a spirited fight for the nomination by the progressive governor of New Jersey, Woodrow Wilson, Champ Clark of Missouri the Democratic Speaker of the House, and Congressman Oscar W. Underwood of Alabama. After forty-six ballots Wilson was nominated and a progressive platform adopted which attacked the Republican protective tariff, promised to regulate the trusts, endorsed a constitutional amendment for the direct election of senators, and advocated a law to protect labor from prosecution under the Sherman Anti-Trust Act.

While the Democratic convention was in session in Baltimore, debate raged among progressive Republicans in the state of Washington over the proposal to form a third party. In Spokane the dominant sentiment was against leaving the Republican party. Horace Kimball, speaking for the Spokane Republican committee, wired Poindexter, insisting that it was unnecessary to form a third party in Washington because the progressives could win the Republican primaries. Poindexter agreed with Kimball completely. The senator urged Kimball to prevent the formation of a third party in Washington, and he pointed out that it would be quite legal to nominate Roosevelt electors separately at a state progressive convention so that Roosevelt's electors would be on the presidential ballot. Local progressives should run as candidates in the Republican party. Poindexter's position was endorsed by C. B. Kegley, C. R. Case of the AFL, and several progressive candidates. Poindexter's argument, like Kimball's and fellow progressives' in the Senate, was simple: he was a professional, and he had no stomach for an unpredictable third-party adventure.38

But on the same day that Poindexter's answer to Kimball appeared in the *Spokesman-Review*, Poindexter's leading spokesman in Seattle, Tom Murphine, came out for the formation of a third party, and so did a number of progressive Republican candidates. Poindexter objected vigorously to this course of action. There was good "prospect of securing absolute control of the republican organization." He insisted that Roosevelt could be supported without the formation of a new party: "It is not important what the movement is called or whether it is considered a new party or otherwise; it is the fact which is important." Poindexter's arguments persuaded some closest to him, and he reported to Roosevelt that the Washington progressives would remain in the Republican party and support his candidacy on a separate Progressive slate, since of course Taft would be at the top of the Republican ticket. Roosevelt accepted this decision, though he made it clear that he preferred "a straight out third party fight."39

The third-party advocates in Washington, however, could not be stopped. They formed the state Progressive party in Tacoma in late July on their own and issued a call for another meeting to be held August 7. This was a most upsetting development to Poindexter. "I do not know any way of preventing these people from holding their convention if they want to. I certainly shall not take part in it nor in their plan of campaign," he wrote Murphine. It was obvious that this move would divide the progressives into two groups if Poindexter and his followers remained in the Republican party. In Spokane where the progressive forces already controlled the party organization, Poindexter's position seemed to carry the day, but elsewhere, especially in counties where the Taft Republicans were in control, sentiment to form a Progressive party was overwhelming.[40]

Poindexter and the eastern Washington Republicans still resisted the formation of a new state Progressive party when the national Progressive party convention opened in Chicago in early August amid emotional and rosy predictions that a new day was dawning in American politics. Poindexter, busy in the Senate, was the last of the Washington delegation to arrive in Chicago. He was quickly elected honorary chairman of his state's delegation, and when the Washington delegation marched into the convention hall, each member proudly displayed a white silk badge reading "Washington Comes Back." The badge referred to the refusal of the Republican convention in July to seat this delegation, or, as the *Spokesman-Review* put it, to "the crime of June 18th."[41]

Poindexter and fourteen other progressive leaders escorted Theodore Roosevelt to the platform on August 6 to accept the Progressive nomination for president. The *Spokesman-Review* informed its reader that Poindexter was "the most conspicuous man on th platform" except Roosevelt and Senator Beveridge, who delivered the keynote address. After Roosevelt delivered his "Confession of Faith" and the convention ended, leaders of the Washington delegation conferred with Roosevelt and Senator Dixon, the Progressive National Chairman. At this meeting apparently Poindexter was persuaded that a state convention of all Washington progressives should meet to decide the third-party question.[42]

Undoubtedly the decision of the Seattle and western Washington progressives to form a new party on their own was responsible for Poindexter's change. The nomination of a splinter Progressive ticket in addition to a progressive slate in the Republican primary would certainly have divided the progressive vote and guaranteed victory for the regular Republicans. Poindexter (later, in 1915) explained his decision in a letter to Senator Works of California. He pointed out that he had "strongly opposed the formation of a separate Progressive Party." However, he was not in his state at the time and was "overruled." Since most of the progressive element decided to join the new party, Poindexter recalled, "I was compelled to act with them."[43] He decided, in short, that to avoid splitting the progressives into two groups, he had to join the Progressive party.

Poindexter's resistance to the third-party movement was overcome completely on August 13 when the progressive delegates to the Aberdeen convention, the leaders of the third-party faction, and the delegates to the national Progressive convention conferred in Seattle. They decided to form a Progressive party in Washington, and they set September 1 as the date of the convening of the first Progressive party convention in the state. According to the *Post-Intelligencer*, the action was taken by the leaders of the Poindexter faction which "changed front" and "rode rough shod over the original third party advocates." After the Seattle conference, all progressives who had filed to run in the Republican primary were advised to withdraw within ten days if they desired progressive support. Displeasure and irritation at this outcome was very evident in Poindexter's letter to Horace Kimball. He thanked Kimball for his help and advice, "especially in view of the apparent lack of experience, and good judgment of a number of those who are aggressive in the movement."[44]

The senator's reasons for opposing the formation of a third party seemed sound for the reform movement as well as for the senator's own political career. The progressive faction probably could have controlled the Republican party in Washington in the primaries and, from a practical standpoint, a bolt seemed unnecessary. It was the western and especially the Seattle and Tacoma factions of the progressive Republicans which insisted upon the bolt from the Republican party. The eastern,

Spokane-dominated branch headed by Horace Kimball and O. C. Moore opposed the bolt because they controlled the local Republican organization. In Seattle, Tacoma, and elsewhere on the coast, on the other hand, the party organization remained in the hands of Taft men. Where experienced and practical leadership seemed lacking, the third-party movement revealed its strength.

The professional politicians in Spokane were overruled, nonetheless, and a new Progressive party was formed in Spokane County with Horace Kimball as county chairman. On September 10 a state Progressive convention met in Seattle where state and congressional candidates were nominated. The meeting was honored by the presence of Theodore Roosevelt, himself, who delivered an hour-long oration. The crowd was so enthusiastic, the *Spokesman-Review* reported, that when the minister prayed for divine blessing for Roosevelt, it erupted spontaneously with cheering and applause. After the state convention Senator Poindexter campaigned throughout the state. He declared on October 14 that only the election of Roosevelt would bring federal control of "combinations and capital." Corporations "are necessary to develop the resources of the nation," he admitted, "but can only be controlled by the federal government." At the final Progressive rally of the campaign at Spokane, Poindexter received a "tremendous oration" as he rose to deliver his first public speech in Spokane since the campaign of 1910. He delivered a two-hour roasting of the "bosses" and political "machines" of both the Democratic and Republican parties. "Roosevelt," he exclaimed, "is the common enemy of them all!" He called for political reforms to return the government to the hands of the people because, "You can't put into effect these great social and industrial reforms until you adjust the agencies of government so the people can control them." To prevent his audience from thinking him radical, he added, "The progressive party does not object to property or big business, because big business is needed to carry on the big business of the country, but what it does object to is big business in control of the government."[45]

The day after Poindexter's speech, the Progressives closed ranks to carry Washington for Roosevelt. He received 35 percent of the popular vote, Woodrow Wilson was second with 27 percent, and Taft received 22 percent. The remaining 16 percent was cast for Socialist Eugene V. Debs and other minor candidates. Thirty-two of thirty-nine counties were carried by either Roosevelt or Wilson, the candidates recognized as Progressives, and together they polled 62 percent of the vote. Roosevelt carried the largest number of counties, and he was strongest in the urban counties dominated by Spokane, Seattle, and Tacoma. Taft, who was labeled as the opponent of reform, received 22 percent of the total vote and carried only seven counties.[46]

Examination of the county distribution of the voting returns in 1912 in Washington gives convincing evidence of the stability of the state's sectional voting habits. The pattern seems essentially consistent with the sectional distribution in previous elections in Washington, if it is assumed that counties which cast their pluralities for Roosevelt and Wilson were voting for a reform candidate and those which gave Taft the largest share of their vote were the least sympathetic to reform candidates. In this sense the 1912 distribution was strikingly similar to the distribution of the presidential election of 1896 when Bryan swept the same counties that supported Roosevelt and Wilson in 1912 and lost to McKinley the counties which Taft carried in 1912. The Roosevelt and Wilson counties in 1912 were by and large the same as those carried most overwhelmingly by Turner in the gubernatorial campaign of 1904 and by Poindexter in the Republican senatorial primary in 1910. By 1912 the strength of support for reform candidates, especially in the counties of eastern Washington, had been demonstrated many times over a sixteen-year period. These results should have left little doubt that in the near future at least the prospects for a conservative or antireform candidate in Washington were poor indeed.

But the Progressive victory was not as overwhelming as it at first appeared. Of five seats in the House of Representatives to be filled, only two Progressives, J. W. Bryan and J. A. Falconer, were elected, and they were elected at large. The first, second, and even the eastern Washington third district elected Republicans. There were nine state offices contested; the gubernatorial contest went to Ernest Lister, the Democrat, by a very slim plurality, the Republican incumbent Hay was second, and Robert T. Hodge, the Progressive, a rather poor third. All other state offices were won by Republicans. Although progressive sentiment was strong in the presidential and congressional at-large contests, other state races showed that the strong Republican tradition in Washington had not been broken.[47]

On the national scene, Wilson was elected president with about 42 percent of the total popular vote. As in Washington, although Theodore Roosevelt received more votes than Taft, the Progressive party had not exhibited great national strength. One Progressive candidate for governor and only a few Progressive candidates for Congress were elected, and it has been estimated that the Progressives won only about 250 of the countless state and local elections which they had contested.[48]

The problems which Poindexter experienced in attempting to put organization and direction into the progressive Republican campaign in Washington illustrated the immense difficulties involved in the formulation of the Progressive party on the state and local level. There were few recognized progressive leaders in western Washington, no established political institutions which the progressives could utilize, and far too many progressives who wanted to run for office. Everything had to be created and organized at once amid the confusion of a campaign. The result was personal victory for Roosevelt but failure for the third party. For Poindexter, the election awakened great expectations for his own future and for the future of the Progressive party and at the same time placed him in an awkward political situation in the Senate for when the Senate convened in December 1912, Poindexter was the only member who professed to belong to the Progressive party.

5.
The New Freedom

THE EMOTIONS of the campaign of 1912 stimulated Poindexter to take a prominent role in the fight for progressive reform during the Sixty-third Congress. He declared shortly after election day that the nation was in need of laws "which will put the great Interstate, industrial and transportation agencies under the more effective control of the Federal government," and he called for laws "which will . . . put the Federal government under the more effective control of the people." These reforms, Poindexter reasoned, would make the federal government "at the same time more responsible in its powers and more responsible to a well ordered and regularly expressed public opinion."[1] To symbolize his militancy, Poindexter was the only senator to list himself as a member of the Progressive party. In the first Wilson Congress, the Sixty-third, however, Poindexter usually voted with the progressive Republican bloc in support of progressive reform legislation as in the previous Congress. He supported the major legislative achievements of Wilson's "New Freedom" including the Underwood Tariff, the graduated or progressive income tax, the Federal Reserve Act, the Clayton Anti-Trust Act, and the Federal Trade Commission Act. He also introduced two major reform proposals of his own, a bill to create a federal industrial army to solve the problem of national unemployment and a bill to provide for the federal construction and operation of coal mines in Alaska and a transportation system to market the coal. Neither of Poindexter's proposals received a serious hearing by the Senate, and it was not until the 1930s that federal projects, such as the Civilian Conservation Corps and the Tennessee Valley Authority, attempted social experiments on the grand scale Poindexter envisioned at the height of the Progressive era. Even though Poindexter's two rather advanced and ambitious proposals received little support, they served at least to identify him as one of the most extreme members among the Senate progressives. On the whole, however, Poindexter's record was less deviant than in the previous Congress, and this was true of the other progressive Republicans as well. Examination of the roll-call votes reveals that only nine Republicans voted less than 80 percent of the time against the party majority, and in general Republicans seemed more capable of combining to oppose or modify Democratic legislation than they had been in uniting to support the recommendations of the Taft administration. The Democrats even though their ranks had been enlarged considerably by northern senators elected in 1910 and 1912, continued to exhibit greater party cohesion than the Republicans; and it was the Democratic majority which provided the votes necessary to enact the legislation of the "New Freedom."[2]

After the election of 1912 and before Wilson's inauguration, the Sixty-second Congress met in its last "lame duck" session, but Poindexter and his wife left their son Gale to prepare for his entrance examinations to the United States Naval Academy and traveled to Panama to relax and to observe the construction of the Panama Canal, then nearing completion. The senator was back in his seat, however, late in January 1913, to carry on his crusade for progressivism. He joined LaFollette and Bristow of Kansas in a successful effort to prevent President Taft from making thirteen hundred last-minute federal appointments,[3] and he delayed the beginning of Woodrow Wilson's inaugural ceremonies on March 4, 1913 by seizing the Senate floor to deliver a lecture on women's rights. "He talked on and on and on," reported the *Chicago Tribune*, and his speech, the *New York Times* pointed out in a decidedly huffy tone, held up Wilson's inauguration twenty-five minutes: "It was a severe strain on the patience of the crowd, but there was not a murmur."[4]

The day after Wilson's inauguration, the president convened the Sixty-third Congress in special session to consider the first reform bill in his "New Freedom" program, the Underwood Tariff. Since the Democrats were in control of the House and the Senate and Poindexter was no longer a Republican, he was obliged to look to the new Democratic majority for his committee assignments. Most of them were the same as in the previous Congress—he was returned to the Committee on Naval Affairs and Mines and Mining, and he became chairman of the Committee on Expenditures in the War Department. "I consider myself quite fortunate in having a large number of good committees and also a chairmanship," he wrote a friend in Spokane. "In this transition period of realignment and readjustment of great parties one is fortunate not to be ground to pieces in the mills."[5]

With organization problems settled, the new Democratic Congress began in early April 1913 to deliberate the Underwood Tariff bill which proposed major reductions in tariff duties. The House of Representatives quickly passed the bill, and forwarded it to the Senate. Again it was in the Senate, as in 1909, where the struggle for tariff reform was more difficult. Wilson, however, persuaded the Democratic Senate caucus to make the bill a party measure; and when voting on amendments began on July 19, it was evident that the president's efforts had been successful. Democratic party cohesion on the Underwood bill was even higher than in 1909, and Democrats from all sections voted in a solid bloc time after time to resist Republican efforts to break Democratic cohesion.[6]

Poindexter and the Senate progressive Republicans voted more frequently with the regular Republicans on this Democratic measure than on the 1909 Republican bill, for the Democrats proposed drastic reductions in the tariff, and the Republicans—Insurgents and regulars alike—were, after all, protectionists. This can be seen by comparing the voting record of Poindexter and seventeen progressive

Republican senators on duties for items produced in large quantities in states represented by these western and midwestern senators shown in table 3, with a distribution of the voting of the same western and midwestern senators on selected articles not produced to any great extent in the states they represented in table 4. All of these senators except Works of California voted regularly and consistently for higher duties on the articles produced in the West and Midwest. On items not produced in large quantities in the West or Midwest, twelve of the nineteen senators tended, on the majority of votes, to support lower tariffs. On these latter products, furthermore, there was ample evidence of disinterest. Only nine reformers voted more than ten times out of a possible sixteen on items not produced in the West and Midwest.[7]

The voting of the progressive Republicans in 1913 on amendments to the Underwood Tariff was similar in nature to the voting of the House Insurgents in 1909 on the Payne bill. On both occasions the progressive Republicans tended to vote for protection of the products of their own region. This observation was acknowledged and justified in 1913 by some prominent members of the Senate reformers including LaFollette, Borah, and Poindexter. Borah opposed the Underwood bill because, he argued, the measure continued to discriminate against western products: "I think it is one of the most sectional tariff bills that was ever passed by Congress. There is not an important product of the farmer or producer that is not put upon the free list. He is placed upon a free trade basis for everything he sells and upon a protective basis for everything which he buys." LaFollette spoke vigorously on the Senate floor against the Democratic intention to put wool on the free list. LaFollette insisted that he favored a general reduction of protective duties, but he admitted that if he had any prejudice, he was "sure that it was in favor of the producer of the raw material." To remove the duty on wool completely, he argued, "is an unwarranted discrimination against the farmer."[8]

Poindexter, like LaFollette, objected to particular discriminations he found in the bill. In the past, Poindexter frequently had called for

TABLE 3
UNDERWOOD TARIFF. VOTING OF PROGRESSIVE REPUBLICANS ON SELECTED FARM AND LUMBER PRODUCTS
X = Vote for higher duty
0 = Vote for lower duty

	Barley	Butter	Cattle	Eggs	Flax	Flaxseed	Fruits	Hay	Hemp	Horses/Mules	Logs	Meats	Posts/Poles	Potatoes	Seeds	Sheep	Shingles	Skins	Wheat	Wool	Totals X	Totals 0
Borah	X	X	X	–	–	X	–	X	X	X	X	–	–	–	–	X	–	0	X	X	11	0
Brady	X	X	X	X	X	X	X	X	X	X	–	X	0	X	X	X	X	–	X	X	17	1
Bristow	X	X	X	X	X	X	X	X	X	X	–	X	0	X	X	X	0	–	X	X	16	1
Clapp	X	X	X	X	–	X	–	X	X	X	–	X	0	X	X	X	–	X	X	X	11	4
Crawford	X	X	X	–	X	–	–	X	X	X	X	X	0	X	X	X	–	0	X	–	13	1
Cummins	X	–	X	–	–	X	–	–	X	–	X	–	–	–	–	X	0	0	–	0	8	2
Fall	–	–	–	–	X	–	–	–	X	X	X	–	–	–	–	–	–	–	–	–	4	2
Gronna	X	X	X	X	X	X	X	X	X	X	–	X	0	X	X	X	X	X	X	X	12	1
Jones	X	X	X	X	X	X	X	X	X	X	X	X	X	X	X	X	X	X	X	X	20	0
Kenyon	X	X	X	X	X	X	X	X	X	X	0	X	0	X	X	X	0	X	X	X	17	3
LaFollette	X	X	X	X	X	X	X	X	X	X	–	X	0	X	X	X	–	–	X	–	16	2
Nelson	X	X	X	X	X	X	X	X	X	X	X	X	–	X	X	X	X	X	X	X	17	1
Norris	X	X	X	X	X	X	X	X	X	X	0	X	0	X	X	X	0	0	X	0	16	4
Perkins	X	X	X	X	X	X	X	X	X	X	X	X	–	X	X	X	X	X	X	X	18	1
Poindexter	X	X	X	X	X	X	X	X	X	X	X	X	–	X	X	X	X	0	X	–	16	1
Sherman	X	X	X	X	X	X	X	X	X	X	X	X	–	X	X	X	–	X	X	0	16	2
Sterling	X	X	X	X	X	X	X	X	X	X	–	X	0	X	X	X	X	X	X	X	19	1
Townsend	X	X	X	X	X	X	X	X	–	X	X	–	–	X	X	X	–	X	X	–	12	1
Works	–	–	–	–	–	X	–	–	–	–	X	X	–	–	–	–	0	–	–	–	3	1
Total votes for higher duty	17	16	17	14	14	16	12	16	16	17	10	14	1	14	14	16	5	7	16	10		

TABLE 4

UNDERWOOD TARIFF. VOTING OF
PROGRESSIVE REPUBLICANS ON SELECTED
MANUFACTURED PRODUCTS AND RAW MATERIALS
X = Vote for higher duty
0 = Vote for lower duty

	Aluminum	Automobiles	Shotguns, etc.	Castiron Pipe	Coal tar Distillates	Cotton Cloth	Cotton Hosiery	Cotton Thread	Cutlery	Iron	Lead Ores	Needles	Scissors/Shears	Steel Forms	Thread	Totals X	0
Borah	–	–	0	0	–	X	0	X	–	0	X	–	–	–	X	4	4
Brady	0	–	0	–	X	–	X	X	–	–	X	0	–	X	X	6	3
Bristow	0	0	0	0	0	X	0	X	0	X	X	0	0	X	X	6	9
Clapp	0	X	–	0	0	–	–	X	–	–	0	0	0	–	X	3	6
Crawford	0	0	0	0	–	–	0	X	–	0	–	–	–	X	X	3	6
Cummins	–	0	0	X	0	–	–	–	0	X	–	–	–	X	–	3	4
Fall	–	–	–	–	–	–	–	–	X	–	–	–	–	–	X	2	0
Gronna	–	0	0	X	0	–	–	X	0	0	X	0	0	–	–	3	7
Jones	0	0	0	X	0	X	0	X	X	0	X	0	0	X	X	7	8
LaFollette	0	X	0	0	0	–	–	X	0	0	–	0	0	–	X	3	8
Kenyon	0	X	0	0	0	X	0	X	0	0	0	0	0	X	X	5	10
Nelson	X	X	–	X	–	X	X	X	X	X	X	X	X	X	X	13	0
Norris	0	X	0	–	0	X	0	X	0	0	0	0	–	X	X	5	8
Perkins	X	X	0	X	0	X	–	X	–	X	X	X	–	X	X	10	2
Poindexter	0	–	–	0	0	X	0	–	–	–	X	–	0	X	–	3	5
Sherman	–	0	0	X	–	X	X	X	X	0	X	X	X	X	X	10	3
Sterling	0	0	0	X	0	X	0	X	0	–	X	X	0	X	X	7	7
Townsend	–	X	0	–	0	–	–	X	X	X	X	–	–	–	X	6	2
Works	0	–	0	–	0	X	–	–	–	–	–	0	–	X	X	3	4
Total votes for higher duty	2	7	0	7	1	11	3	15	5	5	11	4	2	13	16		

reductions on manufactured goods. In 1912, for example, he severely criticized the attempts by eastern senators to raise the tariff on woolen cloth, and he insisted that if the Congress continued "indefinitely to ignore and repudiate the sentiment of the country, the whole system is bound to fail—not only the tariff system, but the Government itself." During the debate on the Underwood bill, however, he focused almost exclusively upon obtaining increased protection for Washington products. To illustrate, on August 15 he proposed an amendment to raise the duty on hay from $2.00 to $3.00 per ton, "I admit that $3.00 per ton duty . . . is a substantial duty," he said. "It is a protective duty." Then he explained that he had "no hesitation whatever in offering this amendment when I compare the rates on agricultural products with the rates fixed in this bill on manufactured products which the farmer is compelled to buy and consume." In his view, in short, Poindexter sought merely to secure a more equitable rate structure for his section, not an end to protection.[9]

Poindexter's voting on the Underwood Tariff bill was quite similar to that of the progressive Republican senators', and, as he readily admitted, he aimed at winning concessions for Washington state's products—barley, butter, cattle, eggs, hay, hemp, horses and mules, lead-bearing ores, logs, meat, sheep, shingles, wheat and wool. If failure to vote is an indication of lack of interest, then he was not concerned about rates on the items of little importance to the Washington economy, for he voted only nine of the total sixteen votes analyzed.

One of the most controversial sections in the Underwood bill was the one which provided for the graduated or progressive income tax. This was the first income tax enacted under the 16th Amendment that had been ratified in 1913. Many Senate progressives, both Republicans and Democrats, criticized the House bill because the tax rates were set too low, and a bipartisan group of advanced progressives proposed a series of amendments intended in general to raise the rates on higher incomes. Most Democrats opposed all amendments, and of the few votes cast for the amendments to increase income tax rates most were cast by western Republicans.[10]

Two of the amendments to increase tax rates were Poindexter's. One proposed to insert, in lieu of the Democratic provision, a 10 percent tax on net income exceeding $500,000 and a 20 percent tax on all net income over $1,000,000. The second proposed to raise the tax on net incomes of $1,000,000 or over from 7 to 8 percent. Both were defeated, opposed by most Democrats and most Republicans.[11]

In justifying his income tax proposals, Poindexter emphasized, as he had many times before, that his goal as a progressive reformer was intended to restore honesty and equality of opportunity to American society. The "principal vice" of the Democratic bill's tax provisions, he said, "is that the principle of graduation upon which the income tax is based stops before it reaches the excessive fortunes" that "have been acquired by special privilege of one kind or another." As examples of special privilege, Poindexter pointed to the "discrimination and special favor in transportation rates" and "the acquirement through special favors, of the natural resources," two kinds of special privilege that would occur quite naturally to a spokesman of the legal-business establishment in Spokane, Washington. The efforts of Poindexter and the other progressives probably had some effect on the Democrats. Four progressive Democrats demanded that the Democratic caucus reconsider its vote on the LaFollette amendment which had proposed a 10 percent tax on all net income over $100,000. The result was a compromise in which the Democrats agreed to raise the maximum rate from 3 to 7 percent.[12]

The Senate passed the Underwood Tariff on a final vote that was highly partisan. Only Poindexter and LaFollette joined with the Democrats to support the new tariff, and when each voted "aye," he was warmly applauded by the galleries. Poindexter explained his vote for the new tariff by asserting that it provided more than ample protection for manufactured goods. "Its principal defect," he said "is its free-listing of some of the great staple so-called raw materials." Because the bill contained these discriminations against "raw materials," voting for it "was a matter about which I had grave doubts, but upon final consideration I could not bring myself to cast a vote to continue in effect the extortionate and outrageous Payne-Aldrich bill."[13]

Poindexter's vote for the Underwood Tariff won him additional public recognition among progressives. President Wilson expressed his "sincere admiration of the independence and personal conviction which you are so conspicuously illustrating in the Senate"; the *Chicago Tribune* gave him a headline and quoted him at length; and *Collier's Weekly* declared that Poindexter's vote had shown him to be "A Courageous Man." By supporting Washington products on the crucial amendments and by voting for the Underwood bill on the final vote, Poindexter had executed skillfully; he had both defended the economic interests of his Washington constituents and maintained his reputation as a leading reformer.[14]

The second major Democratic proposal enacted by Congress in the Sixty-third Congress was the bill to provide more effective federal regulation of the national banking system by the creation of the Federal Reserve System. Concern about the concentration of banking in the hands of Wall Street financiers had stimulated calls for federal regulation of banking since the Populist movement in the 1890s. At the end of Roosevelt's administration Congress established the National Monetary Commission to analyze the national financial system and make recommendations to Congress. The Commission, headed by Senator Aldrich of Rhode Island, submitted a proposal, the Aldrich plan, that would have established a national bank with fifteen local branches essentially in the control of the national banking community.

Hostile reaction to the Aldrich plan came immediately from progressive Democrats and Republicans who interpreted it as an attempt by Wall Street bankers to strengthen further their control of credit and currency. Both the Democratic and the Progressive party platforms in 1912 denounced the plan, and the Progressive platform declared that control of the financial system should be lodged in the hands of the federal government and protected from control by Wall Street or other special interests. Further hostility to the Aldrich plan and increased incentive for banking reform developed during 1912 and 1913 when the Pujo committee, an investigating committee of the House of Representatives, disclosed findings suggesting that there was a higher degree of concentration of control of the financial system by Wall Street bankers than most had realized.

The demand for banking reform seemed widespread, and Woodrow Wilson, shortly after the election, began to work closely with Carter Glass of Virginia, chairman of the House Banking Committee, to draft a bank reform bill that would be acceptable to the majority in Congress. The bill, when approved by Wilson and submitted to Congress in June 1913, provided for a Federal Reserve system of regional banks governed in policy matters by a Federal Reserve Board. The House passed the banking bill in September 1913 and sent it on to the Senate where it was passed in December 1913.

Poindexter, like most western progressives, was convinced of the need for banking reform, largely because he desired to eliminate eastern financial domination of Washington banks and businessess. He had protested strongly against the Aldrich plan—"another name for a Central National Bank and . . . one of the most insidious and dangerous propositions proposed in many years." He charged that the "most pronounced danger in our national monetary situation is the possibility of the credits and the currency being absolutely controlled by a very small group—or even by one man. Of course, this financial power centers at present in Wall Street." The Aldrich plan, said Poindexter, would turn over to Wall Street bankers "the monstrous power of creating panics at will . . . and other illegitimate purposes" and "would simply give the added sanction of the law and the government to this monstrous power."[15]

As a substitute for the Aldrich plan, Poindexter called for the adoption of a system "which would tend in the opposite direction," or, in other words, which would free the nation from the domination of eastern financial interests. He suggested legislation to provide "legitimate aid direct from the government in time of financial stress or panic" to "the independent banks of the country, wherever located." This plan, concluded Poindexter, would "tend towards decentralization or in other words freeing the local banks . . . from the absolute domination and control of New York."[16] Poindexter's reaction to the administration's banking bill was favorable: "it does not go as far as I would like to have seen it go towards the decentralization of the control of money and credits," he said, but, "it is a step in that direction." Furthermore, said Poindexter, "my opinion of the bill has lately been enhanced by the attacks made upon it by certain banking interests." He could not, however, understand why some small banks opposed the bill; they "seem to be controlled even against their own interests by the great banks of New York City."[17]

Poindexter was one of only a handful of Republicans to vote for the Federal Reserve Act, but he insisted that it would benefit his section of the nation: "I do not expect that the passage of this bill will bring instant relief," he admitted. "I do think, however, that when the country has gradually adjusted itself to the new central reserve bank plan it will make money much easier and relieve the outlying states from the financial slavery they have been under so long from New York." Several progressive Republicans, by contrast, did not share Poindexter's evaluation of the new banking act. "Under this system," explained Borah, "the great banking interests of New York, Chicago, Boston, and San Francisco can absolutely inflate and contract the currency at will." Works of California agreed; the Act constituted, he insisted, a "complete surrender . . . to the money trusts."[18]

Poindexter's attitude toward banking reform served as another illustration of his general effort to free the West from eastern "colonialism." In this respect, his view on conservation of natural resources (he aimed to regulate eastern "trusts" and to prevent them from using the natural resources) and his views on the tariff (where he sought to eliminate alleged discrimination in favor of the East) were quite similar to his views on banking reform. Furthermore, Poindexter's reaction to banking reform demonstrates once again that he desired to make only minor adjustments in the economic system. He seemed only to desire to improve existing institutions and to restore equality of opportunity.

With the passage of the Federal Reserve Act, the first year of the Wilson administration came to a close, and Poindexter reflected with his friend Rufus Woods upon Wilson's achievements. "While there is a fundamental difference between us and the Democratic party," he wrote to Woods, "yet the President has in a number of instances done good progressive work and where he does he is entitled to credit and support in the various measures."[19]

Poindexter was asked sometime later by *Harper's Weekly* to write an evaluation of Wilson's achievements. His article asserted that President Wilson "has a wonderful record of accomplishments." There was much more legislation needed, he added, and he wondered if Wilson would support "the political liberation of women." He also noted that Wilson had yet to take direct action "to check private monopoly, to prevent discrimination, to subject the giants of industry to obedience to the law"; but he readily admitted that Wilson on the whole had done well.[20]

The Wilson administration and the Democrats also won Poindexter's approval in their successful enactment of two measures to regulate the corporation in 1914. Additional legislation to control big business had seemed necessary to all major presidential candidates during the election of 1912, but attention focused upon a major difference between Theodore Roosevelt and Woodrow Wilson on the proper method of federal regulation of business. Roosevelt, in defining "New Nationalism," insisted that since monopolies could not be broken up by legislative action and were in many ways beneficial, the government should cease trying to restore free competition and begin instead to regulate the trusts. Wilson, on the other hand, advocated, as an important part of "New Freedom," strengthening the Sherman Anti-Trust Act to restore free competition and limit the size of combinations.

The measure which reflected the "New Freedom" emphasis upon the restoration of free competition was the Clayton Anti-Trust bill. It declared many unfair trade practices illegal, made owners and directors of businesses responsible for violations of the antitrust regulations, and in other ways attempted to preserve free competition. While the Clayton bill was under consideration, Wilson, influenced by progressives who were more in sympathy with Roosevelt's proposal to regulate rather than dissolve the trusts, was persuaded to support as well a Federal Trade Commission bill that also had been submitted to the Senate in 1914. This bill gave broad powers to an appointed commission of five members to investigate and prevent unfair competition by the issuance of cease and desist orders. It was given priority over the Clayton bill, and both were enacted into law in the summer of 1914.

Poindexter seemed more interested in the Clayton bill, but he supported the Federal Trade Commission also. He took no part in the Senate discussion of the Trade Commission bill, although he had said in March 1914 that he would like to see such a commission given "the power to fix prices" and "to adjust wages." He claimed, in fact, that there was no important distinction between the kind of federal regulation afforded by a trade commission and that provided by antitrust legislation. He had given "a great deal" of thought, he said, to "the supposed conflict between such commission regulation and the Sherman Anti-Trust law" and had concluded that "there is no real conflict." He explained: "The Sherman Anti-Trust law is . . . not inconsistent with industrial governmental regulation through such a commission, but the proper enforcement of it requires such a commission."21

The Clayton Anti-Trust Act, in the meantime, had generated considerable criticism from labor and farm groups because it failed to exempt unions and farm organizations from antitrust prosecution. Labor groups were particularly determined to obtain this exemption, and during most of 1913 and 1914 Samuel Gompers and the American Federation of Labor worked for passage of the Bacon-Bartlett bill which provided for an explicit antitrust exemption. Poindexter had been pressured for some time by labor unions in Washington to support the Bacon-Bartlett bill, and as early as December 12, 1913 he informed the secretary of a printer's union that he favored the "principle" contained in the bill. Elsewhere, however, he indicated that he supported exemption only for "voluntary organizations"—labor and farm groups which were "not organized for financial profit, and not in any sense commercial, business or industrial organizations." He favored antitrust exemptions only for groups that were "more social and fraternal in their spirit and purposes." Clearly this was not the unqualified antitrust exemption labor demanded, and in fact a spokesman of the Spokane Fruit Growers Company informed Poindexter that such an exemption was of little or no value to a farm organization either. A successful farm organization, he said, "must be a business organization and has got to have capital stock and under the last analysis has got to operate for profit."[22] Most of the correspondence to Poindexter in support of the antitrust exemption, however, came from labor unions.

When it became obvious that the Bacon-Bartlett bill could not pass, labor and farm groups endeavored to have some form of antitrust exemption incorporated into the Clayton bill. They were partially successful, and when the Clayton bill passed the House it met some of labor's demands. Labor unions in Washington overwhelmed Poindexter with pleas that he support the exemption in the House bill. For example, M. T. Alliman, secretary of the Everett Trades Council, informed Poindexter that twenty-three unions in Everett demanded passage of the Clayton Act with the exemptions; and the secretary of the Seattle Central Labor Council demanded passage of the Clayton Act exactly as passed by the House.[23]

During the spring and early summer of 1914 Poindexter was also deluged with telegrams and letters from businessmen who opposed the antitrust exemption for labor unions. The president of a lumber company in Leavenworth, Washington, declared that "when they [the Democrats?] legislate against any one class . . . we think they are going beyond their rights in order to gain political advantage." The manager of the Employers' Association of Washington, the New Seattle Chamber of Commerce, and the Spokane Chamber of Commerce sent earnest pleas to Poindexter to oppose the examptions, and brother-in-law R. L. Rutter sent Poindexter a telegram charging that the labor exemptions were "most pernicious unfair and unreasonable."[24] Poindexter responded to most of this correspondence with a noncommittal form letter, but he took special pains to answer Rutter. In general he agreed with Rutter's position: "Of course, any special favors or exemptions to any class would be intolerable." However, Poindexter assured his brother-in-law that the labor exemption that he supported did not grant "special favors" to unions. "My impression," Poindexter continued, "was that the exemptions referred to were general in their nature and related to all associations not organized for commercial profit, and applied to every class and condition alike." A few days later, Poindexter repeated his views of the exemption clause to another Spokane businessman: "Of course, there ought not to be any special privilege for any one—farmers, labor unions, or anyone else. The distinction seems to be between any organization for commercial profit. I certainly am not in favor of allowing one set of men to do what another set . . . are prohibited from doing."[25]

When the Clayton bill reached the Senate floor, it contained the provision which Poindexter had promised to support, that is, it exempted from prosecution under the antitrust laws, farm, labor, and other organizations not organized for profit. Dissatisfied with this exemption, Senator Cummins of Iowa obtained the floor on September 2 to offer an amendment to the bill which would have added a sentence that seemed to be the amendment Gompers and other labor leaders demanded: that nothing in the Clayton Act "shall be construed to forbid the existence and operation of labor organizations having for their objects bettering the conditions, lessening the hours, or advancing the compensation of labor." The Cummins amendment was defeated twenty to thirty-nine, and Poindexter voted with the majority against Senator Cummins, organized agriculture, and organized labor.[26] Faced with a sharp, emotional conflict between small businessmen on the one hand and labor organizations on the other, Poindexter yielded to the urgings of his friends in the business community by opposing the Cummins amendment. But he did support, on the other hand, the "weak" Democratic labor exemption, although even this exemption seemed radical to Rutter and other Washington businessmen. Poindexter's loyalty and ultimately his own point of view rested with Rutter and his Spokane colleagues, but he was also aware of the need to adjust to new industrial conditions, and he needed to maintain the support of both businessmen and union members.

The farm-labor exemption clause was, of course, only one section of the Clayton bill. The sections which seemed more important to Poindexter were those which dealt directly with the problems of trusts and monopolies, and throughout the debate he showed himself to be a staunch defender of free competition and an uncompromising foe of combinations in restraint of trade. This was made evident when Senator Cummins on August 27 proposed an amendment to the bill providing some exceptions to the prohibition against the holding of stock in competing corporations. Poindexter objected strenuously, arguing that the law "ought to be absolute and without exception!"[27] In short, Poindexter displayed in this debate no indication that he had been influenced by Theodore Roosevelt's contention that under some circumstances combinations in restraint of trade ought to be permitted to exist.

Poindexter proposed two amendments of his own to the Clayton bill. One proposed to set higher penalties for violations of the bill, and the second would have spelled out more explicitly the prohibitions against railroad ownership of stock in subsidiary companies. Both were voted down, and soon afterward the Clayton Act was passed. Poindexter and eight Republicans joined with the Democrats to pass the bill. All but one of the eight Republicans were, like Poindexter, from states west of the Mississippi River.[28]

In supporting most of the Wilson administration's legislative proposals to the Sixty-third Congress, Poindexter established his claim to be one of the foremost advocates of progressive reform in the Senate, and he made it rather clear that he felt that Wilson's "New Freedom" bills had not gone nearly far enough. He submitted two proposals of his own that reveal more precisely other problems which he felt should attract the concern of the federal government. In 1913, while the Underwood

Tariff was under discussion, Poindexter proposed that the federal government assume a major share of the responsibility for unemployment in the United States by creating a federal "industrial army" to provide work relief. The idea was suggested to him by R. A. Dague, a former editor of the *Santa Paula* (California) *Chronicle*, who characterized himself as an "enthusiastic socialist." Dague proposed that the "industrial army" be used to construct highways, ships, and other public works, and, in some respects, his project seems similar to the Civilian Conservation Corps and other federal agencies established in the 1930s.[29]

Poindexter incorporated these ideas into a bill he introduced to the Senate in June 1913. It was immediately referred to its burial place in the Committee on Education and Labor, but Poindexter was not one to give up easily. He insisted upon the need for an "industrial army" to deal on a prolonged basis with the problem of perpetual unemployment which he felt was an unavoidable by-product of industrialization: "We are accumulating in our youth a lot of libidinous [*sic*] of an old nation, such as millions of people whom the government must care for and protect in some way whether it accords to our abstract theories of government or not." Inevitably, he maintained, industrial unemployment will require the federal government to move "more and more in the direction of what you call paternalism,—that is we will gather a larger and larger horde of what you call misfits, failures . . . and as a community we would be compelled to take care of this."[30]

Poindexter continued to press for consideration of his industrial army bill until at least 1916 without success. He insisted that city and county governments had done the same thing for years in the form of poorhouses. His bill, he argued in a letter to President Wilson in 1914, "simply provides for a more efficient and comprehensive system of dealing with the unemployed as a substitute for the inefficient and pauperizing methods of dealing with the unemployed poor as paupers and vagrants." In January 1915 he declared that "the question of the unemployed is a most important one," but, he admitted, "I have not been able so far, to make even a dent in the Conservatism of Congress on that subject." On this occasion he blamed congressional reluctance upon the influence of "Big business" which "is . . . having too much to say in regard to our government and it is time that more consideration and attention should be given to the common people." Later in 1915, Poindexter urged that the government should "employ ten thousand men as soon as they could be gathered" to be put to work on coal mines, on a railway in Alaska, and on road, river, and harbor improvements in the United States; and in December 1915 and again in April 1917 he reintroduced his bill into the Senate; but never did it receive consideration.[31]

Poindexter's industrial army bill was probably one of the most advanced pieces of labor legislation proposed to the Senate during an era when there was little evidence of congressional concern about urban and industrial problems. The proposal, in fact, seemed directed more fundamentally to the conditions of the poorest, most underprivileged segment of the working population in the United States than most of the reforms proposed at the time by leading urban social reformers, and it marked Poindexter as one of the very few members of the Senate who seemed genuinely concerned about the problems of the chronic unemployed. It did not seem, however, that Poindexter acted primarily from compassion or from humanitarian concern for the unemployed, and certainly there is no evidence that he was in any way influenced here by organized labor. As has been seen, in the conflict over an exemption from the antitrust laws for labor unions, Poindexter showed no sympathy for the views of organized labor. Poindexter's defense of the industrial army idea consistently stressed the danger of a permanent body of "misfits and failures" to the social order, and he presented his proposal as a practical, hardheaded solution to an "inevitable" product of industrial conditions.

Poindexter also championed a proposal, similar in some respects to the industrial army bill, to save Alaska's natural resources, especially its coal deposits, from eastern corporations. After a trip to Alaska with Gifford Pinchot in 1911, Poindexter had promised a crowd in Spokane that he would work for the creation of a project in which the United States government would build, own, and operate a railroad and a coal mine in Alaska to save it from "the Syndicate" and to provide the people of the Pacific coast with inexpensive coal. Although such a proposal as Poindexter envisaged seemed unlikely to receive serious attention by the Senate, it was, nonetheless, an appealing prospect even to the most rabid Poindexter-haters in the Puget Sound area where the Alaskan trade was an important economic asset. Seattle businessmen had been interested in promoting the development of the Alaskan economy, and in November 1911, just after Poindexter's speech in Spokane, the New Seattle Chamber of Commerce had dispatched its chairman, John L. Wilson, to Portland, Los Angeles, San Diego, San Francisco, and other large towns on the Pacific Coast to urge upon local businessmen the advantages to be gained by the development of Alaska. Another member of the New Chamber of Commerce, M. D. Leehey, praised Poindexter's proposal. "Several of us," he wrote, "are at work now in an effort to organize a campaign along these lines through the commercial bodies of Seattle. I believe that we can procure the unanimous endorsement by all our local commercial bodies, of your plan for such a railroad."[32]

Poindexter introduced his bill to save Alaska from "the Syndicate" in 1913. It authorized the president to operate coal mines in Alaska and to provide for transportation of the coal by a government-owned and operated railroad and a fleet of ships. To offset any argument that his bill would restrict the possibilities for private investment, he pointed out that his bill "leaves ample opportunity for individual enterprise and at the same time by government competition prevents private monopoly." Poindexter's desire to open Alaska was shared by the Wilson administration, and in 1913 a Democratic Alaskan railroad bill was introduced to the Senate by Senator Chamberlain, a Democrat from Oregon. This bill, however, was hardly as ambitious as Poindexter's, and it merely authorized the federal government to construct an Alaskan railroad.[33]

Although Poindexter's bill was favorably received by some businessmen in Seattle, he was encouraged, as a more practical course, to support the administration's measure. M. D. Leehey, who in 1911 had supported Poindexter's Alaskan proposal and in 1913 was chairman of the Alaska Day Committee of the Seattle Arctic Club, praised Poindexter for being "one of the first to advocate the construction of government railways in Alaska," but it was clear that Leehey wanted Poindexter's bill withdrawn. It was too radical, and it threatened to divide the ranks of those in favor of a government-built railroad. The *Post-Intelligencer* less tactfully also asked Poindexter to "abandon, at least for the time being, any attempt to secure government direction of all human activities in the North." A government-built railroad, the editorial continued, "is the first need. Other things can follow in natural sequence as they seem needed for Alaska's development." Poindexter responded to the pressure to support the administration measure by promising that he would "certainly not undertake to obstruct any progressive legislation. If we can get nothing better I shall support the Committee bill," but he insisted that his own bill was much more desirable.[3]

The Democratic Alaskan bill was debated by the Senate in January 1914. Poindexter offered his bill as a substitute, as he had said he would, but it found no sympathetic hearing. Without a recorded vote, his proposal was quickly rejected, and the Senate then passed the Democratic Alaskan railroad bill. Although it was a Democratic measure, many western progressive Republicans joined Poindexter to support it, and the news of the bill's passage was received with joy in Seattle. "Action of Senate Means Prosperity," predicted the headlines in the *Post-Intelligencer*.[35]

Poindexter won the approval of many of his constituents by his efforts to open Alaska. Even the *Post-Intelligencer*, one of his most vociferous critics, admitted after the passage of the Alaskan railroad bill that although the men who represented Washington were of different political factions, "when the time came for united action all differences were laid aside and forgotten. They were one."[36]

Thus Poindexter won even the approval of the chief opposition newspaper in his efforts to stimulate th economic development of Alaska with federal funds, and he managed this achievement while remaining consistent with his record as a champion of the conservation of natural resources. He could still maintain that his efforts had the effect of preventing the "exploitation" of Alaska by the "syndicate" (eastern corporations) in the interests of the "people" (local businessmen). It was evident, however, that Poindexter saw other social advantages as well that could be secured through a massive federal Alaskan project. The lessons learned from government projects in Alaska, he argued, will "be of inestimable value to us in the United States proper when we inevitably will reach an acute stage . . . of social and economic problems developing so fast around us."[37] In short, Poindexter anticipated that his federal Alaskan project would serve, like the industrial army, to hire the unemployed. In this context, again, Poindexter emphasized his apprehension about the future of the American social order, and his comments suggested rather strongly that Poindexter shared Theodore Roosevelt's fear of social revolution, and hoped that the industrial army, a federal project in Alaska, and perhaps other reforms would offer the impoverished working class greater opportunity and ward off or at least ameliorate the "acute stage" which Poindexter believed to be just over the horizon.

Further clarification of Poindexter's attitudes on reform and social order erupted during an angry speech on the Senate floor in the summer of 1913 in response to the *Post-Intelligencer*'s charge that the senator was guilty of nepotism. The newspaper reported that Poindexter's son Gale had been appointed to Annapolis by Congressman LaFollette of Washington in exchange for Poindexter's appointment to West Point of another Spokane boy, whom LaFollette intended to appoint. In addition, the newspaper claimed that through the senator's influence, his brother Fielding Poindexter had been reinstated in the army after a physical disability retirement, that brother William Poindexter served as a clerk in the Senate, and that the senator had attempted unsuccessfully to get Ernest Poindexter a government position. The *Post-Intelligencer* named additional people on the government payroll whom it said were Poindexter's relatives, and concluded that there was "sufficient proof that almost a dozen of the Virginia Poindexters are indebted to their illustrious relative for their positions."[38]

Poindexter answered the *Post-Intelligencer*'s charges on August 28 when he asked that one of the newspaper's articles be printed in the *Congressional Record* and announced that he wished to make a personal statement. He admitted that there had been an agreement between himself and Congressman LaFollette to appoint Gale to Annapolis. His only defense for this was to say that LaFollette had thought the arrangement was "proper and fair." The senator conceded also that he had appointed his brother William "to a position in the folding room," but he emphatically denied any connection with positions held or favors received by any other relatives.[39]

Poindexter, characteristically, did not remain long on the defensive. He called the *Post-Intelligencer* the "principal exponent" of the "political ring" which governed the state of Washington and insinuated that this personal attack on him was motivated by a desire of the "ring" to discredit his campaign for progressive reform. In this emotionally charged barrage, he then went on to try to explain why he supported progressive reform. He maintained that "This ring and the interests they represent seem to want to make this a war of extermination," and he wondered why they thought "that in such a war they will be the ones who will survive." They could not survive, he exclaimed, because they violated the law: "It is singular that the proprietors of these property interests can not see that when they leave the safe highway there is no other way by which they may be saved. When they pack juries and corrupt elections, as they have done so often, they are striking at the foundations of their own castle." Newspapers of "this same type," he continued, had recently incited sailors to mob the IWW hall in Seattle. "It was a fine example of obedience to law and respect for the flag!"[40]

But to prevent any impression that he was improperly sympathetic with the IWW, Poindexter explained that all elements should obey the law, with no special favors for any group. "There shall be no discrimination as to persons, whether the disturber of the peace be a thriving corporation, an I. W. W. wind jammer, an incendiary mob, or a libelous newspaper. The ignorant and poverty-stricken alien who talks lawlessness should be punished, but for every year of his incarceration the bandit of big business and their literary prostitutes, . . . should serve 10 years in prison."[41] In Poindexter's opinion (a view he subsequently would change) "big business" more often broke the law than did the IWW, but his ideal was to maintain equality under the law and to defend the social order, or as he put it, "the people," from the activities of any "special interest."

While this outburst provoked by the *Post-Intelligencer*'s personal attack was not a carefully constructed exposition of Poindexter's social attitudes, it was nonetheless a fairly coherent statement of his progressive ideology. He contended that he spoke for the established social order, the "people," against its enemies. He focused above all upon corporations as the principal threat to the "people," but clearly any person or group which failed to conform to the law threatened the "people." Obedience to the law and a law-abiding citizenry obviously ranked high in Poindexter's value system, and the "I. W. W. windjammer," the "incendiary mob," and the "poverty-striken alien" all represented potential, if not immediate, threats to the "people." His support of bills to provide federal jobs for the unemployed merely manifested his anticipation of future dangers to the social order and his desire to solve these problems before they reached, as he put it, an "acute stage."[42]

The *Post-Intelligencer* accepted Poindexter's denials "at face value," though it still wondered how all the Poindexters got on the government payroll. As for Poindexter's attack, the *Post-Intelligencer* responded with words which many of Poindexter's opponents must have approved. "Such false, demagogical outcries as he gave renewed vent to in the senate are his stock in trade," the newspaper declared. "He would not be Miles Poindexter if he ceased his imaginary grappling with the Guggenheims, 'the ring' and 'the interests,' or paused in his flight from political goblins in general. His occupation would be gone. He would then be miraculously turned statesman."[43] The *Post-Intelligencer* touched upon one of the essential ingredients of Poindexter's temperament, for both before and after 1916 he seemed almost incessantly to be "grappling" with his opponents. Whether Poindexter's statements were "demagogical" or not probably depended upon one's values; certainly his supporters did not think him a demagogue. Others, to be sure, including Roosevelt, Beveridge, LaFollette, and Borah, also seemed at times to use similar, though perhaps not such extreme, language.

By the time the Sixty-third Congress adjourned in early 1915 Congress had enacted most of the major legislation of Wilson's "New Freedom" program. Although Wilson's achievements had been possible primarily because of the loyal support and cohesion of the Democrats in Congress, Poindexter had played an important role in shaping and passing the Underwood Tariff, the Federal Reserve Act, the Federal Trade Commission Act, the Clayton Anti-Trust Act, and he had promoted his own bills to create an industrial army and to provide for a federal project to mine and transport coal in Alaska. His record as an advanced progressive reformer was without challenge. But even as Poindexter struggled in the Senate to secure the passage of effective reform legislation, he also worked to establish his identity as one of the leading personalities in the Progressive party and to place the new third party on a sound basis both in Washington state and nationally.

Shortly after the election of 1912 Poindexter attended a Progressive party conference in Chicago. Theodore Roosevelt spoke to the gathering and, although he privately felt pessimistic about the future of the new party, he publicly reaffirmed his faith in the principles of the 1912 Progressive platform. In a mood of optimism the conference adopted a plan of permanent organization, with headquarters in New York and a publicity bureau in Washington, D.C.

Poindexter felt the conference had been a "great success." His conversion to the third party had been a reluctant one, resulting from absolute political necessity, but once the decision had been made, Poindexter plunged himself into Progressive party activities with tremendous energy and, in contrast to Roosevelt, with optimism for the future.[44] Poindexter's letters to his fellow Progressives after November 1912 were filled with optimism and encouragement. He predicted that "the Progressive party . . . must before a great while become the dominant political party of the Nation," and he hoped to secure the development of a political organization. "Every real progressive should now co-operate in quietly but systematically perfecting a National, State and County organization." In his opinion the Progressive party "in some miraculous way seemed to spring from the ground fully panoplied and equipped in the campaign just passed," but he doubted the same could happen in 1914 without "organization." Then he concluded, "The sacred fires must be kept burning. There is work worthwhile ahead."[45]

There were many Progressives like Poindexter who insisted that the Progressive party had a future. Former Senator Beveridge, for example, in an article in the *Saturday Evening Post*, denounced the proposal to amalgamate the Progressive and Republican parties which the Progressive publisher Frank Munsey had advanced in February 1913. William Allen White informed Theodore Roosevelt, after White had completed a tour through the southwest, "I find the Progressive sentiment in those states stronger than it was before the election. In Kansas, I think matters are in splendid shape." In California in early December 1912, the progressive Republicans led by Hiram Johnson testified to their faith in the future of the Progressive party by withdrawing from the Republican party and joining the Progressives.[46]

There were, however, many indications that all was not well. Much depended upon the ability of the Progressives to entice into their new adventure the progressive Republicans who had not supported Roosevelt in 1912. Albert Beveridge, in sending Poindexter "heartiest congratulations" for the

Progressive success in Washington, revealed his concern about efforts of his former Republican colleagues to keep the progressives in the old party: "The papers say Taft, Hadley, and one or two other gentlemen, are framing up a scheme to rehabilitate the Republican party, by getting our Insurgent Senators to take a hand. I hope that most of our fellows will do as you have done in this matter, and not lend themselves to any such time serving plan."[47] Poindexter agreed wholeheartedly: "The spirit of the rank and file, as well as the leaders of our Progressives, is that this great organization which has sprung into existence almost as if by magic, is too great a power for good to be abandoned."[48]

Efforts to woo most progressive Republicans into the Progressive fold were not successful, however. Senator Works of California, a consistent supporter of progressive legislation, had refused to support Roosevelt in 1912 and did not associate himself with the Progressive efforts led by Hiram Johnson and Chester Rowell in his own state. It was Works's view that the formation of the new party had been a serious tactical blunder, because, as he pointed out in January 1914, "The Progressives in the Republican party had obtained complete control of the party in California, and in several other states, and would, if they had held consistently to their course have controlled it as a national party by 1916 and elected a Progressive Republican president. Poindexter, it will be remembered, had advanced a similar argument against the formation of the Progressive party in Washington. Works, furthermore, stated emphatically that he would not become a Progressive: "I do not think the Progressive Party has accomplished any good or that it ever will. . . . It was started wrong, has been unfortunately managed by the wrong kind of men and has gone to extremes in some of its ideas."[49]

Works was perhaps not as important to the Progressives as Senator Cummins of Iowa, who was regarded as one of the leaders of the progressive Republicans in the Senate. In July 1913 Senator Clapp of Minnesota, who had backed Roosevelt in 1912, and Beveridge exchanged lengthy letters to convince one another that Cummins should become a

Progressive, and in September Clapp informed Beveridge that Cummins "is still of the opinion that regeneration can come only through the old party. There is no use talking to him and yet, everytime a real issue comes up, the old line is drawn as sharply as ever." When Beveridge sent Poindexter an editorial from an Indianapolis newspaper predicting that Poindexter would soon withdraw from the Progressive party, Poindexter vehemently denied the charge and assured Beveridge that "conditions for the Progressive Party were never so encouraging as at this moment," and he hopefully predicted that Cummins and Senator Kenyon of Iowa were on the verge of joining the crusade.[50]

Poindexter's prediction was in error, however, for less than a month later Cummins informed Beveridge that he had not changed his mind. In fact, it had been rather clear for some time that the leading progressive Republicans did not intend to change parties. Senators Borah, Norris, Bristow, Kenyon, and Cummins, and former Governor Hadley of Missouri, declined invitations to visit with Roosevelt, and in May 1913 Hadley and Cummins organized a conference in Chicago of progressive Republicans aimed at furthering progressive reform within the Republican ranks. This effort seemed to end any realistic hope that more Republicans would join the Progressive party.[51]

Nonetheless, when Poindexter wrote Horace Kimball early in January 1914, he persevered in his optimism. "We are much enthused today in Victor Murdock's very prompt challenge to Senator Bristow," he said, referring to the senatorial race in Kansas, and, obviously in good spirits, Poindexter added, "There is a growing feeling here that there is brewing an inevitable split in the Democratic Party between the Reactionaries and Progressives. So far the reactionaries . . . have suppressed their animosity towards Wilson, but as patronage gives out, it is bound to appear . . . tending to bring Progressive Democrats into the claims of the Progressive party." Poindexter repeated this optimistic forecast in a speech which he delivered in April 1914 before the Indiana Progressive convention where Beveridge was nominated to run for the Senate. Poindexter called for the nomination and election of Theodore Roosevelt in 1916 as the first Progressive president; he declared that the Progressive party stood for "enlarged and extended" powers of the federal government; and he denounced "monopoly" and declared that it could only be regulated effectively by the federal government.[52]

Roosevelt, in contrast to Poindexter and Beveridge, publicly revealed a lack of faith in the Progressive party late in the summer of 1914 when he offered his support to Harvey D. Hinman, a Republican candidate for governor of New York. Hinman refused to accept Roosevelt's conditions, but the entire episode gave the impression to many Progressives that their leader was pulling out. Beveridge denounced Roosevelt's action, but Poindexter, always reluctant to criticize Roosevelt, remained silent.

Every effort to nudge the Progressive party into the grave was exerted by the Taft Republicans in Washington state where Senator Wesley Jones, Poindexter's colleague, was running for reelection. Scott C. Bone, editor of the Seattle *Post-Intelligencer*, took the position that there was no need for a third party in Washington. Bone informed Albert J. Beveridge that Washington "through the Republican party, has acquired about all the reform measures that the new party advocates, [and] there really seems less reason for the party's activity here than anywhere else in the union." Senator Jones was even more anxious to close ranks with the Progressives. He informed the Republican lieutenant governor of Washington "that a spirit of the utmost reconciliation should be shown in the attemp to get the Republicans together. The fact that a man did not vote the Republican ticket last fall either in whole or in part should not interfere with his being recognized as a Republican if he claims to be such who is willing to enlist with us. S. A. Perkins, a leading Taft-Republican, as early as April 1913 was hopeful. He assured Jones that "Progressive Republicans are gradually coming back to the fold" and he added, "we are endeavoring to make it as easy for them as possible, which is the policy I think should be pursued all over the country."[53]

Poindexter continued to oppose a return to the Republican party, but some of his friends in Spokane seemed ready to end the schism. A Progressive meeting held in Spokane to consider amalgamation was attended by A. W. Doland and O. C. Moore, Poindexter's allies and friends for several years. Doland endorsed amalgamation and declared that "the progressive vote of 1912 was largely a personal Roosevelt vote, and the progressive party allowed itself to be led into a great mistake by thinking otherwise." The state Progressive chairman, L. Roy Slater, spoke against amalgamation, but privately Slater was worried because, in contrast to 1912, only a small number of Progressives were willing to run for office. Poindexter tried to bolster his spirits: "when the movement has displayed its permanency to everyone . . . I do not think we will be bothered so much . . . as leaders will be developed."[54]

Despite his optimistic statements about the future of the Progressive party, Poindexter was well aware of the difficulties which the new party faced. There was considerable dissatisfaction among western Progressives who felt they received scant consideration from party headquarters. Medill McCormick of Illinois was especially outspoken in his criticism of the New York headquarters. He informed Poindexter on April 1 that he had just seen W. H. Parry of Seattle, chairman of the King County Progressive League, who was on his return from a visit to national headquarters. "Parry . . . complained that there was no Chicago office and New York seemed indifferent to the correspondence from the state of Washington," wrote McCormick. He added, "Will White of Kansas talks in the same strain." McCormick urged that the executive committee be reorganized and the committee meetings be held in Washington, D.C., so that western congressional delegates like Poindexter and Congressman Victor Murdock of Kansas could participate. This arrangement, thought McCormick, "would represent the western feeling as against the exclusively eastern feeling."[55]

The same dissatisfactions were expressed by Parry himself to Poindexter. Parry wrote that he had met Bainbridge Colby, who was chairman of the Committee to Preserve American Rights in the Panama Canal and a leading Progressive. Colby, Parry complained, "like myself, was groping in the dark and wondering what, if any, program the Executive Committee had in mind." Parry pointed out he had become acquainted with many party leaders from all sections of the nation "and found them earnest and loyal; but disheartened over lost opportunities and lack of leadership." Parry also told Poindexter of his visit to Progressive party headquarters in New York. After a long wait, he said, he talked with a party official whose most important problem was how to pay carfare for three speakers to go to Brooklyn. "I did not feel warranted in adding to his troubles by telling him of our needs in the State of Washington," Parry added. "It was useless to talk with a man who was willing to take five dollars worth of time to discuss a thirty cent proposition." Parry had not talked to George Perkins, the chairman of the National Committee, because "Mr. Perkins was at Palm Beach directing operations at long range." Perkins's assistant either knew nothing or would tell Parry nothing, which led Parry to conclude, "If a man comes all the way from Montana or Maine to get a little counsel or encouragement there should be someone besides a clerk or hired man to talk with him."[56]

Poindexter reacted quickly to Parry's discouraging letter. "I do not see any remedy for these conditions," he answered, "short of a complete and fundamental reorganization of the executive committee." Poindexter also felt that party headquarters should be transferred to Chicago, and added that he was urging the formation of a "national committee of ability and understanding. We cannot let the matter go through neglect, as the situation is ripe and crying out for just such a party as ours is." He felt that "national cooperation for campaign purposes" was "totally lacking" and that there was no successful intraparty communication. "Perkins seems to think that everything is in perfect condition and I think that state of mind is solely due to the fact that he is wholly without experience and without conception of what is needed."[57]

Progressives had been seriously divided over the role of George W. Perkins since 1912. Perkins was a member of the J. P. Morgan firm and a director of International Harvester Company and the United States Steel Company, and he was greatly distrusted by many Progressives. As early as December 1912, Amos Pinchot had urged Roosevelt to remove Perkins as "titular head" of the Progressive party, but Roosevelt defended Perkins enthusiastically; and in May 1914, Pinchot, in an open letter to Senator Dixon, brought the antagonism against Perkins into the open by demanding his resignation. Roosevelt was indignant, threw his support behind Perkins, and kept him in office; but Roosevelt's action failed to quiet the opposition to Perkins.[58]

Although Poindexter was himself critical of Perkins's political skills, he was not willing to join with Pinchot in demanding Perkins's removal. Loyalty to Roosevelt and to the party seemed to be the reason for his action. Poindexter told Beveridge, who also supported Perkins, that the "Pinchot-Perkins matter is just like a number of others we have had to deal with . . . where a man seems to be willing to wreck a great cause because of his personal dislike of an individual." Perkins, said Poindexter, forgetting for the moment his own criticism of Perkins, "is doing good work for the Progressive Party and is entitled to be judged by his actions."[59]

Perkins, in fact, had been and continued to be one of the chief sources of financial support for the Progressive party, but he alone could not furnish all that was needed to build a new party. The Progressive party in Washington was desperately in need of financial assistance, and the party controlled almost no patronage. W. H. Parry reported on April 17 that state chairman Slater had just resigned because of lack of funds and that a rally held at Bellingham was a "flop." In the southwest counties, he added, "we have no organization at all, and in others the organization is inactive." Somewhat earlier, a Seattle Progressive contacted Chester Rowell in California, hoping in vain through him to persuade Hiram Johnson to address a statewide conference. "They say that . . . they have an uphill fight there and very much need your help," Rowell informed Johnson.[60]

But in face of dissent, lack of funds, and the early desertion of close friends like A. W. Doland and O. C. Moore, who ran for Congress in the 1914 Republican primary, Poindexter stubbornly maintained that the future of the Progressive party was bright. His ambitions for the Progressive party, however, were not based solely upon his concern for Progressive principles. Poindexter had convinced himself that he could be elected president of the United States, and he saw the Progressive party as the avenue for attaining his goal. Poindexter's plans were not well formulated, and he never explicitly expressed them, presumably because of his fear that anything he put in writing might be used against him; but there is sufficient information in the correspondence between Poindexter and his closest friends, Horace Kimball and Rufus Woods of Wenatchee, to indicate that he entertained serious intentions to run for president in 1920 as the national leader of the Progressive party.

Poindexter was convinced that the dominant mood of the nation was Progressive, and he hoped that his role as a leader in the national movement would bring him to power. He also expected to use issues such as intervention in Mexico, the repeal of the Panama Canal tolls, and his support of a large navy, as he suggested to Kimball, to "strike a flame of public opinion." While in Washington, probably after the election of 1912, Poindexter and Rufus Woods discussed the possibility that Poindexter might become the Progressive presidential nominee in a few years. Woods later wrote Poindexter "about the presidential prospects," and Poindexter told him that "the subject has been suggested to me several times. . . . and I think it will be a good plan simply to bear it in mind and quietly confer about it among our most intimate friends for the time being. Of course, there are all sorts of possibilities in the matter if handled properly."[61] Not once in his letter did Poindexter use the word president or presidency; it is only by reading Woods's letter that the senator's can be understood.

Later in three separate letters in 1913 and 1914 the senator discussed his plans with Horace Kimball He explained his reticence to discuss the plan in writing, and he said he wanted to get home to confe with Kimball, for, "I know nothing that I would enjoy more than a good talk, or rather a lounging around and a series of talks with you." Then he went on to write guardedly of his plan. "The old Republican organization," he said, "is completely at sea," and he predicted that the Progressives would do well in the midterm election in 1914. He said that he expected Roosevelt to run as a Progressive in 1916 and "gain at least the second place vote for the Presidency." In 1920, he continued, "we ought to be able to land it with a candidate whom events will produce between now and then."[62] Poindexter could not bring himself to add, even in a letter to Kimball, that he thought that he might be the Progressive party nominee in 1920, but surely this is what he meant.

Poindexter did not permit Rufus Woods to forget his presidential ambitions either. He reminded Woods of their previous discussions about the presidential election of 1920 in a letter written in November 1913. After discussing the election of 1914, Poindexter added, "If we win out in the meantime, we might begin later on a propaganda for 1920 on the proposition you suggested sometime ago." Since Washington was "the leader of the United States in this progressive movement," Woods told Poindexter later in 1914, "this state ought to be in line for important recognition. Miles Poindexter, as the chief Bull Mooser of the State, ought certainly to be in line for the leadership of the national organization." Clearly Woods had pleased Poindexter: "I am in hopes we can make a sweeping victory in the state in 1916, and then we will be on pretty solid ground to make a plan for whatever we may determine on in 1920."[63]

But before Poindexter could plan realistically to run for president on the Progressive ticket in 1920, he had to see to it that the Progressive party survived the election of 1914. That task, as it turned out, was one which proved too difficult for him. When the election results in Washington were counted, Senator Jones had been elected over both the Democratic candidate and Ole Hanson, the Progressive. To Poindexter's consternation, Hanson finished third with only 24 percent of the total vote, compared to 38 percent cast for Jones. In addition, every Washington seat in the House of Representatives went to the Republicans except the eastern Washington fifth district which was carried by a Democrat, C. C. Dill. The Progressive party had failed in Washington, and the editor of the *Post-Intelligencer*, Scott C. Bone, in congratulating Senator Jones, summed it up: "The Republican situation in the state is most promising for the future. . . . I really think the day of demagogy has passed."[64]

The voting in Washington in the senatorial contest in 1914 again revealed a sectional pattern similar to the pattern found in many elections since 1896. The Democratic senatorial candidate was strongest in eastern Washington where he carried six counties, and Senator Jones carried every other county, except three on Puget Sound, which were carried by Hanson, the Progressive. The disaster which befell the Progressive party in Washington was repeated in state after state across the continent. Some of the most well-known Progressives, Beveridge, Murdock, Gifford Pinchot, Bainbridge Colby, and others, all went down to defeat; only Hiram Johnson and the Progressives in California weathered the storm. Poindexter's prediction that 1914 would be a critical year for the Progressive party was proven correct, but hardly with the results that he had anticipated.

6.

Foreign Affairs: A Progressive "Realist"

ON DOMESTIC issues in the Progressive era Poindexter reacted on the whole in a manner consistent with the interests and values of an eastern Washington politician, and his record in Congress identified him as one of the western and southern members of the progressive coalition in the Senate. Poindexter indicated, particularly in his comments about social and labor problems, however, that probably he was in some important respects unlike most others in the progressive coalition. His position on foreign affairs in the Taft and Wilson years made these differences with his fellow progressives in Congress considerably more obvious. In contrast to many of the progressives, including both LaFollette and Norris, he welcomed an American concern and involvement in foreign affairs, and he espoused a well-developed and integrated set of attitudes toward foreign affairs which suggested that he had taken foreign policy matters seriously for many years. His attitudes were very similar to those of Theodore Roosevelt and Albert J. Beveridge, and like Roosevelt he reacted to the problems of world affairs in a way which Robert E. Osgood has described as "realism." As a "realist" Poindexter tended to emphasize the overpowering influence of national self-interest and to view international relations as a Darwinian jungle where the struggle for power inevitably outweighed all moral, ethical, or legal considerations. He seemed to assume that war was an inevitable condition of man's existence and that national survival depended in the final analysis upon the national capacity to make war.[1]

Poindexter attempted to express some of his views and concerns about world affairs to his constituents in a speech he delivered in Springfield, Washington, in 1913. Those remarks help explain his response to specific foreign policy issues that came before Congress in the Progressive era. He attempted in that speech to awaken his listeners to the dangers facing the United States abroad and at home, a theme he also had touched upon in his defense of his industrial army bill, and elsewhere. The United States, he asserted, was in an "age of sodden commercialism," of "centralized wealth gained by unfair and corrupt methods, with its accompanying luxury and licentiousness," and without "patriotism." Such conditions, he warned, would bring "disaster." The United States was in danger of losing in "the eternal struggle for survival." Man's history, he maintained, "is the history of the subjugation of wealthy and degenerate aristocracies, by younger, sturdier, more patriotic peoples moved by the spirit and stirred with the nobler impulses of principle." He avoided mentioning specifically the millions of immigrants that had been pouring into the United States annually since the beginning of the century from eastern and southern Europe and from Asia, but he apparently had the immigration problem in mind as he pointed to the dangers from abroad to an American population about to succumb to "luxury and licentiousness." The United States, he went on, is "confronted with overcrowded lands, virile and hungry people, forced to look abroad for means of livelihood. They are looking to America." If the United States is to survive, he insisted, it must arm itself for the impending conflict; it must prepare itself to resist "by force . . . the mighty assaults from the teeming hordes of Europe and Asia." He was repeating, in short, a message commonly found in the "Social Darwinist" literature of the time: the United States was in danger of growing weak and decadent and incapable of resisting the imminent inundation by allegedly inferior but more primitive and virile peoples.[2]

To prepare the United States for the eventual onslaught of the "teeming hordes of Europe and Asia," Poindexter vigorously promoted a much greater national commitment to military, and especially naval expansion. His second choice in Senate committee assignments was the Naval Affairs Committee (next to Foreign Relations) and, while it was important for a senator who represented communities on Puget Sound to be on the Naval Affairs Committee, to Poindexter the ideological reasons to be on that committee were even more compelling. Expansion of the navy, from his point of view, was critical to the future capacity of the United States to survive.

Poindexter's commitment to naval expansion probably was reinforced by his knowledge of the writings of Admiral A. T. Mahan. Admiral Mahan had been president of the Naval War College at Annapolis during the 1890s when he became America's leading exponent of the significance of sea power in history. Mahan's ideas had been enthusiastically promoted by Theodore Roosevelt and Roosevelt's close friend, Henry Cabot Lodge, the regular Republican from Massachusetts.[3] Poindexter, too, was much impressed by Mahan's arguments. He urged the admiral in 1912 to write a history of the United States: "I would like exceedingly if you could apply especially to the United States the result of your studies as to the effect of the sea-power upon history. . . . Let us hope you will give the world, and especially our own country, the benefit of it." He also attempted to instruct his Senate colleagues on the need for a larger navy in 1912 during a debate over naval appropriations, by drawing arguments from Mahan's writings. "I regard an adequate fleet as insurance against loss by war," he declared, and he said that he saw no reason "which would prevent this Nation from building a fleet as great as that of England," though he maintained that he did not advocate such a policy. "It is only commonplace," he reminded his colleagues, that the United States had been successful in past wars "because of our Navy." As further proof of the need for a large navy, Poindexter cited the need to uphold the Monroe Doctrine: "The only way we can maintain it is by the possession of a sufficient military force."[4]

Poindexter's public statements on the use and expansion of the navy led to an exchange of views in May 1913 with Roosevelt. Roosevelt responded to a statement in which Poindexter apparently argued that the American fleet should keep more ships in the Pacific. Roosevelt agreed that "from time to time—and the time has certainly come now—our whole Navy should be transferred to the Pacific so as to make it understood that the Pacific is as much our home waters as the Atlantic." He warned Poindexter, however, that until the Panama Canal was opened it would be "a criminal mistake to divide the fighting fleet" between two oceans. Poindexter agreed emphatically with Roosevelt. The "Atlantic fleet should be kept intact." To explain his earlier remarks, he added that he actually "contemplated the development of a separate and distinct fleet" for the Pacific. He pointed to the British Empire as an example of what he had in mind: "Our interests are now so 'far-flung' that, like England, we will have to likewise extend our power." Poindexter closed his letter by praising Roosevelt for sending the navy around the world in 1908. The peaceful international situation that resulted, he observed, "was due in large part to your statesmanship."[5]

Poindexter's reaction to President Taft's arbitration treaties of 1911 also places him along with Roosevelt squarely with the "realist" camp. The treaties, negotiated with Great Britain and France, provided that the signing powers would arbitrate all differences that could be settled by the application of "the principles of law and equity"; and for his initiative in the matter Taft was widely acclaimed by those who believed in the use of international law, arbitration, and other institutional and legislative methods to achieve peace. The leading critics of Taft's "idealistic" proposal included Theodore Roosevelt and Henry Cabot Lodge. Roosevelt was unsparing in his condemnation of the treaties: "I should regard it as a capital misfortune and a disgrace if this country ratified the unamended treaties."[6]

Like Roosevelt, Poindexter had only contempt for Taft's treaties. They were "utterly bad," he exclaimed, because in the treaties "the United States agrees that every question of whatever nature (it may involve for instance the free admission as immigrants to this country of all Orientals, or the Monroe Doctrine, or any other question of the most vital nature) is subject to debate and consideration as an international question." The Monroe Doctrine, Poindexter declared, was "not subject to debate." If the United States ratified these treaties, he argued, it "would throw away every question of however vital nature affecting our honor, our national integrity, or even our independent national existense. . . . Such a proposition is utterly intolerable to me." Poindexter then attacked advocates of arbitration in words which anticipated his stand on the League of Nations later. They "advocate an international armed force" to enforce the rulings of the International Court of Justice at The Hague and threaten "our independent national existence."[7]

Taft's idea that international affairs could be regulated by arbitration treaties seemed hopelessly foolish to Poindexter, for it ignored man's inability to curb his instincts. "Peace," he argued in a letter to a supporter of arbitration in March 1912, "does not, never did, and never will depend on treaties. . . . The demand of the people forced us into the War with Spain, and no treaty on earth could have stopped it." He challenged the view that international differences could be settled by law just as personal differences were settled. Personal differences, as well as international confrontations, he asserted, are settled "by force," that is by the legal and police system. "We constantly maintain an armed force," he went on, "to maintain domestic peace."[8] The Senate voted on Taft's treaties in March 1912 and amended them so radically that when they were ratified, Taft refused to submit them to the British and French and in effect abandoned his effort to advance the cause of world peace through arbitration.[9]

Poindexter's reaction to events related to the Mexican revolution gives further illustration of his "realistic" foreign policy attitudes. The Mexican revolution erupted under the leadership of Francisco Madero in 1910 when Madero named himself provisional president and promised political, social, and economic reforms for the Mexican people. President Taft adopted a neutral policy toward Mexican internal affairs, but he did mobilize American troops on the border and he proclaimed an embargo on arms shipments to Mexico. Shortly after the outbreak of the revolution, in March 1911, Poindexter demonstrated an interest in the Mexican situation by traveling with his wife to the Mexican border on his way from Washington, D.C., to Spokane. After arriving in Spokane, he predicted that "there will be no invasion of Mexico by our troops," and he expressed no criticism of Taft's policy of neutrality: "It would be unworthy of the United States to attempt to suppress the pending political and military conflict among the Mexican people."[10]

But the worsening situation in Mexico soon altered Poindexter's views. The Madero government was overthrown, and Madero was assassinated in 1913 by one of his generals, Victoriano Huerta. War between Huerta and his opponents erupted, and Mexico slipped into the chaos of revolution. These events rendered a shock to Poindexter's high regard for "obedience to the law," and he demanded American intervention. In February he submitted to the Senate a resolution which called upon President Taft to report to the Senate what measures he had taken to protect American citizens in Mexico. The resolution was referred to the Foreign Relations Committee where it died, but a few days later Poindexter firmly asserted "that law and order would not be permanently established in Mexico without the intervention of the United States. . . . Taking that then as conceded, the question remains as to how and when we should proceed."[11]

Poindexter justified intervention into Mexico by invoking the Monroe Doctrine, or more precisely, by invoking Theodore Roosevelt's interpretation of the Monroe Doctrine, the Roosevelt "corollary." "The Monroe Doctrine, as we have applied it, is uncontrovertibly an act of ultimate sovereignty over the entire Western Hemisphere," he asserted. "After assuming this authority, to the exclusion of European nations, it follows necessarily that we are burdened by the responsibilities incident to such a position." Poindexter stressed the fact that European powers did not recognize the Monroe

Doctrine, and he warned that "a failure on the part of the United States, in Mexico or elsewhere, to fulfil the responsibilities" of the Monroe Doctrine would encourage other nations to intervene, and he specifically mentioned his concern about Germany. The possibility of German intervention in Latin America, incidentally, also had long concerned Theodore Roosevelt.[12]

After Woodrow Wilson became president in early 1913, Wilson withheld diplomatic recognition of Huerta's regime and attempted to pressure Huerta to provide for the election of a government acceptable to the United States. When this policy failed, Wilson attempted to drive Huerta from power by aiding Huerta's opponents and by diplomatic pressure, and he reluctantly ordered American forces into the port of Veracruz in 1914, after an incident at Tampico where Mexican officials allegedly had insulted the United States.[13]

Poindexter joined with other Republican "realists," such as Roosevelt and Lodge, to demand military intervention in Mexico and to denounce Wilson for failing to act more aggressively against the Huertan Government. "We have all been pretty patient on this Mexican business . . . to give the Administration a chance," Poindexter stated in March 1914. "But it is now evident we are getting deeper into a humiliating situation every day." He proposed that the United States should "stop shipment of arms" to Mexico and "seize all seaports and frontier towns." Even before the incident at Tampico, as a matter of fact, he came very close to advocating war: "War is a last resort, but Mexico and any other country should be made to understand that . . . this nation stands for justice and is not afraid to insist upon its proper demands."[14]

A resolution to grant Wilson the authority he requested to intervene in Mexico with force was debated in the Senate on April 21, 1914, and support for intervention was almost unanimous. The only difference of opinion centered on the precise wording of the proposed resolution. Debate over the resolution continued until far past midnight, and it was 2:00 a.m. when Poindexter obtained the floor to offer his amendment. He simply proposed to declare war against Mexico! His amendment, he declared, "recites merely the actual existing condition of affairs," and he pointed out that it would give the president the advantages of a belligerent power under international law. He attacked Wilson's intervention policy and criticized the president for having declared that the United States objected only to Huerta and not the Mexican people. This, argued Poindexter, was a "false position" and an "artificial distinction." He criticized Wilson and the wording of the House resolution for placing the justification for intervention on narrow grounds. The arrest of a "half dozen" sailors, he insisted, was not sufficient reason and was "far from being the only" cause for intervention. Poindexter's justification for intervention was the Monroe Doctrine. Because of the Monroe Doctrine, he said, "I shall vote for this resolution, regardless of the blunders which have been made by our diplomacy and the paradoxes which are contained in the resolution."[15] Soon after Poindexter completed his remarks his war amendment was rejected without a roll-call vote. On the amendments that were voted on, senators generally voted along party lines, and Poindexter voted with the Republican minority except on the final vote when he voted with the Democrats to give Wilson the authority he had requested.[16]

The prolonged and bitter debate over seemingly trivial differences served to highlight the sharp differences on foreign policy issues between Poindexter and many other progressive Republicans. LaFollette, for example, voted in opposition to Poindexter on three of the five votes, and LaFollette's amendment to the resolution irritated Poindexter most because, had it passed, it would have disclaimed any intention on the part of the United States "to exercise sovereignty . . . or control over Mexico." Poindexter explained his opposition to the LaFollette amendment in a letter to C. B. Kegley. "Whatever we may deem it advisable to do," Poindexter wrote to Kegley, "it is folly to mortgage the future and tie our hands in advance."[1]

The sharp differences in attitudes toward intervention in Mexico in 1914 displayed by the members of the progressive Republican bloc in the Senate reflected a more general lack of agreement among members of this group on foreign policy. Attitudes of progressive Republicans in the Senate or of progressives more general has been, in fact, examined by several studies. While these studies define important terms somewhat differently and present other difficulties in comparability, they do focus on more or less the same individuals and the same foreign policy issues and in general support the view that there was no progressive consensus on these issues. For example, Bernstein and Leib found that while most of the progressive Republicans in the Senate, as they define this group, did not seem to be actively "committed to aggressive, expansionist policies," only three, LaFollette, Norris, and Borah, actually qualified as "leaders in the Senate of anti-imperialism." John Milton Cooper, Jr., writing more generally about all progressives but including progressives in the Senate, concluded that a few progressives shared the "nationalism" of Theodore Roosevelt and Albert J. Beveridge, and that by 1917 progressives could be found advocating a wide range of points of view on foreign policy, including "internationalism, isolationism, and self-interested nationalism." Examination of the Senate voting record in these Congresses more generally, furthermore, shows that the most salient characteristic of voting alignments on foreign policy questions was partisanship. Foreign policy was among the most highly partisan of all issues considered by the Senate between 1909 and 1915. The progressive Republicans, as defined in this study, furthermore, often did not vote together on these matters, and Poindexter found more in common on foreign policy with regular Republicans such as Henry Cabot Lodge than he did with insurgents such as LaFollette, Norris, and Borah who did not share the more aggressive, expansionist views of the Republican majority.[18]

Even before the Senate had granted Wilson's request for authority to intervene in Mexico, the president had given orders to the American squadron off Veracruz to seize the customs house. This was done in the face of stiff Mexican resistance, but when the Argentine, Brazilian, and Chilean governments offered to mediate on April 25, Wilson quickly accepted; American troops were withdrawn in November 1914; and the controversy subsided. Poindexter's views on the American response to the Mexican revolution illustrated that he had reacted in complete harmony with Roosevelt. Though for a time Roosevelt refrained from attacking Wilson on this issue, until after the election in November, he assailed Wilson in December 1914 in the *New York Times*,[19] and he continued to hold Wilson's reluctance to use force and his willingness to submit the difficulties at Tampico and Veracruz to arbitration with deep contempt. Poindexter and Roosevelt held very similar views on other issues related to Latin America, and it is probably accurate to conclude that Roosevelt's attitude toward Latin America had no more vigorous defender in the Congress during the Taft and Wilson years than Miles Poindexter.

Poindexter was not in complete agreement with Roosevelt, however, in the controversy over the Panama Canal tolls. This issue originated in 1912 when Congress exempted American ships engaged in the coastwise trade from paying tolls to use the canal. Even before President Taft signed the Act, the British government objected and a few months later submitted a statement arguing that the exemption violated the Hay-Pauncefote Treaty of 1901 which had provided British approval of an American built canal in Central America in return for à pledge that all nations would be permitted to use the canal on the same basis. Roosevelt's initial reaction to the British government's contention on August 14, 1912 was that it was "wrong" and "only in the interest of the Canadian Pacific R. R." However, in December 1912 he admitted that the Taft government should arbitrate the dispute, because the United States had pledged itself to arbitrate such disputes and ought not go back on its word.[20]

President Wilson was committed to support the American tolls exemption by the Democratic platform of 1912, but he became convinced that the British contention was correct. In the interests of party harmony, Wilson delayed action on the British protest until the passage of some of his more important reform legislation, and in early 1914 he appeared before a joint session of Congress, asked for repeal of the tolls exemption, and concluded that he would "not know how to deal with other matters of even greater delicacy and nearer consequence if you do not grant it to me in ungrudging measure."[21]

Opposition to repeal of the tolls exemption had been expressed in the state of Washington soon after the British protest had been delivered to the State Department in late 1912. As early as January 1913 the New Seattle Chamber of Commerce sent Poindexter a resolution stating that it "emphatically opposed" charging tolls for American ships. Similar sentiments came also in January 1913 from the Tacoma Chamber of Commerce and the Raymond, Washington, Commerce Club. Articles in the *Post-Intelligencer* explained why businessmen in Seattle and other Washington towns on Puget Sound so vehemently opposed repeal of the exemption. It would give British Columbian shippers an advantage over American shippers. Because the law provided that the American coastwise trade be carried only in American ships, the *Post-Intelligencer* argued, merchants in Puget Sound were forced to pay higher shipping charges than British Columbian shippers who could ship in cheaper foreign ships. Therefore, continued the *Post-Intelligencer*, although Washington and British Columbia were "identical in character," the British Columbian products, admitted duty free by the Underwood Tariff, could be sold cheaper in the eastern United States. Such an arrangement, said the *Post-Intelligencer*, gave to British Columbia "the largest possible advantage over the state of Washington."[22]

If businessmen in Washington were angry, Poindexter was furious, for Wilson's proposal challenged his position in two important ways: 1) It violated his concept of the proper way to conduct foreign policy, and 2) it appeared to be another example of the struggle between "the people" of Washington and the "special interests."

Wilson's proposal to repeal the American exemption was, in Poindexter's mind, a capitulation to the British. "This question really involves the Monroe Doctrine" and "national integrity itself," Poindexter declared. The tolls controversy, Poindexter insisted, "really involves a question as to whether American or English influences are to be predominant in the Western Hemisphere." His answer to the question was clear: "The hegemony of the United States in all of the Americas must be strictly maintained." In the movement to repeal the toll exemptions, Poindexter thought he perceived the influence of what he called the "Tory party." It is "more powerful now than ever before, swollen with privileges and power." It was essentially a disloyal element, he charged, which for profit "would willingly consent to haul down the American flag and . . . establish a foreign authority over our country." It seemed natural to him to conclude "that some of the interests which one way or another control the great transcontinental railroads . . . are the sinister influences back of the canal tolls agitation" and "would willingly surrender the Monroe Doctrine and our national interests if by so doing they could destroy the full usefulness and free competition of the canal."[23]

Encouraged by the favorable response in Washington to his efforts, Poindexter proposed a resolution to the Senate which demanded that Wilson explain to the Senate what he meant by the words "greater delicacy" that Wilson had used in his speech recommending the repeal of the tolls exemption. Poindexter called Wilson's proposal "an object very much desired by the railroads of this country," and he charged Wilson with interfering in the business and duties of Congress. As soon as Poindexter had returned to his seat, Senator Brandegee, Republican from Connecticut, moved to table Poindexter's resolution, a motion according to the *New York Times*, that became a test of strength on the tolls question. The Brandegee motion carried easily, and in the voting party lines were blurred: nine Republicans and twenty-six Democrats voted "yea," while nineteen Republicans, seven Democrats, and Poindexter, voted "nay." All the Republicans voting to table the Poindexter resolution except Perkins of California were representatives of landlocked or eastern states, and of the seven Democrats who voted with most Republicans against tabling, four, Ransdell of Louisiana, Vardaman of Mississippi, and Lane and Chamberlain of Oregon, represented seacoast states. The few senators who broke partisan ranks, in short, appeared to be reacting to geographic and economic considerations.[24]

Poindexter was not alone in the use of progressive rhetoric to justify what appears to have been merely a conflict of sectional, economic interests. At least one very powerful supporter of the tolls repeal, the *Chicago Tribune*, used the same slogans and prejudices to justify the interests of its own section. Chicago was, of course, a railroad center which stood to gain by an increase in costs of coastwise water transportation. The *Tribune* described the opponents of repeal as spokesmen of a "Lobby" and the "interests." It was the "ship combine" which attracted most of the *Tribune*'s ire—although it did note that "Dishonest jingoism is raising false issues"—and it called upon "the people of this city and this great region of the middle west whose interests are . . . hurt" to act. The tolls exemption, it charged, is an "unjust privilege granted to the fat-fed beneficiaries of the shipping trusts." The mayor of Chicago, in April 1914, also denounced the tolls exemption and called for support of the president's bill, and the president of the Illinois Manufacturers Association branded the exemption as "class legislation" and discrimination against the "central west."[25]

During the debate on the Panama tolls bill, an amendment was offered by Senator Reed of Missouri that apparently would have met Washington shippers' main objection to repealing the Panama tolls exemption. The Reed amendment provided that the discrimination against foreign-owned ships in the coastwise trade be eliminated, but it was the only amendment to the tolls exemption bill which was opposed by a majority of both parties. Senator Jones of Washington supported the amendment, but Poindexter voted against it. Superficially his vote seemed inconsistent, but in fact it demonstrated his priorities. He wanted to assist the business interests in Seattle, but not at the expense of the American merchant marine. The discrimination against foreign ships, in his mind, was a means to further the development of American sea power, a goal more important to Poindexter than even the economic interests of his Puget Sound constituents. Except for the Reed amendment, voting on repeal of the tolls exemption in the Senate was predominantly along party lines, and on most votes Poindexter voted with the Republicans against the bill.[26]

The controversy over the Panama Canal tolls and other foreign policy issues were quickly overshadowed in importance by the beginning of World War I in Europe, late in the summer of 1914. The war began with the German invasion of neutral Belgium and France, and Europe set about destroying itself in a holocaust of fire and steel. President Wilson reacted with a proclamation of neutrality, and he seemed to achieve, as Link has suggested, a greater degree of impartiality than most contemporary public leaders. But it was not possible for many, perhaps most, Americans to remain neutral. Most active political leaders soon began to express sympathy with the Allies, and one of Wilson's leading critics, Theodore Roosevelt, soon abandoned his own early attempts at neutrality to denounce Wilson for not "acting emphatically" in the defense of Belgian neutrality.[27]

Poindexter's sympathies, too, were with the Allies from the very beginning of hostilities. He had long believed, as he had informed a friend in 1913, "that our great danger is from Japan and Germany"; and in October 1914, just after the war began, he told a German-American correspondent in St. Louis that while he admired "enormously the German people," he sympathized "most deeply with the French in the splendid struggle they are making for the right to exist." Poindexter thought Germany was a threat to American national interests, and he predicted shortly after the war began that "if Germany should win the United States would ultimately have to meet that force." This led him to conclude in private that "some justification might be found for our intervention at this time," but he recognized that "Such a step . . . involves such tremendous consequences that it would not be sustained by public opinion." Hence his public remarks on the issue of American intervention in the war were cautious and evasive.[28]

The question of the neutrality of the United States was involved in one of Wilson's legislative proposals laid before Congress when it convened in December 1914. A curtailment of foreign shipping resulting from the war led the administration to introduce a bill to provide for a government-owned and operated shipping line. Prepared by Secretary of the Treasury William McAdoo, the bill provided that $30 million be appropriated for the purchase of ships, and although it was not stated publicly, McAdoo intended to purchase German ships which had been bottled up in American harbors by the British navy when the war broke out.

Republican opposition to the McAdoo bill in the Senate was led by Lodge and Root of New York, because they opposed the extension of the government into competition with private enterprise, and they maintained that the purchase of German ships would create a diplomatic controversy with the British. Root informed Taft that the bill "is one of the worst bills that I have known" and Senator Borah agreed "it would be better if we would take forty million dollars and pour it into the middle of the sea."[29]

Wilson's ship-purchase bill initially attracted Poindexter's support. He had demanded such governmental activities as this in many areas of the economy, including a proposal that the government build and operate a fleet of ships for the Alaskan trade, and of course he was an ardent advocate of a large American navy and merchant marine. In addition, Root and Lodge were the leaders of the Republican opposition to reform, and the honeymoon period between the president and Poindexter had not ended. When the administration bill was introduced into the Senate in December 1914, Poindexter endorsed it as a progressive reform. He took note of "the violent and almost venomous opposition to this bill on the part of some of the Senators," and he charged that their position "undoubtedly reflects the interest of the great ocean ship combines." A few days later, he declared that the ship-purchase bill "will tend to break the tremendous power and reduce the extortions of the present foreign shipping combines and monopolies."[30]

The Democratic caucus voted to make the shipping bill a party matter, and the *New York Times* predicted that the debate would be "an endurance test," since most Republicans were adamantly against the bill. The *Times*'s prediction was correct, for by early 1915 Republican opposition had succeeded in killing it. The Republican effort to defeat Wilson's shipping bill, in fact, provided progressives and regular Republicans common, partisan ground for cooperation against Wilson and the Democrats. Roosevelt was in complete accord with Lodge, Root, and Borah on the bill, and at their suggestion he brought his great influence to bear by writing to some progressive Republicans, including Poindexter. His first letter to Poindexter—prepared the day the Democrats made the ship-purchase bill a party matter—declared that the shipping bill was "vicious" and would help only "the foreign (mostly German) shipowners and the business firms interested in the sale." Also, he pointed out that the bill aided Germany, threatened to embroil the United States with the Allies, "and gives the lie to Wilson and Bryan's ostentatious professions of neutrality." Roosevelt concluded his letter with a comment about Wilson. He said there had never been a "worse or more un-American stand in foreign affairs than in this Administration," and he hoped that "Progressives will make evident their fundamental opposition to its foreign policy."[31]

Poindexter promptly responded, "I agree with you entirely as to the almost inexpressible weakness and inefficiency of the Administration's foreign policy," and he recognized the force of Roosevelt's argument by admitting that "the bearing which the purchase of ships under the pending bill would have on our relations to the belligerents constitutes a real danger." Then he explained why he supported Wilson's measure: "Otherwise than this difficulty I have been inclined to accept the measure as apparently the only possible practical means of extending our merchant marine." To this Roosevelt quickly and curtly answered, "If nothing else can be done, can you not get an amendment put on that bill forbidding the purchase of any ship of any of the belligerents during the present war?" Then he took another shot at Wilson and Bryan: "What unutterable hypocrisy President Wilson and Secretary Bryan have shown!"[32]

Roosevelt dispatched a third note to Poindexter on January 30, but it was unnecessary. The day before, when many Republicans absented themselves from the Senate, evidently to delay consideration of the shipping bill, Poindexter joined them. When the Senate took up the shipping bill again, Poindexter stood with the Republicans, and the voting was very partisan. Poindexter explained his reversal of position on the following day by claiming that he had "fatal objections" to the shipping bill "in the present form." The most serious defect in the bill, he said, was that the Wilson administration planned to purchase German ships. The very same day, he wrote to Roosevelt indicating that he had completely accepted Roosevelt's argument: "If ships are required they ought to be built in American navy yards, and operated by the government on such lines as are free from the European war complications."[33]

Despite Republican charges that his policy was pro-German and might lead to war with Britain, Wilson and Secretary of State Bryan continued to press for American neutrality. Wilson protested against British interference with American shipping, and he sent Edward M. House to Europe in January 1915 to attempt to negotiate an end to the war. The most serious obstacle to continued American neutrality was Germany's submarine policy. The Germans proclaimed a submarine blockade of the British Isles in February 1915, shortly after the British instituted their naval blockade, and Wilson protested to both powers against their violations of American rights. The first crisis over German submarine policy occurred in May 1915 when a German submarine sank the British passenger liner, the *Lusitania*, with almost twelve hundred on board, one hundred and twenty-eight of them Americans. Reflecting the shock which affected many Americans, Wilson sent a note to Berlin which seemed too harsh to Secretary of State Bryan, and then a second, even sharper note. Warning that Wilson was pursuing a policy which would lead to war with Germany, Bryan resigned in protest.

Before Bryan's resignation, Poindexter, like Roosevelt, criticized Wilson's policy of neutrality though certainly, for Poindexter, the criticism was unusually mild. After Bryan's resignation, Poindexter even praised Bryan's integrity, but obviously he had no sympathy for Bryan's position. Poindexter said he did not know the contents of Wilson's second note, "but if it is . . . a determined stand for the honor and rights of the United States and its citizens as a neutral nation, the President will have practically the universal support of the people of this country in maintaining that position." But he was careful to point out that "this does not mean, of course, that we will be involved in war with Germany. The physical situation and the conditions make that impossible at this time."[34]

Wilson's pressure on Germany particularly alarmed the opponents of Wilson's policy who feared that Germany would attack another allied vessel with Americans on board and create a new war-crisis. With this possibility in mind, Senator Gore of Oklahoma and Congressman McLemore of Texas introduced resolutions in both Houses of Congress intended to stop Americans from traveling on all armed, belligerent merchant ships. The president and the great majority of congressmen opposed the resolution, and at the last moment in the Senate Gore, realizing his resolution would be badly beaten, reworded it so that it declared that the death of an American citizen caused by the sinking of an armed merchant ship would be "just and sufficient cause of war," apparently an attempt to force Wilson's supporters to admit to the consequences of his submarine policy. Gore's resolution was tabled by an overwhelming vote.[35]

Even though the meaning of the Gore resolution was confused, the voting demonstrated once again that the Republican supporters of progressive reform were not in agreement on a foreign policy issue. Ten of the fourteen senators who voted against the tabling of the resolution were Republican supporters of reform, but four, including Poindexter, voted with the majority to table Gore's resolution. Every Democratic senator except O'Gorman of New York supported the administration, while the Republican party divided.[36]

The debate over the Gore resolution, the arguments over neutral rights, and the alarming news of the fighting in France led many Americans during the winter of 1914-15 to join a preparedness campaign, as it was called, to improve and strengthen the army and navy. Preparedness societies were organized and military groups such as the Navy League acquired new prestige and members. The sinking of the *Lusitania* and the growing possibility of war with Germany gave great impetus to preparedness, and reluctantly even President Wilson became convinced of the need to strengthen American military forces. In October 1915 he approved a five-year-plan to greatly expand the navy, and he endorsed a proposal to enlarge the army and to form a national reserve force of four hundred thousand men. Wilson presented his plan to the nation in a speech delivered in November 1915 in New York City, and in December in his message to Congress he recommended his preparedness program, along with his ship-purchase bill.[37]

The opposition of those who felt that Wilson's preparedness program was unnecessary came from many progressives, such as Borah, Norris, and LaFollette. Most of them were among the more advanced progressive reformers who believed that wars were caused by "big business" financiers and munitions makers— the villains of so much reform-minded oratory before 1916—and they were most reluctant to play into the hands of their traditional enemies. Senator Borah at first cautiously endorsed "a reasonable program of preparedness," but by November 1915 he was not so sure. "I begin to believe," he informed the editor of the *New York Evening Post*, "that we are losing our heads on the subject." Senator John D. Works of California, as late as early 1917, was unalterably opposed to preparedness. It was in his judgment a "step . . . in the direction of militarism and will serve to burden the people of this country with a large standing army and an unnecessarily large navy."[38]

Poindexter, by contrast, joined the preparedness movement enthusiastically. "There is no doubt in my mind," he exclaimed in January 1915, "but that some investigation should be made as to the preparedness of our navy and army and that we should maintain our navy upon a sufficiently strong footing to protect us in case of necessity." Though he probably supported intervention into the war as well, Poindexter did not admit that he favored war until much later in 1917. That he was engaged in a campaign for reelection at the time no doubt caused him to exercise great caution in his choice of words on so controversial an issue. "I do not contemplate a war in which we shall take the offensive," he wrote, but "we must be ready to defend ourselves and the time is ripe for a proper inquiry into these matters."39

The senator also did not attack Wilson on neutrality and preparedness, as he had criticized Wilson's handling of the Mexican question. Poindexter was aware, apparently, of Wilson's popularity in Washington. Therefore, he did not make a major speech on preparedness, but in his private correspondence he spoke strongly for an expansion of the armed forces. He strongly supported Roosevelt's proposal to adopt universal military training as a means of instilling into the youth of the nation the Spartan-like military virtues which in his world view seemed so essential to national greatness and survival: "I really think that some such plan as that, based upon a modification of the Swiss and Australian systems, is the most important feature in the entire program." He was acutely aware, of course, of the violent opposition in the United States to such a plan. "I am afraid," he admitted, "it will be impossible to enact it now, but by agitation we may prepare public opinion for it."40 When Wilson's preparedness bills reached the Senate floor, Poindexter consistently backed efforts to expand the armed forces. He joined with a combination of Democrats and Republicans who on May 13 passed an army bill which seemed to include almost everything Poindexter realistically could have hoped for. The regular army was more than doubled, the National Guard was increased and integrated into the federal defensive organization, and volunteer training camps were established. Likewise, the navy bill, a triumph for the "big navy" advocates, also passed in the summer of 1916. It was, in the opinion of two scholars, "the most comprehensive piece of naval legislation thus far passed."41

Senate voting on Wilson's preparedness legislation offers an opportunity to determine the precise makeup of the groups in the Senate which supported and the groups which opposed the president's program. Thirty-nine Democratic senators supported the president's preparedness program, and only three, Vardaman of Mississippi, Robinson of Arkansas, and

Lane of Oregon, voted against it. So far as Democratic senators were concerned, the issue was primarily a party matter. Republican senators, by contrast, were divided again. Twenty Republicans voted for preparedness, and seven of them were supporters of progressive reform. Eight Republican senators voted consistently against preparedness, and all were supporters of progressive legislation.[42] Poindexter supported preparedness on nineteen out of twenty votes. He agreed with progressives such as Theodore Roosevelt, and on this and most foreign policy issues of the Taft and Wilson years he disagreed strongly with LaFollette, Norris, Gronna, Borah, and many of the more advanced progressive Republicans who usually opposed an interventionist foreign policy.

A review of Poindexter's actions and statements related to foreign policy provides a rather clear set of attitudes, or perhaps an ideology, that identify Poindexter as a "realist" in foreign policy matters. To Poindexter, increased national power and a great navy were essential, for only by constantly growing in strength could the United States maintain or increase her status among the powers of the world. "I would say," he wrote in mid-1915, "that not only is it necessary for the growth of the United States in influence and power that her military and naval forces be strengthened, but I am strongly of the opinion that she will relatively decline in influence among the powers of the world unless this is done."[43]

National strength and virility were also necessary, in Poindexter's view, to protect the nation, because "we must be prepared to fight if we would have peace and honor." All men preferred peace, he continued, "But . . . there would remain those weaknesses and rival interests of human nature which cannot always be reconciled." Thus he believed that "it will always remain necessary for any people . . . to preserve that virility, manhood, and character characterizing the man who is able to fight for his rights."[44]

It was to guarantee that American "virility" and to prevent national decadence that Poindexter so ardently supported a program which would provide a military reserve "of citizens trained in camp life."

Military training represented to him the very best a nation could offer its young men, and in December 1915 he endorsed a program of military training in the public schools. Such a program Poindexter suggested, should develop "the physique of our young men inculcating in them habits of obedience, respect of authority, improvement of manners and deportment" and "lay the foundation for military material in case of the necessity of war."[45] Without national virility and a powerful military establishment, Poindexter predicted national decay and decline, a recurring motif in his speeches and writings.[46]

Poindexter, in summary, held convictions regarding foreign relations that were very similar to Theodore Roosevelt's. They shared views which have been described as "modern," "realistic," and "Social Darwinist," all terms that describe essentially the same set of attitudes. Changes in the world balance of power were a matter of concern to both Roosevelt and Poindexter, and both shared a fear that Germany had predatory designs upon Latin America, an area which Roosevelt had defined as part of the American sphere of influence. They also shared what a critic might call an exaggerated sense of national honor and a feeling that the horrors of war were sometimes overestimated. Poindexter placed great importance upon Roosevelt's interpretation of the Monroe Doctrine, and in his reaction to the Mexican revolution Poindexter vigorously supported a major military role for the United States in Latin America. Like Roosevelt, Poindexter seized upon the wartime crisis after 1914 to promote the expansion of the American military establishment. Military virtues—obedience, discipline, sacrifice, and loyalty—rated high in the value systems of both men, and they shared a belief in the desirability of universal military training to build character and to foster national defense.[47]

The importance which Poindexter placed upon Roosevelt's judgement was graphically demonstrated during the debate over Wilson's shipping bill. Before Roosevelt's letter opposing the bill arrived, Poindexter described the opponents of the bill as men acting in "the interest of the great ocean ship combines." After Roosevelt's letter, the bill was suddenly transformed into "a real danger" in international affairs and perhaps an instrument by which the proposed shipping board could come to the aid of "the Trust ships now interned." It is little wonder that in 1916 Roosevelt declared that Poindexter was one of the two men (the other was Senator Fall of New Mexico) "with whom I have been able most cordially to cooperate among all the people at Washington."[48]

Poindexter also shared many personal characteristics in common with Roosevelt. Both came from old American families; both were robust physical types; both loved the outdoors, fishing and hunting; both were advocates of the strenuous life; and both were successful Republican politicians, aggressive, ambitious, and driven by a desire to win and to exercise political power. It would be appealing to conclude that perhaps in some way these personal characteristics which Poindexter shared with Roosevelt were common to other "realists," and that perhaps these characteristics help explain the similar attitudes of these men toward foreign affairs. The causal tie between personal characteristics and foreign policy attitudes, however, is most obscure and unproven. Carefully designed research using a much larger sample might show more conclusively that a causal relationship existed, but the present state of knowledge in this area permits no definitive conclusions.

7.

Return to the Republican Party

ALTHOUGH ISSUES related to World War I must have seemed very important to Poindexter in 1915 and 1916, given his interest in foreign affairs, he seldom spoke out publicly on these matters until after his reelection in 1916. Probably he sensed that these divisive and controversial issues should be avoided in an election campaign especially since Poindexter's prospects for reelection were already clouded by the disastrous defeat of the Progressive party in 1914. At any rate, he played only a minor role in the debate over preparedness legislation, and in 1915 and 1916 he concerned himself, so far as his constituents could tell, with other matters. Poindexter displayed considerable interest during this period however, in two other foreign policy questions: further intervention in Mexico and the status of the Philippine Islands. He also supported efforts to secure passage of a more stringent immigration law, and he cooperated with other progressives to secure passage of the Federal Farm Loan Act. He showed little concern for other issues debated during this session.

The Mexican revolution continued to attract Poindexter's attention even after the Tampico incident in 1914. He obtained the floor of the Senate on January 12, 1915 to deliver a long and bitter attack on Wilson's "do nothing" Mexican policy. If such policy had always been followed by Americans, he exclaimed, "the value and the distinction of being a citizen of this country" would not exist. He ridiculed Democratic Senator Thomas of Colorado, who defended Wilson, by noting that Thomas "confined himself very largely to painting a picture of the horrors of war." If we do anything, we will become involved in war; war means death and loss and destruction; nobody wants war. Does the Senator from Colorado mean to say that nothing can be done to maintain the value of American citizenship?" Poindexter, of course, had the answer to his question. "No nation," he maintained, "no set of men, ever arrived at success through a policy of backing out and surrendering and giving away."[1]

After Pancho Villa attacked a group of Americans in early 1916 in Northern Mexico, Poindexter made another attack on Wilson's policies despite the fact that Wilson had dispatched a force under General Pershing into Mexico after Villa. Poindexter demanded more stringent measures in Mexico, and in private actually endorsed annexation of Northern Mexico! When a correspondent recommended that Lower California be annexed to the United States, Poindexter responded, "My own opinion is we ought to have more than that. I think the northern tier of states of Mexico could very readily be induced to agree to become territories of the United States with the possible future opportunity of becoming states."[2] However, with the election of 1916 at hand, Poindexter did not persist in his attack on Wilson on this ground as he had in 1914: and in 1917, with the coming of the World War, he gradually lost interest in the Mexican question.

Another matter of foreign policy which gave Poindexter cause to be irritated with Woodrow Wilson was the legislation strongly endorsed by the president to grant an increased measure of self-government and, eventually, independence to the Philippine Islands. The Jones bill, as it was called, was debated in January 1916, shortly after the Sixty-fourth Congress met. The Democrats threw their support behind the Clarke amendment which committed the United States more specifically to an early granting of independence to the Philippines, and to an effort to negotiate guarantees of Philippine independence from other nations.

Poindexter had firm and long-standing views about the ultimate disposition of the Philippine Islands. "I am in favor of extending the privilege of self government in the Philippines as rapidly and as liberally as is consistent with peace and order," he declared in 1913, but he emphasized that "This . . . is quite a distinct matter from entire independence." The Jones bill, stated Poindexter, intends "that we shall give the Philippines independence in international affairs and guarantee it." This proposal, argued Poindexter, is "illogical." "I do not see how we can assume responsibility for their international affairs unless we reserve some right to direct these international affairs."[3]

During the debate on the Jones bill in the Senate in January 1916, Poindexter delivered a lengthy speech in which he called upon the Democrats to be more practical, and he denounced their proposal to grant independence to the Philippines as a break in "traditional" American policy. "It seems to be the idea," Poindexter told the Senate, "That there is a moral obligation . . . for the United States of America to go cruising around the world to find a people we think need a common language, who we think ought to have their country put in a sanitary or hygenic condition, who we think are not capable of governing themselves, and to do that work for them and to teach them how to govern themselves and then abandon them." Poindexter scorned those who wished to conduct American policy on this basis. It "is not in accordance with common sense!" "We all know," he continued, "that international relations are not, in our time at least, and, so far as I can see, will be at no time in the near future, determined by principles of brotherly love." He called upon the Senate to support a more realistic policy by pointing out that the Democrats proposed to grant Philippine independence and then guarantee that independence. "Are we going to saddle upon the next generation," he asked, "the responsibility of plunging this country into war or else of dishonoring itself by abandoning its treaty obligations because we have entered into a treaty with foreign countries for the neutralization of the Philippine Islands?"[4]

The Senate passed the Jones bill on February 4, 1916 with the Clarke amendment in the bill, but in the conference committee the House refused to accept the Clarke amendment, and the bill passed without establishing a time when independence would be granted. Republicans solidly opposed the bill and the voting was highly partisan, but on six votes which seemed to present to the Senate a clear-cut choice between supporting or opposing independence for the Philippines, the progressive Republicans divided into two distinct groups, six for independence and six against.[5] Poindexter was one of those progressives who opposed Philippine independence on all six votes, but others in the Republican reform group shared the views of Senator Borah of Idaho who declared in early 1916, "I may be old-fashioned and altogether wrong but I do not think this Republic is at all fitted for the work of imperialism."[6]

Poindexter also spoke out vigorously in support of the Burnett Immigration bill. It included a provision for a literacy test (which both President Cleveland and Taft had vetoed earlier) and was approved by the House in February 1914 and by the Senate in January 1914. President Wilson, who also objected to the literacy test, vetoed the bill, but the supporters of the bill reintroduced it in 1916. Immigration restriction was a popular issue on the Pacific Coast where Oriental immigrants had come to live in relatively large numbers. West Coast sentiment against the Japanese had led to the 1906 effort by the San Francisco school board to segregate Oriental students, and only President Roosevelt's personal intervention brought an end to the practice. Hostility toward Orientals in Washington seemed equally strong, and pressure on the West Coast congressional representatives to support the Burnett bill was powerful.[7]

Poindexter needed no pressure to support the Burnett bill. He strongly opposed immigration, especially Asian immigration, and in 1909 he declared that he was "in entire sympathy with the efforts which the city of San Francisco has made to protect its public schools from race contamination." Poindexter, in fact, placed himself "strongly in favor of rigid exclusion of general Asiatic immigration." He elaborated: "There is no question in my mind that if an opportunity was offered, the

Pacific Coast would be overrun with Japanese and Chinese, and we would have repeated here all the difficulties and humiliations of a race problem which has been a curse to the South. Even a little consideration of the future ought to induce us to guard against such a calamity." One year later, Poindexter declared that one of the reasons he opposed Joseph G. Cannon as Speaker of the House of Representatives was because Cannon had successfully defeated an effort to include literacy tests in an immigration bill. Typically, Poindexter explained Cannon's action by pointing out that the Speaker had acted in behalf of the steamship companies, the railroads, and other companies which desired cheap foreign labor.[8]

After Poindexter entered the Senate, he was an outspoken and consistent supporter of immigration restriction. In 1913, for example, he assaulted the Carnegie Endowment for International Peace by declaring that "Mr. Carnegie's Peace Society . . . wants us to abandon California in its struggle for race integrity . . . yield to the Japanese and to abandon the policy of building a navy; and submit every question whether it involves our national existence, honor, or vital interests to unconditional arbitration before some foreign tribunal." In 1914 Poindexter predicted a racial war with Asiatics in language common to many Social Darwinists of the time who shared the senator's fear of the "Yellow Peril." "Now that the march of the races westward has come to the end of the continents and completed the circuit of the globe," he declared, "there is bound to be a stupendous conflict or otherwise—between these two great portions of the human race."[9]

Poindexter spoke vigorously for the Burnett immigration bill in the Senate in July 1916. He lamented that immigration of "cheaper labor" was undermining the American protective tariff system, and he warned that immigration from Japan amounted to a fifth column designed to undermine American defenses. These people, he said, "quietly and insidiously come into the currents of our life, bringing with them their cheaper and perhaps lower, at least, different methods of work and of living." The issue at stake was the future of Western civilization, and Poindexter once again warned of national decay—decadence would come to America if Oriental immigration continued. American defenses "will be undermined," and the nation will "crumble into ruins."[10] The view that the influx of "inferior" races would lead to decline in national fitness and in the national capacity to survive was an essential ingredient of Poindexter's Social Darwinist world view. Physical fitness, self-discipline, and the outdoor life seemed to him to go hand in hand with aggressiveness, ambition, and drive, and they resulted in personal achievement. The influx of a race of people which Poindexter thought lacked these qualities meant decay for the "Anglo-Saxon" and for American society and nation.

To implement his views on immigration, Poindexter on December 13, 1916 proposed an amendment to the Burnett bill which provided for the exclusion of all aliens who were ineligible to become naturalized citizens. Obviously this was aimed at the Japanese. When Poindexter's amendment was discussed, Senator Smith of South Carolina immediately came to the aid of the Wilson administration, which had the responsibility for maintaining the Gentlemen's Agreement with Japan. Smith pointed out that such an amendment was in violation of an agreement with a foreign power and "can only give offense." Poindexter countered by declaring that his amendment applied "to every nation," and then he turned his attack to treaties and international agreements in general: "I for one am getting weary of the limitations which we find ourselves hedged around with in attempting to legislate upon purely domestic matters—and this . . . is purely a domestic matter." Besides, he insisted, his amendment merely endeavored to protect the United States "in the ever intensifying struggle for existence" by preventing the entry of "a horde of aliens who have not the essential elements which will enable them ultimately to become merged into the currents of American citizenship."[11]

Voting on the Burnett immigration bill in the Senate offers another opportunity to compare Poindexter with his fellow Republican supporters of reform. The recorded votes on immigration restriction were scattered throughout the years 1914 to

1917, and on these votes not a single progressive Republican supporter of reform could be properly described as a serious opponent of immigration restriction.[12] Norris of Nebraska voted most frequently against immigration restriction, but even his voting record did not indicate strong opposition. Poindexter, Wesley Jones, his colleague from Washington, Cummins, Works, Nelson and Sterling seemed the staunchest supporters of restriction and, inexplicably, Perkins of California appeared by the voting to have opposed restriction half of the times he voted. This result should not, of course, be surprising, for all the progressive Republican bloc, and most Democrats as well, represented agricultural states, essentially rural and small-town America, where little sympathy for the plight of the immigrant was likely to be found.[13] But in voting for immigration restriction, the Republican supporters of reform were acting in accord with the dominant sentiment in the Congress, for in early 1917 Congress overrode Wilson's second veto and the Burnett bill became law.[14]

While the Senate wrangled over the immigration bill during 1916, Poindexter worked to secure passage of a bill to provide easier credit for farmers. Since the beginning of the Populist revolt of the 1890s, a federal system of long-term credit for farmers had been a major objective of agricultural groups, and in the 1912 election the Democratic, Republican, and Progressive parties all included a plank in their platforms favorable to this proposal. A bill to provide rural credits was submitted to Congress in 1913 by the Democratic House and Senate banking committees, but it was not until February 1916 that the bill was reported favorably to the Senate.

Poindexter, representing an agricultural area where Populist and progressive reform had been and was still popular, had long been a staunch advocate of rural credits. As early as February 4, 1912 he assured C. B. Kegley of the Grange that he favored including "rural credit" in the Postal Savings Bank plan, and in 1914 he introduced a bill to provide for farm loans by the postal savings banks. He repeated his desire to provide easy credit for farmers in 1913 during a discussion of the Federal

Reserve bill by pointing to the necessity for "relief from the extortions of the money trust" and to make "money easier and cheaper to our farmers."[15]

Not many days after he introduced his farm loan bill Poindexter received a strong protest from R. L. Rutter, who opposed competition in the farm loan business from the federal government. "Fine business provided that the government goes into the farming business and sells us farm products at cost!" commented Rutter sarcastically. Poindexter disagreed: "I do not think I can go that far with you, but the government already being in the banking business, what better use can it make of its deposits than to loan them as proposed in the measure referred to?" Despite Rutter's objections to farm credits, Poindexter reintroduced his bill when the Sixty-fourth Congress convened in December 1915, and it was again referred to committee. This brought another protest from the Spokane and Eastern Trust Company, although this time not written by Rutter. Poindexter assured the bank that "There is no intention to set up new banking institutions" or to threaten the interests of banks. Federal loans with a "long period for repayment and low rates of interest," he explained, would not compete with banking interests because they would be granted to "the poor settler or land owner" for improvements that could not be financed through normal financial institutions. Instead of losing money, he maintained, the banks "would be the first to benefit by the increased prosperity and improvement of all the rural districts."[16]

When the Democratic Farm Loan bill was voted on in the Senate on May 4, 1916 Poindexter joined with the Democrats to help pass it. The sectional split in the Republican party was sharp, for of the sixteen Republicans (including Poindexter) who voted for the bill, only two, LaFollette of Wisconsin and Townsend of Michigan, represented states east of the Mississippi River. All five of the votes cast against the bill were cast by eastern senators.[17]

Although the Farm Loan bill, the Jones bill, the Burnett bill, as well as foreign policy issues that were considered by the Senate during the early part of 1916, were important to Poindexter, the demise of the Progressive party and his campaign for reelection became overriding considerations by mid-1916. Poindexter had been greatly discouraged by the 1914 election results. His aspirations for national prominence at the head of the Progressive party were smashed, and in their place was regret. He should never have permitted himself to be dragged into the third party, he thought, and it was not long after the election that he recalled in a letter to Works of California that he had opposed the formation of the Progressive party in Washington. A few months earlier, in a private letter to Rufus Woods, Poindexter indicated that he was ready to amalgamate. "It may be necessary to let the separate party arrangements go," he told Woods. "As you may remember," he reminded Woods, "I opposed it at the time it was organized."[18]

The strategy which Poindexter planned to use to return to the Republican party was worked out as early as December 1914. In a letter concerning the campaign of 1916 he stated that "In all probability I will be a candidate for reelection," and he assured his correspondent that he would "still be a candidate as a Progressive whether there is a separate Progressive Party, or the fight is made as we did in 1910."[19] The "fight in 1910" of course had been carried out in the Republican primaries, and, it must be emphasized, Poindexter treated the decision to return to the Republican party as a change in method, not a change in principle. The problem of maneuvering back into the Republican party was also discussed in an exchange of letters with R. L. Rutter in December 1914. Rutter had sent Poindexter a clipping from a Spokane newspaper which predicted that Poindexter would run for president in 1916 to promote progressive causes. Poindexter retorted, "Actually I have no desire whatever to be such a martyr nor experimental victim as described in the article. I do not think it is necessary, and will endeavor to do something more practical."[20]

Word began to filter out that Poindexter was ready to amalgamate, and prospects for reelection seemed bright. The unfriendly *Walla Walla Union* warned its readers that Poindexter may "ooze" back into the Republican party, and a supporter reported from Spokane "local conditions . . . are extremely favorable for your continued success." This correspondent felt that the primary would develop quite similarly to the 1910 contest when several candidates from west of the Cascades ran against Poindexter, the only candidate from eastern Washington. Poindexter promised, "we will continue to stand as progressives," and he added, "I fail to see why the union of progressives and progressive republicans, and the settlement of the question of control of the party, could not be had in the republican primaries."[21] This was, it will be remembered, the solution which Poindexter had advocated in 1912 before he had been forced to leave the Republican party.

Poindexter notified George Perkins at national Progressive headquarters on April 8, 1915 that he would run for reelection to the Senate in the Republican primary, and on April 18 the senator announced publicly that he would run as a Republican. A few days later, Poindexter advised Perkins to promote national amalgamation and passed on his thinking about the presidential nomination in 1916. His idea of who should be the Republican candidate was no surprise: "Confidentially, would say that in my judgement clearly the only practical and proper thing to do under the circumstances is for all Progressives to unite in a movement, quiet at first but systematic, for the nomination of Mr. Roosevelt on the Republican ticket."[22] It is likely that despite the defeat of the Progressives in 1914, Poindexter had not abandoned his long-range ambitions to run for president. If in 1916 the Progressive element could nominate Roosevelt as a Republican, why not Poindexter in 1920? But if the idea of running for president as a Republican in 1920 was still on the senator's mind during 1915 and 1916, he did not refer to it in his correspondence.

Poindexter's announcement that he would return to the Republican party was timed apparently so that he could be in Washington for an extended period after the announcement, for after a short session of Congress which ended in March 1915, the Senate did not reconvene until December 1915. Most of this time Poindexter spent in the state of Washington attempting to rekindle the fire he had ignited in 1910. In August 1915 he went East to confer with

Roosevelt who approved of his recent decision, and to no one's surprise, Poindexter announced after the meeting that "there was nothing in my conversation with Colonel Roosevelt to change my views." Poindexter declared that the Republican party "if united is overwhelmingly progressive," and he called upon all "Progressives to make their fight in the Republican party for its control" and to unite in the nomination of "an independent, liberal progressive candidate" for president in 1916. There is no doubt whom he had in mind.23

Roosevelt confirmed his approval of Poindexter's course of action in July 1916 when he observed that "although we had retained the nucleus of a party in Washington, it was potent only to do mischief to the Republicans; it could not do anything for itself." Roosevelt, too, was in the process of amalgamating and thinking seriously of the possibility of the Republican nomination. The outbreak of war in Europe in 1914 had pushed a concern for reform into the back of his mind and had made it easy to cooperate with regular Republicans and old friends, such as Henry Cabot Lodge and Elihu Root, who held compatible views on matters of foreign policy. By contrast, many progressive reformers, such as Senator LaFollette, Amos Pinchot, Jane Addams, and George Norris, had so disgusted Roosevelt by February 1916 that he told Lodge "that the worst crowd we have to deal with is the progressive senators and their followers."24 It was most convenient to Roosevelt, and to Poindexter, that when the Progressive adventure was over, foreign policy issues emerged to bridge the gap between themselves and the Taft Republicans.

With the election of 1916 and the difficulties related to amalgamation on his mind, Poindexter returned to Washington, D.C., in December 1915 for the first session of the Sixty-fourth Congress. At this session, Poindexter made his amalgamation with the Republican party official, and he found the experience humiliating. The day the Senate convened Senator Lodge wrote to remind Poindexter that "Last year the Democrats gave you a minority chairmanship This year they leave your assignments to us and also leave to us the minority chairmanship which you held." A few days later Lodge informed Poindexte that according to seniority his chairmanship (it was the Committee on Expenditures in the War Department) would go to "Senator Jones . . . as the Senior Republican next entitled to a chairmanship." Lodge asked Poindexter what other committee assignments he preferred. Poindexter asked to be placed on the committees on Foreign Relations, Judiciary, and Interstate Commerce in that order; and, referring to the notification that he could not have his chairmanship, he added, "you can realize the embarrassment to me of being deprived of such assignment already held." But Poindexter's embarrassment did not move Henry Cabot Lodge. When assignments were made, not only was Poindexter deprived of the chairmanship, he did not receive appointment to any of the three committees he had requested. His major assignments included Expenditures in the War Department, Mines and Mining, Naval Affairs, and Pensions, and he was appointed chairman of the committee on Additional Accommodations for the Library of Congress. It was a painful lesson in the costs of political independence.[25]

The campaign for reelection in 1916, however, concerned Poindexter more than his committee assignments in the Sixty-fourth Congress. He was opposed for the Republican nomination by the Taft Republican Congressman William E. Humphrey who had served in the House of Representatives since 1903 and had the endorsement of the regular Republicans. Senator Jones supported Humphrey, although Jones did not wish to announce his position publicly. He feared Poindexter would seize upon this endorsement as a "combination" formed "to dictate" Humphrey's nomination. "There is no reason to put a club of this kind, however small or large, in Poindexter's hands," he explained. Jones was willing, on the other hand, to urge another candidate, E. A. Bryan, president of Washington State College, to withdraw. Jones warned Bryan of "what is likely to result when there are three or four or more candidates for nomination to the Senate," and he added, "I would regret this very much." Bryan, however, was unwilling to withdraw, and the 1916 senatorial primary campaign took on an appearance similar to the primary election of 1910 when the multiplicity of regular Republican candidates had worked to Poindexter's advantage.[26]

The *Post-Intelligencer*, by contrast, displayed none of Senator Jones's timidity. In a caustic editorial on May 23, 1915 it threw all its influence behind Congressman Humphrey and expressed the deep antagonism which Poindexter had engendered among Taft Republicans. Humphrey's "Republicanism," it said, "is not of the variable, uncertain, bridge-burning, unstable sort that trims its sails to meet each passing breeze, or, with demagogic versatility, readily adapts itself to free trade one day and runs to cover of protection the next, regardless of effects save upon his political fortunes."[27] Poindexter had by 1915 changed sides and parties so frequently—from Democrat to Republican, from regular Republican to Insurgent, from Insurgent to Progressive, and from Progressive to Republican—that his enemies could easily describe his actions as "demagogic versatility." Regular Republicans like Jones, Humphrey, and the individuals who had been loyal to President Taft between 1910 and 1912 in the face of overwhelming opposition to that unfortunate man, could now in 1915 and 1916 present themselves with great credibility as men of principle.

In other states as well, sentiment among Progressives to return to the Republican fold was strong. For example, in California, where Progressive strength had been about as strong as in Washington, there was a pronounced movement toward amalgamation, and Progressives were reported to be returning to Republican harness in large numbers. At a meeting of the Progressive National Committee on January 10, 1916, a declaration of principle was adopted which stated that if an acceptable candidate was nominated by the Republicans, the Progressives would support him. The one essential element necessary for the complete reunion of the two parties seemed to be the nomination of a Republican presidential candidate who could appeal to both groups.

Poindexter's candidate, Roosevelt, was probably the choice of the vast majority of Progressives, but he was unacceptable to the regular Republicans. Ex-President Taft, whose feelings on the matter were no doubt indicative, wanted to see Wilson defeated, but he was not able to forgive Roosevelt

for 1912. Taft's choice for the nomination was
Supreme Court Justice Charles Evans Hughes. Few
Republican officeholders were for Roosevelt, and
he, himself, told William Allen White later that
"In Congress . . . the only two men who supported
me were Poindexter in the Senate and Gus Gardner
in the House." Senator Lodge said he was not
opposed to Roosevelt's nomination, but he felt that
Roosevelt was unacceptable to most Republican
leaders. Lodge endorsed the favorite-son candidate
from Massachusetts, Senator Weeks; but early in
May 1916 he predicted that Hughes would be nominated. Borah was not for Roosevelt, and as early
as April 1916 he, too, predicted that Hughes's
"nomination is practically as certain . . . as
Wilson's." Poindexter apparently felt the strength
of the Hughes bandwagon as well, for he admitted
that other than Roosevelt, "Hughes is the most
valuable man from a progressive republican standpoint."[28]

The Progressive and Republican conventions convened simultaneously in June 1916 in Chicago with
the threat of war in the background. Only the month
before Congress had passed the president's army
preparedness bill, and the situation in Mexico,
where Pershing's force was pursuing Villa, threatened to erupt into full-scale war. Because of "certain political conditions," Poindexter was unable
to get a ticket to attend the Republican convention,[29] and since he had left the Progressive party,
he had no convention to attend. Some Progressives
came to their convention determined to nominate
Roosevelt and to ignore the action of the Republican convention, but George Perkins, who worked
closely with Roosevelt, kept the Progressive convention in check. The platforms produced by the
two parties were almost identical except that the
Progressive document called for universal military
service, and the reform proposals which had dominated the 1912 Progressive platform were in 1916
almost obscured by paragraphs supporting a high
protective tariff and increased national preparedness.

When consulted by the Republicans, Roosevelt
suggested as possible Republican nominee the names
of General Leonard Wood and Henry Cabot Lodge, and

when advised that Wood was not acceptable, Roosevelt endorsed Lodge as the nominee of both the Progressive and Republican conventions. Lodge, of course, was completely unacceptable to the Progressives—the suggestion, to Amos Pinchot, was "almost too bizarre to be credited—and the Republicans proceeded to nominate Hughes. The Progressives insisted stubbornly upon nominating Roosevelt despite the frantic efforts of Perkins to stop them; but Roosevelt declined their nomination, and the history of the Progressive party came to an ignominious end.30 Many leading Progressives were dismayed and disappointed with Roosevelt's behavior. Hiram Johnson was disgusted, Beveridge disillusioned, and William Allen White teary-eyed. But not Miles Poindexter. He was of the opinion that Roosevelt's refusal to accept the Progressive nomination was a "very patriotic one," and he confided to O. C. Moore, "I have had no doubt that he would take this attitude."31

A few days later, at the Democratic convention, President Wilson was renominated by his party. Working with Democratic leaders, he prepared a platform which among other things seemed to be an appeal for Progressive support and which promised a neutral foreign policy and "reasonable" preparedness. To counteract the criticism which Republicans and Progressives, such as Roosevelt, Lodge, and Poindexter, had leveled against what they called Wilson's weakness in foreign policy and his reluctance to promote preparedness, Wilson desired that the Democrats should stress "Americanism" in their campaign. Yet sentiment for a strong antiwar campaign dominated the convention.

The Democratic effort to appeal to the Progressives of course had no effect on Poindexter. He seemed to suffer no regrets for having gone back to the Republican party with Roosevelt. "The Progressive Party . . . accomplished a great purpose," he said, "but the mass of its membership have considered themselves as Republicans and that Party is merely a wing of the Republican Party." He predicted that the Progressives would fall in line with Hughes and the Republicans: "Hughes is noted for his independence of the machine, and really, after all, that is really the basis of progressivis so far as party organization is concerned."[32] However, in Washington state there were indications that some Progressives did not accept Poindexter's appraisal of the situation. George Dilling observed that in Seattle Hughes's nomination "has not created a great deal of enthusiasm" and that there was "considerable disappointment among the Progressives over the fact that they will not have an opportunity to vote for Colonel Roosevelt." Dilling predicted "that a very large percentage, perhaps one half, of the active Progressives here will support President Wilson."[33]

In the regular Republican camp there was concern that Poindexter would be able to carry out his change of parties successfully. Senator Jones confided to the Republican state chairman, M. T. Hartson, that Congressman Humphrey "is considerably worried" about his primary race with Poindexter, and Jones ruefully admitted that Humphrey had reason to be worried. Although Jones and Hartson continued to oppose Poindexter, they welcomed his followers back into the Republican party. Hartson reported on June 16, 1916 that he had talked with Progressive leader L. Roy Slater "with the idea that there should be no Progressive candidate in the field." He added that Slater had stated that "some of their extreme people" would support the Democrats, but that most would support the Republicans provided "nothing is done to further widen the breach." There was little chance of that happening, since Republicans feared they could not carry the state for Hughes. Hartson informed Jones that he proposed to call a meeting of the State Republican Executive Committee in order to appoint former Progressives to the membership of that body. "As I have heretofore expressed it," he added, "I am of the opinion that we should look to the future and forget the past. I believe that by doing so we can again amalgamate all branches of the Republican party and go forth to victory."[34]

Toward the summer's end, Poindexter could stand to stay at work in the Senate no longer. He arranged a pair with Senator Shafroth of Colorado and boarded a train for Spokane, arriving August 9. He was greeted by a crowd which included most of his old friends—Kimball, Rutter, Kegley, and Moore, and the gathering was described by the friendly *Spokesman-Review* as the largest political gathering of the campaign. Though exhausted from his busy summer and from the long train ride, Poindexter delivered a few remarks at the train station which constituted an appeal to Progressives and members of the "rejuvenated" Republican party to work together.35

A few days later, on August 13, Charles Evans Hughes arrived in Spokane on his special campaign train, and in the group of Republicans serving as Hughes's welcoming committee was Horace Kimball, evidently representing Poindexter. During the Republican parade Poindexter sat in Hughes's open car. With the tall, slender ex-Progressive on one side and the Taft leader of the 1912 Aberdeen convention, S. A. Perkins, on the other, Hughes moved through downtown Spokane. On the speaker's platform, intermingled with regular Republicans, sat many who had figured in the leadership of the Progressive party including L. Roy Slater, Horace Kimball, and Poindexter. In Spokane County, the Republicans seemed superficially at least, quite amalgamated.36

The management of Hughes's campaign in Washington seemed to achieve much greater harmony than did the management of Hughes's campaign in California where a similar political situation existed. In both states the Progressives had been led by strong figures, Hiram Johnson and Poindexter; in both, the Progressives had been strong enough to dominate their state at least for a short time; and in both, the Progressive leaders, Johnson and Poindexter, were running in the Republican primary for nomination to the Senate. In California, however, when Hughes arrived Johnson was not given nearly as much consideration as Poindexter had received in Washington. Although a regular Republican was permitted to ride on Hughes's train in California, Johnson was not; and just before Hughes left California, he accidentally snubbed Johnson.37 The Hughes organization in California ignored even Senator Works who had supported Taft and opposed the bolt in 1912. "They undertook to ignore entirely not only the Progressives," wrote Works, "but the progressive Republicans like myself." However, it would appear that the difference in the treatment of Poindexter and Johnson in their respective states was not of great consequence, since the election results in November were essentially the same in both: both Johnson and Poindexter were elected to the Senate and Hughes failed to carry either state.[38]

Hughes's campaign in Washington was not pleasing to M. T. Hartson, who expected Wilson to carry the state. Hughes, wrote Hartson, "is not much of a campaigner as Taft or Roosevelt, nor have his speeches the degree of punch in the talks of the latter." Hartson also disliked the manner in which Hughes criticized Wilson, for the accomplishments of Wilson's administration had been pleasing to many reform-minded voters in Washington. He observed that the "Wilson people seem very touchy of criticism, and even some of our Republican friends are of the opinion that Wilson and his administration . . . ought not to suffer any criticism, but ought to be commended."[39]

A few days after Hughes departed from Spokane, the Poindexter campaign was put into motion by the organization of a Spokane Poindexter club with old friends prominent at the meeting. Poindexter left Spokane very soon afterward to stump the state in his fashion. His remarks during the primary campaign were generally not reported in the major newspapers because he was campaigning in the rural counties, but judging from letters he wrote before he began his tour of the state and from the speeches of his leading opponent, Congressman Humphrey, who was given good publicity in the *Post-Intelligencer*, Poindexter was on the defensive for having voted for the Underwood Tariff. While still in Washington, D.C., Poindexter pointed out that he was aware that this vote would be used against him, and he pointed to the fact that he had defended the interests of his constitutents: "I would like to get it before the voters of the state . . . that I voted for a duty upon lumber, shingles, hay, wool, butter, eggs, and agricultural products generally, and against very many of the provisions of that bill, particularly where it placed the raw products of the west on the free list."[40] This was, of course, an accurate representation of his stand on the tariff.

No longer did Poindexter defend himself as the leading advocate of progressivism; his claim for reelection was based largely upon what he had done in the past six years for Washington's economic interests. He said he was on "the most friendly terms with the President and with his Cabinet," and had been "instrumental" in the passage of the Alaskan railroad bill. He pointed to his defense of local interests in the Panama tolls fight and in the Bremerton Naval Yard bill; and he mentioned his position on conservation. He had opposed "the giving away in large quantities of the public lands," he claimed, in order to see that it was preserved for homesteads.[41]

Congressman Humphrey did not return from the East to enter the primary campaign until several days after Poindexter did, and the *Post-Intelligencer* could not fail to note that "Poindexter preferred to risk the criticism for leaving his work at the national capital, to hurry home" while Congressman Humphrey stayed on the job. Humphrey arrived in Spokane on August 28 and opened his campaign there. He was introduced by the regular Republican, D. T. Ham, as "a Republican from principle, and not for office." According to the report of the meeting in the *Spokesman-Review*, Humphrey devoted most of his speech to attacking Poindexter's tariff record, and he repeated these criticisms in subsequent speeches.[42]

Humphrey's evaluation of Poindexter's behavior was mild in comparison with some attacks that appeared in the *Post-Intelligencer*. In an editorial entitled "Pickwick Poindexter" on August 23, the paper seized upon Poindexter's frequent changes in political parties and compared him to Dickens's Mr. Pickwick, who advised a friend "to do what the mob does." Poindexter's behavior, said the editorial, earned for the senator the title recently given him by the *Saturday Evening Post*, "'Psychological Miles'": "He could always accommodate himself so readily to any situation that promised to be popular. If insurgency happened to be in vogue, he insurged louder and longer than any other of the insurging clan. . . . When the Progressive party boomed large and made strides towards becoming dominant, the psychological senator burned all bridges behind him and . . . proclaimed that the . . . G. O. P. was dead and buried." But after 1914, the editorial pointed out, Poindexter then "psychologically softpedaled his insurgency" and rejoined the Republican party with "watchful waiting ambitions."[43]

But despite the *Post-Intelligencer* editorials and the attacks by Congressman Humphrey, Poindexter remained the leading candidate for the Republican nomination as the primary campaign closed. He returned home to Spokane on September 10 to await the outcome of the election, and in his final statement to the *Spokesman-Review* he correctly declared that "on every occasion" he had voted "to raise the schedules of the Underwood bill on our western products." He did not remind the voters of his progressive record; in fact he did not use the word *progressive* at all.[44]

When the primary election returns had been tallied, Poindexter had won; but his election was hardly the overwhelming 58 percent of the total vote he had received in the 1910 primary. He received only 42 percent of the total vote, and Humphrey received over 37 percent. The county returns indicated, however, that voting in Washington continued to display a sectional pattern somewhat similar to the pattern of elections since the 1890s. Although Poindexter had not based his campaign on his record as a supporter of reform, he carried by and large the same eastern Washington counties that he had carried in the primary in 1910 and that Bryan had carried in 1896.[45] The *Spokesman-Review* was pleased by the election results although officially it had remained neutral in the senatorial primary. Henry McBride, former governor and the antirailroad candidate of 1904, won the nomination for governor, so the *Review* felt that the victory had been essentially a victory for reform, and it predicted that the Progressives in Washington would vote the Republican ticket in large numbers.[46]

The national Democratic campaign was officially opened on September 30 by President Wilson. Returning to the theme that had appeared so popular at the Democratic convention in June, he charged that the Republicans were the war party and that a

Republican victory would mean intervention in Mexico and Europe. The slogan "He kept us out of war" became a dominant note in the campaign of many Democrats. The Republican Hughes, throughout his campaign, attacked Wilson's handling of the Mexican revolution. He also criticized Wilson's reluctance to support military preparedness, but he generally avoided discussing the European war.

In only one speech reported in the newspapers during the campaign did Poindexter rely to any extent upon the progressive rhetoric of his first term in the Senate. This occurred in Pullman where in previous years Populists, antirailroad reformers, and Progressives had received heavy majorities. There Poindexter endorsed Hughes because Hughes was for "progressive Republicanism" and "vigorous Americanism." But in most of his speeches Poindexter avoided the familiar progressive slogans, and in their place were appeals to "Americanism" and Republicanism. No longer was he the lone wolf; he had joined the pack. But whether joining or fighting the pack, he was always, as the *Post-Intelligencer* correctly observed, "in the very thick of the fray."[47]

The *Post-Intelligencer*'s editorials were an indication that the Taft Republicans had resigned themselves to supporting Poindexter, for after all, there was little else to do. Thus, on September 26 S. A. Perkins, state Republican chairman, instructed C. P. Lund, Spokane state committeeman, to call a meeting of all defeated senatorial aspirants to endorse Poindexter. Perkins concluded, "I will attend such a meeting if it is held, get busy." The Republican chairman of Spokane County followed Perkins's lead, and on September 28 he reminded local Republicans that it was Poindexter, not eastern Washington Democratic Congressman C. C. Dill, who had pushed the decision to open the Colville Indian reservation to homesteading through the Department of Interior.[48]

Poindexter's Democratic opponent was George Turner who, it will be remembered, had been a leading Silver Republican, former United States senator, and in 1904 unsuccessful Democratic candidate for governor. Turner's campaign theme was similar to that used by Congressman Humphrey in the

Republican primary. He reminded a crowd in Seattle on October 2 that Poindexter had supported a reduced tariff in 1913 and in 1916 but now called for higher Republican protection; and Turner repeated Humphrey's charges about Poindexter's frequent changes of political parties. He recalled that Poindexter had great hopes for the Progressive party, and added that "the election of 1914 . . . dissipated that cheerful prospect, and he [Poindexter] hastened to seek the cover of republican regularity." But in 1916 Turner had no better claim to the "reform vote" than did Poindexter, and he was a Democrat in a state which, when all things were equal, elected Republicans.[49]

On election day in November it seemed that Washington had again been carried by the reform candidates. Wilson carried the state with 48 percent of the total vote, to 44 percent for Hughes, and nationally Wilson was reelected by a very narrow margin. Poindexter was reelected to the Senate with a solid fifty-five percent of the total vote. There was, however, a considerable difference in the geographical distribution of Wilson's and Poindexter's vote. Wilson's vote was sectional. Most of the eastern counties were solidly in Wilson's camp, and they, together with seven western counties, including urban King (Seattle) and Pierce (Tacoma), made his victory in Washington possible. The Hughes counties were the Pacific Coast and Columbia River counties of the southwest. In other words, Wilson captured the "reform counties": he carried almost identical sections of the state which had gone for Bryan in 1896 and for Poindexter in the Republican primaries of 1910 and 1916; he lost the same geographical section which Bryan lost in 1896 and Poindexter lost in the 1910 and the 1916 primaries. Evidently, Wilson's success in passing reform legislation since 1912 somehow had convinced the progressive voters of Washington that he represented the same cause which Bryan and Poindexter had represented before him.[50]

Poindexter's vote in 1916 by county was quite different from both Wilson's vote and from the vote in his own primary. The sharp sectional split did not appear, and the distribution was very similar to the county distribution of the vote cast for Taft in 1908. Poindexter's strength was rather evenly distributed all over the state except that Turner carried one county, Ferry, in eastern Washington, and Poindexter's plurality was below 50 percent in four eastern Washington counties. Poindexter carried eleven counties by 60 percent or over; all eleven were in western Washington, and none of them had been in the block of eastern counties which had supported Bryan so strongly in 1896 and Poindexter in the 1910 and 1916 primaries. Unlike Wilson's vote in the same election, and unlike his own vote in the 1910 Republican primary or the September 1916 Republican primary just past, Poindexter was stronger in the West and weaker in the East.[51]

The difference between the pattern of Wilson's and Poindexter's election vote in 1916 can perhaps be understood by emphasizing again that the pattern of the vote cast for Taft in 1908 was very similar to Poindexter's in 1916; in both elections the Republican candidate apparently captured the support of the "normal" Republican vote which was generally stronger in the southwestern counties and weaker in the eastern counties. Secondly, George Turner probably revived loyalties from the past in eastern Washington and animosities in western Washington. Furthermore, judging from the narrow margin by which Poindexter defeated Humphrey in the primary, Poindexter probably had lost support from reform groups.

The outcome of the election was a deep relief to Poindexter. "Our victory under the circumstances was very remarkable," he wrote. "The great outstanding feature of the election was the independence of the voters." He was sorry that Hughes had lost, and he placed the blame for it upon "the blindness of the old reactionary crowd. . . . They threw the election away." But regardless of Poindexter's private criticism of the regular Republicans, publicly he had made his peace with them. Amalgamation had been achieved, and Poindexter had succeeded in his bid for reelection. Now he could turn his attention to the national arena where foreign policy and war issues threatened to dominate his second term as domestic reform issues had dominated his first.[52]

The election of 1916 provides a convenient point to review Poindexter's career as a supporter of progressive reform and to assess his role in terms of the politics of the Progressive era more generally. Quantitative analysis of the voting record in the Senate during the Progressive era indicates that the progressives represented the states of the South and West. Most of the votes required to enact the major progressive legislation of the years of Poindexter's first term were provided by the Democrats. Democrats, furthermore, provided the leadership and the discipline to hold their forces together in the face of frequent Republican efforts to destroy Democratic cohesion. Poindexter and the other progressive Republicans were a colorful but undisciplined handful from Wisconsin and the West, who voted with the Democrats sometimes but with the regular Republicans more often. Their agreement with the Democrats tended to occur on issues such as banking and railroad regulation, rural credits, parcel post, certain kinds of tariff reform, and other issues of importance to the farm states of the South and West. There is good reason to agree with Samuel P. Hays's observation that "Sectional economic conflict ran deep during the Progressive Era and produced widespread political repercussions."[53]

Poindexter was similar to most of the reformers, then, in that he represented a section of the nation which elected a large number of progressive reformers to Congress. The economic and geographical problems of the businessmen and farmers of Spokane and eastern Washington clearly played a dominant role in shaping and directing Poindexter's progressivism, and apparently fellow insurgents, such as Borah, LaFollette, and Norris, were moved in large part by similar considerations.

Poindexter saw no conflict between progressive reform and support of the economic interests of his constituents; in his example the two merged. This is seen in his behavior relating to the Payne-Aldrich and Underwood tariffs, his efforts to regulate the railroads, his support of the Alaskan railroad and coal mining bills, his opposition to the repeal of the American exemption from the Panama Canal tolls, and in his support for the Farm

Loan bill. In this respect, Poindexter's behavior seemed quite similar to the behavior of other Republican supporters of reform, and the voting record of Poindexter and his fellow progressives on the Underwood Tariff in particular makes it difficult to agree completely with Professor Goldman's View that the willingness "to place the good of society above any selfish interest" has "been common among reformers" and has "not especially characterized standpatters."[54] The reformers in the Senate were reformers mainly because they were defending the interests of their section of the country against eastern "colonialism."

It would be an oversimplification, however, to try to explain Poindexter's progressivism solely on the basis of economic and sectional considerations, for the words he used to explain and justify his actions indicate that he felt the fears and shared the anxieties of others of his social class in Spokane and across the nation. Progressivism, said Professor Hofstadter, represented "the spirit and desires of the middle class" and "stood for a dual program of economic remedies designed to minimize the dangers from the extreme left and right."[55] This generalization fairly accurately characterized the position of Miles Poindexter. He explained his actions consistently over the years between 1908 and 1916 as an effort to protect "the people" from the "interests." By "the people" he meant the middle class (however that amorphous term be defined) and by "the special interests" he referred to the corporations—eastern controlled railroads, banks, and other trusts—and also at times he seemed to include labor unions, socialists, the urban working class, and, of course, the immigrants.

Before 1916 Poindexter concentrated his attack upon the big business "interests," for the corporation seemed the most immediate danger to "the people." He stated in 1909 that "The great issue of the day . . . is, whether the special private interests shall exploit the government for themselves, or whether it shall be administered in the interests of the public." "The issue today," Poindexter declared during his campaign in 1910, "is whether the people of the United States shall take charge of their own business or whether the interests shall continue to run the government." After publication of the findings of the Pujo committee in 1913, Poindexter declared, "There is no doubt that a few private individuals in this country exercise a greater control over the social and economic conditions of the people than has ever been exercised before." In defending his Alaskan railroad bill in 1913, he predicted that "Great interests . . . will violently assail this bill and will attack me in every possible way. . . . However, it is a part of the common warfare in which we have been engaged for several years." During the controversy over the repeal of American exemption from the Panama Canal tolls, he charged that "the insidious opposition of the transcontinental railroads" had hindered the construction of the canal, and that "There is a most formidable phalanx of those who would lay the burden of tolls upon the consuming public."[56]

That Poindexter also feared the growth of radicalism is clear. His reforms were intended to preserve and strengthen the economic and political system, thereby weakening the appeal of radicalism. He stated in 1909 that the lack of "popular influence in the government" was "largely responsible for the growth of socialism and other radical movements," and he warned in 1911 that unless the "abuses" of the system were corrected, "there will be serious trouble among our people." In the same year, he pointed to "a growing disrespect for the laws of this country," and he feared "the country can not be maintained unless the confidence and respect of people in law is maintained." During the Lawrence strike in 1912, as well, Poindexter was concerned that "this condition at Lawrence is but a symptom of a far-reaching social and political danger which, if aggravated . . . may at any time assume alarming proportions." Later in 1912, Poindexter pointed to the many "social and political questions which must be solved if we are to avoid the deluge." In addition, he opposed the imprisonment of a Socialist editor in 1913 because, he said, "fearful struggles . . . will inevitably ensue if such acts of tyranny become frequent."[57]

It was to head off "the deluge," it appears, that Poindexter proposed his industrial army bill, for in 1913 he defended his bill by pointing to the growing "horde of what you call misfits, failures" in the United States and insisting that the government was "compelled to take care of this." Defending the same measure in 1915, Poindexter asserted that "The question of the unemployed is a most important one," and he noted, in 1913, that "all lawlessness and violence is not on the side of the property interests, but the workers also, and some of their leaders talk and act lawlessness." But Poindexter added, "I attach the greater blame . . . to the great business interests, because they have no excuse whatever for their criminal conduct." Poindexter summed up his position rather succinctly: "the people . . . have decreed . . . that the law shall be supreme; that there shall be no discrimination as to persons, whether the disturber of the peace be a thieving corporation, an I. W. W. windjammer, an incendiary mob, or a libelous newspaper." No matter what group was guilty, violations of the law had to be checked in defense of "the people."[58] Until 1916, however, it is clear that Poindexter considered the greatest threat to "the people" to come from big business, the "special interest" of the Right.

In foreign affairs Poindexter was best described as a "realist" and a Social Darwinist, and he was one of the progressive reformers Leuchtenburg and Hofstadter had in mind in asserting that the progressives were "imperialists" and "militarists."[59] They erred, however, in suggesting that the Roosevelt point of view was shared by most progressives, for there was a marked difference of position on the foreign policy questions of the years 1911 through 1916 among the progressive Republicans in the Senate. Indeed, most of the more advanced progressive Republicans in the Senate opposed "imperialism." Poindexter's views were close to those of Roosevelt and perhaps Beveridge, but almost diametrically opposed to the position taken by LaFollette, Norris, Clapp, and Gronna on nearly every foreign policy question. Roosevelt had good reason in 1916 to be "delighted with Poindexter's victory in Washington."[60]

Poindexter's views on foreign affairs and domestic affairs, in sum, were both grounded on the same assumptions about the nature of human affairs. In domestic politics Poindexter did not appear to be motivated primarily by a sense of humanitarian compassion for the unemployed immigrant or the poor farmer or farm laborer of eastern Washington in his support for progressive reforms. His industrial army bill, which was indeed an advanced proposal that anticipated legislation not to be enacted until the depression of the 1930s, was supported out of fear of a decline of American power, fear of being swamped by the "teeming hordes of Europe and Asia." Poindexter shared Roosevelt's "morbid fear of social violence,"[61] and Henry Pringle's observation that Theodore Roosevelt "was led to radicalism by his desire to perpetuate the existing order" was a very accurate description of Poindexter's position.[62] So long as social revolution seemed no immediate threat Poindexter found it possible (especially during the heady days of insurgency after his victory in 1910) to defend radical labor groups like the IWW and the striking immigrants in Lawrence. After World War I and the Russian revolution, however, the activities of domestic radicals would quickly loom as a threat, in Poindexter's view, to "the people," and he would react violently, in fear again, against these "special interests" of the Left. The complex attitudes which Poindexter held as a progressive Republican, in short, help explain why after 1917 he became a conservative, even reactionary, Republican, for he had never shared many values or attitudes with progressives, such as LaFollete and Norris. The intensity of his transformation after 1917 probably was accentuated by his temperamental inclination to assume an extreme, authoritarian position, as he had before 1917, but the direction of the change in his political position after 1917 was quite consistent with Poindexter's prewar progressive ideology.

8.

World War I: Disruption of the Progressive Coalition

FRESH FROM a hunting trip and a much-needed rest, Poindexter returned to the Senate when the second session of the Sixty-fourth Congress assembled on December 4, 1916. Although still pledged to defend progressive ideals and policies, he was no longer the lone Progressive. He had made an uneasy peace with the Republican organization in his own state and was prepared to make amends with his fellow Republicans in the Senate. Indications are that the Taft Republicans, as well, were willing to forget the past, for three months later, when the Sixty-fifth Congress convened, Poindexter was appointed by Senator Lodge to the powerful Committee on Committees. He retained most of his previous committee assignments including Naval Affairs, Interstate Commerce, and Mines and Mining, and he was made chairman of the Committee on Indian Depredations.[1]

As Poindexter arrived in Washington, President Wilson dispatched a note to call the warring nations of Europe to the peace table, and on January 22, 1917 Wilson went before Congress to define his peace objectives in one of the most important speeches of his career. He called for "peace without victory"; he urged that each nation be given the right to determine its own future; and he ended with a call for the formation of an international "concert of power." Shortly after

Wilson's speech, on January 31, the German government in effect rejected his efforts to mediate and announced that it intended to carry on unlimited submarine warfare against all shipping in the war zone. Wilson retaliated by severing diplomatic relations with Germany, and two months later, on April 2, 1917, he asked Congress for a declaration of war against Germany. He did not justify his decision on the basis of national rights or security, as Poindexter or Roosevelt would have done. He stressed "idealistic" reasons—to defend democracy, to achieve world peace, and for humanity. His war aims from the beginning were totally unacceptable to Poindexter.[2]

Poindexter figured very little in the Senate debates on foreign policy and the European war during early 1917. He offered a bill in February to provide for the construction of eighty coastal and twenty fleet submarines, to be built on the west coast, and he also joined with most of his Senate colleagues in March to vote against the LaFollette filibuster to prevent Wilson from arming American merchant ships. By the end of March, however, Poindexter had grown impatient with President Wilson's reluctance to go to war with Germany. Poindexter welcomed hostilities. "Of course," he said, "all right thinking people are for peace and will go to the last point consistent with decent self-respect to preserve it," but he felt that sometimes war was necessary. "We know . . . from observations of the relations of men, both individually and nationally, that the devil is not yet dead, that evil still exists, that war is an actual condition." Wilson's fear of war, and his efforts to bring the war to an end without American military intervention, seemed to Poindexter a sign of weakness and lack of understanding: "We cannot effectively meet this condition by preaching the doctrine of pacifism, or abstract principles of morality." The only answer, he said, was the use of "force."[3]

Poindexter was more than ready to support Wilson's request for war when it finally came. The war resolution passed overwhelmingly in the Senate with only six, three Republicans and three Democrats, voting in opposition. All six had been consistent supporters of progressive reform, but most of the progressives, including most Democrats of course, voted for war. Poindexter's main criticism was that Wilson had delayed the request so long: "We ought to have settled the Mexican question and the German question both when the trouble first started."[4]

To meet the wartime emergency the role of the federal government was vastly expanded in 1917 and 1918. Congress created a selective service system, provided for federal control of the railroads, and passed legislation which imposed unprecedented national regimentation of civil liberties. Congress appropriated huge sums for the construction of army camps, for procuring supplies, and for the manufacture of war materials. Poindexter supported all of these measures wholeheartedly, and he added his own amendments in several instances to promote the most vigorous and effective conduct of the war. He cooperated with the unsuccessful Republican effort in Congress to force President Wilson to commission Theodore Roosevelt to take a volunteer fighting force similar to the "Rough Riders" of 1898 into the trenches in France, and in general Poindexter followed the leadership of Roosevelt just as he had before the war. The war, in fact, seemed to bring out even more distinctly than before the basic agreement between Roosevelt and Poindexter. To Poindexter the war seemed in a sense a Darwinian test of the nation's will to survive. He expected total conformity and a Spartan-like commitment from every citizen to the most resolute conduct of the war, and his extremely nationalistic views left no room for dissent or nonconformity. Those who doubted the wisdom of war with Germany and her allies or the arbitrary methods adopted by the government to conduct the war were, in Poindexter's view, disloyal.[5]

Disloyalty, or opposition to the war, in fact, became from the very beginning the issue that most aroused Poindexter's fighting instincts. His reaction to the wartime loyalty issue laid bare the intensity of his hatred for pacifists and antiwar radicals, and foretold the part he would later play in the postwar Red Scare. The impact of the war, moreover, rapidly cooled Poindexter's commitment to progressive reform, and by war's end he spoke and voted as a loyal member of the Republican party. He was, nonetheless, perhaps more successful than Roosevelt and most Republicans in curbing his partisanship in the early months of the war. As the war entered its second year and it became apparent that Wilson intended to negotiate a "soft" or "idealistic" peace with Germany, however, Poindexter plunged aggressively into the unrestrained Republican assault on Wilson which culminated in the emotion-laden midterm election of 1918. Poindexter's wartime behavior, in short, amply demonstrated Seward Livermore's conclusion that political partisanship during the World War "was intensified by the war hysteria."[6] Poindexter's actions show, furthermore, how "war hysteria" transformed a radical progressive into a conservative, Harding Republican.

Opposition to the war or to any of the war measures immediately violated Poindexter's notion of proper conduct by a citizen during wartime. He viewed the considerable criticism of the Selective Service Act, for example, as an indication of disloyalty. When two parents in Spokane wrote to him objecting to the draft and the fact that their sons would be drafted, he responded by implying that they were among the "many bitter enemies of the United States living in the United States who desire apparently to see it dominated by a foreign country or destroyed by internal dissention." Like most Americans, he also expressed suspicion of foreigners, particularly German-Americans and their culture. While he said he believed that most German-Americans were loyal, he maintained "that we ought to have a single language in this country and while the use of foreign languages ought not to be proscribed their permanent and regular use . . . ought to be discouraged." He also displayed, as did many others, an exaggerated and jingoistic sense of American history. When a critic of David A. Muzzey's history of the United States pointed out to Poindexter that in a book of over six hundred pages, Muzzey devoted only seventeen to the American Revolution, that neither Nathan Hale nor John Paul Jones was mentioned, and that only one sentence was devoted to the battle of Bunker Hill, Poindexter expressed astonishment that the book was in use, and he concluded that the war "will serve a useful purpose" by ferreting out such "alien influences." One effect of the war, he predicted, will be the development of "a sharp issue between the patriots and the disloyal residents of this country. . . . I have confidence in the ability of the body politic to purge itself of alien elements."[7]

Poindexter eagerly assumed a leading role in eradicating or suppressing such "alien influences" in American society that opposed the war with Germany, opposed wartime legislation, or held "unpatriotic" views—he rarely used the term "un-American." There was also the need to establish a means of censoring the publication of news concerning sensitive military information. These considerations led many others, as well, to feel a need for federal censorship. President Wilson created the Committee on Public Information headed by George Creel early in the war to censor the publication of war information and to assume the responsibility of explaining the government's programs and war aims to the public, and soon after the creation of the Creel Committee, Congress passed the Espionage Act, which imposed far greater limitations upon traditional civil liberties. This Act prohibited false statements to aid the enemy, the inciting of rebellion in the armed forces, and the obstruction of the draft. Furthermore, it empowered the Postmaster General to remove from the mails any materials which in his judgment advocated treason, insurrection, or the use of force to resist the law.

The latter provision of the Espionage Act, which has been severely criticized by civil libertarians and historians ever since, was attached to the administration's bill in the Judiciary Committee by Senator Poindexter. Before the bill emerged from the Senate Committee on April 16, 1917, the *New York Times* reported that the "most important" change in the committee's bill was Poindexter's amendment, which the *Times* published in full. It provided for a fine of not more than $5,000 and/or not more than five years imprisonment for anyone who sent through the mails any printed matter which was "in violation of any of the provisions of this act, or intended or calculated to induce, promote, or further any of the acts or things" declared unlawful by the Act; and, in addition, it excluded from the mails printed material "containing any matter of a seditious, anarchistic, or treasonable character." Poindexter's explanation of the purpose of his amendment illustrated his general view toward the opponents of the war. "Now that we are at last, after so much soul racking procrastination, committed to defend our citizens and protect the honor and dignity of the country," he declared, "I believe that a most decisive and even stern attitude ought to be taken by the government and patriotic citizens against those who are attempting to throw a monkey-wrench in the machinery."[8]

When the Espionage bill reached the Senate floor, many of Poindexter's former progressive Republican allies denounced it vehemently. "There are parts of this Espionage Bill," said Hiram Johnson, "that . . . make it the most outrageous, shameful and tyrannical measure ever passed by a free government." Borah was in full accord: "It seems to me to be so utterly at war with every principle of free government." And Senator Cummins declared that the power delegated to the government under this bill "extends the operation of secrecy to every energy of the American people." Although a provision was added guaranteeing the right to criticize the government, many felt that this was only a thin coating of sugar for a very bitter pill.[9]

Poindexter placed himself in total opposition to these progressives in the debate. He delivered a lengthy speech in defense of the bill, arguing for the necessity of vigorous censorship during wartime. He denied the charge made by the bill's opponents that the traditional right to criticize the government was prohibited by the bill and pointed to the special guarantee cited above. He was interrupted by Norris who argued that the special guarantee was nullified by the censorship provisions, but Poindexter brushed Norris's objections aside. "To say that because we are a free people and have in our Constitution a guaranty of the liberty of the press we must have along with our headquarters newspaper reporters . . . who, under this constitutional guaranty claim the constitutional right to spread that information abroad to the world, is to say that democracy is inefficient and incapable of preserving itself." An overwhelming majority of the Senate agreed with Poindexter, and the Senate bill was passed seventy-seven to six. Four of the six voting against the bill were progressive Republicans.[10]

The Espionage Act soon appeared inadequate to Poindexter, however, because he became convinced that the law had failed to silence the opponents of the war. The antiwar group which particularly aroused Poindexter was the Industrial Workers of the World even though at the time of the strike in Lawrence, Massachusetts, in 1912, it will be remembered, Poindexter vigorously had championed the "Wobblies." Their outspoken opposition to the war totally changed his attitude, however. This transformation can be dated accurately, for as late as January 1917 Poindexter expressed sympathy with the IWW. This was in response to an armed clash which had taken place in Everett, Washington, between members of the IWW and the local police. At that time he told the secretary of the Socialist party in Anacortes, Washington, that he favored a fair investigation of "the labor trouble at Everett" by the Wilson administration, and if this did not materialize, he promised to take the issue up in Congress. In response to a letter from President Wilson, who feared that the "Wobblies" would not get fair trials in Washington, Poindexter described, furthermore, the Everett incident as "unfortunate," and he assured Wilson "of the absolute fairness and justice of our local courts."[11] In none of his remarks about the Everett clash did Poindexter express criticism of the IWW.

Poindexter's change in attitude toward the IWW developed quickly after the outbreak of war in April 1917, when he began to receive charges that IWW members were sabotaging the war effort. He reacted angrily. He told one correspondent in mid-July 1917 that the state government should act "in preventing the violence threatened by the I. W. W. organization—the burning of wheat fields, the destruction of machinery, etc., at least, such is reported to be the case." If the Washington state government failed to act, concluded Poindexter, "The federal government undoubtedly will intervene under its war power, but it ought not to be necessary for it to do it."[12] In another letter Poindexter argued that bad working conditions were no excuse for the conduct of the IWW. "Wages are fairly good now . . . and the people resent under these circumstances the threats of violence and destruction of property." By the end of the summer of 1917 Poindexter had become so incensed by the activities of the IWW that he devoted considerable time on the Senate floor to a discussion of their "disloyal" activities in Montana and Washington. He cited a letter from a lumber company executive in Washington to show that the IWW engaged in acts of sabotage that interfered with lumber production. Poindexter assured the Senate that he did not oppose a "legitimate labor union," but only "the advocates of murder and dynamite that are leading the Industrial Workers of the World organization."[13]

Poindexter's fear of the IWW and other radical groups was greatly intensified by the news of the Bolshevist revolution in Russia. The Russian Bolshevists seized control of the Russian government in November 1917 and immediately began negotiations with the Germans, leading to a Russian withdrawal from the war. Civil war broke out in Russia simultaneously, and to Poindexter and many Americans Russia seemed in 1918 gripped in a Bolshevistic terror.

Within weeks, in early 1918, Poindexter began to link the obstructionist activities of the IWW and the antiwar efforts of some Socialists and other radicals as a part of an international Bolshevist conspiracy to overthrow the capitalist system. "The people" were once again in danger, but this time from their enemies on the Left, and Poindexter responded to this threat as he had responded earlier to the threat from the "special interests" of the Right. The impact of the Russian revolution seemed to convince Poindexter that a much greater threat now existed from the Left than had ever threatened "the people" in the prewar years. The fact that the opponents of the war were largely radical or at least liberal or progressive served to intensify his hostility and to provide a linkage in his view between being antiwar ("disloyal") and supporting the international Bolshevist conspiracy. He was particularly alarmed about the IWW which, he declared, "is a revolutionary 'direct action' (meaning physical force) organization, and ought to be suppressed with an iron hand in the interests of liberty and law." He had become convinced that there was a relationship between the IWW, the Russian Bolsheviks, and the Germans: "One curious circumstance of the times is that the Prussian military kulture, the Russian bolsheviki, the American I. W. W., the anarchists, and so-called direct action Socialists are fundamentally all the same,—that is, they believe in accomplishing their desires by ruthlessness and destruction, which means that they repudiate Christianity and the teachings of a thousand years of civilization." The answer to the problem, said Poindexter, was to give these revolutionaries "their own medicine,—force," and he promised to introduce new legislation that "would reach scoundrels of this kind and papers that print their mouthings."[14]

Many Americans shared Poindexter's conviction that more stringent legislation was required to curb the activities of the IWW and other opponents of the war, even though under the Espionage Act of 1917 many opponents of the war had already been effectively silenced and jailed. A more severe Democratic measure to curb sedition was taken up in April 1918. At the same time Poindexter introduced his own loyalty bill, part of which the Judiciary Committee incorporated into the Senate sedition bill. The *New York Times* praised the committee, in an editorial, for correcting the "astonishing defects" in the Act of 1917 by adopting Poindexter's amendment. The Poindexter amendment, the *Times* concluded, "proscribes penalties severe enough to be really deterrent."[15]

Poindexter's amendment provided that a maximum penalty of twenty years in prison and $10,000 fine be made against any person who expressed

> disloyal, threatening, violent, abusive, or seditious language about the Government, the Constitution, the President, the flag, or the uniform of the army and navy . . . or any words calculated to bring the

Government or its institutions into contempt or disrepute, or calculated to incite resistance to Federal authority or to hamper the efforts of the Government in the prosecution of the war. . . . [and the same penalties for] whoever shall by word or act support or favor the cause of the German Empire or its allies in the present war or by word or act oppose the cause of the United States therein.[16]

To insure that his amendment remained in the bill unchanged, Poindexter took a very active part in the debate. When Senator Gore charged that Poindexter's provision prohibiting criticism of the government or the Constitution violated "the charter of our liberties," Poindexter admitted that "Many of the things that are proposed to be punished by this bill might very well go unnoticed and be of trivial public importance in times of peace." But he reminded the Senate that "the bill ought to be judged by its application to the emergency that confronts the country." Gore retorted that Poindexter magnified "trivial things . . . into serious breaches of the law or the Constitution." Poindexter countered, "Mr. President, that is very beautiful rhetoric that the Senator from Oklahoma has entertained the Senate with, but it is not very practical in the solution of the problem of this war."[17]

A major test of Senate opinion on the Sedition bill was provided by the vote on the amendment offered by France of Maryland which provided that nothing in the act should be interpreted to prevent a person from speaking the truth. The France amendment was opposed by supporters of the bill, including the Attorney General's office, because it would have presented difficulties in obtaining convictions under the law; it was defeated, thirty-one to thirty-three. Both parties divided to some extent as most Republicans voted with ten Democrats to support the France amendment, while the nay votes were cast by most Democrats and six Republicans. Poindexter was one of the six to vote with the Democrats against the amendment; he was joined by three progressive Republicans, and opposed by five. On the only vote on the Sedition bill as a whole the bill passed the Senate forty-eight to twenty-six, and although the voting was largely partisan, eleven Republicans crossed party lines to vote with most Democrats.[18]

Although the Sedition Act was denounced at the time and is still criticized as an even more severe limitation upon freedom of expression than the Espionage Act, Poindexter was barely satisfied with it. He had found it very difficult to secure approval of his ideas in the Judiciary Committee and the Senate, he said, but "I do not think the measure will do any harm, and we may, at some future time, be able . . . to go further." His ultimate desire was "to shoot or hang a few of those who are guilty of treason, or of being spies. I would like to have the opportunity of enforcing even the laws that are already on the statute books for a few weeks."[19]

Poindexter's position on the Sedition Act contrasted sharply with the views of many of his former progressive Republican colleagues. Seven of them had voted against the bill and seemed to share the view of the *Nation* that "it goes farther . . . than any similar legislation abroad—even in Prussia." Certainly this was the attitude of Hiram Johnson who informed C. K. McClatchy, another California progressive, that the Act "seeks to stifle all criticism, and certain Republicans voted for it, because there are so many hysterical people now in the land anxious to shoot anybody forthwith who says anything at variance with these hysterical individual's ideas. I am very glad consistently to have fought this sort of thing."[20]

Not many days after the passage of the Sedition bill, Poindexter's ire was further aroused by organized labor in Seattle. The secretary of the militant Seattle Central Labor Council, James A. Duncan, sent the senator a resolution passed by a construction union in Seattle calling for a general strike in Seattle on May 1, 1918, in protest agains the conviction of Thomas Mooney. Mooney and Warren K. Billings had been indicted and convicted in California for a 1916 bombing during a preparedness parade. Some, primarily radical labor groups, thought Mooney was innocent and that he had been convicted because he was a labor radical. His conviction became to some labor groups a symbol of labor's fight for fair play and equal rights, and President Wilson had intervened to request that the governor of California commute Mooney's sentence. To many other Americans, including Poindexter, however, Mooney's guilt and the justice of his conviction seemed undeniable. Duncan's letter informed Poindexter that all Seattle unions had been asked to join the proposed strike which would begin May 1 and last until "the victimized Mooney case defendants are unconditionally freed."[21] Poindexter, up to this point, had been rather careful not to antagonize organized labor, but this threat to strike during wartime on behalf of a convicted radical forced Poindexter into the antilabor camp where, unfortunately for his political future, he remained.

The letter from Duncan and the accompanying resolution was read to the Senate, and then Poindexter opened a long tirade which surpassed in venom any he had delivered previously against either the "special interests" during his progressive years or the opponents of the war. He flatly declared that an international Bolshevist conspiracy was at work in Seattle. The Duncan letter and accompanying resolution, he charged, "exemplify and illustrate a movement of certain lawless elements in the United States and in other countries, particularly in Russia, which if not arrested will plunge the world into anarchy and bloodshed." He charged explicitly that the Seattle Labor Council was influenced by the Bolshevists: "And so it is from the anarchists and bolsheviki of Russia that this movement has originated, culminating in an organized threat at Seattle, Wash., to tie up the war industries of the United States on the 1st day of May, 1918." The Seattle unions, he maintained, threatened the nation with "bolshevistic terrorism," and he linked together a series of violent incidents around the world—in India, Spain, Russia, New Jersey, Pennsylvania, Oklahoma, San Francisco, Quebec, Butte, Montana, and "the sabotage in the wheat fields in Dakota and Washington"—to the Bolshevist conspiracy. These events, he believed, "are all a part of one connected movement to overturn the foundations of society and set up a hobo government in its place." Poindexter concluded his fiery oration with an appeal to the loyal elements of the nation to strike "with an iron hand" against "every traitor who seeks to cut off supplies from our armies in the field."[22]

This speech, Poindexter later maintained, was proof that he was the first American to see the great danger of the "international communist conspiracy." Of course, such a contention would be most difficult to prove, but it is safe to say that with this speech Poindexter became one of those responsible for the launching of what later was to be known as the Red Scare. The speech is also significant because it dramatically marks the point when Poindexter turned against organized labor. His characteristic intolerance combined with a wartime compulsion to obtain national unity dulled his political sensitivity.[23]

Poindexter's speech attracted considerable attention. It was discussed by the *New York Times*, by Samuel Gompers, the *New Republic*, and the Seattle newspapers. Gompers, the head of the AFL, was prompted by Poindexter's charges to criticize the Seattle Central Labor Council for its action and to declare that a general strike would violate the law and the interests of the workingman. The *New Republic*'s reporter in the national capital described the Poindexter speech as "an inadequate and prejudiced account of the Mooney case." The *Seattle Post-Intelligencer* featured Poindexter's speech with a picture of both Poindexter and James A. Duncan, and Duncan's reply. "Poindexter must be crazy," he said. "There is only one way to allay unrest and suspicion and that is not to rave and rant as to the effects, but to remove the cause." Duncan maintained that union labor in Seattle was not disloyal and was not against the war; it supported a strike only to dramatize the injustice done Mooney. The general strike in Seattle did not take place, however. At Mooney's personal request it was canceled, but the threat to strike on Mooney's behalf was more than sufficient evidence to convince Poindexter that many labor organizations were "disloyal" and Bolshevist-inspired.[24]

The activity of these radical and "disloyal" elements was also used by Poindexter to attack the

Wilson administration. He accused the administration of leniency toward "pro-German" radicals in a letter on January 29, 1918 to Wilson's attorney general, T. W. Gregory. Poindexter asked why Gregory had not created an "alien enemy zone" and why "no attempt has been made to separate alien enemies from employment." The very next day he sent Gregory another letter to inform him there had been a meeting at Carnegie Hall on January 22, 1918 addressed by a man whose speech "was pro-German, anti-war, and pacifist." On that same date, he continued, "the theaters of New York were closed under the fuel administration, while this pro-German meeting was allowed to proceed."[25] Poindexter also expressed these charges in a speech in March 1918 when he joined in a Republican attack on Wilson's conduct of the war. Poindexter brought up Wilson's speech to Congress the previous January when the president had first enunciated his famed Fourteen Points, including the call for a League of Nations. Poindexter equated Wilson's internationalism with Bolshevism, and he suggested that Wilson had expressed sympathy with the Russian revolutionaries in that speech of January 8: "the President of the United States . . . offered encouragement to this misnamed government of Russia."[26]

When a Spokane voter challenged Poindexter's insinuations, the senator retreated slightly. "I do not know that anybody has expressed the idea that the President is in improper sympathy with the I. W. W. or bolsheviki, certainly, I have not," he answered. "But," he added, "it was, perhaps, that certain acts of his, even though they might have been with the highest motives in the world,— such as his effort to free convicted dynamiters and his commendatory references to the Bolsheviki Government, were mistakes from the standpoint of governmental policy." Nonetheless, Poindexter continued in his private correspondence to charge that the Wilson administration had been guilty of "leniency" in its handling of "seditious and disloyal persons." He referred to Wilson's interference in the Mooney case, and he deplored the president's "friendship for the bolsheviki, traitors, anarchists, spies, and German hirelings of Russia."

Poindexter was not by any means alone in suspecting that Wilson was sympathetic with the opponents of the war and the "Bolsheviki," and one who also expressed this view was Theodore Roosevelt. He, like the senator, was absolutely convinced of Mooney's guilt, and in mid-December 1917 Roosevelt denounced "the I. W. W. and similar movements in this country" for taking "the same position" as the Bolsheviks. The month after Poindexter's speech on the Mooney case found Roosevelt writing that Wilson "has favored the Bolshevists in every way that he could," and in October 1918 Roosevelt charged that "Wilson is leading the forces of Bolshevism."27

The efforts by Poindexter to promote legislation and government action to silence the opponents of the war and to promote the most effective conduct of the war coincided with a decline in his enthusiasm for progressive reform. This can be illustrated by studying Poindexter's response to the War Revenue Act of October 1917. Senate differences over income tax rates in this measure reflected the prewar controversy over the progressive or graduated income tax, and in 1917 most of the prewar progressives favored a tax structure that would lay the heaviest burden of financing the war upon the upper income brackets. When the bill was signed by the president, it met many of these objectives and also imposed new taxes on excess profits, luxuries, and services.

On the issue of increasing the personal income tax rates in the upper income levels, Poindexter agreed with the progressives as he had in 1913, because, he said, he felt it was right that the wealthy "should be made to pay largely" for the war. In the voting on the tax bill Poindexter voted consistently with most of the progressive Republicans for increases in personal income tax rates. Six roll-call votes related to amendments were offered by progressives to increase income tax rates, and on each Poindexter voted for the higher rate, along with most progressive Republicans.28

On a related issue, the war profits tax, however, Poindexter differed sharply with many of the progressive Republicans. Eight were of the opinion that there should be a very high war profits tax in the bill, and working with a handful of Democrats, they secured nine votes on amendments to the bill involving this tax.[29] "By this amendment," exclaimed Hiram Johnson, referring to his own proposal to push the war profits tax up to 73 percent, "we seek . . . to touch these swollen profits; profits that have come from disaster; that come . . . from this crisis in which we find ourselves." Most Republicans, as well as most Democrats, were opposed to this tax. Theodore Roosevelt, for example, wrote Senator Johnson only four days before Johnson introduced his war profit tax amendment, to attempt to soften the California progressive's position. Roosevelt agreed with Johnson that "What is most needed at present is a very heavily graduated tax on the excess profits," but he warned Johnson that "it would be a calamity to restrict profits so as to reduce production."[30]

Poindexter agreed with Roosevelt, and on September 5 he spoke at length against the war profits tax. He, too, viewed it as a threat to the war effort, for "the war industries of the country" are "essential to the conduct of the war." The war industries deserved large profits, said the senator, because their business "must come to an end when the war is over," and besides, "many of them are . . carried on by individuals and small business concerns," not corporations. Such a tax, he insisted, "will not contribute to the success of the war." The greatest need, added the senator, was unity: "the investment of the rich, and the toil of the poor, all exerted together in the most vital service of the Nation in its greatest need." The wartime need for unity, in sum, had considerably softened Poindexter's opposition to the corporation and the very wealthy, and the progressive Republicans as a group divided sharply on the issue.[31]

The decline in Poindexter's willingness to pursue prewar progressive goals was probably related, in part at least, to changes in his personal and political associations in the Senate and elsewhere. Most of Poindexter's closest allies before the war were progressive Republicans, but after 1917 they became opponents of the war (Gronna, LaFollette, and Norris) or inconsistent in their support for war measures (Borah, Cummins, Kenyon, Sherman, and

Johnson). They became, to Poindexter, disloyal persons and a threat to the national security. The attitudes of more radical groups such as pacifists, Socialists, and the IWW, moreover, were in Poindexter's eyes, even more reprehensible. Further cooperation with these persons and groups on progressive measures became increasingly difficult. Most prewar opponents of progressive reform, on the other hand, supported the war and tended to react to the war issues and the fear of Bolshevism as Poindexter did. Hence it became easier for Poindexter, as the war progressed, to work with individuals such as Senator Lodge and with the Republican majority, and, indeed, by early 1918 Poindexter can more accurately be counted as a regular Republican. This can be illustrated by his active participation in a seemingly well-orchestrated Republican attack upon President Wilson's conduct of the war, that began in early 1918 and continued on through the armistice negotiations and the election campaign of 1918.

In the early months of the war Poindexter and most Republicans had joined with the Democrats to enact the major bills requested by the Wilson administration to conduct the war. Unfortunately, the mere passing of laws was only the beginning of the gigantic effort required to mobilize American society, and as 1917 ended much remained undone. Neither airplanes nor ships were being produced in any significant number, the transportation system seemed hopelessly disorganized, soldiers in training camps were not well equipped or clothed, and American troops had not made a significant contribution to the fighting on the western front and would not do so until the early summer of 1918.

Poindexter, like most Republicans, long before the outbreak of war had been critical of Wilson's handling of foreign affairs, and he automatically interpreted the delays and setbacks as conformation of his earlier suspicions that Wilson was incompetent, a pacifist, and temperamentally incapable of achieving quick, vigorous mobilization. Theodore Roosevelt quickly became a leading spokesman of this view, and the administration's refusal to permit Roosevelt to lead a division of volunteers into the trenches only reinforced the conviction that Wilson was incapable of vigorous wartime leadership

Poindexter tried valiantly during the first year of the war to refrain from partisan criticism. In August 1917 he disagreed sharply with a correspondent who had suggested that Wilson's "previous weakness" be forgotten in the interest of winning the war, but he conceded that "it is a time to be silent about it." But Poindexter was incapable of suppressing his exasperation with what he perceived as Wilson's incompetence. As early as May 1917, during a debate concerning censorship of newspapers, Poindexter demanded military action: "My opinion about this war is that, as is very often the case, the best defensive is an offensive. . . . and it would be desirable to prevent the publication of news not of German troops landing in America but of American troops landing in Europe."[32]

The assault on Wilson's conduct of the war, however, did not intensify until late in 1917. Most of the criticism came from Republicans and was aimed at the president, although his secretary of war, Newton D. Baker, was often the target of Wilson's critics. Those favoring a reorganization of the government unified behind a bill proposed by Senator Chamberlain, a Democrat from Oregon and chairman of the Military Affairs Committee. His bill proposed the creation of a War Cabinet of three citizens that would be independent of the cabinet and responsible only to the president. The plan retained a semblance of bipartisanship because of Chamberlain's role, but it was supported mainly by Republicans. The idea apparently was to force Wilson to appoint Theodore Roosevelt or other prominent Republicans to the War Cabinet.[33]

There was actually no possibility that Wilson would bring Roosevelt or any leading Republican critic into the administration. In response to the demands for reorganization of his conduct of the war, a Democratic bill designed to undercut the support for the Chamberlain bill was introduced by Senator Overman of North Carolina. Overman's bill gave the president sweeping authority to reorganize the executive branch and it was passed overwhelmingly by the Senate in April 1918. Poindexter was one of the few senators to vote against the Overman bill, and in this way, apparently, he threw his weight behind Roosevelt's effort to force Wilson to appoint him or some other Republican to the War Cabinet. Poindexter's role in this entire affair, however, is difficult to piece together. He did not deliver a major speech on the Chamberlain bill, his name is not prominent in the newspaper accounts, and he rarely mentioned the issue in his correspondence. He did defend the right of Chamberlain's committee to conduct its investigation—"it has dealt with evidence tending to show lack of diligence, undue delay," and he criticized Wilson for bypassing the Senate in appointing members of his War Cabinet. But on so momentous an issue he was uncharacteristically silent.[34]

This reluctance to join publicly with Roosevelt may be explained perhaps by Poindexter's strong conviction that internal dissension should be kept to a minimum. In fact, in defending the Military Affairs Committee's investigation of the conduct of the war, he added, "we should avoid mere captious wrangling among ourselves in the face of a common enemy."[35] But if his desire to maintain national unity explains his unusual silence in January 1918, then the senator changed his mind rather sharply soon thereafter, for beginning in March Poindexter became a most outspoken and extreme Wilson critic.

The change in Poindexter's attitude toward Wilson was undoubtedly influenced by military events. The German spring offensive on the western front was launched on March 21 and appeared so threatening to the Allies that on March 26 they agreed to unify command in the hands of the French General Foch. More significantly, the election of 1918 was approaching, and Poindexter had no desire to see Wilson and the Democrats win another victory at the polls, if it could be prevented. On the very day that Foch was made commander of all Allied forces, Poindexter joined in a concerted Republican assault on Wilson that the *New York Times* called "the bitterest debate the Senate has known since America's entry into the war."[36]

Poindexter opened his "aggressive attack" upon Wilson after Senator Lodge had finished speaking. He took up Lodge's point that the United States had failed to produce a sufficient number of airplanes at this dark hour. "The substantial, fundamental fact in the situation is that we have been engaged for a year in this war . . . and we have no airplanes!" Poindexter exclaimed. When Senator Hitchcock, Democrat of Nebraska, attempted to explain the delays, Poindexter cried, "it is a great deal of satisfaction . . . when defeat stares us in the face, to be confronted with the excuse that the schedule that was made for the equipment of the armies of this country was somewhat in fault." To be told that production was behind schedule only ninety days was hardly satisfactory: "this great battle that is now on in France will not last 90 days!"[37]

At this point, for the first time in public, Poindexter hinted that there was disloyalty in the Wilson administration. He told the Senate that a "gentleman high in the organization of the airplane construction board" had said "that there seemed to be in the effort to produce airplanes some mysterious unknown influence that was putting a blight upon the entire effort of the board." Poindexter declared that there was plenty of spruce in the state of Washington for airplane construction and that he had presented to the airplane board lumbermen who could produce the spruce. "They were unable to get permission to produce spruce, and yet it is said that the reason why we have no airplanes is because they could not get spruce." The same result had occurred, added the senator, when he had presented lumbermen to the shipping board earlier.[38] The theme of disloyalty in the Wilson administration would appear more explicitly in the months to follow, but as early as March 1918 insinuations that Wilson was pro-German, pro-Bolshevist, and sympathetic with radical antiwar groups began to appear in Poindexter's speeches and writings.

The Wilson administration was not without its defenders. Several members of the president's party were active in the Senate exchanges, and the *Nation* on April 4, 1918 was very critical of the Republicans. "But even granting the truth of every charge made by Senator Lodge and Senator Poindexter and Colonel Roosevelt, what good purpose can be served by emitting helpless moans?" it asked. The *Nation* provided more emphatic support for Wilson later in the summer by charging that the Republicans were seeking desperately for issues to use against the Democrats in the 1918 congressional campaign and that Republican leadership was "bankrupt." "If we turn to Congress, the utter lack of statesmanship is even more appalling for loyal Republicans," the *Nation* maintained.[39] But these defenders of Wilson had little effect on the fiercely nationalistic and combative senator from Washington who felt only disgust and contempt for an administration that seemed incapable of contributing to the battle raging in France during the spring of 1918.

The barrage of criticism leveled upon Wilson by the Republicans in 1918 laid them open to charges of fomenting dissension and obstructing the war effort—the same charges Poindexter used against the opponents of the war. In fact, Senator Stone, Democrat from Missouri, asserted in January that Roosevelt was "the most seditious man of consequence in America," and the *Nation* pointed to the inconsistency in the Roosevelt-Poindexter view of freedom of speech in wartime. The issue, said the *Nation*, was "who does the criticizing." Criticism of the government was acceptable to this group, said the *Nation*, "provided that the critics came from the thoroughly conservative among us and are convinced in their own minds that they are the only ones in whom bubbles up undiluted wells of patriotism."[40]

Such comments provoked Poindexter to justify himself. He was featured in an article in the Sunday *New York Times* in April as a Republican who favored "Honest Criticism" of the conduct of the war. He insisted that criticism of the government was legitimate only if based upon "honest and patriotic motives." This kind of criticism, he maintained, "is an entirely different thing from propaganda in favor of the Kaiser." Referring to his own bill to curb "seditious" expressions, that would become part of the Sedition Act, he added, "Legislation must be provided to stamp that out or the people may take matters into their own hands."[41]

To further this line of argument Poindexter and Theodore Roosevelt found common ground on which to attack the Wilson administration in May. Roosevelt had charged in an article in the *Kansas City Star* that the administration through Postmaster General Burleson punished newspapers that had upheld the war and failed to punish antiwar publications. Burleson denied the charge and dared Roosevelt to name specific publications to prove his allegations. Roosevelt responded to Burleson's challenge in a letter to Poindexter "so as to get . . . [it] into the permanent record." His letter, dated May 22, 1918, included a copy of an editorial in *Metropolitan*, which he said the New York post office "attempted to suppress," copies of his articles on the freedom of speech, and a very long rebuttal to Burleson.42

Roosevelt's documents were placed in the *Congressional Record* by Poindexter on May 25, and it was not many days before he was called upon to defend himself and Roosevelt to a constituent who wondered if Poindexter had not become the Colonel's mouthpiece in the Senate. "I do not represent him or speak for him as to his political action or conduct in any way whatever, although I am a great admirer of him," responded the senator. "One of his chief characteristics is the courage with which he applies his opinions and impulses in attacking what he deems to be vicious and wrong." The senator reminded his correspondent that he did sometimes differ with the Colonel and pointed to the recently passed Sedition Act as an illustration.43 But the contradiction which Poindexter's critics found in his almost fanatical zeal to silence the opponents of the war but, on the other hand, to maintain the right of "loyal" Republicans to criticize the Wilson administration apparently continued to disturb Poindexter. In December 1918, after the armistice had been concluded, he published an article in *Forum* to sum up his position. He was, he said, "in entire accord" with the wartime censorship laws, and he emphasized the fact that he was the author of "that section which penalizes the support of the German cause or opposition to the cause of the United States." This did not mean, he stressed, as many unfortunately thought, "that it is disloyal and unlawful to criticize public officials, and especially the President." He felt the distinction rested simply upon loyalty, and "What is disloyal and seditious is not difficult to determine." Freedom of expression, he believed, was more important than ever before, and he predicted that "the people" would not "blind themselves" and "surrender all rights of judgement and discrimination."[44]

Republican criticism of Wilson's conduct of the war in the spring of 1918 was premature, for by midsummer Allied forces were on the offensive, and victory seemed imminent. Thus the Republican focus shifted, as the summer progressed and the election of 1918 approached, from a criticism of Wilson's conduct of the war to an assault upon his "idealistic" peace proposals. The significance of the midyear elections was obvious. If the war was drawing to a conclusion, the Congress to be elected in the fall would play a critical role in the making of the peace. The president had stated his peace aims clearly in January 1917 when he called upon the warring powers for "peace without victory," and in his war message of April 1917 when he described American belligerence as an unselfish effort to secure world peace and to make the world safe for democracy. Further evidence that Wilson intended to persevere in his "idealistic" war objectives appeared in the president's message to Congress in January 1918 when he enunciated his Fourteen Points.[45]

Poindexter totally rejected Wilson's "idealistic" war aims. To the senator the war was a struggle for national interests, and he instantly aligned himself in the "realist" camp with Roosevelt and Lodge. "Our war with Germany is not a disinterested one," he told the Senate. "It is a fundamental struggle for liberty and for democracy, not in the abstract only for other people, but in the concrete and for our own people." During an exchange with Senator Borah later on the Senate floor, Poindexter predicted that if Germany defeated the Allies, she would invade the Western hemisphere. Borah agreed, but he remarked that "many" (obviously a reference to Wilson and his supporters) thought this a war for the "rehabilitation of Europe." "For humanity," Poindexter chimed in sarcastically, and then Poindexter succinctly presented his own war aims: "It is a war of self defense. It is a war for the material welfare of the American people, and not for the spiritual ideals of the world." The idea, he wrote later, "that there should be peace without victory . . . is utterly repulsive."[46]

Most Republicans shared Poindexter's aversion to Wilson's "idealism." They demanded an unconditional German surrender, and they feared that Wilson would, in the closing days of the war, agree to an armistice with Germany that would make the total victory they longed for impossible. As early as September 30, Lodge wrote Roosevelt that he was "living in a constant anxiety now of a sudden plunge of the Administration for a negotiated peace. At this point, if we make an armistice we have lost the war and we shall leave Germany about where she started."[47] Republican fears were very real indeed, for on October 6 the German government appealed to President Wilson for an armistice based on the Fourteen Points. Poindexter reacted with alarm, along with Lodge and Roosevelt. On October 7 he seized the Senate floor to alert the nation. Wilson, he claimed, proposed to grant terms to the Germans so lenient as to sacrifice all that had been won on the battlefield. He charged that Wilson planned to require merely that the German army withdraw from Belgium and France before negotiations could begin. Such leniency, Poindexter raged, was "an insidious menace to the vital interests of this Nation." He demanded that the war go on until the German army had been totally crushed and American troops were on German soil; he demanded "the execution of some of the murderers and robbers who have laid waste Belgium and France"; and he demanded a court-martial for the kaiser. "What they want is not justice, but mercy; and that is what they ought to ask for," he cried. Again, on October 10, 1918, Poindexter repeated his views by praising the previous remarks of Senator Lodge. Wilson's armistice terms, he said, meant "a German victory." About two weeks later Poindexter introduced a resolution that proposed to make it unlawful for any American official to negotiate with Germany until that country surrendered unconditionally. It was referred to committee and never acted upon.[48] Poindexter's actions were heartily endorsed by Roosevelt. "As compared to Republican Senators like Messrs. Lodge and Poindexter and their associates," Roosevelt declared on October 15, "the President has been infirm of purpose and vacillating in conduct; and to increase their strength is to strengthen this nation's attitude towards the war."[49]

Republican outrage at Wilson's initial negotiations with Germany may have influenced him, because his second note made harsher demands than had been spelled out in the first note. Poindexter later argued that Republican pressure was responsible for this, and Poindexter claimed that his resolution to prohibit further negotiations "had the effect, apparently, of causing the President to abandon his negotiations . . . on the 14th of October." He was mistaken in the details at least. His own resolution was not introduced until October 21, but it is possible that his conduct coupled with that of other Republicans did influence Wilson to increase his demands on Germany.[50]

Roosevelt shared Poindexter's interpretation of the Republican effort to force Wilson to make more harsh demands upon Germany, and he favored using this issue against the Democrats in the election. In a letter to Will H. Hays, national chairman of the Republican party, who was preparing a statement calling for the election of Republicans, Roosevelt instructed him to call for the election of "men who will do as Kahn, Poindexter, Lodge, and their associates have done." He also noted that Wilson's efforts to negotiate with Germany "was stopped only by the vigorous protests of men like Lodge and Poindexter, who have been the staunchest upholders of the war, and that it is our war, and that it is our business to send Republicans to Congress now, to avert the danger of any improper yielding by the Democrats." Roosevelt appealed to Poindexter, Lodge, and Johnson in a public telegram on October 24 to oppose Wilson's Fourteen Points "in their entirety" as a basis of the peace negotiations and to insist upon "peace based on the unconditional surrender of Germany."[51]

With his policies subjected to such severe attack, President Wilson yielded to the appeals of Democratic party leaders and on October 25 requested the voters to elect a Democratic Congress. The Senate Republicans responded on October 28 in a series of speeches, as if Wilson's request had introduced partisanship for the first time since

April 1917. Poindexter was the last to speak. He found it "extremely distasteful" to discuss a partisan matter, but President Wilson, said Poindexter, "has projected a partisan discussion into the affairs of the Government." Poindexter now intended to present to the nation "a fair understanding" of the issues that would be involved in the fall elections. Wilson, he said, will insist upon treating Germany as "an equal partner"; he "will endeavor to form a league of nations with Germany and save her from due punishment and retribution for the wrongs she has done to mankind." This, then, was the question for the voters: a victorious peace or "a weak peace."[52]

After Wilson's note to Germany of late October, which implied that a new democratic government would receive more consideration in the peace negotiations, in early November the German kaiser abdicated. Soon afterward, the German army surrendered and agreed to withdraw to the German border. The debate in the United States over the nature of the armistice proceeded simultaneously with the diplomatic negotiations and the campaign of 1918. In that campaign Poindexter's activities served to show that his efforts had won approval from regular Republicans. On May 27, 1918 the new national Republican chairman, Will H. Hays of Indiana, wrote to Poindexter to inform him that he had been selected to serve on the senatorial campaign committee. Senator Gallinger, who had been one of the leading opponents of reform before 1916, had suggested Poindexter's name, said Hays. In addition, Senators Wadsworth and Calder of New York, New of Indian, Smoot of Utah, Kellogg of Minnesota had been asked to serve; none of these had been a member of the prewar progressive Republican group except Poindexter.[53] Poindexter did not play an active role in the 1918 campaign in Washington state, but nationally, for the first time in his career, regular Republican party leaders seemed anxious to have him on their side. He was asked by the National Committee to speak in Wyoming, Idaho, Ohio, Rhode Island, Oregon, and Washington; there were, said the chairman of the congressional committee on speakers, "many demands for you." In addition to requests for him to speak, Poindexter was also asked to write a statement on election issues, that was circulated nationally to Republican newspapers.54

Across the nation the election of 1918 was a major setback for the Democrats. The results insured that the Republicans would control both Houses in the next Congress; and because of Wilson's unfortunate appeal to the voters in October, Republicans claimed that Wilson's leadership had been repudiated. In eastern Washington's Fifth Congressional District, as well, victory was with the Republicans. Democrat C. C. Dill, the incumbent who was accused of being an opponent of the war by the Republicans, was defeated by a very slim margin by J. Stanley Webster. Dill, however, carried four counties, and two of these counties gave him 60 percent of the vote. There was, in sum, considerable Democratic strength in eastern Washington in 1918 even though Dill was accused of being "disloyal," and these results might have served as a warning to Poindexter that his antilabor, antiradical tirades might serve to alienate groups that had supported his campaign as an insurgent Republican in 1910 and 1916.55

Poindexter accepted with due modesty some credit for the Republican party's successes, and he insisted that the election of 1918 was a progressive victory: "After all these years this is the fruition of the Progressive struggle ending with complete control of the Party." Probably Poindexter was quite sincere in seeing the 1918 Republican victory as a victory for progressivism, for in his view he supported the same values and groups he had always supported. But from the perspective of those who knew little of his ideological values, he seemed to have shifted in only a very few years from being an extreme progressive reformer to an extreme conservative. By the end of the campaign of 1918, Poindexter, indeed, had switched from one wing of the Republican party to the other. Furthermore, other reform leaders, such as Theodore Roosevelt, apparently ceased supporting reform at approximately the same time Poindexter did. They were all, it seems, affected by what Otis Graham, Jr., has called "the war induced alteration of the reform mentality in the direction of ideas and impulses at once less confident and less generous."56

Poindexter's change also seemed influenced by his fundamental disagreement over the conduct of the war with some of the leading prewar reformers in Congress. Poindexter on one occasion, in private, called LaFollette one of "several so-called Pacifist and pro-German Senators," and undoubtedly he also had in mind Borah, Norris, and several other members of the progressive Republican bloc, as well. The totality of the division of the prewar progressive Republicans can be illustrated by examining the response of these senators to selected votes on issues related to the conduct of the war. Table 5 shows how members of this group stood on these votes. They can be divided roughly into three groups, those that opposed these war measures, those that supported all or most of these measures, and the moderates.[57] Poindexter, along with nearly half of the progressive Republicans, steadfastly supported the war, but clearly Gronna, LaFollette, and Norris can in these terms be classified as opponents of the war. The remainder, including Borah and Hiram Johnson, could at best be considered only lukewarm in their support of the war. In contrast to these progressives, most regular Republicans, business groups, and industrialists whom Poindexter had labeled "special interests" before 1916 supported the war loyally. Thus, by the summer of 1918, Poindexter had come to defend war industries from what he said were confiscatory tax rates and to ally himself with former Republican opponents of reform, such as Senator Lodge, to denounce the administration's conduct of the war.

The breakup of the prewar progressive Republican bloc over the conduct of World War I and related issues, helps explain how the war contributed to the demise of the progressive reform effort in the Senate. While Democrats had provided the organizational leadership, party cohesion, and most of the votes to enact the progressive reform legislation of the Taft and Wilson years, the progressive Republicans had contributed some votes and a great deal of emotional enthusiasm. Never an entirely effective voting bloc, in part because of the strong ideological commitment to "democracy" and "individualism," and because of their antipathy to party discipline, the progressives in the Republican

TABLE 5

VOTE OF PROGRESSIVE REPUBLICANS ON SELECTED WAR MEASURES

	1*	2	3	4	5	6	7	8	9	yes	no
Borah, Idaho	yes	yes	yes	–	yes	no	no	no	no	4	4
Cummins, Iowa	no	no	yes	–	yes	yes	–	no	–	3	3
Curtis, Kans.	yes	no	yes	yes	yes	yes	yes	–	no	6	2
Fall, N.Mex.	–	–	yes	yes	–	yes	yes	yes	yes	6	0
Gronna, N.Dak.	no	no	no	no	no	no	no	–	no	0	8
Johnson, Calif.	–	–	–	–	yes	yes	no	no	no	2	3
Jones, Wash.	–	yes	yes	yes	yes	yes	no	yes	yes	7	1
Kenyon, Iowa	–	no	yes	–	yes	yes	no	–	no	3	3
LaFollette, Wis.	no	no	no	no	no	no	no	–	–	0	7
Nelson, Minn.	yes	yes	yes	yes	yes	yes	yes	no	yes	8	1
Norris, Nebr.	no	no	no	yes	no	–	no	no	no	1	7
Poindexter, Wash.	yes	yes	yes	yes	yes	yes	yes	yes	yes	9	0
Sherman, Ill.	no	yes	yes	yes	yes	no	yes	no	no	5	4
Sterling, S.Dak.	yes	yes	yes	yes	yes	yes	yes	yes	yes	9	0
Townsend, Mich.	–	no	yes	yes	yes	yes	–	–	–	4	1

*The numbers correspond to war issues as follows: 1) against LaFollette filibuster of 1917; 2) for preparedness; 3) for war declaration; 4) against LaFollette amendment to draft act; 5) for draft act; 6) for espionage act; 7) against war profits tax; 8) against France amendment to sedition act; and 9) for sedition act.

party splintered into at least two hostile groups after 1917. Poindexter became as intensely nationalistic and intolerant of the opponents of the war as any senator in either party. Gronna, LaFollette, and Norris became outspoken critics of the war, guilty, in Poindexter's view, of disloyalty, perhaps even treason, and Borah and Johnson, whose support of the war had been lukewarm at best, were only slightly more tolerable. It would be a mistake, however, to exaggerate the significance of the dissolution of the progressive Republican bloc, for later in the 1920s the group reappeared as the Farm bloc, with about as much unity as before 1917, although Poindexter would no longer be with them. The war and other factors diminished Democratic party solidarity as well; in fact, a few of the opponents of the war were Democrats. Decline in Democratic cohesion, combined with a major decline in the number of Democrats in Congress after the elections of 1918 and 1920, undoubtedly contributed much more to the demise of the progressive reform effort in Congress than the disintegration of the progressive Republican bloc. Nonetheless, their inability to continue to cooperate after 1917 was a contributing factor to the disruption, if only for a few years, of the progressive coalition in the Senate.

9.

The Struggle Against Internationalism and Bolshevism

IN THE year after the election of 1918 Poindexter concentrated primarily upon two major issues, Woodrow Wilson's peace program and the activities of the "Bolsheviki," the IWW, and organized labor. He insisted, in fact, that the two issues were related, and occasionally he actually equated Wilsonian internationalism with Russian bolshevism. To Poindexter the most alarming element of Wilson's peace program was the proposal that the United States should become a member of the League of Nations. The idea of an international organization to preserve peace had been proposed by Wilson as one of his Fourteen Points, and he made it clear, even after the Democratic defeat in the election of 1918, that he intended to play a major role in the peacemaking by announcing that he would personally attend the peace conference at Versailles. Wilson departed for France in December 1918, and he did not return until February 1919, after he had persuaded the allied representatives at Versailles to include the League of Nations Covenant in the peace treaty. The League Covenant provided for an international organization with a Secretariat, a Council, and an Assembly, and the League was dedicated to encourage international cooperation and maintain peace. To preserve peace and security, article 10, which Wilson felt was the heart of the Covenant, pledged the member nations to uphold the principle of collective security.[1]

Poindexter identified himself with the irreconcilables—the small group of senators who opposed American membership in the League of Nations and ratification of the Treaty of Versailles in all circumstances—soon after the signing of the armistice. His central objection to the League was that he saw it as a threat to American national independence. Poindexter predicted that the adoption of Wilson's League would place American sovereignty "in the hands of Europe"; he stressed the danger of a League to the Monroe Doctrine; and he warned of the power of "a very large and growing class of socialists and radicals who minimize the value of nationality." The idea of such an international government also violated Poindexter's Darwinian concept of reality. He ridiculed a Democratic senator for assuming that "the same passions and ambitions that have actuated the governments of nations in the past are not going to be in full play in the evolution of the future." Human nature, he explained, could hardly be changed so simply. "The necessity for expansion and colonization are not matters that are determined by the form of government or by the terms of peace. They are governed by fundamental influences, the primal instincts of man, and they are going to be in as full play after the terms of peace between Germany and the allies have been settled as they were at the time the Monroe Doctrine was set up by American statesmen of a previous generation."[2]

In his private correspondence, Poindexter hammered continually at the idea of a League, with basically the same two themes: nationalism and "realism." Poindexter stressed repeatedly the idea that the League "means an end of the independence of the United States." He ridiculed the supporters of the League as "theoretical gentlemen, professors and others . . . who have had no practical experience either in private business or government affairs." Jane Addams, who supported the League, he reminded W. H. Cowles of the *Spokesman-Review*, "has been confined to work among poor children," and she speaks only for ladies who dabble in "'parlor socialism.'"[3] Poindexter predicted that the League would violate American traditions established by President Washington; he used historical arguments—all similar attempts to end war in the past had ended in war; and he feared that the rest of the world would "dictate" American immigration policy.

The leader of the Senate opposition to Wilson's League was the new chairman of the Committee on Foreign Relations, Senator Henry Cabot Lodge. He and Roosevelt were convinced that it was unwise for Republicans to reject the idea of a League outright. They endeavored to convince the irreconcilable Albert J. Beveridge of the wisdom of this approach, but apparently neither Lodge nor Roosevelt made any effort to dissuade Poindexter from joining the irreconcilables. Roosevelt did, however, congratulate the Washington senator for his first speech against the League. "You are always doing such admirable things nowadays that I bid fair to become your constant correspondent," Roosevelt wrote. "I wish heartily to thank you for what you have been saying about the Peace League." Roosevelt went on to say that he was willing to accept a "common sense Peace League with our allies, if we don't promise too much." But he said he was unalterably opposed to membership for Germany.[4] Not many weeks later, Roosevelt died, and the leadership of the Republican opposition to Wilson's League was left in Lodge's capable hands.

The publication of the first draft of the Covenant touched off a series of speeches by the Senate irreconcilables. Poindexter led the way with a three-hour tirade on February 19. Again, his central theme was the League's threat to American national independence, but toward the conclusion of his speech Poindexter added a new dimension. He linked the supporters of the founding of an international organization to preserve peace with the Bolshevist revolution. "Mr. President," he declared, "there is an internationalism abroad in the land— an internationalism of the elite and an internationalism of the proletariat," and he charged further that "Germany is supporting both." The two internationalist groups, he said, consisted of the "idealists and peace-at-any-price pacifists" and, in the second group, "the Industrial Workers of the World and their Bolshevist allies throughout

the world." The goal of both groups was the same—
"an international and despotic government of the
world." The *Chicago Tribune* reported that Poindexter was listened to with the "closest attention,"
but the *New York Times*, which supported the League,
concluded that Poindexter's "points . . . were the
old and obvious criticisms that occurred at the beginning to everybody averse to the idea."[5]

Outside the Senate, Poindexter joined with other
irreconcilables to speak against Wilson's League
at every opportunity, and his furious efforts to
educate the public as to the danger of "internationalism" managed to antagonize many of the
friends of the League. William Howard Taft—who
had good reason to remember earlier unpleasant encounters with Poindexter—was active in support of
the League of Nations, and Taft was appalled at
what he called "the explosive ignorance of Poindexter." Echoing Taft's judgment, the *New Republic*
declared that Poindexter and Democratic Senator
Reed of Missouri, another vocal critic of the
League proposal, were "known as far as Thibet and
Timbuctoo as mere empty sounds in a desert of inanities." Poindexter, Borah, and Reed, the *New Republic* maintained, "ignored the implacable political and economic conditions which demand the establishment of international government." The *New York
Times*, critical but not so blunt, appeared to consider Poindexter the most intransigent of the irreconcilables, for in April 1919 an editorial professed to see a softening of attitude of some
League critics. "Soon," it predicted hopefully,
"Mr. Poindexter will find himself alone."[6]

With the League proposal under intense fire,
Wilson returned briefly to the United States in
February 1919. He then invited members of the House
Foreign Affairs and Senate Foreign Relations committees to dinner, but his efforts to convince and
conciliate were unsuccessful. Shortly after that
meeting with Wilson, Senator Lodge read into the
Record a statement signed by thirty-seven senators,
more than enough to prevent ratification of a
treaty, which declared that the consideration of a
League of Nations ought to be postponed until a
peace with Germany had been secured. Poindexter was
one of those who signed this "round Robin," as

Lodge's statement was called, and it gave Wilson early warning that enough Republicans to defeat the Versailles treaty were willing to cooperate with Senator Lodge.

Wilson responded in a speech in New York on March 4 that the League would continue to be an integral component of the treaty, but later he did make important concessions to the League's critics. A new draft of the League Covenant, revised at Versailles in part to meet the objections of the Senate, and made public on April 28, contained a provision to enable nations to withdraw from the League, exempted domestic issues (as defined by the League Council) from the League's jurisdiction, and removed the Monroe Doctrine from the League's authority. These concessions were by no means sufficient to many of Wilson's critics, and as the new Congress which would consider the Treaty of Versailles gathered, the most severe opponents of American entry into the League of Nations worked desperately to find a way to prevent ratification of the treaty.

The new Senate, the Sixty-sixth, had a Republican majority of two seats. This meant that Senator Lodge would be chairman of the Committee on Foreign Relations and that the committee would be in the hands of Wilson's enemies.[7] President Wilson submitted the treaty with the League incorporated in it to the Senate in July 1919. Soon afterward the Foreign Relations Committee opened hearings, but not until September 10 was the majority report, which recommended many amendments and reservations, reported to the Senate. In the voting on the League in the Senate in November 1919, there were about sixteen Republican irreconcilables, including Poindexter, and two Democrats. Nine of the Republican irreconcilables had been progressives: Borah, Gronna, LaFollette, Norris, Poindexter, Sherman, and Fall had been supporters of progressive legislation before 1917, and Johnson and Medill McCormick of Illinois had been members of the Progressive party. The presence of so many moderate and advanced progressive Republicans among the irreconcilables cannot, however, be taken to mean that these prewar reformers shared common attitudes toward foreign affairs. Poindexter, as has been seen, was an irreconcilable because of his extreme nationalism, a point of view almost diametrically opposed to the views of Borah, LaFollette, and Norris, and probably some of the other progressives. Poindexter and the "isolationists" voted together, but for very different reasons, and in no way could Poindexter's opposition to American membership in the League of Nations be interpreted as "isolationism." Poindexter's view probably was closest to the ideological position of Lodge, Beveridge and, had he lived, Roosevelt.[8]

Partisan politics played a significant role in the voting which ended with the defeat of the treaty, as it usually did in foreign affairs. Reservations were added to the treaty by an almost solid block of Republicans. With the reservations incorporated, the president, who had collapsed during a speaking tour in behalf of the treaty, stubbornly insisted that the Democratic senators vote against the revised treaty. Democratic votes coupled with the votes of the irreconcilables, who had voted for most of the reservations, defeated the revised treaty. The treaty without reservations received nearly unanimous Democratic support, but the irreconcilables combined with most Republicans to defeat the Democratic draft. Although there were only sixteen irreconcilables, Wilson's treaty was defeated. In February and March 1920 the treaty was taken up again, but in general the results were the same. The League of Nations had been rejected by the Senate and Miles Poindexter, voting with the irreconcilables, played an important part in this fateful decision.[9]

Even before the voting on the treaty began, Poindexter had been faced with the charge that his action was motivated by political considerations. He denied this charge emphatically. "Politics, in the sense of seeking artificial party advantage, so far as I am conscious, never occurred to me," he said. "What I have said about the League of Nations and about the President is based on the strength of my conviction and upon propositions which I am convinced are absolutely demonstrable to a moral if not a mathematical certainty." This was a fair and accurate description of Poindexter's position, for he, like Senator Beveridge, had declared against a

League of Nations before it had become associated with Woodrow Wilson and the Democratic party. Since entering public life Poindexter had consistently held a "realistic" attitude toward foreign policy, and his objections to the League of Nations stemmed from this conceptual framework. But the Washington senator was a partisan to the core, ambitious and, at times, ruthless in the treatment of his political enemies, as his attacks on Wilson showed. Poindexter was running for the presidency in 1919, and he used his fight against the League as one of the central themes of his campaign. But partisanship seemed only to intensify this attack, and Poindexter surely would have spoken vigorously against the League no matter who proposed it, or when. In 1919 and 1920 Poindexter's convictions and his partisan ambitions pulled together hand in glove.[10]

The fight against the Treaty of Versailles, as Poindexter described it, was a struggle for national existence against an "internationalism of the elite," but he felt that American society was under an equally serious domestic threat from what he called "an internationalism of the proletariat." Poindexter of course referred to the Bolshevist revolution in Russia and to his belief that American pacifists, antiwar radicals, and at least some labor leaders were under the influence of the so-called "international communist conspiracy." Poindexter's concerns apparently were fostered by the founding of the Third International in Moscow in early 1919 and, a few months later, by the organization in the United States of the Communist Labor and Communist parties. After the war's end, furthermore, a significant increase in militant labor activity greatly aggravated his fear of radicalism. But in general his hostility to the Reds after the war seemed only a continuation of the fight he had made during the war to suppress antiwar groups. Fundamentally, it seemed the major cause was Poindexter's nationalism, swollen to extreme proportions during the war, that spilled over into the immediate postwar years.[11]

One of the first major postwar labor efforts, which Poindexter and many others thought was Communist-inspired, was the Seattle general strike of January 1919 in Poindexter's own state. It began when the Seattle shipyard workers broke their contract with the Emergency Fleet Corporation to strike for higher wages and shorter hours. The Seattle Central Labor Council, which had threatened a general strike the year before on behalf of Thomas Mooney, called on the entire Seattle labor force to strike in sympathy with the shipyard workers. On February 6 approximately sixty thousand men stopped work and the city's activities came to a standstill. The Seattle mayor, Ole Hanson, who had been an unsuccessful Progressive candidate for the Senate in 1914, requested troops and declared that the strike was a revolutionary plot. Federal troops were hastily moved into Seattle from nearby Camp Lewis, and the strike was crushed, a complete failure. Newspapers informed their readers that the aims of the strike were revolutionary and that it had been instigated by the Bolshevists, and many national and state leaders raised their voices against the Bolshevists, none with more vigor than Senator Poindexter.[12]

During early 1919 Poindexter concentrated on the attack upon Wilson's League of Nations, but even before the Seattle strike Poindexter had charged that the IWW had been "catered to by the Administration . . . and to that I think is due their activity." Just two days before the Seattle Central Labor Council called the strike, Poindexter obtained the Senate floor to introduce a resolution clearly intended to suggest that the administration and particularly the Attorney General, Thomas W. Gregory, was unwilling to take legal action against radicals. His resolution pointed out, among other things, that it was the Attorney General's responsibility to enforce the laws against sedition, treason, violence, and insurrection, and that on February 2 and 3 at Poli's Theater in Washington, D.C., there had been public meetings where speakers "advocated the course of the present Bolsheviki government of Russia." Then the Attorney General was asked to inform the Senate "what, if any, steps he has taken to enforce the laws of the United States." The Senate passed the resolution on February 5, without objection and without a vote.[13]

After the Seattle strike Poindexter joined forces with western Washington employers who had been early advocates of the open shop movement. He exchanged views on the open shop, for example, with Alex Polson, president of the Polson Logging Company of Hoquiam, Washington. Poindexter claimed that the Seattle strike "was an international rather than local movement—a mere incident of the incipient world-wide social revolution which the communists are attempting to bring about." He suggested to Polson that "the employers of the state, or those who are interested in preserving law and order" should investigate the nationality and beliefs of labor leaders: "it would be of great value in dealing with the subject." Furthermore, he roundly denounced the closed shop, one of the most important aims of organized labor. Men should be free to work whether they belonged to the union or not, he told Polson, and he said there was grave need to protect "labor . . . from the bolshevik tyranny which is getting control of it apparently."[14]

One day later Poindexter expressed essentially the same sentiments to the Secretary of the National Association of Manufacturers. The position of that organization in support of the open shop was of course well known. Poindexter reiterated his charge that the Seattle strike was "merely an incident in the world-wide, internationalized, social, revolutionary movement"; he reminded the secretary of labor's efforts to free the radical Thomas Mooney; and he criticized "the authorities," obviously the Wilson administration, for "espousing the cause" of Mooney. "The result has been," said Poindexter, "to encourage the communistic movement and out of it has come . . . the Seattle strike." He observed that the Association of Manufacturers had no plan to stop the growth of this "menace," and he called upon "the manufacturers of the country" to "take some part in shaping public opinion and in giving their support to the government in adequate measure for its protection against anarchy and ruin."[1]

During the remainder of 1919, Poindexter sustaine a persistent bombardment of the Wilson administration for its alleged sympathy with the Bolshevist movement. Much of his criticism was leveled at the new Attorney General, A. Mitchell Palmer, a progressive Democrat from Pennsylvania, after Palmer was appointed early in 1919 to replace Gregory.[16]

The senator's charges did not pass unchallenged, however, and in May his speech to the Republican Club of Cambridge, Massachusetts, was brought to the attention of the Senate by Senator Robinson, Democrat from Arkansas. Robinson cited Poindexter's speech as an example "of the partisanship displayed by Republican Senators." Robinson said he referred specifically to a statement in which Poindexter had asserted that Wilson was cooperating with the IWW to destroy American independence. Poindexter snatched up the gauntlet immediately. In the "Fourteen Points" speech on January 8, 1918, Poindexter insisted, Wilson had praised the Russian Bolshevist representatives to the Brest-Litovsk discussions by saying that they challenged "'the admiration of every friend of mankind.'" This speech, claimed Poindexter, was reprinted in Bolshevist pamphlets. "I assume as I said in Massachusetts, that eulogy of the Bolshevists by the President used in that way is of great benefit to the communist movement." Poindexter added that the covenant of the League of Nations was further evidence to support his charges against Wilson. This was the admission Robinson desired, for he responded, "All of you who heard him know he has justified the charge to which I have referred solely on the ground that the President is advocating the league of nations." Such comments, said Robinson, were proof that Poindexter was attempting "to raise prejudice."[17]

Few people seemed to take Poindexter's accusations about Wilson seriously, but Poindexter's charge that some labor unions were Bolshevist-led was evidently widely believed. In August, the striking Boston police force was accused of being influenced by bolshevism, and similar fears were expressed about the steel workers' strike in September in Gary, Indiana, where rioting and violence led the governor of Indiana to summon federal troops. Not many weeks later, the United Mine Workers called for a strike to begin November 1, and the coal miners, too, were immediately condemned as revolutionaries.

As these events unfolded, Poindexter continued his attack upon the administration's handling of radicalism, and the alleged relationship between supporters of the League of Nations and international communism. Attorney General Palmer, Poindexter charged in September 1919, had failed to prosecute radicals and to deport radical aliens. "If the laws already on the statute books for the punishment of sedition, anarchy and deportation of anarchists, aliens and aliens preaching sedition were rigidly enforced," he said, "much of the difficulty . . . would immediately be suppressed."[18]

Poindexter submitted a resolution to the Senate on October 14 aimed at the Attorney General's failure to act against radicals. This resolution requested that Palmer explain to the Senate why the Department of Justice had failed to take legal action against "various persons . . . who . . . it is alleged have attempted to bring about the forcible overthrow of the Government of the United States." In addition, the resolution asked why the Justice Department "has failed to take legal proceedings for the arrest and deportation of aliens, who, it is alleged, have . . . committed the acts aforesaid." To explain his resolution, Poindexter pointed to the steel strike. The purpose of the strike in Gary, he declared, "reaches to the scheme of subverting . . . the authority of the Government. . . . In other words, it is a revolutionary movement." He warned his fellow countrymen "that we have now reached a point . . . at which it behooves the Government . . . not only to take action but to take vigorous action to suppress anarchy and revolution and to defend itself." Poindexter said he understood that President Wilson and Attorney General Palmer resented his resolution, but he concluded that it was no time to consider personal feelings.[19]

Poindexter's resolution was well timed, for the next day, October 15, the *New York Times* announced to its readers that the army had uncovered an IWW plot in Gary, Indiana, to destroy government property and organize a revolution in the Midwest. Directly under the headlines—"EXPOSE I. W. W. PLOT TO SEIZE POWER"—was, in heavy type, "Poindexter Urges Action." The *Times* discussed fully Poindexter's speech attacking Palmer's failures to act against the IWW, and it reprinted the full text of the Poindexter resolution which was considered by the Senate on October 17. After the adoption of some minor changes to soften the condemnation of the Attorney General, the Senate adopted it unanimously. In an interview with a *New York Times* reporter after passage of his resolution, Poindexter promised to give another major speech soon on "red" activities, and in closing the interview, he observed without comment that all but eight of the sixty or more aliens arrested, and interned at the immigrant reception center at Ellis Island after the Seattle strike, had been freed.[20]

Three weeks later Palmer launched the first of the infamous raids conducted by his office during the "Red Scare." Several hundred members of the Union of Russian Workers were arrested in twelve cities. Poindexter expressed approval of Palmer's action and claimed credit for it: "I am glad to note, as the apparent result of the resolution which passed on my introduction, increased activity by the Department of Justice in enforcing the laws against anarchists, both alien and domestic." He believed that a new and more severe law to curb radicalism was needed, but he maintained that Palmer had "ample statutory authority for suppressing the revolutionary movement."[21] The Attorney General responded directly to the Poindexter resolution by submitting to Congress on November 15 a new bill for the regulation and prosecution of radicals, but it failed to satisfy Poindexter who submitted his own bill to suppress radicalism on the seventeenth—it was referred to the Judiciary Committee and never acted upon. Poindexter continued his attack against Palmer in an article on radicalism in the *New York Times*. "Poindexter Charges That Present Laws Have Not Been Properly Used," commented the *Times*, and it featured photographs of both Palmer and Poindexter and called the Washington senator the "Leading Critic of the Department of Justice."[22]

Further drastic action against the "Red menace" was taken by the Attorney General on December 21, 1919, when two hundred and forty-nine aliens were deported under his direction. Then on January 2, 1920 over four thousand persons suspected of being "Reds" were arrested in thirty-three cities. Palmer immediately was hailed as a national hero, but in the years since the emotions of the "Red Scare" have subsided, he has been severely criticized for flagrant disregard of personal rights and civil liberties.

There is some reason to believe that the Poindexter resolution was in fact directly responsible for stimulating Palmer to act against the "Reds" in 1919 and 1920. Poindexter's charges that Palmer was not alarmed by the "Red menace" before the Poindexter resolution was passed by the Senate were partly correct.[23] Palmer had, in fact, indicated after his appointment as Attorney General in March 1919 that he felt too much had been made of "disloyalty" and "sedition." On March 31 Palmer warned private "patriotic" societies that their vigilante-type efforts to ferret out seditious persons "is entirely at variance with our theories of government." Because of this statement, Palmer was admonished by the *New York Times* and praised by the *New Republic* and the *Nation*. After a bomb exploded mysteriously in front of his house, Palmer still seemed restrained—particularly when his remarks are compared with Poindexter's; and the *Nation* again complimented Palmer for his moderation even under such trying circumstances. Apparently it was only after the Senate adopted the Poindexter resolution that Palmer revealed any public concern about the "Reds."[24]

During the weeks that Poindexter assailed Palmer for laxity toward "Reds," he also participated in a major debate in Congress over the relationship of the federal government and the national railroad system. Poindexter's position on this issue illustrated the degree to which he had come to speak and to vote as a member of the regular Republican bloc in the Senate. The Railroad Brotherhoods in 1919 proposed that the federal government, which still operated the railroads under the McAdoo Federal Control Act of 1918, continue to control the railroads after the war. The proposal, usually known as the Plumb Plan, named after its originator Glenn Plumb, an attorney of the railroad unions, was endorsed by the national convention of the American Federation of Labor in 1920, and it received the support of Senator LaFollette and a few other congressmen. Majority sentiment in the new Republican Congress, however, was clearly opposed to it. The bill which ultimately passed, the Esch-Cummins Transportation Act, was sponsored in the Senate by Cummins of Iowa, one of the prewar progressives. It provided for the restoration of control of the railroads to private ownership and a temporary federal guarantee of railroad profits. Cummins's bill included many provisions the prewar progressives had fought for, but it abandoned the wartime experiment in federal railroad management.[25]

The leading critic of the Cummins bill was Senator LaFollette. LaFollette rejected the popular contention that government management during the war had been inefficient, and he maintained that the Cummins bill for the most part yielded to the interests of the railroads. Instead, the Wisconsin senator favored a two-year extension of federal operation, and he was supported by a few of the old progressive Republican group—Johnson, Norris, Gronna, and Borah.[26] Most of the prewar reformers, however, stood with Cummins and the Republican majority.

Poindexter was unalterably opposed to the Plumb Plan despite the fact that about a year before he seemed at the least willing to consider the possibility of federal ownership of the railroads. But by January 1919 the senator had changed his mind. "Our people talk of government ownership as though some mysterious and magic benefit to our citizens would come from it," he said, and he rejected that point of view. "I would say," he wrote the Secretary of the Brotherhood of Locomotive Firemen and Engineers, "that the socalled [sic] Plumb Plan . . . would lead to the ruin of the railroads and possibly the ruin of the country."[27]

Before the railroad bill reached the Senate floor, the Interstate Commerce Committee adopted an antistrike provision that provided a penalty of a fine and/or imprisonment for any two or more persons convicted of attempting to obstruct railroad operations and for persons who counseled, aided, or ordered such acts. This provision immediately attracted the determined opposition of organized labor. Samuel Gompers of the AFL charged that the antistrike amendment "would reintroduce industrial servitude in the United States," and the Railroad Brotherhoods insisted that the Interstate Commerce Committee reconsider the amendment. The Committee voted unanimously to reject the Railroad Brotherhoods' request, and Poindexter, a member of the Committee, defended its decision. "Mr. Gompers," he charged, "claims to be a conservative leader, yet . . . he goes as far as the most radical, proposing to eliminate the government, which is equivalent to direct action and syndicalist doctrine of anti-statism." Poindexter explained his position more carefully to a shipyard labor leader in Tacoma who said he had always voted for Poindexter and could not comprehend why "the man we placed our faith in to such a degree as we have in you, should call us by all the vile names they [newspapers] give you credit for." Poindexter insisted that his "attitude is most friendly towards organized labor and has always been so." But he objected to "the use . . . of the labor unions in this country by radical anarchist, or bolsheviki, or syndicalist leaders who are, as they express it, 'boring from the inside.'" He closed his letter with a generalization similar to those he had used to defend his progressivism before 1917: "I have opposed the undue control of government by capital, and . . . would oppose likewise undue control of the government by any other class."[28]

During the debate on the Cummins bill in mid-December 1919, Poindexter played an active role. He spoke briefly on December 15 against the Plumb Plan—it "would inevitably lead to the paralysis of the [railroad] business"; but he concentrated most of his attention on two other issues, the rate-making powers of the Interstate Commerce Commission and the antistrike provision.

Poindexter expressed the longstanding concern among the business and farm groups in Spokane about discriminatory freight rates in his remarks about the rate-making provisions of the railroad bill. In Committee he attempted to substitute a measure of his own to prohibit absolutely railroad discrimination against the short haul, but his amendment failed. Then on the Senate floor on December 16 he proposed what appeared to be the same amendment. Again the amendment was defeated, and almost all of its support came from senators from west of the Mississippi River, the region which had produced most of the prewar progressive Republicans. Thus

Poindexter sided with the prewar progressives on at least some kinds of railroad regulation; but he no longer used the "progressive rhetoric" of the prewar years, and he ceased to attack the "special interests." His argument was a frank statement on behalf of the economic interests of Spokane and eastern Washington. "You realize the obstinacy and bitterness of the fight," he told the secretary of the Seattle Chamber of Commerce. "It is simply a question of dollars and cents on all sides, with the difference that we are asking for the removal of discrimination while the other side is enjoying favorable discriminations, which it does not desire to give us."[29] The economic problems remained the same, but Poindexter's approach to them had changed considerably.

In the debate over the antistrike provision in the Cummins bill, Poindexter added nothing new to his general criticism of organized labor except that he attempted to explain more fully how his position in support of the antistrike clause was consistent with earlier fights for progressive reforms. He said he perceived the antistrike provision as the same fundamental question he had faced before 1917 in his fight against the "special interests." The United States government should not, he continued, be permitted to come under the control of "any special class, whether it is that of business or of capital or of organized labor."[30] In other words, Poindexter's views in 1919, as he saw it, were the same as they had been in 1912. As before, he saw himself as a defender of "the people" against the "special interests."

Voting on the Cummins bill began on December 17 with thirteen prewar progressive Republicans participating. A comparison of the voting of each of the prewar progressives with Senator Cummins demonstrates that the prewar progressive Republicans no longer agreed on railroad legislation, an issue that had been central to the progressive program in the Senate before 1917.[31] Of the thirteen, nine voted more or less consistently with Cummins and four against him. Poindexter, with one exception, voted with Cummins, but Borah, Gronna, LaFollette, and Norris usually voted against Cummins. Those who most frequently opposed Cummins (and Poindexter) on the railroad bill were of course the same progressives who had opposed the war or had supported it only halfheartedly. The bitter feelings engendered by wartime issues now made it more difficult for the progressive Republicans to cooperate. The voting suggests, moreover, that Poindexter was not the only member of the prewar progressive Republican bloc in the Senate to break with LaFollette and the other critics of the war. The division in progressive Republican ranks was apparently not irreparable, however, since some of these same individuals worked together later in the 1920s as members of the Farm bloc, but the voting does suggest that in the immediate postwar years the progressive Republicans were not voting together on an issue that before 1917 would probably have united them.

The Senate passed the Cummins bill on December 20, 1919, and Poindexter served as one of the conferees appointed to meet with representatives of the House. A major difference between the House and Senate bills was the antistrike amendment. Poindexter worked vigorously to save that provision, but after lengthy negotiations, the conference committee eliminated it. Congress then quickly passed the bill, and it was signed by Wilson in February 1920.[32] By then, the campaign of 1920 was well under way, and Poindexter had become a serious contender for the presidential nomination on the basis of his leadership in the struggle against Wilsonian internationalism and the international Communist conspiracy. He clearly hoped that his position on these issues would attract the support of business groups, regular Republicans, and antilabor interests—elements he had not appealed to before 1917—and enable him to capture the Republican nomination in 1920.

As early as 1914, Poindexter had dreamed of running for president in 1920. At that time, he planned to base his platform on his record as a leading progressive. In 1920, Poindexter of course had ceased to advocate progressive reforms, but he still wanted to be president. The death of Roosevelt left the Republican party in 1920 short of leaders with a national reputation, and none of the three leading candidates for the nomination,

General Leonard Wood, Governor Frank Lowden of
Illinois, and Senator Hiram Johnson of California,
seemed to Poindexter strong enough to capture the
nomination. Poindexter hoped that his prominence
in the fight against internationalism and bolshevism, combined with his earlier reputation as a
leading progressive, would give him the leverage
he needed to seize the nomination for himself.[33]

To many prewar progressives Johnson seemed the
best choice. The leading California progressive
Republican, he had been in the Senate since 1917,
had taken an active role as an irreconcilable in
the fight on the League of Nations, and on the conduct of the war he had been moderate. In assessing
his own chances for the Republican nomination,
Johnson made some perceptive observations about
Poindexter's place in the Republican party, and
about the state of the party as the 1920 campaign
approached. Johnson wanted the Republican nomination, but he realized that the odds were against
him. The progressives were weak, he admitted in
February 1919, and, "The present attitude of our
standpat brethren is that they don't need any aid
from Progressives." Furthermore, he observed, the
progressive reformers "have grown weary of being
outcasts politically and want to be regular again.
They don't want to be classed as Progressives
only as Republicans, and they have no stomach for
a fight now." Johnson identified Poindexter as one
of those he had in mind. With the progressives
split, Johnson predicted, the "reactionaries" will
"take one of their own and nominate him for President." Poindexter, Johnson thought, "will probably
be a candidate, but nobody takes him seriously."[34]

Poindexter, nonetheless, received encouragement
for his candidacy, but primarily from his own state.
W. H. Cowles, owner of the *Spokesman-Review*, in
February 1919 assured the senator of his support.
"If your candidacy is developed by your friends to
large proportions, we want to do what we can to
help you," wrote Cowles. However, Cowles was skep-
tical of Poindexter's prospects and added, "at the
same time we want to keep ourselves in the same
position regarding General Wood." Poindexter
answered Cowles immediately: "As to the Presidential matter, I find that it is developing itself to

very large and substantial proportions." Referring to Wood, Poindexter added, "I note what you say about another candidate and the matter has been fully discussed by friends of his and mine with the result that a number who were at first inclined to support him will support me."35

Some political leaders in Washington who had been active in the Progressive party quickly joined the Poindexter campaign, and leading Taft Republicans in Washington also agreed to cooperate with Poindexter. D. T. Ham of Spokane, who had been a bitter foe since 1909, pledged his support in August 1919. S. A. Perkins, the man who had been instrumental in the defeat of the Roosevelt delegates in the state convention in 1912, also backed Poindexter. Added assurance that Republicans in Washington were united in Poindexter's support came from Horace Kimball. A luncheon had been held, wrote Kimball, at which Perkins, Slater, Sam Walker, a Seattle ex-Progressive, W. H. Cowles, and other leading Republicans attended. "We all made strong statements on your behalf," said Kimball, and he added, Perkins "is most sincere in his support."36

Efforts were also made by Jonathan Bourne, former progressive Republican senator from Oregon, to carry Oregon for Poindexter, and the senator also received encouragement from two New York businessmen, Jules S. Bache and William H. Todd, who provided over half of his campaign expenses. Bache, a New York banker and director of seventeen corporations, donated or raised $26,800 for Poindexter's campaign, and Todd, a shipbuilder who owned shipyards in Tacoma and Seattle, donated or raised $20,000 for Poindexter's campaign. The remainder of Poindexter's campaign expenditures came largely from people in the state of Washington, although Jonathan Bourne contributed $10,000.37

Assured of the loyalty of his own state's Republicans and with some financial backing, Poindexter dispelled any doubts about the seriousness of his campaign in October 1919 by publicly announcing his decision to run. He delivered the first official speech of his campaign in Lowell, Massachusetts, on October 31, where he focused on the "Red" menace. He warned that the industrial strikes that were sweeping the nation were part of a plot by "anarchistic agitators." He attacked the Wilson administration for aiding the Bolsheviks, and he declared that this issue had become the key political issue of the day. He denounced Samuel Gompers for defending the striking Boston policemen, and he defended the open shop, declaring that the state and federal governments should guarantee the working man the right to join or not to join a union as he chose.[38]

Only a few periodicals covered the senator's presidential campaign. A friendly article in the *Literary Digest* in December 1919 noticed that he was not like most presidential candidates who coyly wait until they are called upon to run. The article described the senator as "a blunt outspoken man" who "believes in direct methods." It observed that he had always been independent of tradition and political parties, and, although Poindexter had been a member of the Progressive party, the article assured its readers, Poindexter was not a "radical." In *Collier's*, Mark Sullivan surveyed the presidential candidates and devoted a few words to Poindexter's candidacy. Poindexter, wrote Sullivan, had made his debut into national politics as one "of the more extreme Insurgent sort," but the senator had become "strongly impressed with what was in his judgment the danger to American institutions, involved in the radical labor activities of his own State."[39]

There were, however, as Hiram Johnson said, some who could not take Poindexter's campaign seriously. The *New York Times* declared in December 1919 that Poindexter "has no more chance of breaking into the Middle West than of carrying Siberia," and added, "He must know this so well that it becomes a matter of speculation why he is seeking the nomination." The *Times* felt that most men from the lesser populated states who said they were presidential candidates were actually running for the vice-presidential nomination, "but Mr. Poindexter's methods are so unlikely to make him a good man to agree on that this supposition must be eliminated in his case." It criticized his efforts to show that General Wood was not a Roosevelt Republican, and the *Times* also ridiculed Poindexter's attempts to maintain that he was still a progressive. "If any member of the Borah-Johnson group is nominated, it will almost certainly be Senator Johnson himself, and in any case it will not be Mr. Poindexter."[40]

The *Seattle Union-Record*, a labor paper, also ridiculed Poindexter's candidacy. When the senator campaigned in Seattle in April 1920, the *Union Record* wondered if Poindexter had "got the presidential microbe when growing up in Old Virginny. He has shown some of the traits of the old-fashioned southern politician." It repeated the familiar charge that Poindexter was a political opportunist and declared, "We cannot conceive of him, for example, standing up like Senator LaFollette, for principle, while the people were going away from him. He is not the stuff that makes martyrs." Then the editorial concluded: "As to labor, he is not a student of economics, is not familiar with Labor's movements, is off in regard to radicalism in the ranks of Labor, and talks like one who had inherited his economics from ante-civil war days, and his views from the Chamber of Commerce."[41]

Poindexter entered presidential primaries in three states, South Dakota, Oregon, and Michigan, although he later withdrew from the Oregon contest. He campaigned in South Dakota in early December 1919 just before the Republican state convention was scheduled to meet. He launched a "sharp attack" on General Wood who, according to the *New York Times*, would be the nominee of the Republican state convention that was scheduled to meet before the primary. Poindexter declared that "steam roller methods" and the "gag law" were being used to defeat him, and in one address he questioned Wood's claim to be Theodore Roosevelt's choice. Nonetheless, the convention selected Wood to be the officially designated choice of the state convention on the South Dakota ballot; and a few days later, Poindexter filed to run against Wood in the primary, according to South Dakota law, as an independent Republican.[42]

The primary election, however, revealed most emphatically that Poindexter had campaigned in vain, and on March 26 Wood carried the South Dakota primary easily. His closest competitors were Lowden and Johnson, in that order. The *New York Times* took pleasure in noting that Poindexter had not at the time the news report was filed received one thousand votes.[43] In the Michigan primary, as well, Poindexter failed to attract meaningful support. He endeavored to secure the support of bankers and industrialists on the basis of his antilabor record, but the strategy failed. Hiram Johnson carried the Michigan primary, Wood was second, and after him came Lowden, Hoover, and General Pershing. Poindexter received only 2,662 votes! "As for Poindexter," the *Seattle Union-Record* gloated, "in his trips to Washington, he evidently did not take the Michigan Central often enough to become well known."[44]

Poindexter's single preconvention success was achieved in his own state. The Washington state Republican convention convened in Bellingham on April 27, endorsed Poindexter for president, and instructed its delegation to the national convention "to use every worthy means to bring about his nomination." Thus Poindexter presented himself to the national Republican convention in Chicago with only his home state behind him. He professed optimism nonetheless. "Our situation as regards securing the nomination at Chicago is most excellent, especially since the returns from Michigan came in, as you can easily figure for yourself," he assured a correspondent in Boston. Poindexter's unfounded optimism is perhaps explained by noting that Hiram Johnson carried Michigan and that Poindexter based his strategy on the prospect of winning the support of Johnson delegates when that senator failed to receive a majority.[45] As the convention delegates began to assemble in Chicago, the *Literary Digest* issued the final results of its public opinion poll. Poindexter was not even listed. The poll of the week before, however, had ranked him thirteenth. Poindexter's campaign had obviously failed to attract massive support.[46]

Seemingly undismayed by the adverse results of the primaries and the *Literary Digest* polls, Poindexter arrived at the convention in Chicago on June 4 and immediately went into conference with the leaders of the Washington state delegation. Jules Bache, a member of the New York delegation, appeared before the Washington delegates to assure them that Poindexter could be nominated. Poindexter, dressed in a light gray suit, displayed enthusiasm and energy as he bustled about his campaign headquarters talking to delegates and tending to the many details which concern a presidential candidate. Delegates Poindexter lacked, but energy, enthusiasm, and optimism he had in abundance.[47]

Not until after the party platform had been drafted and submitted to the convention were the nominating speeches delivered. The most troublesome issue before the convention was whether the United States should become a member of the League of Nations, but that plank, written by Elihu Root, was so equivocal that delegates holding almost all shades of opinion on the League were able to accept it. The nominating process began on June 11. Poindexter was nominated by George H. Walker of Seattle, the ex-Progressive who had recently been elected state chairman of the Republican party in Washington. Walker emphasized Poindexter's postwar record as an opponent of the "Reds" and the League of Nations. On that day four ballots were taken. As was expected, Wood had the most support with Lowden and Johnson holding second and third places. On the first ballot Poindexter received twenty votes: one from Louisiana and one from New York; two from Hawaii and two from Alaska; and fourteen from Washington. On the second ballot only the Washington delegation and the single New York delegate, evidently Jules Bache, supported him. On the third and fourth ballots his strength remained unchanged. After the fourth ballot, the convention, unable to agree upon a nominee, recessed.[48]

The night of June 11 was one filled with political discussion and bargaining, but nothing remains to indicate what Poindexter was doing during this time. The much-discussed meeting of leading Republican senators at the Blackstone Hotel was evidentl not attended by Poindexter; and there is no indication that he was considered as a possible nominee by this group which knew him best. It is possible that his name was mentioned, since Senator Calder of New York and Watson of Indiana, who were friendl to his candidacy, were at this meeting; but probabl his candidacy was not taken seriously.[49] At this meeting, apparently no decision was made by the men in attendance to unite in support of any other candidate should Lowden or Wood fail to secure the nomination, but Warren G. Harding's name was frequently mentioned as the best compromise candidate. On the following day the senator from Ohio was nominated on the tenth ballot. Poindexter's strength remained almost the same until the final ballot. The Washington delegation remained steadfastly behind him, but the effort was in vain. "We were disappointed, of course," wrote Poindexter a few days later. "The people who largely influenced the nomination that was made, were pledged to us, as well as many others, but contingencies intervened apparently at the last moment, which changed the situation. . . . it well might have been different."50

Poindexter's chances of winning the Republican nomination for president, as his critics had pointed out, faced tremendous odds. He represented a western state with a relatively small population, and he was not well known outside his own state, as the results of the South Dakota and Michigan primaries showed. Moreover, Poindexter's claim to represent the policies of Theodore Roosevelt was no more valid than Leonard Wood's, and certainly Hiram Johnson's credentials as a progressive were more persuasive than Poindexter's. Poindexter did correctly predict that the convention would deadlock, but he was not the only one to do this. After the deadlock, Poindexter's candidacy had little to offer in comparison to Harding's. Harding represented a more populous state which had already produced a number of Republican presidential and vice-presidential candidates, and Harding had made few enemies in any group of the Republican party. As a party regular he was well liked and quite acceptable to the leaders of the party. By contrast, Poindexter had made many enemies. Lodge and Brandegee could still remember him as a strident Insurgent, and Taft surely had not forgotten Poindexter's defiance and disloyalty to the party before 1917. Many progressives like Borah, Gronna, LaFollette, and Norris, on the other hand, would not have considered the nomination of Poindexter as a meaningful gesture to their group. Outside the state of Washington, in short, it was difficult to find any except a few of the most extreme antilabor, anti-"Red," and anti-League elements who supported Poindexter's nomination. He was an extremist in a political situation where extremists usually have been counted out.

After the nomination of Calvin Coolidge, the governor of Massachusetts, as Harding's running mate, the Republican convention adjourned. Poindexter had been named chairman of the senatorial campaign committee, and he returned immediately to Washington, D.C., where he threw himself into the task of insuring the election of a Republican president and Congress in November. Although Elihu Root, Herbert Hoover, and other Republican supporters of the League maintained that Harding supported United States membership in the League, Poindexter and most irreconcilables insisted that the election of Harding and a Republican Senate was necessary to prevent American entry into the League. Poindexter campaigned through the West in August. In Portland he claimed the West for Harding because the Democratic presidential candidate, James M. Cox, would "embroil" America "in European affairs," and upon his return to Washington, D.C., he predicted a Republican Senate would be elected—"the people . . . are so indignant at the conduct of the present Administration." A day later, he sent campaign instructions to a Republican in Washington who was to make a speaking tour through Pacific Coast states for the senatorial committee: "What we want to emphasize is the tremendous importance of saving the independence of the United States against the proposed consolidated League of Nations government, and that this question may depend upon the election of a Republican Senator in any one state." Poindexter also indicated that he would pursue the same theme in his own speeches he had scheduled in New York, St. Louis, Des Moines, and several western states.[51]

Republican efforts were rewarded in 1920 with landslide majorities. Harding polled 60.3 percent of the total vote, and the Republicans won decisive control of both houses of Congress. Harding carried the state of Washington, but his majority there was not as impressive as his national majority—he carried Washington with 56 percent of the total vote. This probably was in part because a militant new third party, the Farmer-Labor party, dominated by radicals and labor unions, polled 19 percent of the Washington vote, while the Democrats captured only 21 percent. In the senatorial contest Senator Jones was reelected, and in both the senatorial and gubernatorial elections the Farmer-Labor candidates finished higher than the Democratic candidates. The Farmer-Labor party in Washington represented a combination of dissident groups—Socialists, the Washington AFL, the Washington State Grange, the Railroad Brotherhoods, and the Non-Partisan League—but it was, according to one study, primarily "a labor rather than a farmer party." In Washington, it manifested the reaction of west coast labor to the antilabor atmosphere of the Red Scare, and to other labor grievances, and nationally the party seemed to represent similar feelings of discontent with the general atmosphere of repression and antiunion sentiment.[52]

If Poindexter examined Washington's 1920 election returns, he might have been tempted to soften his attack against organized labor, for the vote indicated that prounion and radical political views were strong in heavily populated western Washington. Western counties where organized labor was strong gave the Farmer-Labor candidates substantial support. The Farmer-Labor party finished second in every county on Puget Sound but two. Probably the source of this third-party strength was organized labor in heavily populated King (Seattle), Pierce (Tacoma), and in the other western counties where lumberjacks, mill workers, and dockworkers in the aftermath of the Seattle general strike were militant, angry, and organized.[53] The farm counties in eastern Washington, by contrast, seemed in 1920 to present no evidence of concern to Poindexter, for of the twelve counties which gave Harding over 60 percent of their vote, eight were in the wheat-producing area of eastern Washington, the area which between 1896 and 1920 had voted consistently for populist and progressive candidates. In 1920 these predominantly farm counties showed little enthusiasm for the Farmer-Labor party. It was clear, nonetheless, that organized labor was quite effective in 1920 and could be expected to mobilize its forces against Poindexter's stand for reelection in 1922.

10.

A Harding Republican

THE FIRST Congress of the Harding administration, the Sixty-seventh, was the last Congress in Miles Poindexter's second term in the Senate, and it probably was the most satisfying for him. The Republican party controlled the presidency and both Houses of the Congress with comfortable majorities, and for the first time in his political career Poindexter was genuinely welcome at the White House. Poindexter ranked in seniority among the top one-third of the Senate, and held very good committee assignments. He never succeeded in securing his coveted appointment to the Foreign Relations Committee—perhaps he was still paying for the displeasure he had caused Lodge and the regular Republicans before 1917, but he was chairman of the Committee on Mines and Mining, a member of the Interstate Commerce Committee, and, most important to him, acting chairman of the Committee on Naval Affairs. In general his behavior and his voting record identified him as a loyal party regular—a Harding Republican.[1]

To Poindexter the most important issues of Harding's first Congress were in foreign affairs. Serving as chairman of the Senate Naval Affairs Committee, he became actively involved in the debate over naval expansion and the Washington Disarmament Conference. Poindexter shared the Navy Department's desire to continue the naval expansion program inaugurated by the preparedness legislation of 1916, and he agreed with the navy that one of the principal reasons to maintain a program of naval expansion in the 1920s was the increasing power of Japan in the Pacific. The collapse of Germany and Russia and the weakened postwar position of France and Great Britain, as the big-navy advocates saw the world, left only the United States as a major counterbalance to the Japanese. American naval power was not equal to the task, however, according to this argument, and American possessions in the Pacific were defenseless. To attempt to alter the Pacific power balance, Poindexter and the members of the Naval Affairs Committee in December 1920, at the close of the previous Congress, had substantially rewritten the House naval appropriation bill to bring it more into line with the recommendations of the Navy Department. American talk of naval construction alarmed Japan and tended to stimulate Japanese efforts to enlarge their navy and led the British Admiralty, which still commanded the largest navy in the world, to plan new naval construction as well. A new armaments race seemed to be a real possibility.[2]

The prospect of an armaments race alarmed those in the United States who had long advocated disarmament as a means to prevent war, and when the Senate first considered the naval appropriation bill in the Sixty-sixth Congress, Senator Borah introduced a resolution which called upon the president to negotiate an end to naval construction with Great Britain and Japan. Later, in early January 1921, as the Senate Foreign Relations Committee considered his first resolution, Borah introduced and secured passage of a second resolution which requested the Naval Affairs Committee to advise the Senate whether naval construction should be suspended six months to give the president ample time to secure a disarmament agreement.[3]

Poindexter responded to Borah's second resolution for the Naval Affairs Committee in February 1921. His sympathy for naval expansion of course was well known. He submitted a committee report that concluded that "there should be no suspension of the present building program of the Navy." As expected, the committee's report failed to convince Senator Borah who moved that his resolution urging the president to arrange for a disarmament conference be attached to the navy bill.[4]

Poindexter met Borah's criticism by insisting that the majority of the Naval Affairs Committee favored disarmament too, but he argued that the United States should not suspend its naval expansion program until after a disarmament agreement had been negotiated. To disarm beforehand, Poindexter argued, would place the United States "in a position of inferiority in the negotiations." A few days later, in private, Poindexter denounced the Borah-led assault on naval expansion in less diplomatic language: "The pacifist movement is very strong and the country is full of defeatists as it was before and even during the war. The argument is boldly made that we ought to reunite ourselves with Great Britain and that her Navy will take care of us. I regard it as one of the most dangerous matters of attack we ever had to confront."[5] Borah and the opponents of the naval appropriations bill then, in effect, filibustered to prevent its passage in the Sixty-sixth Congress.

After Harding's inauguration in March 1921, the naval appropriation bill was one of the first issues to be considered by the Sixty-seventh Congress. President Harding sympathized with the Naval Affairs Committee's work and shared Poindexter's opposition to Borah's disarmament resolution. In his address to Congress he endorsed "approximate disarmament," but he maintained that "prudence forbids that we disarm alone."[6] In response to Harding's plea, the Republican majority in the House of Representatives, ignoring Borah's resolution, on April 28 passed the administration's naval appropriation bill. With the Senate about to take up the naval bill, Poindexter, accompanied by Senator Hale of Maine, went to the White House to confer with the president. After the conference, the two senators informed reporters that Harding opposed the attempts of Congress to force his hand in disarmament negotiations.[7]

The sentiment for disarmament, however, could not so easily be ignored. The *New York Times* pointed with alarm to the apparent intention of the Harding

Republicans to disregard the popular clamor for disarmament, and it charged that there existed in Washington a group determined to push naval expansion "until the United States has the most powerful navy afloat, Great Britain taking second place." All indications were that the *Times*'s hostility to naval expansion was widespread, and the public pressure in support of Borah's resolution was irresistible. On May 14 Harding privately informed Poindexter that he was ready to capitulate. The president prefaced his remarks with a statement of his interpretation of the duties of the president. He believed that it was not "essential that the Executive should give an opinion on the desirability of such action" because Congress had the power to express its opinion on such matters. "Indeed," Harding wrote, "Congress has the power to enforce what is popularly referred to as a 'Naval Holiday,' by simply withholding appropriations." Furthermore, Harding insisted that while he did not intend that the United States should "disarm alone," he also favored disarmament negotiations and did not oppose an expression of the view of Congress on disarmament: "If the Congress believes the progress of such a movement will be facilitated by legislative expression previous to conference with the naval powers with whom we ought to cooperate, there is no reason to oppose such action."[8]

Three days after Harding's letter was written, on May 17, Poindexter changed his position too. During one of the several exchanges he had with Borah, Poindexter announced that he did not oppose the Borah resolution. In fact, he maintained he had never opposed it! Borah, however, was quite surprised. He asked Poindexter to repeat his statement. The *New York Times*, likewise, treated Poindexter's announcement as a complete reversal in position, and the *Times* guessed correctly that Poindexter acted with the "sanction" of Harding. According to the *Times*, after Poindexter's announcement, word was passed to the supporters of the administration to vote as they pleased on Borah's measure.[9]

Voting on the naval appropriation bill took place late in May 1921, and the Senate passed the bill on

June 1. The progressive Republicans again demonstrated their disagreement on foreign policy by dividing into two groups. Borah, Kenyon, LaFollette, and Norris voted against Poindexter's position on almost every vote. The Borah resolution was adopted seventy-four to nothing, with twenty-two not voting. A more severe test of opinion on naval disarmament, however, was a vote on a motion by Senator Pomerene, Democrat from Ohio, to suspend the rules so that he might offer an amendment to authorize the president to suspend the naval building program six months while he tried to arrange the meeting of a disarmament conference. Both Poindexter and Lodge argued that the amendment was out of order, and it failed, twenty-nine to thirty-six.10 "Here was a definite scheme one would expect to commend itself to disarmers in earnest. Such the Administration Senators had professed themselves to be," said the *New York Times*. It quoted Poindexter's statement that such a delay would cost the taxpayers millions and added, "That is a favorite argument of Senators who are really cold to an international disarmament agreement, though posing as friends of limitation of armaments."11

The reaction of the general public to the Borah resolution is impossible to gauge, but the enthusiasm of pressure groups was evident. Senator Borah was deluged with letters praising his action; women's organizations endorsed his efforts; in Chicago a group of clergymen held a Congress on the Reduction of Armaments; the president was presented with a petition in favor of disarmament by the AFL on June 18; and between May 5 and June 22, over five hundred petitions for disarmament were entered into the *Congressional Record*. In this atmosphere the United States government in August issued invitations to attend a conference on disarmament to be held in Washington, D.C., to the major naval powers. It was agreed that the conference would consider Far Eastern problems and disarmament on a more unrestricted basis than Borah had contemplated. As the American representatives to the conference, the Harding administration selected Secretary of State Charles Evans Hughes, Senator Henry Cabot Lodge, ex-Senator Elihu Root, and Senator Oscar W. Underwood, a Democrat from Alabama.[12]

During the preliminary negotiations Poindexter's mind was filled with dark forebodings, for his ambition to make the American navy the greatest in the world remained unshaken. "Personally," he wrote, "I do not want to see this country in a helpless and contemptible situation." He attacked the organizations behind the disarmament movement by declaring that they were part of a "movement in this country which undertakes to ridicule the idea of national patriotism which, up to the present moment, has been generally regarded as the highest motive which could actuate an American citizen." But after the names of the American delegates had been announced, Poindexter was somewhat reassured. "We have able representatives in the conference, and I trust satisfactory results will be achieved. This does not mean, of course, that we will agree, as some propose, to leave other nations armed while we make ourselves helpless and at their mercy."[13]

The Washington Conference opened on November 12 with a dramatic speech by Secretary of State Hughes who captured the imagination of many Americans by proposing a scrapping of some existing capital ships, a ten-year holiday in the construction of new capital ships, and a ratio of 5-5-3 in replacement tonnage for the United States, Britain, and Japan. When reached by a reporter from the *New York Times*, Poindexter was dismayed: "We are already enjoying a naval holiday, as the appropriation is about used up and the shipyards where our program is being carried to completion are running only about ten percent of their normal capacity." Most senators, however, said the *Times*, praised Hughes's proposal.[14]

Poindexter analyzed Hughes's disarmament plan on November 20, in an article in the *New York Times*. It was one of his most thoughtful and intelligent criticisms of the disarmament movement, written with unusual tact and moderation. Since everyone was for peace, he commented, the great publicity given disarmament raised "a false issue." "The real question is not whether we favor peace or favor war," he pointed out, "but as to the discovery of some means by which the chances of war will be lessened and the era of peace in the world lengthened." He gravely doubted the value of disarmament as a deterrent to war. There were wars, he said, "before armament was invented," and "a certain amount of armament is absolutely essential to curb and restrain the evil impulses of men and nations and to administer justice." He was aware of the "great burden upon the economic resources of the people" which naval expansion created, and he admitted that unlimited naval expansion would "inevitably tend toward conflict in the end."15

But to Poindexter, disarming at a time of instability and conflict risked even greater danger. He pointed to the waste which would result if ships then under construction were abandoned. What will the United States do about Japanese expansion and the Anglo-Japanese alliance, he asked. He pointed to the defenseless condition of American bases in the Pacific and observed that "in order to protect them [the United States] must have bases from which her fleets can operate." Japan, he noted, had proposed that the United States construct no additional bases in the Pacific, but since Japan had sufficient bases in the Pacific, such a concession would leave "the United States at a great disadvantage." More important in securing peace than disarmament, he concluded, "is sufficient amount of good-will among the nations to bring them to an agreement as to future programs." These observations of course were very familiar since they repeated ideological assumptions and values of the "realists" that Poindexter had promoted since his early days in the Senate. The remarks serve to show the consistency of his position, but also to point up his willingness to stand nearly alone in an atmosphere dominated by the utopian attitudes of Borah and the advocates of disarmament.16

Support for Borah's position came from several of the prewar progressive Republicans, and none was more ardent than Hiram Johnson. Both Johnson and Poindexter had been irreconcilables on the League of Nations issue, but they had done so for very different ideological reasons. Johnson heartily endorsed Borah's efforts and looked forward to the Conference with hope. "The Conference has possibilities of limitless good," he wrote, for "out of it may come something which will relieve the world from heavy taxation coincident with large armaments." Unlike Poindexter, Johnson did not approve of the members of the American delegation—they "view disarmament cynically"; but he was sure that "the irresistible force of public opinion" would triumph.[17]

The Washington Conference produced two treaties which seemed significant to Poindexter, the Five Power and the Four Power pacts. In the Five Power Naval Treaty the United States, Great Britain, Japan, France, and Italy agreed to a ten-year naval holiday in the construction of capital ships and accepted the replacement ratios suggested by Secretary Hughes. The ratios were accepted by Japan only because the United States and Great Britain agreed to limitations in the future construction of naval fortifications in certain areas of the Pacific, thereby leaving Japan the dominant power in that area. The Four Power Treaty eliminated the Anglo-Japanese alliance and substituted an agreement between the United States, Britain, Japan, and France to respect each other's possessions in the Pacific. Poindexter particularly approved of the Four Power Treaty. He confided privately to his friend J. W. Bryan of Bremerton, on January 21, 1922, that the Four Power pact was quite acceptable to him, and a day later the *New York Times* published another of his articles praising the "practical" results of the Conference. He congratulated Secretary Hughes for having put the Conference on "a very concrete and specific basis." In this respect, he declared, "it had the advantage of other world conferences which undertook the vague and rather impossible task of setting up an entire 'new order' for the government of the world." The Four Power Treaty, in contrast, "is a most excellent achievement." It "imposes no new or extraordinary obligations, either legal or moral, and it does not establish any new agencies or government whatever"; and, above all, it was "the exact antithesis of the League of Nations" and "has not fallen into the unreasoning pacifist and Socialist error."[18]

In the Senate debate over the ratification of the various treaties of the Washington Conference, Poindexter defended the Four Power Treaty vigorously.

He contrasted it with the League of Nations; he emphasized that it did not threaten American independence; and he noted that the Monroe Doctrine was not challenged. "One of the chief virtues, if not the chief virtue of this agreement," he insisted, was "that which makes it a practical working arrangement, and that is that it is limited in its scope both as to the subject with which it deals and as to the area which it covers." His approval of this product of the Washington Conference is understandable in view of his general approval of power politics, for the Four Power Treaty amounted to an alliance—no matter how much this was denied by its defenders—between four nations for a specific purpose. When Senator Tom Watson of Georgia wondered what the people of the Pacific coast thought of a treaty which recognized Japanese equality in the Pacific, Poindexter answered that the United States Navy was there to protect them, and that the British and French were committed "to use their influence to prevent an aggression" in the Pacific. This, he added, "tends to remove or to minimize the probabilities of an attack upon them."[19]

Poindexter admitted privately, though, that the American agreement not to strengthen fortifications in Guam or the Philippines "is . . . in my opinion dangerous." He worried that the Japanese commitment to respect American possessions would be too readily accepted by the public as a substitute for sea power: "There seems to be a powerful and almost universal illusion on the subject of international good will and the pacifist proposition of depending on that." He echoed this fear on the Senate floor by appealing to "the people of my country . . . not to be misled by the illusion or the delusion, so that they could disband their Army, throw down their arms, and deprive themselves of the power of self-defense because some other nations had signed an agreement that they would respect their rights."[20]

Unlike Poindexter, several of the prewar progressive Republicans opposed the Four Power Treaty. Borah, LaFollette, and Hiram Johnson recognized this agreement as an alliance pure and simple, and they feared that it would involve the United States in the affairs and problems of the far-distant Pacific. "There is no difference in principle between the League of Nations and the new treaty," declared Johnson, and it "is nothing else . . . than an alliance with Great Britain and Japan in the Pacific." If it is agreed to, he predicted, "it will nt [*sic*] be difficult . . . to take us into another relating to Europe."[21] The objections of Johnson notwithstanding, the Four Power Pact was ratified by the Senate on March 24, sixty-seven to twenty-seven. Poindexter, along with most Republicans, voted for ratification, and among the remaining prewar progressive Republicans, only Borah, Johnson, and LaFollette opposed it.[22]

Poindexter also supported the Five Power Treaty which produced the disarmament ratios, despite his grave reservations about disarmament. He did find one important provision in the treaty which appealed to him: the treaty placed the United States, theoretically at least, on a par with Great Britain. Moreover, he had come to realize that an attempt to build a navy exceeding Great Britain's was out of the question. "It is already evident," he wrote in March 1922 in the *New York Times*, "that there will be a struggle to prevent the maintenance of a navy on the basis provided in the treaty, and the probabilities are that instead of having our naval power curtailed by the treaty we will not fully develop the naval power . . . which we are especially authorized to do under the terms of the treaty." The Five Power Treaty, then, had the reluctant support of the junior senator from Washington when it was ratified overwhelmingly by the Senate, seventy-four to one.[23]

In supporting the disarmament agreement Poindexter refrained from breaking with the Harding administration, but this did not mean that Harding could always rely upon him. The year before the disarmament agreement was ratified, Poindexter, in fact, was one of a handful of Republicans to oppose a treaty with Colombia negotiated by the Harding administration. The history of this treaty went back to 1914 when President Wilson's administration negotiated a treaty with Colombia that expressed the regret of the United States government for the 1903 events in Panama that preceded the construction of the Panama Canal. It provided Colombia with special privileges in the Panama Canal, and it promised to pay that country $25 million; in return Colombia agreed to recognize Panama's independence. At that time a determined Republican opposition protested vehemently against this implied criticism of Theodore Roosevelt, and it was not until March 1917 that the treaty was reported favorably to the Senate by the Democratic-controlled Foreign Relations Committee. A minority report signed by Lodge and the Republican members protested against it, and the Republicans were able to prevent the treaty from coming to a vote. But after Harding became president, Secretary of State Hughes and Secretary of Interior Albert B. Fall, who before 1920 had opposed the treaty, actively worked for its ratification, with the apology to Colombia eliminated. Republicans in the 1920s saw the issue differently because of their interest in opening oil reserves in Colombia for American exploitation.[24]

Poindexter's loyalty to the memory of Theodore Roosevelt was not affected by the change in the official Republican position on this treaty, nor by the appeal of more oil from Colombia, and on April 18, 1921 he stated angrily on the Senate floor that the Colombian treaty had stamped "with the stigma of shame an act of President Roosevelt's." He pointed out that Lodge and other Republicans had opposed the treaty in 1917, and he wondered what had happened to change their minds. On this particular question, Poindexter found common cause with most of the prewar progressive Republicans. Borah shared Poindexter's estimation of the treaty with Colombia, and he said that he was "greatly disappointed that the President has asked for its ratification. . . . It takes $25,000,000 out of the taxpayer's money . . . and turns it over to a lot of political adventurers in Colombia . . . and in doing so, dishonors the name of Roosevelt and puts the brand of shame upon our own country." Senator Johnson agreed: "it seems incredible that the first act of the administration shall be to put this thing over."[25]

Despite the progressive opposition, the Colombian treaty received Senate ratification on April 20,

1921, sixty-nine to nineteen. Most of the prewar progressive Republicans—all those who voted except Curtis of Kansas and Sterling of South Dakota—united to oppose the administration.[26] They seemed still loyal to the memory of Theodore Roosevelt and/or less concerned than some Republicans with improving relations with Colombia.

Poindexter's reactions to the Colombian treaty and the Washington Disarmament Conference demonstrated that his views about foreign affairs had not changed since he had gone to the Senate in 1911. He remained a "realist" throughout his career. But his deep concern with the events in foreign affairs during his last years in the Senate probably contributed to his undoing, for as Poindexter concentrated on foreign policy, the voters of his state grew increasingly concerned with domestic problems.

The spirit of reform that had dominated domestic politics in the Progressive era ended for Miles Poindexter and perhaps for the majority of Americans sometime after the beginning of the World War. The election of Warren G. Harding as president seemed a decisive victory for the opponents of reform and signaled, as Harding put it, a return to "normalcy." Relaxation of the federal regulation of business, economy in government, tax reductions for the upper income brackets, and a protective tariff for American business were the major policies of the Harding years. These policies represented, by and large, a turn away from the reform achievements of the prewar years. For most middle- and upper-class Americans, furthermore, the 1920s were a very prosperous decade when rising incomes, an increased standard of living, and the availability of luxuries and amusements seemed irrefutable evidence to the well-to-do of the wisdom of the probusiness policies of the Republican administration.

Most working men and farmers, however, did not share in the general prosperity of the 1920s. Labor had almost no political power in Washington in the twenties, but the representatives of the farm states constituted a major portion of the seats in Congress, and early in the 1920s they began to demand federal support for distressed farmers. Farm prices, that had been high during the war, dropped sharply during 1920 and 1921, and farmers quickly brought pressure to bear upon their representatives in Congress for assistance. Congressmen from the West and the South—the same states that had elected the prewar progressives—voted together and worked together on certain issues in the interests of agriculture. New senators from the South and West joined the Farm bloc, as this group was often called in the 1920s, but some of the most active members of the Farm bloc were the prewar progressives—LaFollette, Norris, Borah, and Kenyon, and most Democrats.[27]

Few states were more affected by the depression in agriculture in the early twenties than Washington, especially the eastern counties. While the emergence of the Farmer-Labor party in 1920 in Washington seemed largely in response to labor dissatisfaction, some farmers were active in the movement, and one Farmer-Labor leader, William Bouck, had been the head of the state Grange since the death of C. B. Kegley in 1917. Apparently because most farmers objected to his collaboration with organized labor, Bouck was suspended by the National Grange in 1921 and later expelled, but shortly thereafter about one-third of the membership of the Grange in Washington withdrew from the organization.[28] A political revolt in the magnitude of the one which brought Poindexter to the Senate in 1910 seemed to be brewing in Washington.

As farm and labor groups in Washington grew more radical after 1917, Poindexter became more hostile toward radicalism. His record on domestic legislation during 1920-22, moreover, was not the kind to win the approval of aroused farmers and workers. Poindexter had become a Harding Republican, opposed to any extension of federal control of business, in favor of the tax policies of the administration, and unfriendly to the efforts of the Farm bloc to provide federal assistance for distressed farmers.

As a Harding Republican, Poindexter had come to share the attitude of the majority of Republicans in Congress toward federal regulation of business. When in 1921 a voter pointed to the need for further business regulation, the senator recollected that "The Federal Trade Commission was created for

the very purpose of doing just such things as you
suggest, but nothing important . . . has come of
it . . . as the abuses seem to be about as rank as
ever." Furthermore, he defended the Standard Oil
Company, which, he said, "has cheapened instead of
increased the cost of products they have to sell."[29]
Poindexter's attitude toward federal regulation of
business was further demonstrated by his reaction
to the efforts of farm representatives to improve
the federal regulation of the meat-packing industry
in 1920 and 1921. These efforts included a bill
sponsored by Senator Gronna to create a federal
livestock commission, which passed the Senate in
January 1921 but was never passed by the House,
and the Packers and Stockyards Act of 1921, which
granted further power to the Department of Agriculture to inspect and control the stockyards and
meat-packers. On the final votes Poindexter supported both Gronna's bill and the Packers and
Stockyards bill, but he was in fact probably opposed to both bills. At any rate, he voted against
all efforts by the members of the Farm bloc to
strengthen the Packers and Stockyards bill, and he
actually voted with most prewar progressives only
once during the consideration of that bill. That
was on final passage.[30] Clearly Poindexter did not
share the objectives of the Farm bloc to strengthen
federal regulation of farm-related corporations,
and he probably voted for this measure on final
passage because he thought it was popular with his
constituents.

 Poindexter's attitude toward the relationship between the federal government and business was made
even clearer by his position on the Muscle Shoals
controversy. The Harding administration proposed
to lease two nitrate plants and a partially completed federal dam, constructed at Muscle Shoals
on the Tennessee River during the war, to Henry
Ford, at considerably less than the cost of construction. Senator Norris, chairman of the Senate
Committee on Agriculture and Forestry and a champion of conservation and public power, blocked the
approval of the administration's proposal. Norris's
own bill provided that the federal government continue to operate Muscle Shoals, and it seemed no
more radical than Poindexter's prewar plans for

Alaska. But in 1921 Poindexter adamantly opposed the expansion of Muscle Shoals. "The Muscle Shoals project . . . has already cost the government, or rather the people, $100,000,000, and cannot be sold for anything," he declared in 1921. "It is now proposed to spend an indefinite number of additional millions in the project without the slightest assurance that nitrate will be produced there any cheaper than it can be obtained elsewhere, if any is produced at all."[31]

The senator also supported the Harding administration's tax bill of 1921. The secretary of the treasury in the Harding cabinet, Andrew Mellon, intending to rewrite the progressive tax laws of the Wilson era, in November 1921 obtained passage of a bill which, though by no means all he wanted, eliminated the excess profits tax and sharply reduced the rates on very high incomes. The Mellon plan was severely criticized by some of the prewar progressives who joined with other Republican members of the Farm bloc and the Democrats to force the administration to accept many changes in the bill. Hiram Johnson, nonetheless, was convinced that progressive reform was dead, and he described the Mellon tax bill as it had emerged from the Senate Finance Committee as "a measure for the benefit of those who have . . . [which will] endeavor to take something more from those who have little."[32]

Though Poindexter had once agreed with Johnson on tax legislation, he did no longer. As early as June 1919 he had endorsed a reduction in taxes: the wartime rates were "the most extortionate . . . ever levied upon a people." He had, furthermore, come to doubt the value of taxes that were "supposed to be levied upon wealth," because, "as all taxes inevitably are, they are passed along through increased prices . . . [to] the people." In early 1920 he hoped that taxes would "be reduced as rapidly as possible," and in August 1921, not long before the Mellon bill came to the Senate floor, he repeated his tax views: "What the country needs more than anything else is active business . . . and it is certainly true that this will not take place while the burden of taxation upon proceeds is as great as it is at present."[33] During the voting on the administration's tax bill Poindexter stood consistently with the administration and the Republican majority. Seventy votes on amendments to the bill were taken, and Poindexter voted consistently to keep the Mellon bill unchanged. He supported only fourteen amendments, and eleven of the fourteen proposed further reductions in the tax rates provided in the bill. A comparison of his voting with that of Henry Cabot Lodge also demonstrates his attitude toward tax legislation: of the fifty-two times he and Lodge both voted, they differed only four times. Many of the prewar progressives, on the contrary, voted regularly against the administration's bill. The new tax bill passed the Senate on November 7, 1921. Poindexter voted for it then, and he supported it a second time when the conference report was agreed to on November 23.[34]

Although issues related to tax policies and federal regulation triggered a new response in Poindexter after 1918, his position on tariff legislation remained relatively unchanged, for despite his reform rhetoric, he, like other progressive Republicans, had been a protectionist. He shared the Republican conventional wisdom that the best solution to the postwar farm depression was to pass a new tariff bill. For example, in December 1920 he informed a constituent that "The House . . . is now engaged in framing an emergency tariff and I am in hopes the rates will be placed high enough to meet the emergency and I think it will bring immediate relief." Poindexter referred to the Emergency Agricultural Tariff bill which passed the Senate on February 16, 1921, during the Sixty-sixth Congress. Poindexter voted for that bill, and he generally supported the higher duty on specific rates. The voting record of the other prewar progressive Republicans was very similar, and with few exceptions the group voted for the higher duty on wheat, meats, cotton, sugar, butter, cheese, milk, and condensed milk.[35] The bill was vetoed by President Wilson, reenacted, and signed in June 1921, after Harding's inauguration.[36]

The major tariff legislation of the Harding era, the Fordney-McCumber Tariff, was passed in the Sixty-seventh Congress in August 1922. This bill proposed to replace the low rates of the Democratic

Underwood Tariff of 1913 with high protective duties on both agricultural and manufactured products. Poindexter was in complete harmony with this objective, and during the debate he spoke vigorously for more protection for his state's products. On May 29 he asked for a higher duty on crude magnesite; on July 1 he defended an increase in the rate on split peas; on June 26 he and Senator Jones fought bitterly but in vain to prevent passage of a committee amendment to place shingles on the free list; on July 6 he spoke for Jones's amendment to raise the duty on fish; and the following day he introduced a fish amendment himself.[37]

Like Poindexter, LaFollette and most of the prewar progressive Republicans voted for higher duties on agricultural products (see tables 6 and 7). The record of the members of this group on amendments was rather similar to the record they had made when voting on the amendments to Taft's Canadian Reciprocity bill and to the Underwood Tariff; they exhibited a marked tendency to support the higher duty on products produced in their own geographical sections.[38] On nonagricultural products no clear tendency is discernable, though on these products the number of votes against the higher duty was higher and absenteeism more pronounced.[39] In general, however, Poindexter's voting record on the Fordney-McCumber Tariff differed sharply from the voting record of most of the prewar progressives. Poindexter generally voted with the Republican majority, but some of the others disagreed frequently with the position taken by most Republicans When the bill passed the Senate on August 19, 1922, it had Poindexter's support, and only Borah of the prewar progressive Republicans voted "nay," although LaFollette, it was announced, would have voted "nay" if present.[40]

Further evidence that Poindexter had become a Harding Republican can be seen in his reaction to other efforts of members of the Farm bloc to cope with the agricultural depression. He did not oppose most of these measures—it was pretty clear that eastern Washington farmers were in trouble; but he supported them with a distinct lack of enthusiasm. "The theory of government assistance and socialistic economics is unsound," he asserted in early

TABLE 6

FORDNEY-MCCUMBER TARIFF. VOTING OF PROGRESSIVE REPUBLICANS ON SELECTED FARM AND LUMBER PRODUCTS

X = Vote for higher duty

0 = Vote for lower duty

	Beef	Cattle	Hides	Lamb	Logs	Milk	Pork	Poultry	Shingles	Wheat	Wool	Totals X	0
Borah	X	–	0	X	0	–	–	–	0	X	0	3	4
Cummins	X	X	0	–	0	–	X	–	0	–	0	3	4
Curtis	X	X	X	X	X	X	X	X	X	X	X	11	0
Johnson	X	X	–	X	–	X	X	X	X	X	–	8	0
Jones	X	X	–	X	X	X	X	X	X	X	X	10	0
Kenyon	–	–	–	–	–	–	–	–	–	–	–	–	–
LaFollette	X	X	–	X	–	X	X	X	0	X	–	7	1
Nelson	X	X	–	X	–	–	X	X	0	–	0	5	2
Norris	X	X	–	X	–	X	X	X	0	–	0	6	2
Poindexter	X	X	–	X	–	X	X	X	X	X	–	8	0
Sterling	X	X	X	X	X	–	X	–	0	X	X	8	1
Townsend	X	X	0	X	–	X	X	X	0	X	–	7	2
Totals for higher duty	11	10	2	10	3	7	10	8	4	8	3		

TABLE 7

FORDNEY-MCCUMBER TARIFF. VOTING OF
PROGRESSIVE REPUBLICANS ON SELECTED
MANUFACTURED PRODUCTS AND RAW MATERIALS

X = Vote for higher duty   0 = Vote for lower duty

	Aluminum	Bicycles	Coal Tar Products	Cotton Yarn	Electric Bulbs	Glass	Harness	Horseshoes	Iron/Steel Plates	Knives	Printing Presses	Saws	Shotguns/Rifles	Scissors	Wire	Totals X	Totals O
Borah	0	-	-	0	0	-	-	-	0	-	0	0	0	0	0	0	9
Cummins	X	0	-	-	-	X	0	-	X	-	-	0	-	-	0	3	4
Curtis	X	0	X	X	X	X	0	X	X	X	X	X	X	X	X	13	2
Johnson	-	-	X	-	-	X	-	-	X	-	-	-	X	-	X	5	0
Jones	X	-	X	0	-	X	0	X	X	X	X	X	X	X	X	11	2
Kenyon	-	-	-	-	-	-	-	-	-	-	-	-	-	-	-	-	-
LaFollette	-	-	0	-	0	0	-	-	0	0	0	0	0	0	0	0	10
Nelson	-	-	-	0	-	-	-	-	X	-	0	-	-	-	-	1	2
Norris	-	-	0	-	0	-	-	-	0	-	0	-	-	0	0	0	6
Poindexter	-	-	X	-	X	-	-	-	X	-	-	-	X	X	X	6	0
Sterling	X	0	-	0	0	X	0	X	X	X	-	X	X	X	X	9	4
Townsend	-	-	X	0	0	X	-	-	X	X	X	X	X	X	X	9	2
Totals for higher duty	4	0	5	1	2	6	0	3	8	4	3	4	6	5	6		

1920. "I think myself that any tendency towards these principles is directly away from the fundamentals of American ideals, and ultimately would be complete destruction of our whole system which has been so successful."[41]

Most senators from the West, however, were hardly so reticent in promoting federal aid for agriculture, and as a result of their efforts a resolution passed the Senate during the last days of the Wilson administration directing the Federal Reserve Board and the War Finance Corporation to take certain actions to relieve distressed farmers. The WFC was authorized specifically to spend one billion dollars for transportation and exportation of grains, but President Wilson vetoed the resolution. It would, wrote Wilson, "finance private business at public expense"; but on January 3, 1921, the Senate passed the resolution over Wilson's veto. Poindexter joined with the Senate majority to override the veto, but he seemed decidedly negative about the usefulness of this kind of relief. "I think myself it is of very doubtful expediency but perhaps justified for trial," he wrote.[42]

A few days after the Senate passed the farm relief resolution, it also passed what was known as the Capper-Volstead bill to release farm cooperatives from the restrictions of the antitrust laws. It passed with little debate and no vote. It died before it could be approved by the conference committee, however, was reintroduced in the next Congress, and passed the Senate again on February 8, 1922. "There are greater possibilities in this line than in most others," wrote Poindexter, but his lack of enthusiasm in pushing even this modest effort to extend federal aid to farmers was apparent and served to further identify him with the Harding Republicans.[43]

Probably the issue used more than any other by Poindexter's enemies to publicize his "betrayal" of progressive reform was the Truman H. Newberry case. Newberry had been the Republican candidate for the Senate in 1918 in Michigan and had defeated Henry Ford, a Democrat and a pacifist. Newberry's election was immediately contested on the grounds that in his primary campaign he or his supporters had spent extravagant sums of money, exceeding the limits set by law. Because the division of the Senate was so close in 1919, Newberry's vote was essential to give the Republicans a majority and the power to organize the Senate. Control of the Senate was extremely important in 1918, it will be recalled, because the League of Nations was to be considered. Newberry had been seated, therefore, but an inquiry ordered.[44]

After a prolonged investigation, on January 12, 1922 the Senate passed a resolution which dismissed the case against Newberry but "condemned" the use of "such excessive sums" by a close vote. Poindexter voted for the resolution, and against three efforts to declare Newberry's seat vacant. To several of the prewar progressives, the Newberry case involved election corruption, and Borah, Jones, Kenyon, LaFollette, and Norris voted for all three efforts to unseat Newberry. Poindexter was highly sensitive to the implications of the Newberry case, and on February 3, 1922 he placed in the *Congressional Record* a letter he had written to a constituent defending his vote. He emphasized that Newberry had been "loyal" during the war, that Newberry had been in the armed forces during the election and not in Michigan when the illegal spending was done, and that three of Newberry's sons and a brother had also been in the military service. He stressed the point that Ford "was a pacifist, had opposed the effort to bring the war to a victorious conclusion, was in favor of a compromise peace, and . . . had secured the military exemption of his son." Poindexter reminded his reader that "The campaign was in 1918 . . . at the critical stage of the war, and it was made a war issue."[45] The thrust of his argument, in sum, placed the greatest emphasis upon Newberry's political views rather than on the legal issue, and his arguments were unable to prevent the growing impression that he was a Harding Republican who had betrayed his commitment to progressive reform.

Poindexter grew increasingly conscious of the number of people in Washington who questioned his loyalty to progressivism. The questions upset him, and in late February 1922 he commented on the problem to his brother-in-law R. L. Rutter: "I do not know what their definition of 'progressive' is. My own definition is that it meant free government, not under the control of any clique, interest, or element, but operating independently in the interest of the whole people. It is just as much contrary to progressive principles that Congress should be under the control of a multi-millionaire newspaper syndicate or of the communist party or element as of any other interest, which was opposed in the campaign of 1912."[46] In short, Poindexter seemed to be saying, as he had said many times before, that he was still a "progressive" and had always been one and, as always, he defended "the people" against the "special interests." The "special interests" of 1922, obviously, were not the same "special interests" he had opposed in 1912.

Despite the senator's contention that he had not changed, many people thought he had, and his prospects for reelection in November 1922 were grim. He had lost the support of many eastern Washington farmers; he was fiercely opposed by organized labor; and the mere mention of his name stirred the *Seattle Post-Intelligencer*, recently absorbed by the Hearst syndicate, into a furious outpouring of invective. A perceptive Hearst reporter in a letter that somehow found its way into Poindexter's hands, predicted that he would lose because, "This is a PROTEST year in politics." "Washington is one of the most radical states in the union," the Hearst reporter thought, and he pointed out that "about 75 percent of the slick old time machine politicians of this state are now for him [Poindexter] for the first time in their lives." Moreover, "Farm groups and labor groups, which cast 121,000 votes in this state for Bob Bridges [the Farmer-Labor candidate] for Governor in 1920, are being pretty well swung into line for 'anything on earth to beat Poindexter.'"[47]

The reporter recognized Poindexter's strengths: "We must not forget that Poindexter, himself, is a wonderful campaigner. He has always made votes with that great, hearty booming laugh. He will hang Hearst's hide upon the barn door and fill it full of buckshot. He'll want to know if the people are going to run their own affairs or let a New York publisher run them. He'll make votes by that talk, of course." But the Democratic candidate C. C. Dill, who had been defeated for reelection in the election of 1918 because of his war record, "will carry Seattle and Tacoma . . . and all of the big cities of the state," the reporter predicted. "The war hysteria is over, and his war record isn't going to hurt him."[48] A similar estimation of the Washington political situation came from Rufus Woods who still supported Poindexter: "with a defection of the Scripps papers, the railroad men, the labor crowd, and the old machine of the standpats, it looks like a real scrap this campaign."[49]

The campaign against Poindexter opened early in January 1922 when W. H. Paulhamus, who was a candidate for Poindexter's seat in the Senate and who had been a progressive before the war, denounced Poindexter's vote to seat Newberry and charged that "Senator Poindexter is simply an Opportunist." Paulhamus recalled that although Poindexter had been elected as "a rabid Progressive," he "has not for years been counted on as being in the Progressive column," and "I know it to be the opinion of many of his earlier supporters . . . that Senator Poindexter has shifted his moorings from the Progressive to the Ultra-Conservative column." Paulhamus also used charges that the Hearst-controlled *Post-Intelligencer* would repeat time and time again during the campaign, that Poindexter had accepted money from businessmen—the "interests"—for his presidential campaign expenses in 1920 in return for favors he did them as an influential member of the Naval Affairs Committee. Poindexter thus had voted to seat Newberry because he was controlled by "the interests."[50]

Poindexter seriously considered filing a libel suit against the *Seattle Star* for publishing these charges, but Horace Kimball advised against it. The senator admitted to Tom Murphine that William A. Todd, a New York shipbuilder, and Jules Bache, a New York banker, had contributed to his 1920 campaign, but he denied "that they are interested in any way in the Naval Affairs Committee which Paulhamus refers to." He also said that Todd, who owned shipyards in Seattle and Tacoma as well as on the east coast, had received government contracts to build three cruisers "but I did not know Todd at the time he secured those contracts."[51]

Not only had Todd contributed to Poindexter's campaign fund in 1920, as Poindexter admitted, but Todd also supported Poindexter in 1922 and probably again supplied money. In December 1921 Burns Poe, a Poindexter supporter in Tacoma, wrote Poindexter that he had been asked by Todd "how we will be fixed financially, and I told him that Ed Benn expects to raise some money from the mill men and that we would probably have to get some campaign funds together." Todd, himself, wrote Poindexter in December 1921 regarding the election. He sent along a letter that he had mailed to Mark Davis of Tacoma, who was associated with Todd's shipyard in that city. In his letter to Davis, Todd stated, "As I have said and as you will agree with me it would be a calamity if by any slipHup [sic] that he [Poindexter] should not be returned."[52] Undoubtedly, Todd's enthusiasm for Poindexter was related to the senator's views on naval construction, but there were no grounds to accuse Poindexter of unethical conduct, unless one condemned a nearly universal practice. Poindexter always had sought to secure government expenditures for Washington interests since he had gone to the Senate, and in this he was almost certainly no different from other senators, whether progressive or conservative. His relationship with Todd, Jules Bache, and other eastern corporation interests does not show that he had violated accepted standards of conduct; only that he had aligned himself with conservative businessmen.

Many of Poindexter's friends remained loyal to him and discounted the charges against him. Horace Kimball, Tom Murphine, and others worked actively for him throughout the campaign, and probably most of Poindexter's old friends would have agreed with the sentiments expressed in Rufus Woods's answer to Paulhamus in February 1922: "After I have known a man and his record for ten, fifteen or twenty years, I am not going to ditch him even though he does vote some of the time the way I wouldn't. . . . The main question is: Is he all right on the fundamentals? Fifteen or twenty years' clean cut record is enough for me."[53]

In the Republican primary three candidates contested Poindexter for the senatorial nomination:

Mrs. Frances C. Axtell of Bellingham, a former Democrat who was endorsed by the Non-Partisan League, the State Federation of Labor, and the Railway Men's Political Club; Austin E. Griffiths, a justice on the state supreme court and a leading Seattle reformer since before 1900; and Colonel George B. Lamping of Seattle. Throughout the primary campaign Hearst's *Post-Intelligencer* attacked Poindexter with cartoons, editorials, and articles. Hearst's central objection to Poindexter was that he had deserted progressivism and was controlled by the "interests." On August 5, the paper printed a challenge to him by William M. Short, leader of the State Federation of Labor, to debate campaign issues in order to explain why he had received large campaign contributions in 1920 even though he had no chance to win the Republican presidential nomination. On August 7, the *Post-Intelligencer* printed an editorial entitled "Canny Miles Keeps Silent" which featured Poindexter's reluctance to discuss the contributions of William H. Todd in 1920. On August 9, it charged that Poindexter was tainted with "BIG MONEY"; on August 19 it attacked Poindexter for opposing the veterans' bonus bill; on September 3, declaring that "Americanism Is the Issue at the Primaries," Poindexter was denounced for supporting the Four Power Treaty. Poindexter, concluded the *Post-Intelligencer*, was "a willing servant of the Old Guard in their machinations against the interests of the people."[54]

The militant *Seattle Union-Record* also concentrated its attack on Poindexter. It challenged Poindexter's contention that the unseating of Newberry would have disenfranchised Michigan voters, and wondered why the senator had not used this argument to defend the antiwar Socialist Victor Berger who had been elected twice to Congress by Wisconsin voters and twice denied his seat. "What's the difference, Miles, between Newberry and Berger?" asked the editorial. On the seventh of September the *Union-Record* stated that "Every time he [Poindexter] does or says anything he but serves to recall to the minds of the voters his betrayal of the progressive citizens who elected him to the Senate." On September 8 the paper in very large print urged its readers to "Concentrate Against

Poindexter." It reviewed the field of candidates against him, and concluded that George Lamping seemed the strongest progressive Republican and should be supported by all, or Poindexter would win. "Such a result would be nothing short of a calamity."[55]

The *Spokane Spokesman-Review* and the *Seattle Argus*, on the other hand, supported Poindexter enthusiastically, and the *Seattle Times* also supported him. The *Review* stated that "on the score of ability" Poindexter was superior to his opponents and, in addition, Spokane deserved to maintain control of one seat in the Senate. The *Argus* defended Poindexter's vote to seat Newberry, and it declared that "Senator Poindexter is a big fish who is being attacked by a school of political minnows." The *Times* supported Poindexter, it seems, because it felt he had been very useful to local interests, particularly the Bremerton Naval Yard. On August 30, it printed a cartoon showing a submarine labeled "Foreign-Owned Press" torpedoing a ship labeled "Bremerton" that was being towed along by a tugboat labeled "Poindexter." "Poindexter," concluded the *Times*, "stands out as the representative of un-bossed Republicanism."[56]

Poindexter carried the Republican primary, although his victory was unimpressive. He received only 39 percent of the total vote, although he carried all but six counties; and Lamping finished second with 26 percent of the total. Both the *Post-Intelligencer* and the *Union-Record* were quick to point out, however, that, as the *Post-Intelligencer* expressed it, "State Still Progressive," because the "Combined Totals of Three Progressives Would Exceed That of Opponent."[57]

Poindexter enjoyed only a brief rest before he threw himself into the campaign against the Democratic nominee and former congressman from eastern Washington, C. C. Dill. Poindexter campaigned across the state in October and early November. He received help from the Harding administration in the person of Secretary of Labor James J. Davis who came into Washington to speak for Poindexter and from Senator McNary of Oregon who campaigned for Poindexter in Seattle just before the election. The main theme of the campaign against Dill was his reputation as an opponent of the war and a supporter of radical causes. The *Spokesman-Review* carried on a systematic attack on Dill. On October 13, the *Review* published a statement by Republican State Chairman Charles Hebbard who attacked Dill's war record and Dill's endorsement of the Plumb Plan; on November 4 the *Spokesman-Review* belittled Dill for declaring that he could have achieved more progress in the Senate for the Columbia River Basin project than Poindexter had; and three days later the *Review* examined Dill's war record and his position on current domestic issues and concluded that Dill was a "shifty, untrustworthy politician" who was supported by the "kaiser-worshippers" and "ultra-radical elements."[58]

Dill relied primarily upon issues that had been raised in the Republican primary. In Seattle on November 2 he attacked Poindexter's support of the Esch-Cummins railroad bill, because, according to Dill, that bill was "the worst sin committed by the Republican administration against the common people." Dill pledged himself to support the repeal of this act, to vote to unseat Senator Newberry, to vote with the Farm bloc, and to fight for the Columbia River Basin project. He severely criticized Poindexter's support of the repeal of the wartime taxes, and he emphasized Poindexter's abandonment of progressive reform. In 1916, said Dill, Poindexter had been opposed by "the wealth of Washington and the newspapers that they [the wealthy] could control, but he had with him the men and women of Washington. Today the situation is reversed. Why is it?"[59]

The Farmer-Labor senatorial candidate in 1922 was James A. Duncan who had so aroused Poindexter's ire in 1918 by threatening to call a general strike on behalf of Thomas Mooney. The *Union-Record* supported Duncan vigorously, but on the day before the election it announced that the most important thing in the election was to defeat Poindexter. "Whatever else you do," it instructed the voters, "condemn such tactics [as Poindexter's] by voting for another candidate."[60]

When the election returns were totaled Poindexter had lost by a very slim margin. Dill was the winner with approximately 44 percent of the vote. He carried Spokane County, most of eastern Washington, and the urban Puget Sound counties as well. Poindexter received 43 percent of the vote, and Duncan, the Farmer-Labor candidate, finished a poor third with 12 percent of the total.[61] It is probable, moreover, that Duncan's candidacy prevented Dill from swamping Poindexter, for in all likelihood the Duncan vote was cast by militant labor groups and sympathizers, and it seems inconceivable that many of Duncan's supporters would have voted for Poindexter had Duncan not been a candidate. Dill, on the other hand, may not have been sufficiently militant to satisfy west coast labor, but his record made him much preferable to Poindexter. At any rate, the combined vote for Dill and Duncan amounted to 56 percent of the vote, and most of Washington's voters again had supported reform candidates. Dill's strength was, in general, in the same counties that had supported Bryan in 1896, Poindexter in the 1910 primary campaign, Roosevelt and Wilson in 1912, Wilson in 1916, and Poindexter in the 1916 Republican primary. In other words, Dill was strongest in Spokane and the counties of eastern Washington, while Poindexter carried the southwestern counties that since 1896 had consistently supported the opponents of reform. Elected by reform-oriented counties in 1910, Poindexter was defeated in 1922 by the same counties. "The state has once more given a direct progressive verdict," said the *Post-Intelligencer*; and the *Union-Record* gloated, "The election of Dill is important only in that it resulted in the defeat of a reactionary of the worst type."[62]

Poindexter's defeat was only part of a reaction in the West and Midwest against Harding Republicans. Wisconsin returned LaFollette to the Senate with a resounding victory, and antiadministration Republicans won several seats in the House and the Senate west of the Mississippi River. The Democrats did very well, too; while still in the minority, they picked up six seats in the Senate and seventy-four in the House. Furthermore, organized labor claimed it played a major role in the results. According to the AFL's political committee, the union had contributed to the election of twenty-four senatorial candidates.[63]

The defeat was of course a terrible disappointment to Poindexter and his friends. Jonathan Bourne blamed organized labor for the disaster, and President Harding agreed with Bourne. Poindexter lost, said Harding, because of his "fearless and aggressive fight against labor autocracy." Harding assured Bourne that he would find "some way . . . to properly take care of" Poindexter. "He is an able and highly honorable public servant, and the government could profit in retaining his services." The senator agreed with Harding and Bourne that labor had been very instrumental in his defeat, but he felt that the "insidious propaganda" regarding the Newberry case had been equally damaging. It "was misrepresented and distorted and played up in the most demagogic and unscrupulous way by a powerful and unscrupulous press, spending . . . many times the amount of money that was alleged to have been spent in the Newberry campaign," he said.[64]

Poindexter analyzed his defeat more carefully in a letter to his Uncle William A. Anderson in Lexington, Virginia. The senator pointed out that his defeat had been by only a very small margin, and he repeated his view that the Newberry case and the opposition of organized labor had hurt him. "The radical movement was very strong in Washington as it was throughout the country . . . and especially in the northwest, as indicated by the formation of very socialistic political organizations, such as the Non-Partisan League, Farmer-Labor party, etc." But Poindexter did not regret the actions he had taken or the views he held. "If standing for complete Americanism and constitutional government means defeat," he told Rufus Woods, "I am very glad indeed to pay that price for the privilege of presenting the issue to the country."[65]

11.
The Final Years

AFTER THE election of 1922, rumors that the defeated Washington senator would be appointed to President Harding's cabinet appeared in the press. Instead, in February 1923, the Harding administration announced that Poindexter had been appointed United States ambassador to Peru, and his appointment was promptly confirmed by the Senate.[1] As Poindexter and his wife prepared to leave the United States in March 1923, the Senator served notice to a friend in Spokane that he did not regard this departure as an end to his political career. He hoped that he and his wife would not be forgotten, and he promised that they would be away only "for a limited time" and that he would "return home to take an active part in our public affairs."[2] Poindexter's return to politics, however, was almost certain to be delayed at least six years if he planned to run again for the Senate, for Senator Jones was too formidable to be challenged and C. C. Dill would not be seeking reelection until 1928. The ambassadorship in Peru, then, probably would be a long interlude in Poindexter's life, as he waited to run again against Dill, but he seems to have handled the Peruvian ambassadorship with tact, moderation, and enthusiasm.

The most significant diplomatic responsibility which Poindexter assumed during his tour in Peru concerned a boundary dispute of long standing between Peru and Chile, the Tacna-Arica question. It involved two provinces, Tacna and Arica, which were taken from Peru by Chile at the conclusion of the War of the Pacific, 1879-84. The treaty ending that war provided that Chile would retain the provinces ten years and then a plebiscite would be held to determine their final disposition. But in 1894, Chile refused to permit the plebiscite, and from that time until the day Poindexter arrived in Lima, Peru, the dispute over the two provinces continued to fester relations between the two countries. The Harding administration offered to mediate the dispute in January 1922, and the negotiations were conducted over the following years by Secretary of State Hughes and his successor Frank B. Kellogg. Ultimately both nations accepted the president of the United States as the arbiter, and in 1925 President Calvin Coolidge ruled in favor of a plebiscite.[3]

Poindexter's role in the negotiations was limited largely to transmitting messages between the Peruvian president, Augusto Leguía, and Secretary Kellogg, though during the negotiations he talked with Leguía frequently and seemed to enjoy the president's confidence. By mid-1924, in fact, he seemed to have taken up Peru's cause, and, always a nationalist, Poindexter saw the dispute as a way to strengthen the ties between the United States and Peru and, no doubt, to extend the influence of his cherished Monroe Doctrine. "Should it [the Tacna-Arica dispute] be decided in favor of Peru, as I am firmly convinced it should," he wrote on June 28, 1924, "it will tend towards stabilizing governmental affairs, strengthening President Leguía and the present regime, and afford an opportunity for tremendous development, commercial and industrial, which is bound to be of enormous advantage to the United States as well as to Peru itself."[4] When Secretary Kellogg concluded in a dispatch on January 4, 1926 that neither Chile nor Peru seriously wanted to settle the dispute by means of a plebiscite, Poindexter challenged him, insisting that the Peruvian government thought it would win the election if given a fair chance. He explained that since the plebiscite would be conducted in provinces governed by Chile, the Peruvian government feared that supporters of annexation to

Peru would never have an equal chance to present their case. Hence, Poindexter recommended, the United States should exert every means available to secure a fair plebiscite.[5] When Kellogg asked Poindexter to persuade President Leguía to exercise more restraint in his speeches, Poindexter explained that Leguía's speeches were not inflammatory, only misrepresented by Chilean sources.[6]

Kellogg abandoned the plebiscite as a solution to the problem in early 1926, and in a series of exchanges won the assent of both governments to negotiate a settlement. Wrangling continued, however, until 1928 when President Herbert Hoover, shortly after his inauguration, announced that the dispute at last had been settled. Tacna, the northern province, was awarded to Peru, and Arica remained a part of Chile.[7]

But the Tacna-Arica dispute occupied only a small portion of Ambassador Poindexter's time. He was relatively young at fifty-five when he first went to Peru, and still thin and muscular as he had been when he first was elected to Congress in 1908. The leisure time his position afforded gave him his first real opportunity since his early Spokane days to live the strenuous life, and he spent many weeks exploring, hunting, and fishing. He helped catch what he later described as a seventy-five-ton whale, he killed jaguars in the Andes, and he caught a two-thousand-pound swordfish. The ancient ruins of the Inca civilization especially fascinated Poindexter. He visited many of the sites, and he was awarded a special gold medal by the city of Lima for his extensive travels in the interiors of Peru during 1923 and 1924. He was named an honorary member of the Geographical Society of Lima and a member of the Order El Sol del Peru.[8] Temperamentally unable to accept long periods of inactivity, Poindexter soon was hard at work writing about what he had seen. He had always aspired to be a man of letters, as his early attempt to publish a novel indicated, and during this six-year period, in addition to his other activities, Poindexter wrote three manuscripts, "The Ayar-Incas," "Peruvian Pharaohs," and "Empire of the Amazon." The first two were later published, but evidently not "Empire of the Amazon."

The Ayar-Incas was published in 1930 in two volumes and *Peruvian Pharaohs* in 1938, and they represented an attempt to produce a scholarly and professional explanation of the origins of the Inca civilization. Extensive footnotes were provided, and many references were made to scholarly works in several languages.[9] In both books Poindexter advanced the hypothesis that the Inca civilization, like all "higher" civilizations, was founded by an "Aryan" or "Proto-Aryan" or "white" race which had migrated to South America from Central Asia. He explained his thesis in *The Ayar-Incas*: "The eastern-moving branch of the forefathers of the white race reached America and established the typical culture of the white Proto-Aryan peoples in American before their westward moving archaic kinsmen had carried their religion and arts to Europe."[10] To explain why the Indian population of Peru was no longer "white," Poindexter argued that the "white" or "Aryan" race had been only a small elite in a large society of "darker peoples" and had lost in "the struggle . . . to preserve the purity of its blood." It lost in the struggle because of "the gradual victory of the indomitable appeal of sex" which resulted in "the absorption of the smaller white element in the tide of darker blood." Miscegenation caused the decline of the Inca civilization: "The royal and aristocratic caste was merged with the peon and the coolie, and the noble race was submerged in the downfall of the great structure it had built." This theory of the rise and decline of the Inca civilization would not be accepted by all, Poindexter predicted. "The view expressed here," he said in the preface to volume one of *The Ayar-Incas*, "is not the conventional view"; and for this reason, he added, "invites criticism." But "even where there is disagreement," he concluded, "opinions, based upon years of study and personal observation, tend to elucidation of the truth."[11]

Poindexter's books were well received in some quarters. A review of *The Ayar-Incas* in *Outlook* magazine in 1930 called it "learned, elaborately annotated, indexed and beautifully illustrated" with "convincing guess-work about the Aryan Asiatic origins of the Ayar-Incas." While his volumes are "extremely valuable to students," this review concluded, "it is unlikely that they can interest the general reader." When *Peruvian Pharaohs* appeared in 1938, the *Spokane Spokesman-Review* assured its readers that Poindexter's books were "virtually textbooks on Peru."[12]

On the other hand, Poindexter's work drew rather severe criticism. Ruth Benedict, professor of Anthropology at Columbia University, reviewing *The Ayar-Incas* in 1930, praised Poindexter's "enthusiasm" for his subject and noted that he had explored some prehistoric sites that had never before been examined by an outsider. But as to Poindexter's theories, she declared, "A list of the misconceptions he assembles would almost equal the bulk of his volumes. He naively equates race, which is . . . physical relationship, with language, which has long since ceased to be regarded as direct evidence of racial relationship. . . . It is of course, fantastic." Professor Benedict added that Poindexter's "sublime ignorance" of chronology was "equally fantastic" and that the books were "not only unscholarly" but "disjointed and dull." In the same year, a reviewer in the *Saturday Review of Literature* was at least as critical as Benedict: "Apparently Senator Poindexter does not know what constitutes evidence; and one can only hope that no earnest layman will accept this book as an example of modern anthropology."[13] Although Poindexter's hypothesis was unacceptable to most anthropologists, his convictions about miscegenation and the superiority of the white race expressed in his books seemed consistent with his Southern, rural origins and his views and his voting on issues related to race, immigration, and foreign policy when he had been in the Senate, though never before had they been so elaborately developed.

While Poindexter worked on his books and supervised the functions of the United States embassy in Peru, he waited for C. C. Dill's term to expire in 1928. In the fall of 1927 he returned to Spokane where he announced that he would run for the Republican nomination for the Senate in 1928. He called for farm legislation to ease the economic plight of America's farmers, for a large navy, and for free tolls for American ships in the Panama

Canal. A year later Poindexter resigned his post in Peru and hurried back to Washington to begin a primary campaign against State Superior Court Justice Kenneth Mackintosh of Seattle, a leading contender for the Republican nomination. In Washington in 1928 agricultural discontent remained strong, for American farmers had not shared the general economic prosperity of the 1920s. Under these conditions Poindexter's chances to regain his Senate seat were slim, for he remained labeled as a regular Republican and an enemy of federal aid to agriculture.[14]

To counteract this image, Poindexter opened his campaign with speeches reminiscent of his prewar progressive rhetoric. He reminded an audience in April 1928 that "the great progressive movement . . . restored government to the hands of the people," and he declared that there were "signs . . . that big business, or some elements of it have forgotten the lesson it learned 17 years ago." He endorsed the McNary-Haugen bill, a bill providing for extensive federal aid for farmers, and he called for the expansion of the Columbia River Basin project. But Poindexter's efforts were in vain, and he was defeated in the Republican primary by Judge Mackintosh. Poindexter received 34 percent of the vote, and he carried seventeen counties, fifteen of them in eastern Washington, an indication that he still had strength in the eastern Washington counties, but his Seattle opponent received 48 percent of the vote and carried twenty-two counties, only three of them in eastern Washington. The third candidate, Austin E. Griffiths, carried no counties and polled only 18 percent of the vote.[15] Although Poindexter had received a sizable vote from the eastern Washington counties that had supported him so solidly in 1910, the returns seemed to indicate that he no longer had a future in Washington politics. Poindexter, himself, seemed to accept this verdict, and the senatorial primary of 1928 was the last effort he ever made to seek political office.

Only a year after his 1928 defeat, Poindexter's wife, Elizabeth, died, and soon afterward he returned to the Virginia home built by Judge Anderson after the Civil War as a wedding gift to

Poindexter's mother. He continued to show an interest in political affairs throughout his years of retirement, and until his death he was active, both mentally and physically. Miles Poindexter's death came as a sharp contrast to his stormy public career, for he died in his sleep on September 21, 1946.[16]

Miles Poindexter's career in Congress fell into two rather distinct periods, the years before World War I (1909-17) and the years during and after the World War (1917-23). Before the war Poindexter was an outspoken and well-known member of the progressive Republican bloc in the Congress. He played a major role in the Insurgent revolt against the leaders of the Republican party; he was especially active in the congressional controversies over tariff reform, and the regulation of railroads, banks, and other corporations; and his progressive record in Congress won enthusiastic approval in his own state, especially among his friends and neighbors in Spokane and eastern Washington, who complained throughout these years of being exploited by eastern-controlled railroads and other trusts. There was much justice, to be sure, in the charges that big business discriminated unfairly against Spokane and eastern Washington, but it was also clear that unfair railroad practices and the discriminatory policies of eastern banks and other trusts had not seriously retarded eastern Washington's economic growth. Spokane and eastern Washington were, in fact, prosperous during the Progressive years, and the two groups which exercised the greatest influence upon Poindexter—the local business community and the farmers who controlled the Washington State Grange—seemed especially well-to-do. In essence, the enthusiasm for progressive reform in Spokane and eastern Washington reflected an on-going struggle by local business and farm groups to protect themselves from the domination of more powerful eastern corporations through federal intervention. Miles Poindexter, himself a member of the business-legal elite in Spokane, became the political agent selected through the political process to represent eastern Washington in national politics.

In Congress Poindexter voted and acted with the Republican majority in the Senate most of the time as did other progressive Republicans, but he frequently joined with the progressive Republicans who at times acted as an independent bloc and at other times voted with the Democrats. Most of the Democrats, too, represented agricultural states—the South and the West; and a coalition of Democrats and a few progressive Republicans enacted the major legislative reforms of the Progressive era. These measures, most of them passed after Wilson became president, provided for more effective regulation of railroads and other trusts, and banking, tariff and political reform, all measures which tended to meet the needs and interests of the agricultural West and South. The most serious social and economic problems in the United States during the Progressive era, however, were to be found in the working-class, immigrant neighborhoods of the industrial cities of the Northeast and among the poor black and white tenant farmers of the South. The progressives in Congress during the Progressive era by and large ignored the problems of the rural and urban poor, and Poindexter was no exception to this generalization. He concerned himself primarily with the interests of the agricultural region he represented, and his record before 1917 differed only in personal, idiosyncratic detail from other progressives in the Congress.

There were, to be sure, important personal differences which distinguished Poindexter from his fellow progressive Republicans in the Senate. He seemed compelled to assume extreme, absolutist positions and to denounce his political opponents with a spirit of vindictiveness that at times seemed to violate the unwritten code of conduct which governed the Senate's proceedings. In fact, he may have offended President Taft and the regular Republican leadership more deeply than any other Insurgent. Poindexter's penchant for absolutist positions also probably helps explain why he became swept away in the emotionalism of the Insurgent revolt to the extent that at one time or another he championed Socialists, the IWW, and the striking textile workers in Lawrence, Massachusetts—groups which seemed to be "unnatural" allies for a prosperous middle-class lawyer from Spokane, Washington. While he worked and voted in Congress for the domestic reform program backed by most senators from the farm belt, Poindexter, furthermore, justified his position in rather different terms: he showed a greater interest than most reformers in measures that appealed to working-class groups. He believed that American society faced the possibility of a major social upheaval brought about by the presence of a large, permanently unemployed and poverty-striken class in the population of the large cities. These apprehensions echoed the writings of some contemporary "Social Darwinists" who emphasized the dangers of social decay, racial suicide, and decline of Western society, and Poindexter expressed these apprehensions as evidence of the need to create work for the jobless urban masses through his industrial army bill and a massive federal project to develop the economy of Alaska.

Poindexter's concern about unemployment, however, seemed motivated more by a desire to preserve the social order and to prevent social revolution than by humanitarian compassion for the unemployed factory workers. Poindexter's vigorous support of immigration restriction, in fact, left little doubt that he regarded the most recent immigrants from Asia and Europe (presumably those from eastern and southern Europe) as "inferior," probably incapable of assimilation into American society, and hence a major cause of the social crisis he anticipated. Poindexter's solutions to the unemployment problem were admittedly "socialistic," but he insisted that he proposed the industrial army bill and the Alaskan bill as a result of a hardheaded, realistic, and unsentimental assessment of the crisis facing the United States. His reasons for advancing these measures, in sum, probably would have offended most Socialists and other radicals, but the proposals were, nonetheless, very advanced by comparison to the agrarian-oriented nature of progressive reform in the Congress. But for the most part, Poindexter focused his work upon issues more important to his eastern Washington supporters, and an analysis of the Senate voting record classifies him as one of a small group of western Republican reformers. His speeches and writing, however, suggest that he was ideologically closer to progressives such as Theodore Roosevelt than to progressives such as LaFollette, Borah, and Norris.

Poindexter's attitudes toward foreign policy also identified him with Roosevelt. An uncompromising nationalist and "realist," he ranked foreign policy questions among the most important before the Congress, and he attempted many times without success to secure an appointment to the Foreign Relations committee. Poindexter usually followed the leadership of Roosevelt without question—he endorsed the effort during Roosevelt's administration to involve the United States more aggressively in international affairs; he pushed for a continuation of an "imperialistic" policy in Latin America based upon Roosevelt's interpretation of the Monroe Doctrine; and he favored a major expansion of the armed forces, especially the navy. On these and related matters Poindexter rarely agreed with fellow progressive Republicans in the Senate—men like Borah, LaFollette, and Norris who paid little attention to foreign affairs, at least before the beginning of World War I, and were inclined generally to resist any departure from traditional, nineteenth-century isolationism. Because of the relative insignificance of international affairs in the Congress before the war, differences among the progressive Republicans over foreign policy failed to create a serious breach in solidarity. Issues of the war and the postwar period, however, highlighted Poindexter's disagreements with other Senate progressives and helped bring about his total rejection of the reform movement.

In Poindexter's second term his extreme nationalism, already apparent before 1917, led him to take an active part in the attempt to suppress the opponents of the war and, after the war, the "Bolshevists" and other radicals. By the war's end, Poindexter had developed an intense hostility toward Socialists, the IWW, and organized labor as well, and he found it increasingly comfortable to cooperate with others who had supported the war and shared his fear of radicalism and labor—eastern businessmen and the regular Republicans in the

Senate. In 1920 he campaigned in vain for the presidency by pitching his appeal to the most conservative elements in the Republican party, and in the early years of the Harding administration Poindexter served as a loyal member of the regular Republican team. His change in political alignment appeared to most of Poindexter's former supporters to be a betrayal of progressive principles, and he lost his bid for reelection in 1922, in the same counties in Washington that he had swept in earlier elections, to a Democrat pledged to carry on in the progressive tradition.

Even though Poindexter executed an extraordinary change in his views toward current issues and in his political allies and enemies, he remained consistent throughout his career to his ideological principles. The Social Darwinist concepts which he used to justify his fight to preserve American hegemony in the Western hemisphere and to make America militarily strong were as strongly fixed in his mind in 1921 and 1922 as in 1911. He opposed international organizations, arbitration, and other "idealistic" methods of preserving the peace with the same intensity in 1911 and 1912 as when he fought to prevent the United States from joining the League of Nations in 1919 and 1920, and he was never an isolationist. He viewed American involvement in world affairs as a necessary participation in the worldwide struggle for survival, and he had little patience with his fellow progressives who championed isolationist causes in the 1920s.

In domestic matters, as well, Poindexter remained consistent with his personal beliefs. Before 1917 he had explained his support for reform as a defense of "the people" against "the interests." He defined "the interests" then as eastern corporations and their political spokesmen, but he made it very clear long before 1917 that he would resist organized labor, the IWW, or any other group which threatened the stability of the political and economic system. After the beginning of the war, Poindexter's prewar fear that the unemployed masses in the cities might resort to radicalism and revolution readily converted into an intense hatred and fear of antiwar radicals and then, after the Russian revolution, of most individuals and groups that Poindexter associated with the "bolshevists." Thus labor organizations as well as more radical organizations became to him an even greater danger to "the people" than big business, "the interests" of earlier years. To combat the new danger, he shifted to the antilabor and anti-"bolshevist" camp with as much or more intensity than in the progressive years. Critics who thought Poindexter had betrayed his progressive principles after 1917 disturbed him, and often he attempted to explain the consistency of his position. When informed by Horace Kimball in 1919 that political enemies in Washington claimed that he was no longer a progressive and that he had turned against his former supporters, Poindexter responded: "I have not changed my attitudes towards labor or 'old friends,' and still stand for fair and liberal treatment of labor and for its protection against abuses. New issues, however, have arisen in the support given to Bolshevism by some elements of labor. . . . Of course this means revolution and I am against it regardless of political consequence."[17] Poindexter had always warned of the dangers of revolution, and after 1917 it appeared to him that his prophesies had come true.

In his efforts to curb "bolshevism" and to preserve a stable social order, Poindexter had the company of many other progressives who became conservatives and opponents of political change after 1917. Theodore Roosevelt seemed to grow more conservative, and both A. Mitchell Palmer and Ole Hanson, two who figured prominently in the Red Scare, had been prewar progressive reformers. It appeared, moreover, that several of the senators who had been at least moderate supporters of progressive reform, Bourne of Oregon, Fall of New Mexico, Curtis of Kansas, Nelson of Minnesota, Sterling of South Dakota, Townsend of Michigan, and perhaps Cummins of Iowa, agreed more or less with Poindexter, and on issues related to the war and the postwar period, they tended to vote with him. Most of the more advanced supporters of progressive reform, however, did not share Poindexter's ideology, and the behavior of some—LaFollette, Johnson, Borah, Gronna, and Norris—led Poindexter to observe in 1921, "I have found myself in absolute disagreement with many of our old associates on certain lines."[18] In his own mind, nonetheless, Poindexter remained throughout his political career a consistent and dedicated warrior in "the people's" fight against "the interests."

Notes

Index

Notes

1. Early Years

1 "The Poindexter Family. Notes from Public and Private Records," *Virginia Magazine of History and Biography* 19 (April 1911):215-18. For additional discussion of the Poindexter genealogy see "The Poindexter Family," *Virginia Magazine* 20 (July 1912):440-43; "Robert W. Poindexter, Jr.," *The Encyclopedia of American Biography* (New York, 1929), 38:8-10. F. Poindexter to M. Poindexter, Jan. 25, 1909; M. Poindexter to O. Bowyer, Oct. 8, 1909; M. Poindexter to J. Poindexter, Oct. 5, 1910; M. Poindexter to M. N. Tillman, June 13, 1913; M. Poindexter to S. M. Coleman, Dec. 16, 1913; M. Poindexter to T. M. Anderson, Dec. 19, 1914; M. Poindexter to F. Bowyer, Dec. 24, 1914; M. Poindexter to L. Poindexter, Aug. 12, 1916; and M. Poindexter to B. Dunlap, Feb. 28, 1916. See also Fielding Poindexter, "William Bowyer Poindexter," July 2, 1913, Miles Poindexter Papers. The papers are deposited at Alderman Library, University of Virginia, Charlottesville, Virginia, and are on microfilm at the University of Washington Library, University of Washington, Seattle, Washington. Hereafter Miles Poindexter will be referred to as "MP," and materials cited without reference to a collection are in the Poindexter Papers.
2 F. Poindexter to MP, May 16, 1904; MP to S. M. Coleman, Dec. 16, 1913; MP to T. M. Anderson, Dec. 19, 1914; and F. Poindexter, "William Bowyer Poindexter."
3 MP to M. N. Tillman, June 3, 1913. See also MP to F. Bowyer, Dec. 24, 1914. F. Poindexter, "William Bowyer Poindexter"; Oren F. Morton, *A History of Rockbridge*

Notes to pages 2-5

County, Virginia (Staunton, Va., 1920), pp. 187-98, 567; William B. Poindexter is listed in the alumni directory of 1855-56 and 1859-60. He is also mentioned as an alumnus of the class of 1859-60 in the "Catalogue of the Alumni of the Lexington Law School, and of Its Successor, The Law Department of Washington and Lee University, 1849-1881." Letter to the author from William W. Pusey III, Dean of the College, Washington and Lee University, Lexington, Va., March 19, 1962; and William B. Poindexter, Company Muster Roll, Company C, 1st Virginia Cavalry, Confederate States of America. National Archives. Washington, D.C.

4 F. Poindexter, "William Bowyer Poindexter"; and W. B. Poindexter to F. Poindexter, Mar. 29, 1905.
5 MP to Editor, *Washington Post*, Nov. 24, 1908; MP to F. Bowyer, Dec. 24, 1914; interview with Gale Poindexter, July 25, 1959; and letter to the author from Gale Poindexter, July 27, 1961.
6 W. A. Poindexter to MP, Mar. 31, 1898, June 28, 1901, and May 31, 1907; W. A. Anderson to MP, Mar. 13, 1913; MP to C. D. Gilkeson, Mar. 12, 1913; W. B. Poindexter to W. Poindexter, Jan. 10, 1902; and W. B. Poindexter to F. Poindexter, Aug. 19, 1899.
7 W. B. Poindexter to F. Poindexter, Aug. 19, 1899; F. Poindexter to E. Poindexter, Oct. 4, 1899; and MP to L. Poindexter, Apr. 12, 1915.
8 Francis Thomas Anderson Junkin, "Genealogical Chart Showing the Descent from Several Lines and Some Interesting Family Connections of the Virginia Families of Alexander, Anderson, Aylette, Bruce, Dandridge, Fontaine, Henry, Junkin, Moore, Poindexter, Spotswood, West, & C. & C." printed for private distribution, 1908; *The National Cyclopedia of American Biography* (New York, 1904) 12:423; Frederick A. Virkus, *The Compendium of American Genealogy. The Standard Genealogical Encyclopedia of First Families of America* (Chicago, 1933) 5:609; and O. Morton, *History of Rockbridge County, Virginia*, p. 122.
9 *Rockbridge County News*. See obituary dated Mar. 14, 1912 in the Poindexter MSS; W. B. Poindexter, Aug. 20, 1912; F. Poindexter, "William Bowyer Poindexter"; MP to S. M. Coleman, Dec. 16, 1913; F. Poindexter, "Memorial to Josephine Anderson Poindexter," Poindexter MSS; and *Who's Who in America* (Chicago, 1925), 13:227.
10 *Who's Who in America*, 13:227, and O. Morton, *History of Rockbridge County, Virginia*, pp. 245-46.
11 W. A. Anderson to MP, Jan. 9, 1899; and F. Poindexter to MP, Dec. 8, 1908.
12 MP to S. Poindexter, Feb. 12, 1902.

13 L. M. Harris to MP, Aug. 12, 1912; and B. Bell to MP, June 10, 1911.
14 Letter to the author from W. W. Pusey III, Mar. 19, 1962. MP to H. S. Wilson, Sept. 21, 1910; MP to Editor, *Washington Post*, Nov. 24, 1908; U.S. Congress, *Biographical Directory of the American Congress, 1774-1971* (Washington, D.C., 1971), p. 1553.
15 Interview with Gale Poindexter; *Walla Walla Union-Journal*, Aug. 13, Nov. 12, Nov. 19, and Nov. 25, 1892; and MP to *Washington Post*, Nov. 24, 1908.
16 *Walla Walla Union-Journal*, June 11, 1893; and MP to *Washington Post*, Nov. 24, 1908; and *Who Was Who In America* (Chicago, 1950), 2:427. F. Poindexter to MP, July 2, 1904. A search through *Forest and Stream* turned up no article by Poindexter. Gale Poindexter stated he is not aware that such a manuscript existed. Poindexter's interest in Scott is seen in the fact that in 1901 he purchased a forty-eight-volume set of that author's writings. "Willie" Poindexter in 1920 urged Miles to take up the book again and predicted that it "would help to keep the tradition of Sir Walter Scott alive." W. A. Poindexter to MP, Dec. 27, 1920. F. Poindexter to MP, Aug. 14, 1901; and Harper & Brothers to MP, Dec. 2, 1901. Donohue, Henneberry & Co. to MP, Oct. 20, 1897; Laird & Lee to MP, Oct. 30, 1897; Herbert S. Stone & Co. to MP, Oct. 30, 1897; Harper & Brothers to MP, Mar. 7, 1902; Bowen-Merrill Publishers to MP, Apr. 17, 1902; and Doubleday, Page & Co. to MP, Jan. 13, 1903.
17 U.S. Bureau of the Census, *Eleventh Census of the United States: 1890. Population, Part I*, 1:352-53; James B. Hedges, *Henry Villard and the Railways of the Northwest* (New Haven, 1930), p. 3; and Otis W. Freeman and Howard H. Martin, eds. *The Pacific Northwest* (New York, 1942), p. 345.
18 A. Berglund, "The Wheat Situation in Washington," *Political Science Quarterly* 24 (Sept. 1909):489-503; U.S. Bureau of the Census, *Twelfth Census of the United States: 1900. Agriculture, Part II*, 6: 189; Edwin J. Cohn, Jr., *Industry in the Pacific Northwest and the Location Theory* (New York, 1952), p. 95; and Douglass C. North, "Location Theory and Regional Growth," *Journal of Political Economy* 63 (June, 1955):246.
19 In 1888 the Republican candidate for territorial delegate to Congress carried the state with approximately 58 percent of the vote, and in 1890 the Republican candidate for Congress carried the state with 52 percent of the vote. Secretary of the Territory, "Statistical Report of the Secretary of the

274   Notes to pages 8-12

Territory of Washington." Olympia, Wash., 1888; and Secretary of State, "First Report of the Secretary of State of the State of Washington." Olympia, Wash., 1890. See also Robert C. Nesbit, *"He Built Seattle": A Biography of Judge Thomas Burke* (Seattle, 1961), pp. 57-89; Keith Murray, "Republican Party Politics in Washington During the Progressive Era" (Ph.D. diss., University of Washington, 1946), p. 13. County election data utilized hereafter in this study were made available by the Inter-University Consortium for Political and Social Research. The Consortium bears no responsibility for the analyses or interpretations presented here. State election results are from Congressional Quarterly, *Guide to U.S. Elections* (Washington, 1975), p. 279.

20 H. C. Farnsworth, "Decline and Recovery of Wheat Prices in the Nineties," *Wheat Studies of the Food Research Institute* 10 (Oct. 1933-Aug. 1934):303; O. W. Freeman and H. H. Martin, *The Pacific Northwest*, p. 344; Charles M. Gates and Robert C. Nesbit, "Agriculture in Eastern Washington," *Pacific Northwest Quarterly* 37 (Oct. 1946):283; and G. B. Ridgeway, "Populism in Washington," *Pacific Northwest Quarterly* 39 (Oct. 1948):287-90.

21 Karel D. Bicha, "Peculiar Populist: An Assessment of John R. Rogers," *Pacific Northwest Quarterly* 65 (July 1974):110-17; Thomas W. Riddle, "Populism in the Palouse," *Pacific Northwest Quarterly* 65 (July 1974):97-109; G. B. Ridgeway, "Populism in Washington," *Pacific Northwest Quarterly*, pp. 300-305; and Congressional Quarterly, *Guide to U.S. Elections*, pp. 280 and 435.

22 G. C. Quiett, *They Built the West* (New York, 1934), p. 505; E. J. Cohn, Jr., *Industry in the Pacific Northwest*, p. 27; and U.S. Bureau of the Census, *Twelfth Census of the United States: 1900. Population*, Part I, 1:478.

23 *Spokane Spokesman-Review*, Dec. 11, 1948; N. W. Durham, *A History of the City of Spokane and Spokane County*, 3 vols. (Spokane, 1912), 2:237; and interview with Gale Poindexter. *Spokesman-Review* hereafter to be cited as *S-R*.

24 MP to J. W. Sullivan, Sept. 23, 1910.

25 E. Poindexter to MP, Nov. 25, 1898.

26 Ralph E. Dyar, *News For An Empire* (Caldwell, Idaho 1952), pp. 63-92; *S-R*, Mar. 20, Mar. 23, May 15, May 21, June 6, June 20, June 25, Oct. 1, Oct. 3, Oct. 5, and Oct. 15, 1896.

27 Douglas Smart, "Spokane's Battle for Freight Rates," *Pacific Northwest Quarterly* 45 (Jan. 1954):20; and *S-R*, Mar. 25 and Mar. 26, 1896.

2. The Emergence of a Progressive Reformer

1 *Spokesman-Review*, June 10, 1900, June 30, 1918, July 5, 1925, Sept. 1, 1928, July 16, 1932, and Feb. 12, 1939. Hereafter cited as *S-R*.
2 *S-R*, June 8 and 9, 1900; and K. Murray, "Republican Party Politics," (Ph.D. diss., University of Washington, 1946), p. 52.
3 Congressional Quarterly, *Guide to U.S. Elections*, p. 281 and *S-R*, Nov. 8, 1900.
4 MP to Joe Greenway, Dec. 5, 1901; MP to S. Poindexter, Feb. 12, 1902; MP to E. A. McDonald, Oct. 15, 1902; MP to C. H. Nugent, Apr. 4 and July 30, 1903; and MP to J. H. Bowers, June 15, 1903.
5 R. E. Dyar, *News for an Empire* (Caldwell, Idaho 1952), pp. 123-25; and N. W. Durham, *History of the City of Spokane and Spokane County*, 3 vols. (Spokane, 1912), 1:541.
6 R. E. Dyar, *News for an Empire*, p. 140; and *S-R*, Mar. 26, Apr. 23, Apr. 29, Apr. 30, May 15, June 6, Oct. 3, Oct. 4, Nov. 2, Nov. 5, 1896 and Aug. 5, 1898, Apr. 3, 1899, May 2, June 22, July 7, Oct. 20, and Nov. 7, 1900.
7 D. T. Ham to MP, Nov. 13, 1902; F. W. Cushman to MP, Feb. 4 and Aug. 2, 1901; and A. G. Foster to E. Poindexter, May 8, 1902.
8 MP to L. Ankeny, Dec. 5, 1903; MP to T. D. Page, Dec. 5, 1903; MP to B. D. Crocker, Jan. 11, 1904; and MP to A. C. Foster, Jan. 14, 1904.
9 MP to L. Ankeny, Dec. 5, 1903, B. D. Crocker to MP, Jan. 14, 1904; T. D. Page to MP, Oct. 22, Dec. 17, 1903 and Jan. 27, 1904; K. Murray, "Republican Party Politics," pp. 61-66; W. B. Thorsen, "Washington State Nominating Conventions," *Pacific Northwest Quarterly* 35 (Apr. 1944):113-15; Congressional Quarterly, *Guide to U.S. Elections*, p. 282; Secretary of State, "Abstract of Votes Polled in the State of Washington at the General Election Held November 8, 1904," Olympia, Wash.; and *S-R*, Nov. 20, 1904.
10 J. W. Mc[?] to MP, Jan. 28, 1898; Sec., Banker's Commercial League of America to MP, Apr. 11, 1899; and R. L. Rutter to MP, Feb. 15, Feb. 18, 1899, and Dec. 24, 1901.
11 E. Poindexter to MP, Nov. 9, 1898; T. C. Davis to MP, Feb. 3, 1902; and MP to County Assessor, Walla Walla County, Mar. 17, 1902.
12 G. F. Poindexter to MP, Mar. 17, 1908; R. L. Rutter to MP, Nov. 27, Nov. 29, and Dec. 18, 1899; E. Poindexter to MP, Sept. 21 and Sept. 22, 1906; and W. A. Ritchie to MP, Dec. 6, 1907.

13 B. B. Adams to MP, Mar. 22, 1905; unsigned postcard from Spokane Country Club, May 9, 1905; see invitation to Scandinavian banquet of Oct. 30, 1906; Debate Council, U. of Idaho to MP, Feb. 23, 1907; W. Nichols to MP, Feb. 26, 1907; F. G. Moorehead to MP, Nov. 13, 1907; F. Witt(?) to MP, Nov. 23, 1908; and *S-R*, Nov. 24, 1907 and Feb. 6, 1908.
14 Interview with Gale Poindexter.
15 E. Poindexter to MP, 1903, 1905, and Jan. 14, 1907.
16 Interview with Gale Poindexter and "Senator Poindexter Who Wants to be President," *Literary Digest* 63 (Dec. 6, 1919):80.
17 D. K. Larimer in the *Sioux City* (Iowa) *Tribune*, July 6, 1910, clipping in the Poindexter MSS; "Senator Poindexter," *Literary Digest*, p. 80; and interview with Gale Poindexter.
18 W. A. Poindexter to MP, Aug. 30, 1899; MP to E. Root, Oct. 11, 1901; F. Poindexter to E. Poindexter, May 13, 1898; and MP to E. Poindexter, Jan. 30, 1900.
19 See for example W. A. Poindexter to MP, Mar. 21, 1901; MP to W. T. Hood and Co., Sept. 10, 1901; MP to S. Poindexter, Feb. 12, 1902; and G. F. Poindexter to MP, Dec. 14, 1901, Mar. 25, 1903, Sept. 12 and Oct. 2, 1905.
20 Howard W. Allen and Jerome M. Clubb, "Progressive Reform and the Political System," *Pacific Northwest Quarterly* 65 (July 1974):130-45; Otis L. Graham, Jr., *The Great Campaigns: Reform and War in America, 1900-1928* (Englewood Cliffs, N.J., 1971), pp. 1-51; Samuel P. Hays, *The Response to Industrialism, 1885-1914* (Chicago, 1957); William H. Harbaugh, *Power and Responsibility: The Life and Times of Theodore Roosevelt* (New York, 1961); George Mowry, *The Era of Theodore Roosevelt, 1900-1912* (New York, 1958); and Henry Pringle, *Theodore Roosevelt: A Biography* (New York, 1931).
21 Jerome M. Clubb, "Congressional Opponents of Reform, 1901-1913" (Ph.D. diss., University of Washington, 1963), pp. 1-192. See also Allen and Clubb, "Progressive Reform and the Political Structure," *Pacific Northwest Quarterly*, pp. 130-45; and G. Mowry, *The Era of Theodore Roosevelt*, pp. 224-25.
22 The combined Democratic and fusionist vote for Bryan in 1896 correlated with the Democratic presidential vote in 1900 at .85 and in 1904 at .47, but the correlation of the Bryan vote in 1896 with the Democratic vote for governor in 1904 was .64. The vote for the fusionist candidate for governor in 1896, John R. Rogers, correlated with the Bryan vote in 1896 at .99, and with the Democratic vote for governor in

1900 and 1904 at .81 and .67. Correlation statistics presented here and elsewhere in this study are Pearson product-moment correlation coefficients. The persistence of this sectional pattern in Washington's county election returns is documented in Howard W. Allen and Erik W. Austin, "From the Populist Era to the New Deal: A Study of Partisan Realignment in Washington State, 1889-1950," *Social Science History* 3 (Winter 1979):115-43. See also Secretary of State, "Abstract of Votes Polled in the State of Washington at the General Election Held November 8, 1904." Olympia, Wash.; C. O. Johnson, "George Turner, Part I," *Pacific Northwest Quarterly* 34 (July, 1943):264-66; and William T. Kerr, Jr., "The Progressives of Washington, 1910-12," *Pacific Northwest Quarterly* 55 (Jan., 1964):21-27.

23 Mansel G. Blackford, "Reform Politics in Seattle During the Progressive Era, 1902-1916," *Pacific Northwest Quarterly* 59 (Oct., 1968):177-85; Dorothy O. Johansen and Charles M. Gates, *Empire of the Columbia: A History of the Pacific Northwest*, 2d ed. (New York, 1967), pp. 436-40; William T. Kerr, Jr., "The Progressives of Washington," pp. 66-69; K. Murray, "The Aberdeen Convention of 1912," *Pacific Northwest Quarterly* 38 (Apr., 1947):100; and C. O. Johnson, "The Adoption of the Initiative and Referendum in the State of Washington," *Pacific Northwest Quarterly* 35 (Oct., 1944):295-96.
24 *S-R*, June 4, June 9, and June 11, 1905.
25 Ibid., July 4, July 22, July 26, July 29, July 30, and July 31, 1905.
26 Ibid., Aug. 3 and Aug. 10, 1905.
27 See Poindexter's membership card dated Sept. 8, 1905 in Poindexter MSS; A. White to MP, Dec. 20, 1905; and *S-R*, Nov. 1 and Nov. 16, 1905.
28 F. W. King to MP, Mar. 24, 1906; *S-R*, Nov. 3 and Nov. 25, 1906; and R. H. Rice to MP, June 1, 1907.
29 *S-R*, Jan. 16 and June 6, 1905.
30 A. E. Griffiths to MP, Aug. 11, 1905; F. H. Gaston to MP, Apr. 4, 1904; W. D. Vincent to MP, Sept. 6, 1907 and Jan. 21, 1908; O. Cain to MP, Dec. 19, 1907; and *S-R*, Oct. 21 and Nov. 1, 1907.
31 *S-R*, Jan. 18, 1908.
32 Ibid., Jan. 10, Jan. 14, Jan. 28, and April 11, 1908.
33 W. P. Edris to K. Plunkett, Apr. 20, 1908.
34 Unsigned letter to "My Dear Friend and Juror," Apr. 15, 1908; J. W. Greb to J. Brown, July 1, 1908. See also J. Huffman to W. P. Edris, Apr. 30, 1908; and also R. L. Rutter to MP, June 22, 1908.
35 Secretary of State, "Abstract of Votes Polled in the Primary Election of September 8, 1908," Olympia. Wash.

36 *S-R*, Oct. 6, 1908.
37 Ibid., Oct. 13, 1908.
38 Inland Empire Hardware and Implement Company to MP, Aug. 14, 1908.
39 *S-R*, Sept. 4, 1908.
40 J. B. Shore to MP, Oct. 6, 1908.
41 MP to A. A. Elmore, Oct. 10, 1908; and MP to H. Crass, Oct. 16, 1908.
42 *S-R*, Nov. 1, 1908.
43 Ibid.
44 *Whitman County Directory* (Seattle, 1904), p. 78.
45 *S-R*, Oct. 18, 1908.
46 Secretary of State, "Abstract of Votes Polled at the General Election, November 3, 1908," Olympia, Wash.
47 Richard Hofstadter, *The Age of Reform: From Bryan to F.D.R.* (New York, 1956), p. 161.
48 *S-R*, Oct. 2 and Nov. 2, 1904; and G. Mowry, *The Era of Theodore Roosevelt*, p. 87. Richard Hofstadter's suggestion in *The Age of Reform* that some members of the middle class became progressive reformers because they were "victims of an upheaval in status" has attracted much attention in the years since that book appeared in 1956. Hofstadter's formulation remains intriguing but still neither confirmed nor disconfirmed. For a more complete discussion of Hofstadter's "status revolution" concept and its critics see Jerome M. Clubb and Howard W. Allen, "Collective Biography and the Progressive Movement: The 'Status Revolution' Revisited," *Social Science History* 1 (Summer 1977):518-31.

3. A Hero of Insurgency

1 John D. Baker, "The Character of the Congressional Revolution of 1910," *Journal of American History* 60 (Dec., 1973):679-91.
2 Charles O. Jones, "Joseph G. Cannon and Howard W. Smith: An Essay on the Limits of Leadership in the House of Representatives," *Journal of Politics* 30 (Apr., 1968):617-46; and Samuel P. Hays, *The Response to Industrialism: 1885-1914* (Chicago, 1957), pp. 116-39. A good recent survey of the Insurgent revolt against the leadership of the Republican party is Lawrence James Holt, *Congressional Insurgents and the Party System, 1909-1916* (Cambridge, 1967). On the Taft administration generally see also Paolo E. Coletta, *The Presidency of William Howard Taft* (Lawrence, Kans., 1973).
3 Kenneth W. Hechler, *Insurgency: Personalities and Politics of the Taft Era* (New York, 1940), pp. 32-33 and 42-47.

4 See for example C. W. Fowler to MP, Nov. 6, 1908 and N. Hapgood to MP, Nov. 7, 1908.
5 MP to C. W. Fowler, Nov. 16, 1908; MP to N. Hapgood, Nov. 17, 1908; MP to W. H. Taft, Nov. 10, 1908; MP to T. H. Burton, Nov. 10, 1908; MP to V. Murdock, E. A. Hayes, and G. A. Pearre, Feb. 20, 1909; MP to N. G. Blalock, Mar. 13, 1909; and *S-R*, Mar. 12, 1909.
6 U.S. Congress, House, *Congressional Record* 44, 61st Cong. 1st sess., 1909, 18. The eleven were Congressmen Cary, Cooper, Lenroot, Kopp, Morris, and Nelson of Wisconsin; Davis and Lindbergh of Minnesota; Hubbard of Iowa; Murdock of Kansas; and Hinshaw of Nebraska; ibid., pp. 20-34. MP to L. S. Abbott, Mar. 19, 1909; MP to A. L. Birchard, Mar. 22, 1909.
7 MP to A. Baldwin, Jan. 22, 1909; *S-R*, Feb. 21, 1909. See also MP to H. C. Moore, Feb. 3, 1909; and MP to A. W. Jones, Feb. 16, 1909.
8 *Congressional Record* 44:804-6.
9 Ibid., pp. 806, 1112-19, 1299, 1301.
10 Ibid., pp. 1293-1302. The list of Insurgents used in table 1 is that compiled in Howard W. Allen, "Miles Poindexter: A Political Biography" (Ph.D. diss., University of Washington, 1959), app. 1:600-603. Use of the list produced by Baker's analysis or by the use of party loyalty scores would not change the conclusion that the Insurgents supported higher tariff duties on products that seemed to compete with the products of their own sections of the nation.
11 MP to D. A. Lockwood, Oct. 3, 1909; and *Seattle Post-Intelligencer*, Aug. 16, 1910 (hereafter cited as *P-I*), W. L. Jones to F. E. Jones, Oct. 1, 1910, in Wesley L. Jones Papers, University of Washington, Seattle, Wash.
12 K. Hechler, *Insurgency*, p. 106. For a more recent discussion of the Insurgents and the Payne-Aldrich tariff which essentially agrees with Hechler, see David P. Thelen, *Robert M. LaFollette and the Insurgent Spirit* (Boston, 1976), pp. 69-74.
13 The quotation from the *New York Sun* is found in George E. Mowry, *Theodore Roosevelt and the Progressive Movement*, 2d ed. (Madison, 1947), p. 48. For a discussion of western concern about the tariff on hides, see Louis L. Gould, "Western Range Senators and the Payne-Aldrich Tariff," *Pacific Northwest Quarterly* 64 (Apr., 1973):49-56.
14 *Congressional Record* 44:4754 and 4755.
15 *S-R*, Aug. 14, 1909; and MP to B. Sinclair, Oct. 27, 1909.
16 MP to D. D. Olds, Aug. 21, 1909; MP to B. Sinclair, Oct. 27, 1909; and *S-R*, May 11, 1910.
17 MP to F. E. Allison, June 1, 1909; and Mark Sullivan,

280 Notes to pages 43-50

"The Fight Against Cannonism," *Collier's Weekly* 43 (Mar. 27, 1909):8 and 11.
18 *S-R*, Oct. 4, 1909. See also MP to D. A. Lockwood, Oct. 3, 1909.
19 MP to N. Hapgood, Dec. 30, 1909. A judicious account of this controversy is in James Penick, Jr., *Progressive Politics and Conservation: The Ballinger-Pinchot Affair* (Chicago, 1968). See also Elmo R. Richardson, *The Politics of Conservation: Crusades and Controversies 1897-1913* (Berkeley, 1962), especially pp. 65-144.
20 *New York Times*, Jan. 5, 1910; and MP to J. P. Perkins, Jan. 6, 1910.
21 *S-R*, Jan. 6, 1910; U.S. Congress, Senate, *Congressional Record* 45, 61st Cong. 2d sess., 1910, 314, 325, 399, 404-6; MP to J. P. Perkins, Jan. 29, 1910; and MP to O. C. Moore, Jan. 13, 1910.
22 *Congressional Record* 45:3425-28, 3435, 3436.
23 Ibid., pp. 3438-39.
24 Ibid., pp. 5522-23, 6030-32.
25 The sixteen roll-call votes included in this analysis were in the *Congressional Record* 44:18, 20, 20-21, 21-22, 33-34, 4754-55. Ibid., 45:404, 3426-27, 3428, 3435-36, 3438-39, 6032. A description and classification of each vote is in Howard W. Allen, "Miles Poindexter," app. 1:600-603.
26 J. D. Baker, "The Character of the Congressional Revolution of 1910," pp. 679-91.
27 See Jerome M. Clubb and Howard W. Allen, "Party Loyalty in the Progressive Years: The Senate, 1909-1915," *Journal of Politics* 29 (Aug. 1967):567-84.
28 Computer facilities used for computations presented in this study were provided by the Office of Academic Computing, Southern Illinois University at Carbondale. The roll-call data utilized in this study were made available by the Inter-University Consortium for Political and Social Research. The Consortium bears no responsibility for the analyses or interpretations presented here.
29 Clipping from *Sioux City* (Iowa) *Tribune*, July 6, 1910. The Taft quotation is found in Henry F. Pringle, *The Life and Times of William Howard Taft*, 2 vols. (New York, 1939), 2:562.
30 For discussions of Poindexter's prospects in the election of 1910 see C. A. Reynolds to MP, Sept. 8, 1909; MP to C. Adams, Sept. 11, 1909; K. C. Beaton to MP, Jan. 1, 1910; MP to K. C. Beaton, Oct. 13, 1909; C. B. Kegley to MP, Oct. 27, 1909; MP to R. Woods, Nov. 13, 1909; and Austin E. Griffiths, "Great Faith, an Autobiography of an English Immigrant Boy in America, 1863-1950." Typed manuscript. Seattle,

Wash., University of Washington, pp. 153-54. See also R. C. Nesbit, "*He Built Seattle*," (Seattle, 1961), pp. 413-17.

31 R. Wilson to MP, Sept. 27 and Oct. 24, 1909; W. P. Edris to MP, Oct. 23, 1909; MP to C. E. Blair, E. W. Burrows, K. C. Beaton, J. D. Corselius, R. Woods, and E. Lorton, Oct. 13, 1909; *Seattle Times*, July 3, 1910; *S-R*, Oct. 21, 1909; *P-I*, Nov. 28, 1909; *Who's Who in America, 1926-1927*, 14:2059; N. W. Durham, *A History of the City of Spokane and Spokane County*, 2 vols. (Spokane, 1912), 2:355-56; and Belle C. and Fola LaFollette, *Robert M. LaFollette*, 2 vols. (New York, 1953), 1:283.

32 D. T. Ham to W. L. Jones, Nov. 26, 1909; W. L. Jones to G. Dilling, Mar. 28, 1910; W. L. Jones to A. L. Rogers, Dec. 14, 1909; M. T. Hartson to W. L. Jones, Nov. 23 and Dec. 7, 1909, Jones MSS.

33 *New York Times*, Jan. 5, 1910; W. L. Jones to M. T. Hartson, Jan. 17, 1910; and W. L. Jones to D. T. Ham, Apr. 18, 1910, Jones MSS; R. Wilson to MP, May 3, 1910; and MP to C. O. Erickson, June 1, 1910.

34 J..P. Hartman to W. L. Jones, Apr. 7, 1910; A. L. Rogers to W. A. Major, Mar. 11, 1910; and W. L. Jones to E. L. Brunton, Apr. 21, 1910, Jones MSS.

35 MP to A. E. Griffiths, June 28, 1910. In contrast to the indifference Poindexter displayed in this letter, the *New York Herald* humorously described Poindexter's arrival at Oyster Bay: "Gentleman with rattled look appears at Oyster Bay station. Reporters try to dodge him, but fail." *P-I*, July 9, 1910; and *S-R*, July 5, 1910.

36 *New York Times*, July 6, 1910; *Portland Oregonian*, July 6, 1910; and *P-I*, July 8, 1910.

37 W. H. Taft to R. A. Ballinger, July 7, 1910, Richard A. Ballinger Papers, University of Washington, Seattle, Wash.; and Archibald W. Butt, *Taft and Roosevelt: The Intimate Letters of Archie Butt*, 2 vols. (New York, 1930), 2:434-37.

38 *S-R*, July 12, 1910; and *Seattle Times*, July 16, 1910. See also T. Roosevelt to N. Longworth, July 11, 1910 in Theodore Roosevelt Papers, Library of Congress, Washington, D.C.

39 *S-R*, July 31 and Aug. 4, 1910; and *Seattle Times*, Aug. 4, 1910.

40 *P-I*, Aug. 5, 1910; and *Seattle Times*, Aug. 5, 1910.

41 W. H. Taft to W. L. Jones, Aug. 11, Aug. 22, and Sept. 3, 1910; and W. H. Taft to John L. Wilson, Sept. 3, 1910, Jones MSS; W. H. Taft to R. A. Ballinger, Aug. 24, 1910, Ballinger MSS; and *S-R*, Sept. 5, 1910.

42 *S-R*, Sept. 1, Sept. 4, and Sept. 11, 1910.

43 Ibid., Sept. 1, 1910; and MP to O. C. Moore, June 23, 1910.
44 *S-R*, Aug. 19, Aug. 21, and Sept. 5, 1910; "Poindexter and Why," *LaFollette's Weekly* 2 (July 16, 1910):5-6. See copy of endorsement of Poindexter for U.S. Senator by the Inland Retail Dealers Association in Poindexter MSS; and W. P. Edris to MP, Dec. 21, 1909.
45 H. Johnson to MP, Sept. 12, 1910; R. LaFollette to O. C. Moore, Sept. 10, 1910; A. B. Cummins to MP, Aug. 27, 1910; G. Pinchot to MP, Aug. 16, 1910; A. Beveridge to G. B. Dresher, Sept. 12, 1910; W. J. Cary to MP, June 13, 1910; and S. L. Lenroot to MP, June 11, 1910. A. J. Beveridge to *Seattle Star*, Sept. 12, 1910; and A. J. Beveridge to M. Sullivan, Sept. 13, 1910 in Albert J. Beveridge Papers, Library of Congress, Washington, D.C.; and *S-R*, Aug. 20, 1910.
46 Secretary of State, "Abstract of Votes Polled in the Primary Election Held in the State of Washington on September 13, 1910." Olympia, Wash.; George Mowry, *Theodore Roosevelt and the Progressive Movement*, pp. 128-30; and MP to T. Roosevelt, Sept. 28, 1910.
47 The vote for Poindexter in the 1910 Republican primary correlated with the Bryan vote in 1896 at .45 and with the Democratic vote for governor in 1904 at .57. While these relationships are only moderately strong, it must be remembered that they are measures of association of votes cast in rather different kinds of elections. Furthermore, in view of the length of time between the election of 1896 and the Republican primary in 1910 and the rapid increases in population which took place in Washington in those years, the consistency of the voting pattern seems impressive. It was a pattern, moreover, which persisted until the late 1920s. See H. W. Allen and E. Austin, "From the Populist Era to the New Deal," *Social Science History* 3 (Winter, 1979).
48 *Seattle Times*, July 17, Nov. 5, and Nov. 6, 1910; MP to W. J. Bigger, Oct. 10, 1910; and *S-R*, Jan 18, 1911.
49 A. L. Rogers to W. A. Major, Mar. 11, 1910; W. L. Jones to E. L. Brunton, Apr. 21, 1910; and J. A. Rea to W. L. Jones, June 2, 1910, Jones MSS; see also W. L. Jones to M. T. Hartson, Apr. 25, 1910, Jones MSS. W. W. Robertson to E. Brainerd, Aug. 17, 1910, Erastus Brainerd Papers, University of Washington, Seattle, Wash.

   In addition to Poindexter, five Insurgents represented congressional districts where in 1896 the majority of the counties were carried by Bryan: Murdock of Kansas; Norris, Kinkaid, and Hinshaw of

Nebraska; and Stennerson of Minnesota. See U.S. Congress, *The Congressional Directory*, 61st Cong., 2d sess., 1909, for a list of counties represented by each Insurgent. *The Presidential Vote: 1896-1932* (Stanford, 1947), by Edgar Eugene Robinson, provides the 1896 election statistics.
50 MP to J. W. Sullivan, Sept. 23, 1910; and R. Hofstadter, *The Age of Reform* (New York, 1956), p. 131.
51 Samuel P. Hays, *The Response to Industrialism: 1885-1914*, pp. 116-39.

4. A Senate Insurgent

1 W. A. Smith to A. J. Beveridge, Sept. 15, 1911, Beveridge MSS; editorial in *Sioux City* (Iowa) *Tribune*, July 6, 1910, clipping in Poindexter MSS; Belle C. and Fola LaFollette, *Robert M. LaFollette*, 2 vols. (New York, 1953), 1:323-25; *S-R*, Apr. 22, 1911; and U.S. Congress, *Congressional Directory*, 62d Cong., 1st sess., 1911, 167.
2 Howard W. Allen, "Geography and Politics: Voting on Reform Issues in the United States Senate, 1911-1916," *Journal of Southern History* 27 (May 1961): 216-28.
3 Barton J. Bernstein and Franklin A. Leib, "Progressive Republican Senators and American Imperialism, 1898-1916: A Reappraisal," *Mid-America* 50 (July 1968):165. A more useful and perceptive critique of the methods used in Allen "Geography and Politics," although this study was not specifically discussed, may be found in Allan G. Bogue, "The Radical Voting Dimension in the U.S. Senate During the Civil War," *Journal of Interdisciplinary History* 3 (Winter 1973): 449-54. Additional research has also pointed up other limitations in "Geography and Politics." In the Allen study the perspective was upon the role played by the Republican reformers and their definition of the reform position. Hence neither the critical role played by the Democrats in the enactment of progressive legislation nor the overall importance of partisanship in the Senate voting in the Progressive years received sufficient recognition. See J. M. Clubb, "Congressional Opponents of Reform, 1901-1913" (Ph.D. diss., University of Washington, 1963); J. M. Clubb and H. W. Allen, "Party Loyalty in the Progressive Years: The Senate, 1909-1915," *Journal of Politics* 29 (Aug. 1967):567-84; Howard W. Allen, Aage R. Clausen, and Jerome M. Clubb, "Political Reform and Negro Rights in the Senate, 1909-1915," *Journal of Southern History* 37 (May 1971):191-212;

Howard W. Allen and Jerome M. Clubb, "Progressive Reform and the Political System," *Pacific Northwest Quarterly* 65 (July 1974):132-37; and David Sarasohn, "The Insurgent Republicans: Insurgent Image and Republican Reality," *Social Science History* 3 (Oct. 1979):245-61.

4 Aggregate measures of party cohesion in the Senate for the 1890s are in William G. Shade, Stanley D. Hooper, David Jacobson, and Stephen E. Moiles, "Partisanship in the United States Senate: 1869-1901," *Journal of Interdisciplinary History* 4 (Autumn 1973): 185-205. Cohesion scores for the Senate in the late 1920s and early 1930s are in Richard Brewer, "Party Loyalty in the Senate During the Early Depression Years: 1929-1934" (M.A. thesis, Southern Illinois University, 1969). See also Jerome M. Clubb and Santa A. Traugott, "Partisan Cleavage and Cohesion in the House of Representatives, 1861-1974," *Journal of Interdisciplinary History* 7 (Winter 1977):375-401.

5 For a recent treatment of the Taft administration see Paolo E. Coletta, *William Howard Taft* (Lawrence, Kans., 1973).

6 U.S. Congress, House, *Congressional Record* 46, 61st Cong., 3rd sess., 1911, app. p. 151.

7 Ibid., pp. 2526, 2563-64.

8 C. B. Kegley to MP, Mar. 29, 1911; and C. B. Kegley to Members of Washington Delegation to Congress, Mar. 30, 1911.

9 W. Sumner to MP, Mar. 29, 1911; C. L. Hibbard to MP, May 16, 1911; Pres., Everett Pulp and Paper Company to MP, June 8, 1911; A. von Boecklin to MP, June 28, 1911; A. S. Cory to MP, Apr. 11, 1911; and MP to A. S. Cory, Apr. 19, 1911. See also J. G. Ames to MP, Apr. 12, 1911; and J. E. Manley to MP, July 7, 1911.

10 W. L. Jones to MP, Apr. 5, 1911; Grandview District Fruit Growers Association to W. L. Jones, Apr. 3, 1911; F. W. Olds to MP, Apr. 8, 1911; J. G. Kelly to MP, Mar. 24, 1911; and *S-R*, Apr. 16, 1911.

11 MP to B. C. Holt, May 4, 1911.

12 U.S. Congress, Senate, *Congressional Record* 47, 62d Cong., 1st sess., 1911, 2781, 2782, 2783, 2789, 3168, 3169, 3170, 3171, 3172, 3173, and 3175. See MP to Stranger Creek Grange, #374, Apr. 20, 1911, and to Bonner Barlett and others, Apr. 20, 1911; and E. G. Griffs to MP (telegram), June 22, 1911.

Nineteen amendments were proposed to the Canadian Reciprocity bill apparently to defeat or cripple it. The names of senators and the number of amendments each supported were as follows:

Bristow, Kans.	Rep.	19	Bourne, Oreg.	Rep.	16
Cummins, Iowa	Rep.	19	Kenyon, Iowa	Rep.	16
Dixon, Mont.	Rep.	19	Simmons, N.C.	Dem.	16
Gronna, N.Dak.	Rep.	19	Borah, Idaho	Rep.	14
LaFollette, Wis.	Rep.	19	Brown, Nebr.	Rep.	14
Nelson, Minn.	Rep.	19	Crawford, S.Dak.	Rep.	14
Clapp, Minn.	Rep.	18	McCumber, N.Dak.	Rep.	13
Bailey, Tex.	Dem.	16	Clarke, Ark.	Dem.	12

13 MP to S. Archer, Apr. 25, 1911; and MP to R. C. McCroskey, May 6, 1911.

14 P. McCumber to E. Root, June 14, 1912, in Elihu Root Papers, Library of Congress, Washington, D.C. See also Kendrick A. Clements, "Manifest Destiny and Canadian Reciprocity in 1911," *Pacific Historical Review* 42 (Feb. 1973):32-52.

15 *New York Times*, Jan. 16, 1912. Robert L. Tyler, *Rebels of the Woods: The I. W. W. in the Pacific Northwest* (Eugene, Oreg. 1967), pp. 1-28; Melvyn Dubofsky, *We Shall Be All. A History of the Industrial Workers of the World* (Chicago, 1969), pp. 227-62; and Donald B. Cole, *Immigrant City: Lawrence, Massachusetts, 1845-1921* (Chapel Hill, N.C., 1963), pp. 177-94.

16 Alpheus T. Mason, *Brandeis, A Free Man's Life* (New York, 1946), pp. 361-62; see also L. D. Brandeis to MP (telegram), Feb. 27, 1912.

17 MP to E. J. Tamblin, Mar. 8, 1912; MP to F. C. Ladd, Apr. 12, 1912; and MP to E. H. Gosse, Mar. 5, 1912.

18 MP to F. C. Ladd, Apr. 12, 1912; and U.S. Congress, Senate, *Congressional Record* 48, 62d Cong., 2d sess., 1912, 2445-53.

19 *Congressional Record* 48:2450-51.

20 Ibid., pp. 2445-53, 6000.

21 MP to S. S. Loomis, July 1, 1910.

22 MP to H. A. Simonds, Sept. 25, 1910; and G. P. Hampton to C. B. Kegley, July 5, 1910, in Gifford Pinchot Papers, Library of Congress, Washington, D.C. See also Hampton's letter to MP on the same date in the Pinchot Papers.

23 *Congressional Record* 48:10830; and MP to W. C. Jones, Jan. 7, 1914.

24 The description of Poindexter's stand on political reform measures is based upon the findings of a Guttman Scale analysis in Howard W. Allen, Aage R. Clausen, and Jerome M. Clubb, "Political Reform and Negro Rights in the Senate, 1909-1915," pp. 191-212. The descriptions of Poindexter's stand on the Railroad Workman's Compensation bill is based upon an unpublished Guttman Scale analysis of the voting on that bill.

25 MP to T. H. Jones, June 19, 1911; *S-R*, June 20, 1911; A. J. Cummins to A. J. Beveridge, July 3, 1911, and T. R. Shipp to A. J. Beveridge, June 23, 1911, Beveridge MSS. See also Belle C. and Fola LaFollette, *LaFollette* 1:338.
26 C. B. Kegley to MP, June 21, 1911; MP to J. W. Bryan, Aug. 5, 1911; MP to J. J. Hannan, Nov. 8, 1911; MP to C. B. Kegley, Dec. 22, 1911; and *Seattle Times*, Jan. 4, 1912.
27 *S-R*, Dec. 10, 1911.
28 MP to G. Poindexter, Nov. 2, 1911.
29 MP to L. Dow, Jan. 27, 1912. See also MP to T. Murphine, Jan. 27, 1912.
30 MP to O. C. Moore, Feb. 3, 1912; and MP to H. Kimball, Mar. 21, 1912. A similar report of this conference was sent to Governor Hiram Johnson of California by the president of the Ohio Progressive Republican League. J. D. Fackler to H. Johnson, Apr. 1, 1912 in Franklin Hichborn Papers, University of California, Los Angeles.
31 MP to Ole Hanson, Mar. 13, 1912; and MP to M. Z. Dibble, Mar. 21, 1912. See also T. Murphine to MP (telegram), Mar. 12, 1912; MP to T. Murphine, Apr. 9, 1912; R. P. Hudson to F. Knox, Mar. 19, 1912; MP to E. C. Snyder, Mar. 13, 1912; and MP to G. F. Hannan, Apr. 1, 1912.
32 MP to G. Pinchot, May 11, 1912. See also T. Murphine to MP, Apr. 14, 1912; MP to T. Murphine, Apr. 20, 1912; clippings from the *Seattle Times*, *Star*, *P-I*, and *Tacoma Ledger*, dated Apr. 14, 1912 in the Poindexter MSS; and H. Kimball to MP, Apr. 27, 1912.
33 K. Murray, "The Aberdeen Convention of 1912," *Pacific Northwest Quarterly* 38 (Apr. 1947):101.
34 Ibid., pp. 102-8.
35 MP to G. A. Haynes, May 29, 1912; and MP to E. C. Snyder, June 4, 1912.
36 T. Roosevelt to MP, July 2, 1912, Roosevelt MSS.
37 A. B. Cummins to MP, July 1, 1912; T. Roosevelt to J. C. O'Laughlin, July 9, 1912, Roosevelt MSS. John A. Gable, however, disputes the view "that few prominent politicians joined the Progressive Party." See John A. Gable, *The Bull Moose Years: Theodore Roosevelt and the Progressive Party* (Port Washington, N.Y., 1978), p. 259, see also pp. 19-59.
38 *S-R*, July 4 and July 6, 1912; and *P-I*, July 7, 1912.
39 *Seattle Times*, July 7, 1912; MP to W. J. Biggar, July 11, 1912; N. W. Durham to MP, July 14, 1912; O. C. Moore to MP, July 18, 1912; *P-I*, July 11, 1912; *Seattle Times*, July 12, 1912; MP to T. Roosevelt, July 22, 1912; MP to J. M. Dixon, July 17, 1912. T. Roosevelt to MP, July 23, 1912, Roosevelt MSS.

40 MP to T. Murphine, July 26 and July 27, 1912: O. C. Moore to MP (telegram), July 30, 1912; *Seattle Times*, July 31 and Aug. 1, 1912; and *P-I*, July 30, July 31, and Aug. 1, 1912.
41 *S-R*, Aug. 6, 1912.
42 Ibid., Aug. 7, 1912.
43 MP to J. D. Works, Apr. 24, 1915.
44 *P-I*, Aug. 14, 1912; J. C. Lawrence to MP, Aug. 14, 1912; *S-R*, Aug. 14, 1912; and MP to H. Kimball, Aug. 27, 1912.
45 *S-R*, Sept. 2, Sept. 11, Oct. 10, Oct. 12, Oct. 14, Oct. 15, and Nov. 5, 1912; and *P-I*, Oct. 29, Oct. 30, Oct. 31, and Nov. 1, 1912.
46 Congressional Quarterly, *Guide to U.S. Elections*, p. 284.
47 Secretary of State, "Abstract of Votes Polled in the State of Washington at the General Election held on November 5, 1912." Olympia, Wash.
48 Congressional Quarterly, *Guide to U.S. Elections*, p. 284, and John A. Gable, *The Bull Moose Years*, pp. 146-49.

5. The New Freedom

1 MP to G. T. Odell, Dec. 14, 1912.
2 The nine Republicans who voted less than 80 percent of the time with the Republican majority were:

Fall, N.M.	79.8%		Kenyon, Iowa	76.9%
Borah, Idaho	79.5%		Poindexter, Wash.	71.8%
McCumber, N.D.	79.4%		Norris, Neb.	71.5%
Clapp, Minn.	79.1%		LaFollette, Wis.	65.3%
Jones, Wash.	78.4%			

See J. M. Clubb and H. W. Allen, "Party Loyalty in the Progressive Years: The Senate, 1909-1915," *Journal of Politics* 29 (Aug. 1967):567-84 and H. W. Allen and J. M. Clubb, "Progressive Reform and the Political System," *Pacific Northwest Quarterly* 65 (July 1974):132-37.
3 U.S. Congress, *Congressional Directory*, 62d Cong., 3rd sess., 1913, 128; MP to T. Page, Jan. 10, 1913; and *New York Times*, Jan. 30, 1913.
4 *New York Times*, Mar. 5, 1913 and *Chicago Tribune*, Mar. 5, 1913.
5 U.S. Congress, *Congressional Directory*, 63rd Cong., 1st sess., 1913, 181; and MP to A. W. Doland, Mar. 26, 1913.
6 Arthur S. Link, *Wilson: The New Freedom* (Princeton, 1956), pp. 177-81; see also Frank Burdick, "Woodrow Wilson and the Underwood Tariff," *Mid-America* 50

288   Notes to pages 88-95

(Oct. 1968):272-90.
7 On the method used to select the eighteen progressive senators see Howard W. Allen, "Geography and Politics: Voting on Reform Issues in the United States Senate, 1911-1916," *The Journal of Southern History* 27 (May 1961):216-28.
   Tables 3 and 4 include only the first vote on each item. This means, for example, that only the vote on the first amendment to raise the duty on wheat is included, although votes were taken on five wheat amendments. Whether one included all votes or only the first vote, the general results are the same, as can be seen by comparing the tables on pages 204 and 205 in Howard W. Allen, "Miles Poindexter" (Ph.D. diss., University of Washington, 1959), with the tables presented here. Votes on duties included in table 3 are found in U.S. Congress, Senate, *Congressional Record* 50, 63rd Cong., 1st sess., 1913, 3300, 3302, 3304(b), 3380, 3752, 4079, and 4470. Votes on duties included in table 4 are found in *Congressional Record* 50: 2644, 3102, 3112, 3155, 3161, 3174, 3233, 3261, 3269, 3537, 4137, 4301, 4306, and 4335. An analysis of Senate insurgent Republican voting on the Payne-Aldrich tariff that reached very similar conclusions is in David Sarasohn, "The Insurgent Republicans," *Social Science History* 3 (Oct. 1979):245-61.
8 W. E. Borah to D. J. Trieber, Jan. 21, 1914, in William E. Borah Papers, Library of Congress, Washington, D.C.; and *Congressional Record* 50:4453 and 4458. D. P. Thelen presented a very different interpretation of LaFollette's position on the tariff in *Robert M. LaFollette and the Insurgent Spirit* (Boston, 1976), pp. 52-78.
9 U.S. Congress, Senate, *Congressional Record* 48, 62d Cong., 2d sess., 1912, 9616, and ibid., 50:3408-9.
10 *Congressional Record* 50:3773-74, 3818-19, 3830, 3834, 3836, 3852, 3866, 3872, 3884, 3889, 4420, 4611, 4612, 4613. See also J. M. Clubb and H. W. Allen, "Party Loyalty in the Progressive Years: The Senate, 1909-1915," *Journal of Politics* 29 (Aug. 1967):575.
11 *Congressional Record* 50:3835 and 4613.
12 Ibid., pp. 3835-36; and M. Clapp to A. J. Beveridge, Sept. 4, 1913, Beveridge MSS.
13 *Congressional Record* 50:4613; *New York Times*, Sept. 10, 1913; and MP to E. K. Brown, Sept. 11, 1913.
14 W. Wilson to MP, Sept. 13, 1913; and *Chicago Tribune*, Sept. 10, 1913. See a reprint of the *Collier's* article in *S-R*, Dec. 28, 1913.
15 MP to N. Fine, Nov. 4, 1912.
16 MP to N. Fine, Nov. 4, 1912; and MP to E. P. Jones,

Apr. 7, 1913.
17 MP to E. Pittwood, Dec. 2, 1913; and U.S. Congress, Senate, *Congressional Record* 51, 63rd Cong., 2d sess., 1913, 1230 and 1488.
18 MP to G. E. Becker, Dec. 19, 1913. W. E. Borah to F. Fouch, Dec. 23, 1913, Borah MSS. J. D. Works to R. Spreckels, Feb. 9, 1914 in John D. Works Papers, University of California, Berkeley, Calif. The prominent role played by Wall Street bankers and their advocates in the writing of the Federal Reserve Act, as described by Gabriel Kolko in *The Triumph of Conservatism: A Reinterpretation of American History, 1900-1916* (London, 1963), pp. 217-54 was never mentioned by Poindexter in his correspondence or on the Senate floor. Poindexter's statements, in fact, leave little doubt that he saw the new banking system as a triumph over Wall Street.
19 MP to R. Woods, Dec. 18, 1913.
20 Miles Poindexter, "A Progressive View: The President Judged by the Only Senator Belonging to the Progressive Party," *Harper's Weekly* 58 (Mar. 7, 1914):12-13. For an elaboration of Poindexter's views on "caucus rule and party tyranny," see his article "My Conscience and My Vote" in *Harper's Weekly* 58 (Jan. 24, 1914):20-22.
21 MP to J. C. Lawrence, Mar. 2, 1914; MP to C. T. Clifford, July 20, 1914; and *Congressional Record* 51: 13319 and 14802.
22 MP to E. W. Phillips, Dec. 12, 1913; MP to L. J. Rothwell, Feb. 5, 1914; and O. Dorman to MP, June 9, 1914.
23 M. T. Alliman to MP, July 13, 1914; and R. Loewe to MP, July 22, 1914. See also F. G. Labrash to MP, June 24, 1914; and F. W. Cotterhill to MP, July 10, 1914.
24 G. L. Gardiner to MP, June 26, 1914; E. Constantine to MP, July 9, 1914; C. B. Yandell to MP, July 15, 1914; T. S. Griffith to MP, Aug. 20, 1914; T. Burke to MP, June 19, 1914; and R. L. Rutter to MP, Aug. 15, 1914.
25 MP to R. L. Rutter, Aug. 15, 1914; and MP to G. M. Poddycord, Aug. 25, 1914. See also MP to P. J. Brady, June 25, 1914.
26 *Congressional Record* 51:14585-90.
27 Ibid., p. 14317.
28 Ibid., pp. 14465, 14467, 14468, 14545, 14546, 14610.
29 R. A. Dague to MP, Jan. 7, 1915.
30 *Congressional Record* 50:2119; and MP to R. A. Dague, Aug. 1 and Aug. 30, 1913.
31 MP to T. W. Woodrow, Feb. 9, 1914; MP to J. Mailley, Mar. 3, 1914; MP to A. J. Young, Jan. 30, 1915; MP

to J. D. Quillen, Feb. 8, 1915; U.S. Congress, Senate, *Congressional Record* 53, 64th Cong., 1st sess., 1915, 224; and U.S. Congress, Senate, *Congressional Record* 55, 65th Cong., 1st sess., 1917, 192.
32 *S-R*, Oct. 31, 1911; *P-I*, Nov. 16, 1911; and M. D. Leehey to MP, Oct. 26, 1911.
33 *Congressional Record* 50:52 and 2365; *P-I*, July 11, 1913; and MP to O. A. Case, Aug. 14, 1913. It should be noted that other progressives, particularly Senator Works of California and Gifford Pinchot, were also quite interested in furthering Alaska's development. See W. L. Fisher to J. D. Works, Nov. 3, 1911 and G. Pinchot to J. D. Works, July 29, 1911, Works MSS; and T. R. Shipp to G. Pinchot, Nov. 10 and Nov. 25, 1910, Pinchot MSS.
34 M. D. Leehey to MP, Oct. 23, 1913; *P-I*, Nov. 9 and Nov. 10, 1913 and Jan. 25, 1914; and MP to W. H. Pemberton, Nov. 4, 1913.
35 *Congressional Record* 51:2228-30, 2242-43, and 2250; and *P-I*, Jan. 25, 1914.
36 *P-I*, Apr. 5, 1914.
37 MP to Otto A. Case, Aug. 14, 1913.
38 *P-I*, Aug. 5, 1913.
39 *Congressional Record* 50:3828-29.
40 Ibid.
41 Ibid.
42 Richard Hofstadter's description of Theodore Roosevelt seemed to apply very well to Poindexter. Roosevelt, said Hofstadter, did not become a reformer "from the standpoint of social democracy, not as an advocate of the downtrodden. He despised the rich, but he feared the mob." Thus Roosevelt thought of himself, argued Hofstadter, as "an impartial arbiter devoted to the national good." Richard Hofstadter, *The American Political Tradition and the Men Who Made It* (1948; reprint ed., New York, 1956), pp. 206-37. See also W. H. Harbaugh's discussion of Roosevelt's attitude toward labor unions in *Power and Responsibility* (New York, 1961), pp. 346-48; and John M. Blum, *The Republican Roosevelt*, 2d ed. (Cambridge, 1977), pp. 1-6, 112-15.
43 *P-I*, Aug. 29, 1913.
44 MP to T. Roosevelt, Dec. 16, 1912.
45 MP to W. J. Biggar, Nov. 12, 1912; and MP to E. C. Snyder, Nov. 21, 1912. See also MP to G. Dilling, Dec. 14, 1912.
46 C. Rowell to W. Kent, Dec. 7, 1912; and C. Rowell to R. R. McCormick, Dec. 7, 1912, in Chester Rowell Papers, University of California, Berkeley, Calif. Walter Johnson, *William Allen White's America* (New York, 1947), p. 218; and Albert J. Beveridge, "The

Future of the Progressive Party," *Saturday Evening Post* 185 (Dec. 28, 1912):3-4, 36-37.
47 A. J. Beveridge to MP, Nov. 18, 1912, Beveridge MSS. See also John Braeman, *Albert J. Beveridge: American Nationalist* (Chicago, 1971), pp. 231-39.
48 MP to A. J. Beveridge, Nov. 23, 1912, Beveridge MSS.
49 J. D. Works to A. M. Draw, Jan. 16, 1914; and J. D. Works to F. Pierce, Mar. 14, 1914, Works MSS.
50 M. E. Clapp to A. J. Beveridge, July 1, 1913; A. J. Beveridge to M. E. Clapp, July 16, 1913; M. E. Clapp to A. J. Beveridge, Sept. 4, 1913; and MP to A. J. Beveridge, Dec. 22, 1913, Beveridge MSS.
51 A. Cummins to A. J. Beveridge, Jan. 14, 1914, Beveridge MSS. For a more optimistic view of the future of the Progressive party in 1913 and 1914, see John A. Gable, *The Bull Moose Years* (Port Washington, N.Y., 1978), pp. 157-228.
52 MP to H. Kimball, Jan. 7, 1914; and *New York Times*, Apr. 19, 1914.
53 S. C. Bone to A. J. Beveridge, Nov. 17, 1913, Beveridge MSS; W. Jones to L. F. Hart, July 24, 1913, and S. A. Perkins to W. Jones, Apr. 18, 1913, Jones MSS.
54 *S-R*, Feb. 24 and Feb. 26, 1914; and MP to L. R. Slater, Mar. 2, 1914.
55 M. McCormick to MP, Apr. 1, 1914.
56 W. H. Parry to MP, Apr. 1, 1914.
57 MP to W. H. Parry, Apr. 4, 1914.
58 Amos Pinchot, *History of the Progressive Party, 1912-1916*, ed. Helene M. Hooker (New York, 1958), pp. 184-200. See also John A. Gable, *The Bull Moose Years*, pp. 152-53.
59 MP to A. J. Beveridge, June 24, 1914. See also MP to C. Weile, June 25, 1914.
60 W. H. Parry to MP, Apr. 17, 1914, and C. Rowell to H. Johnson, Feb. 14, 1914, Rowell MSS.
61 MP to H. Kimball, Mar. 6, 1914; R. Woods to MP, undated; MP to R. Woods, Jan. 21, 1913.
62 MP to H. Kimball, Aug. 13, Nov. 22, 1913; and MP to H. Kimball, Feb. 14, 1914.
63 MP to R. Woods, Nov. 13, 1913; R. Woods to MP, undated; and MP to R. Woods, June 4, 1914.
64 Congressional Quarterly, *Guide to U. S. Elections*, pp. 508 and 729; "Abstract of Votes Polled in the State of Washington at the General Election Held November 3, 1914," Olympia, Wash.; and S. C. Bone to W. Jones, Nov. 11, 1914, Jones MSS.

6. Foreign Affairs: A Progressive "Realist"

1. Robert E. Osgood, *Ideals and Self-Interest in America's Foreign Relations* (Chicago, 1953), pp. 9-10, and 102-5; and Richard Hofstadter, *Social Darwinism in American Thought, 1860-1915* (Philadelphia, 1945), pp. 146-73. Richard Lowitt concluded that when Norris entered the Senate he was not interested in foreign affairs, and Bernstein and Lieb stated that most of the progressive Republicans at least until World War I were "largely indifferent to foreign policy." Richard Lowitt, *George W. Norris: The Persistence of a Progressive, 1913-1933* (Urbana, 1971), p. 41; B. J. Bernstein and F. A. Leib, "Progressive Republican Senators and American Imperialism, 1898-1916: A Reappraisal," *Mid-America* 50 (July 1968): 177; and John Milton Cooper, Jr., "Progressivism and American Foreign Policy: A Reconsideration," *Mid-America* 51 (Oct. 1969):268. For Beveridge's interest in foreign policy see John Braeman, *Albert J. Beveridge* (Chicago, 1971), pp. 42-67, and see D. P. Thelen's analysis of LaFollette's foreign policy views in *Robert M. LaFollete and the Insurgent Spirit* (Boston, 1976), pp. 125-54.
2. A copy of this speech is in the Poindexter MSS.
3. R. E. Osgood, *Ideals and Self-Interest*, pp. 29-41; and R. Hofstadter, *Social Darwinism*, pp. 159-63.
4. MP to A. T. Mahan, Sept. 26, 1912; MP to H. D. Cohrman, Sept. 26, 1912; and U.S. Congress, Senate, *Congressional Record* 48, 62d Cong., 2d sess., 1912, 8648-49.
5. T. Roosevelt to MP, May 20, 1913. Roosevelt gave similar advice to Franklin D. Roosevelt, May 10, 1913. Elting E. Morison, ed., *The Letters of Theodore Roosevelt*, 8 vols. (Cambridge, 1954), 7:729. MP to T. Roosevelt, June 5, 1913.
6. T. Roosevelt to E. Root, Jan. 9, 1912, Root MSS.
7. MP to F. C. Morehouse, Dec. 5, 1911; and MP to H. Parsons, Dec. 23, 1911.
8. MP to M. Besterville, Mar. 4, 1912. See also MP to W. D. Eddy, Jan. 6, 1912.
9. W. Stull Holt, *Treaties Defeated by the Senate* (Baltimore, 1933), pp. 230-35; Walter V. Scholes and Marie V. Scholes, *The Foreign Policies of the Taft Administration* (Columbia, Mo. 1970), pp. 9-12; John P. Campbell, "Taft, Roosevelt, and the Arbitration Treaties of 1911," *Journal of American History* 53 (Sept., 1966):279-98; and Paolo E. Coletta, *The Presidency of William Howard Taft* (Lawrence, Kans., 1973), pp. 168-73.

10 *S-R*, Mar. 17, 1911; and P. Edward Haley, *The Diplomacy of Taft and Wilson With Mexico, 1910-1917* (Cambridge, 1970), pp. 11-73.
11 U.S. Congress, Senate, *Congressional Record* 49, 62d Cong., 3rd sess., 1913, 4261; and MP to R. D. Walsh, Apr. 1, 1913.
12 MP to R. D. Walsh, Apr. 1, 1913; and William H. Harbaugh, *Power and Responsibility*, (New York, 1961), pp. 100-101, 288, and 372.
13 A. Link, *Wilson: The New Freedom*, (Princeton, 1956), pp. 346-416; and P. E. Haley, *The Diplomacy of Taft and Wilson With Mexico*, pp. 77-151.
14 MP to L. N. Shanks, Mar. 5, 1914; MP to *Boston Journal*, Mar. 10, 1914; MP to N. A. Medley, Apr. 7, 1914. See also MP to E. C. Sickels, Apr. 14, 1914.
15 U.S. Congress, Senate, *Congressional Record* 51, 63rd Cong., 2d sess., 1913, 6964, 7004-5.
16 Ibid., pp. 7006-8.
17 *Congressional Record* 51:7006-8 and 7014; C. B. Kegley to MP, Apr. 16, 1914; and MP to C. B. Kegley, Apr. 22, 1914. Note Poindexter's insistence upon referring to the Mexican Resolution as a "War Resolution."
18 B. J. Bernstein and F. A. Leib, "Progressive Republican Senators and American Imperialism, 1898-1916: A Reappraisal," pp. 163-205; and John Milton Cooper, Jr., "Progressivism and American Foreign Policy: A Reconsideration," pp. 261-77. Generalizations concerning the Senate voting record on foreign policy matters are based upon Howard W. Allen, "Republican Reformers and Foreign Policy, 1913-1917," *Mid-America* 44 (Oct. 1962):222-29 and J. M. Clubb and H. W. Allen, "Party Loyalty in the Progressive Years: The Senate, 1909-1915," *Journal of Politics* 29 (Aug. 1967):567-84. See also Walter I. Trattner, "Progressivism and World War I: A Reappraisal," *Mid-America* 44 (July 1962):131-45; Walter A. Sutton, "Progressive Republican Senators and the Submarine Crisis, 1915-1916," *Mid-America* 47 (Apr. 1965):75-88; and John Milton Cooper, Jr., *The Vanity of Power. American Isolationism and the First World War, 1914-1917* (Westport, Conn., 1969), pp. 220-40. Most of the studies of the attitudes of progressives on foreign policy seem to have been stimulated by an influential article by William E. Leuchtenburg who argued that most progressive Republicans supported an imperialistic and aggressive foreign policy; but as Joseph M. Siracusa concluded, more recent scholarship has "shattered" Leuchtenburg's thesis. William E. Leuchtenburg, "Progressivism and Imperialism: The Progressive Movement and Foreign Policy,

1898-1916," *Mississippi Valley Historical Review* 39 (Dec. 1952):483-504 and Joseph M. Siracusa, "Progressivism, Imperialism, and the Leuchtenburg Thesis, 1952-1974: An Historiographical Appraisal," *Australian Journal of Politics and History* 20 (Dec. 1974): 312-25. For a recent effort to defend Leuchtenburg's thesis, see Gerald E. Markowitz, "Progressivism and Imperialism: A Return to First Principles," *Historian* 37 (Feb. 1975):257-75.

19 See, for example, T. Roosevelt to H. C. Lodge, Dec. 8, 1914 in Elting E. Morison *Letters of Theodore Roosevelt*, 8:861-63; and T. Roosevelt to K. Roosevelt, Aug. 28, 1915, *Letters*, 8:962-64; and W. H. Harbaugh, *Power and Responsibility*, pp. 465, 473, 479.

20 T. Roosevelt to A. H. Lee, Aug. 14, 1912, *The Letters of Theodore Roosevelt*, 7:597; and T. Roosevelt to C. A. Spring-Rice, Dec. 31, 1912, *Letters* 7:680.

21 Quoted in A. Link, *Wilson: The New Freedom*, p. 310. See also William S. Coker, "The Panama Canal Tolls Controversy: A Different Perspective," *Journal of American History* 55 (Dec. 1968):555-64.

22 See copy of the Seattle Chamber's resolution, dated Jan. 14, 1913 in Poindexter MSS. J. W. McCune to MP, Jan. 20, 1913; Raymond, Washington Commercial Club to MP, Jan. 8, 1913; and *P-I*, Mar. 7, Mar. 9, Mar. 10, and Mar. 11, 1914. For further discussion of the significance of the tolls exemption upon freight rates to the Pacific Coast see D. Smart, "Spokane's Battle for Freight Rates," *Pacific Northwest Quarterly* 45 (Jan. 1954):26.

23 MP to M. Phillips, Mar. 8, 1913. See also MP to C. B. Yandell, Apr. 18, 1913.

24 *Congressional Record* 51:6322-27; and *New York Times*, Apr. 8, 1914.

25 *Chicago Tribune*, Mar. 9, Mar. 11, Apr. 27, and Apr. 28, 1914.

26 *Congressional Record* 51:10158, 10162, 10210, 10225, 10228, 10246, and 10247.

27 Arthur S. Link, *Wilson: The Struggle for Neutrality, 1914-1915* (Princeton, 1960), pp. 1-56 (the quotation is on page 52); W. H. Harbaugh, *Power and Responsibility*, 466-71; and T. Roosevelt to S. Cooley, Dec. 2, 1914, *Letters of Theodore Roosevelt*, 8:852-55.

28 MP to A. W. Doland, May 12, 1913; MP to G. Hinrichs, Oct. 6, 1914; MP to R. Moran, Oct. 19, 1914; and MP to G. Poindexter, Mar. 19, 1915.

29 E. Root to W. H. Taft, Jan. 16, 1915, Root MSS.; W. Borah to W. Van Irons, Feb. 10, 1915, Borah MSS.

30 U.S. Congress, Senate, *Congressional Record* 52, 63rd Cong., 3rd sess., 1914, 46. See also MP to L. A.

Vincent, Jan. 16, 1915; MP to A. Jamieson, Jan. 21, 1915; and MP to A. H. Curtis, Jan. 23, 1915.
31 *New York Times*, Jan. 24, 1915 and Mar. 4, 1915; and T. Roosevelt to MP, Jan. 24, 1915.
32 MP to T. Roosevelt, Jan. 26, 1915; and T. Roosevelt to MP, Jan. 27, 1915.
33 T. Roosevelt to MP, Jan. 30, 1915; MP to E. E. Elemdorf, Feb. 2, 1915; MP to T. Roosevelt, Feb. 2, 1915; and *Congressional Record* 52:2588-92, 2786, and 2787.
34 *New York Times*, June 10, 1915.
35 U.S. Congress, Senate, *Congressional Record* 53, 64th Cong., 1st sess., 1915, 3465. C. C. Tansill, *America Goes to War* (Boston, 1938), pp. 465-78; and Monroe L. Billington, *Thomas P. Gore: The Blind Senator from Oklahoma* (Lawrence, Kans., 1967), pp. 69-77.
36 *Congressional Record* 53:3465. See also H. W. Allen, "Republican Reformers and Foreign Policy," pp. 222-29. J. M. Siracusa found this analysis of the Gore resolution "meaningless"; see his "Progressivism, Imperialism, and the Leuchtenburg Thesis, 1952-1974: An Historiographical Appraisal," p. 319. Of course the precise meaning of the vote on the Gore resolution was unclear, but, given the context of the debate, it still seems reasonable to consider the Gore resolution (no matter what its actual wording at the moment of the vote) as a gesture of protest against Wilson's policy which some feared would involve the United States in an unnecessary war. The central point, however, was that the progressive Republicans did not respond to this foreign policy issue as a bloc. See J. M. Cooper, Jr., "Progressivism and American Foreign Policy: A Reconsideration," pp. 271-72.
37 Arthur Link, *Wilson: Confusions and Crises, 1915-1916* (Princeton, 1964), pp. 15-54.
38 W. Borah to O. G. Villard, Nov. 20, 1915, Borah MSS. See also Borah's letter to W. H. Cowles, editor of the *Spokane Spokesman-Review*, Nov. 2, 1915, Borah MSS. J. D. Works to H. M. Lee, Feb. 7, 1917, Works MSS.
39 MP to H. B. Joyce, Jan. 4, 1915.
40 MP to L. H. Wells, Dec. 20, 1915. See also MP to E. F. C. VanDissel, Jan. 1, and Jan. 6, 1916.
41 Harold H. and Margaret Sprout, *The Rise of American Naval Power, 1776-1918* (Princeton, 1939), p. 340.
42 *Congressional Record* 53:6198, 6345, 6359(a), 6359(b), 6368, 6371, 6372, 6374, 11192, 11367, 11372-73, 11373(a), 11373(b), 11375, 11378, 11379, and 11384, 11483, 11564; and H. W. Allen, "Republican Reformers and Foreign Policy, 1913-1917," p. 226. J. M. Cooper, Jr. reached similar conclusions, "Progressivism and

296 Notes to pages 139-145

43 American Foreign Policy: A Reappraisal," pp. 270-73.
    Typed statement for *New York American*, June 11, 1915. For a general discussion of the relationship between Social Darwinism and foreign policy see R. Hofstadter, *Social Darwinism*, pp. 146-73.
44 Typed statement entitled "The Army," dated 1916 in Poindexter MSS.
45 Statement prepared for the *New York American*, dated June 11, 1915; and MP to H. J. Sessel, Dec. 11, 1915.
46 *Congressional Record* 53:1154; MP to P. S. Darlington, Mar. 16, 1916.
47 Compare Poindexter's statements with W. H. Harbaugh's description of Roosevelt's views in *Power and Responsibility*, p. 99.
48 T. Roosevelt to B. M. Cutting, Aug. 8, 1914, *Letters of Theodore Roosevelt*, 8:1097.

7. Return to the Republican Party

1 U.S. Congress, Senate, *Congressional Record* 53, 64th Cong., 1st sess., 1915, 955.
2 MP to W. W. Seymour, Mar. 30, 1916. See also MP to J. G. Byrne, Mar. 14, 1916 and A. H. Espy, Mar. 23, 1916.
3 MP to R. R. Turner, Dec. 12, 1913.
4 *Congressional Record* 53:1142-58.
5 The list of progressive Republicans is from Howard W. Allen, "Geography and Politics," *Journal of Southern History* 27 (May 1961):216-28. The votes included are listed in appendix 3, page 608 in Howard W. Allen, "Miles Poindexter: A Political Biography" (Ph.D. diss., University of Washington, 1959). The progressive Republicans divided as follows (the first number indicates the number of votes cast for, and the second the number of votes against, Philippine independence):

For Independence		Against Independence	
Borah	(4-0)	Cummins	(1-5)
Clapp	(4-1)	Gronna	(1-5)
Kenyon	(6-0)	Jones	(1-5)
LaFollette	(6-0)	Nelson	(0-6)
Norris	(5-1)	Poindexter	(0-6)
Works	(4-2)	Sterling	(0-6)

6 W. E. Borah to J. H. Gipson, Feb. 24, 1916, Borah MSS.
7 George Mowry, *The Era of Theodore Roosevelt, 1900-1912*, (New York, 1958), pp. 186-89; and Robert C. Nesbit, "*He Built Seattle*" (Seattle, 1961), pp. 166-212.

8 MP to A. E. Yoell, Oct. 30, 1909; MP to W. B. Hale, Feb. 2, 1910. See also MP to C. P. Taylor, Feb. 25, 1910; and Richard Hofstadter, *Social Darwinism in American Thought, 1860-1915* (Philadelphia, 1945), pp. 163-66.
9 MP to A. D. Burrow, May 14, 1913; and MP to F. O. Smith, Mar. 16, 1914.
10 *Congressional Record* 53:11792.
11 U.S. Congress, Senate, *Congressional Record* 54, 64th Cong., 2d sess., 1917, 262-63.
12 For a list of the Republican supporters of reform, see H. W. Allen, "Geography and Politics," pp. 216-28. The votes on immigration restriction are found in U.S. Congress, Senate, *Congressional Record* 48, 62d Cong., 2d sess., 1912, 5023, 5032; U.S. Congress, Senate, *Congressional Record* 49, 62d Cong., 3rd sess., 1913, 3268, 3318; U.S. Congress, Senate, *Congressional Record* 52, 63rd Cong., 3rd sess., 1914, 85, 223, 787, 788(a), 788(b), 803, 805, 807(a), 807(b), 812, 847, 866, 868; *Congressional Record* 53: 12816, 12817; *Congressional Record* 54:208, 209, 210, 265, 315, 316, 997, 2629. For a description and indication how each vote was evaluated, see H. W. Allen, "Miles Poindexter," app. 4, pp. 609-12. On the twenty-seven votes, the progressive Republicans voted as follows (the first number indicates the number of votes cast for, the second the number of votes cast against, immigration restriction):

For Restriction

Borah	15-8	Works	16-7
Bristow	8-1	Gronna	13-11
Crawford	19-8	Nelson	15-10
Cummins	19-8	Kenyon	11-6
Jones	22-5	LaFollette	7-5
Poindexter	17-5	Sterling	14-8

Uncertain

Clapp	12-12
Norris	8-12
Perkins	8-8
Sherman	4-6

13 Richard Hofstadter, *The Age of Reform* (New York, 1956), p. 180. The response of progressive Republicans, and the Democrats as well, to the problems of blacks and other minorities was at best unsympathetic. H. W. Allen, A. R. Clausen, and J. M. Clubb, "Political Reform and Negro Rights in the Senate, 1909-1915," *Journal of Southern History* 37 (May 1971):191-212.

14 *Congressional Record* 53:2629.
15 MP to C. B. Kegley, Feb. 4, 1912; MP to A. M. Brandt, Oct. 8, 1913; MP to L. C. Crow, Jan. 21, 1914; and U.S. Congress, Senate, *Congressional Record* 51, 63rd Cong., 2d sess., 1913, 9931.
16 R. L. Rutter to MP, July 9, 1914; MP to R. L. Rutter, July 18, 1914; C. Malett to MP, Feb. 29, 1916; MP to C. Malett, Mar. 14, 1916; *Congressional Record* 53:224.
17 *Congressional Record* 53:7412.
18 MP to J. D. Works, Apr. 24, 1915; and MP to R. Woods, Dec. 14, 1914.
19 MP to B. C. McCormick, Dec. 14, 1914.
20 MP to R. L. Rutter, Dec. 28, 1914.
21 Clipping from *Walla Walla Union*, dated Jan., 1915; W. H. Hagen to MP, Jan. 19, 1915; and MP to W. H. Hagen, Jan. 25, 1915.
22 MP to G. Perkins, Apr. 8, and Apr. 28, 1915; *P-I*, Apr. 18, 1915; and *New York Times*, Apr. 18, 1915.
23 See typed statement dated Aug. 11, 1915 in Poindexter MSS.
24 T. Roosevelt to D. B. Heard, July 3, 1916; Elting E. Morison, ed., *Letters of Theodore Roosevelt*, 8 vols. (Cambridge, 1954), 8:1083-85. Bella C. and Fola LaFollette, *Robert M. LaFollette*, 2 vols. (New York, 1953), 1:551-52; G. Mowry, *Theodore Roosevelt and the Progressive Movement* (Madison, 1947), pp. 320-21; and Walter I. Trattner, "Progressivism and World War I," *Mid-America* 44 (July 1962):131-39. Roosevelt's quotation is in G. Mowry, *Theodore Roosevelt and the Progressive Movement*, p. 321.
25 U.S. Congress, *Congressional Directory*, 64th Cong., 1st sess., 1915, 137 and 176; H. C. Lodge to MP, Dec. 6 and Dec. 9, 1915; and MP to H. C. Lodge, Dec. 9, 1915.
26 U.S. Congress, *Biographical Directory of the American Congress*, p. 1095; W. L. Jones to E. P. Piper, Jan. 25, 1916; W. L. Jones to E. A. Bryan, Mar. 23, 1916, Jones MSS; and Edgar I. Stewart, *Washington*, 4 vols. (New York, 1957), 2:175.
27 *P-I*, May 23, 1915.
28 Henry Pringle, *The Life and Times of William Howard Taft*, 2 vols. (New York, 1939) 2:884; T. Roosevelt to W. A. White, Jan. 1, 1917, *Letters of Theodore Roosevelt*, 8:1135-37; John A. Garraty, *Henry Cabot Lodge* (New York, 1953), pp. 323-24; W. Borah to M. Austin, Apr. 24, 1916, Borah MSS; Merlo J. Pusey, *Charles Evans Hughes*, 2 vols. (New York, 1951), 1:140-334; and MP to R. A. Hiller, Mar. 2, 1916. See also John A. Gable, *The Bull Moose Years* (Port Washington, N.Y., 1978), pp. 229-52.

Notes to pages 155-161   299

29 Unsigned letter from Poindexter's office to I. Harrington (secretary to Senator Jones), May 22, 1916.
30 Amos Pinchot, *History of the Progressive Party, 1912-1916*, ed., Helene M. Hooker (New York, 1958), pp. 220, 352-54.
31 George E. Mowry, *The California Progressives* (Berkeley, 1951), p. 241; Walter Johnson, *William Allen White's America* (New York, 1947), p. 264; MP to E. Young, June 12, 1916; and MP to O. C. Moore, June 22, 1916.
32 MP to C. R. Stangeland, June 15, 1915; and MP to W. J. Biggar, June 19, 1916.
33 G. Dilling to MP, June 16, 1916.
34 W. L. Jones to M. T. Hartson, June 21, 1916; M. T. Hartson to W. L. Jones, June 16, June 27, and July 11, 1916, Jones MSS.
35 *Congressional Record* 53:13650; and *S-R*, Aug. 9, 1916.
36 *S-R*, Aug. 3, Aug. 14, and Aug. 15, 1916.
37 M. Pusey, *Hughes* 1:341-62. In Washington, in contrast, the question of who was to ride on Hughes's train was settled by having no Republicans from Washington on board. M. T. Hartson explained the solution to Jones in this way: "Poindexter rather expected to travel with Hughes, and it might have been a good plan to have had this invitation extended, but no one seemed to be invited, not even the state chairman, which, of course, did not hurt the matter at all." M. T. Hartson to W. L. Jones, Aug. 18, 1916, Jones MSS.
38 George Mowry concluded, "As for California, it seems probable that Charles Evans Hughes lost the state not because of Hiram Johnson, but in general because of Charles Evans Hughes." G. Mowry, *California Progressives*, p. 277. Theodore Roosevelt was of the same opinion. See his letter to H. Johnson, Feb. 17, 1917, *Letters of Theodore Roosevelt* 8:1153-56. For contrary interpretations, see M. Pusey, *Hughes*, 1: 362, and J. D. Works to C. Curtis, Sept. 18, 1916, Works MSS.
39 M. T. Hartson to W. L. Jones, Aug. 18, 1916, Jones MSS.
40 *S-R*, Aug. 18, 1916; and MP to T. J. Smith, July 26, 1916.
41 MP to A. Hurwitz, May 25, 1916.
42 *P-I*, Aug. 18, Aug. 29, Aug. 30, Aug. 31, and Sept. 1, 1916; and *S-R*, Aug. 29, 1916.
43 *P-I*, Aug. 23, 1916.
44 *S-R*, Sept. 11, 1916.
45 Secretary of State, "Abstract of Votes Polled in the State of Washington at the Primary Election Held September 12, 1916," Olympia, Wash. The vote for

Poindexter in the 1916 primary correlated with his county vote in 1910 at .44, and with the total vote for Bryan in 1896 at .25.
46 *S-R*, Sept. 15, 1916.
47 *S-R*, Oct. 28, 1916; and *P-I*, Oct. 28, 1916.
48 S. A. Perkins to C. P. Lund, Sept. 26, 1916; and *S-R*, Sept. 28, 1916.
49 *S-R*, Oct. 3, 1916.
50 Congressional Quarterly, *Guide to U. S. Elections*, pp. 285 and 507. Wilson's vote in 1916 correlated with the Bryan vote in 1896 at .55, with the Democratic vote for governor in 1904 at .57, and with Poindexter's vote in the Republican primaries of 1910 and 1916 at .65 and .40 respectively.
51 The county vote cast for Poindexter correlated with the vote for Taft in 1908 at .69, and with the Poindexter vote in the 1916 Republican primary at .02.
52 MP to T. R. McAnally, Dec. 13, 1916; and MP to J. H. Chase, Nov. 21, 1916.
53 H. W. Allen, "Geography and Politics," pp. 216-28; J. M. Clubb, "Congressional Opponents of Reform, 1901-1913" (Ph.D. diss., University of Washington, 1963), pp. 34-36, 87-93, 180-92, 279-80; Samuel P. Hays, *The Response to Industrialism, 1885-1914* (Chicago, 1957), p. 116; J. M. Clubb and H. W. Allen, "Party Loyalty in the Progressive Years, The Senate, 1909-1915," *Journal of Politics* 29 (Aug. 1967):567-84; and "Progressive Reform and the Political System," *Pacific Northwest Quarterly* 65 (July 1974): 130-45.
54 Eric F. Goldman, *Rendezvous with Destiny* (New York, 1952), p. x.
55 Richard Hofstadter, *The Age of Reform* (New York, 1956), p. 236.
56 MP to W. H. Kaufman, Sept. 21, 1909; MP to E. T. Tannatt, May 23, 1913; MP to F. F. Zapp, Sept. 4, 1913; MP to J. W. Collins, Mar. 19, 1914; typed statement in Poindexter MSS; and *S-R*, Sept. 1, 1910.
57 U.S. Congress, Senate, *Congressional Record* 47, 67th Cong., 1st sess., 1911, 1641; MP to W. H. Kaufman, Sept. 21, 1909; MP to E. Howerift, Apr. 24, 1911; MP to E. H. Gosse, Mar. 5, 1912; MP to W. F. Johnson, Sept. 5, 1912; and MP to J. Grant, Aug. 29, 1913.
58 MP to R. A. Dague, Aug. 30, 1913; MP to A. J. Young, Jan. 30, 1915; MP to J. Grant, Aug. 29, 1913; and U.S. Congress, Senate, *Congressional Record* 50, 63rd Cong., 1st sess., 1913, 3829.
59 William E. Leuchtenburg, "Progressivism and Imperialism," *Mississippi Valley Historical Review* 39 (Dec. 1952):483-504; and R. Hofstadter, *The Age of Reform*, p. 272.

60 T. Roosevelt to H. Johnson, Sept. 28, 1916, *Letters of Theodore Roosevelt*, 8:1119.
61 John M. Blum, *The Republican Roosevelt* (New York, 1972). The quotation is on page 108, but see 106-24. See also John Milton Cooper, Jr., "Progressivism and American Foreign Policy: A Reconsideration," *Mid-America* 51 (Oct. 1969):261-62.
62 Henry Pringle, *Theodore Roosevelt* (New York, 1931), p. 368.

8. World War I: Disruption of the Progressive Coalition

1 H. C. Lodge to MP, Mar. 7, 1917; and U.S. Congress, *Congressional Directory* 55, 65th Cong., 1st sess., 1917, 179.
2 Arthur Link, *Wilson. Campaigns for Progressivism and Peace, 1916-1917* (Princeton, 1965), pp. 220-301.
3 MP to H. B. Brougham, Mar. 21, 1917; U.S. Congress, Senate, *Congressional Record* 54, 64th Cong., 2d sess., 1917, 4720, 4744, 4764-68, 5013. See Howard W. Allen, "Republican Reformers and Foreign Policy, 1913-1917," *Mid-America* 44 (Oct. 1962):222-29.
4 U.S. Congress, Senate, *Congressional Record* 55, 65th Cong., 1st sess., 1917, 261; and MP to J. Sparling, Apr. 12, 1917. See also MP to B. Everett, Apr. 13, 1917.
5 For a discussion of Roosevelt's wartime role see William H. Harbaugh, *Power and Responsibility* (New York, 1961), pp. 498-522.
6 Seward W. Livermore, *Politics Is Adjourned: Woodrow Wilson and the War Congress, 1916-1918* (Middletown, Conn., 1966), pp. 4-5.
7 MP to Mr. and Mrs. A. E. House, July 27, 1917; MP to T. T. Scheips, Apr. 7, 1917; and MP to F. X. Denty, Sept. 27, 1917.
8 *New York Times*, Apr. 14, 1917. The *Times* referred to an amendment to the Senate bill which Poindexter submitted Apr. 10, 1917. See *Congressional Record* 55: 523. MP to J. A. Ford, Apr. 16, 1917; MP to S. L. Lemmon, July 5, 1917; and Donald O. Johnson, *The Challenge to American Freedoms. World War I and the Rise of the American Civil Liberties Union* (Lexington, 1963), pp. 55-63.
9 *Congressional Record* 55:877; H. Johnson to C. K. McClatchy, Apr. 21, 1917, in Hiram Johnson Papers, Bancroft Library, University of California, Berkeley; and W. E. Borah to H. Freidburg, Apr. 24, 1917, Borah MSS. See also W. E. Borah to G. Trumball, May 7, 1917, Borah MSS.

10 *Congressional Record* 55:2117, 2269-70. They were Borah, Gronna, LaFollette, and Sherman of Illinois.
11 MP to J. A. Baldwin, Jan. 5, 1917; MP to F. C. Kaylor, Dec. 8, 1916; MP to A. F. Ruebenak, Dec. 8, 1916; MP to E. E. Kidder, Dec. 9, 1916; MP to W. Wilson, Jan. 29, 1917; and Norman H. Clark, "Everett, 1916 and After," *Pacific Northwest Quarterly* 57 (Apr. 1966):57-64.
12 MP to A. E. Griffiths, July 17, 1917.
13 MP to L. A. Vincent, July 21, 1917; and *Congressional Record* 55:5949-50.
14 MP to J. P. Hartman, Feb. 18, 1918.
15 U.S. Congress, Senate, *Congressional Record* 56, 65th Cong., 2d sess., 1918, 4359; and *New York Times*, Apr. 3, 1918.
16 *New York Times*, Apr. 3, 1918; and D. O. Johnson, *The Challenge to American Freedoms*, pp. 68-73.
17 *Congressional Record* 56:4631.
18 Ibid., pp. 4826 and 6057.
19 MP to A. E. Galleger, Apr. 9, 1918.
20 *Nation* 106 (May 1, 1918):558; and H. Johnson to C. K. McClatchy, May 8, 1918, Johnson MSS.
21 *Congressional Record* 56:5395-97; Robert K. Murray, *The Red Scare* (Minneapolis, 1955), pp. 114-15; Robert L. and Robin Friedham, "The Seattle Labor Movement, 1919-20," *Pacific Northwest Quarterly* 55 (Oct. 1964):146-56; and Richard H. Frost, *The Mooney Case* (Stanford, 1968), especially 312-13.
22 *Congressional Record* 56:5395-5401.
23 R. K. Murray, *The Red Scare*, pp. 57-61, dates the beginning of the Red Scare with the Seattle General Strike of January and February 1919, over six months after Poindexter's speech.
24 *New York Times*, Apr. 23, 1918; *Seattle Times*, Apr. 23, 1918; "At the Capitol," *New Republic* 15 (May 24, 1918):24; *P-I*, Apr. 23, 1918; and *Seattle Times*, Apr. 30, 1918.
25 MP to T. W. Gregory, Jan. 29 and Jan. 30, 1918.
26 *Congressional Record* 56:4063.
27 MP to C. S. Beer, Apr. 24, 1918; MP to O. E. Beebe, June 1, 1918; T. Roosevelt to H. O. Green, Dec. 12, 1917, T. Roosevelt to J. Bryce, May 22, 1918; and T. Roosevelt to H. Kahn, Oct. 28, 1918, Roosevelt MSS.
28 MP to H. Higday, Apr. 19, 1917; *Congressional Record* 55:6242(a), 6242(b), 6288, 6326, 6732, and 6740. See S. Livermore, *Politics Is Adjourned*, pp. 57-61.
29 *Congressional Record* 55:6503, 6542, 6549, 6560, 6561, 6570, 6620, 6854, and 6879.
30 Ibid., pp. 6492-94; and T. Roosevelt to H. Johnson, Aug. 28, 1917, Johnson MSS.

31 *Congressional Record* 55:6607-9. The list of progressive Republicans used in this analysis is in Howard W. Allen, "Geography and Politics," *Journal of Southern History* 27 (May 1961):216-28. Senator Johnson, Progressive party candidate for vice-president in 1912, is also included. They divided as follows (the first number indicates a vote for the war profits tax, the second number a vote against it):

For The War Profits Tax		Against The War Profits Tax	
Borah	8-1	Curtis	0-9
Brady	7-0	Fall	0-8
Gronna	9-0	Nelson	0-8
Johnson	9-0	Poindexter	0-9
Jones	9-0	Sherman	0-9
Kenyon	9-0	Sterling	0-9
LaFollette	9-0		
Norris	8-0		

32 MP to E. L. Kniskern, Aug. 11, 1917; and *Congressional Record* 55:2118.
33 S. Livermore, *Politics Is Adjourned*, pp. 79-104.
34 *Congressional Record* 56:386 and 5766; and MP to P. J. Drake, Feb. 16, 1918.
35 MP to P. J. Drake, Feb. 16, 1918.
36 *New York Times*, Mar. 27, 1918.
37 *Congressional Record* 56:4059-60.
38 Ibid., pp. 4061-63.
39 *Nation* 106 (Apr. 4, 1918):386; and "The Republican Plight," *Nation* 107 (July 6, 1918):2766.
40 *Congressional Record* 56:1081-83; and "Treason Stalking Abroad," *Nation* 106 (Jan. 24, 1918):80.
41 *New York Times*, Apr. 21, 1918.
42 T. Roosevelt to MP, May 22, 1918, Elting E. Morrison, ed., *Letters of Theodore Roosevelt*, 8 vols. (Cambridge, 1954), 8:1320-35.
43 MP to O. E. Beebe, June 1, 1918.
44 Miles Poindexter, "Your Right to Speak Freely: A Discussion of the Fundamental Rights of Loyal Americans," *Forum* 60 (Dec. 1918):670-76.
45 Robert E. Osgood, *Ideals and Self-Interest in American Foreign Relations* (Chicago, 1953), pp. 266-77; and Arthur S. Link, *Woodrow Wilson: Revolution, War, and Peace* (Arlington Heights, Ill., 1979), pp. 72-103.
46 *Congressional Record* 55:1499 and 5476; and MP to E. L. Kniskern, Aug. 11, 1917. See also MP to C. F. R. Bannister, May 24, 1917.
47 Henry Cabot Lodge, ed., *Selections From the Correspondence of Theodore Roosevelt and Henry Cabot Lodge*,

304   Notes to pages 193-201

1884-1918, 2 vols. (New York, 1925), 2:539-40.
48 *Congressional Record* 56:11155-57 and 11174, 11402; *New York Times*, Oct. 8, Oct. 11, Oct. 22, 1918; S. W. Livermore, *Politics Is Adjourned*, pp. 213-17; and Thomas A. Bailey, *Woodrow Wilson and the Lost Peace* (New York, 1944), p. 39.
49 T. Roosevelt to S. P. Spencer, Oct. 15, 1918, *Letters of Theodore Roosevelt*, 8:1374.
50 MP to C. C. Brower, Jan. 30, 1919.
51 T. Roosevelt to Will Hays, Oct. 16, 1918, *Letters of Theodore Roosevelt*, 8:1375-76; and T. Roosevelt's telegram to Lodge, Oct. 24, 1918, *Letters*, 8:1380-81.
52 *Congressional Record* 56:11497-502. See S. W. Livermore, *Politics Is Adjourned*, pp. 206-23.
53 W. H. Hays to MP, May 27, 1918.
54 C. B. Slemp to MP, Oct. 8 and Oct. 29, 1918; and W. Jones to MP, Oct. 22, 1918.
55 Secretary of State, "Abstract of Votes Polled in the State of Washington at the General Election Held November 6, 1918." Olympia, Wash.; and Congressional Quarterly, *Guide to U. S. Elections*, p. 740.
56 MP to J. L. Aldwell, Nov. 15, 1918; and Otis L. Graham, Jr., *The Great Campaigns. Reform and War in America, 1900-1928* (Englewood Cliffs, N.J., 1971), p. 103.
57 MP to E. L. Kniskern, Aug. 11, 1917. The method of determining positions of senators on the LaFollette filibuster and preparedness are explained in H. W. Allen, "Republican Reformers and Foreign Policy," pp. 222-29; the positions on the war profits tax are described above. The votes used as an indication of opinion on the other war measures are as follows: 1) LaFollette amendment to draft act (to provide for a national referendum on the draft), *Congressional Record* 55:1624; 2) Draft Act, 55:2457; 3) Espionage Act, 55:2270; 4) France amendment (to guarantee the right to publish or speak the truth) to Sedition Act, 56:4826; 5) Sedition Act, 56:6057; and 6) declaration of war, 55:261.

9. The Struggle Against Internationalism and Bolshevism

1   R. J. Bartlett, *The League to Enforce Peace* (Chapel Hill, 1944), pp. 25-47; and Ralph Stone, *The Irreconcilables: The Fight Against the League of Nations* (Lexington, 1970), pp. 1-76; and Burl Noggle, *Into the Twenties: The United States from Armistice to Normalcy* (Urbana, 1974), pp. 122-51.

2   U.S. Congress, Senate, *Congressional Record* 56, 65th Cong., 2d sess., 1918, 11564.
3   MP to T. H. Brewer, Dec. 9, 1918; MP to T. J. Murray, Nov. 25, 1918; and MP to W. H. Cowles, Jan. 10, 1919.
4   T. Roosevelt to A. J. Beveridge, Oct. 16, 1918; H. C. Lodge to A. J. Beveridge, Dec. 3, 1918, Beveridge MSS; and T. Roosevelt to MP, Nov. 16, 1918, Elting E. Morison, ed., *Letters of Theodore Roosevelt*, 8 vols. (Cambridge, 1954), 8:1395-96.
5   U.S. Congress, Senate, *Congressional Record* 57, 65th Cong., 3rd sess., 1919, 3746-56; *New York Times*, Feb. 20 and 21, 1919; and *Chicago Tribune*, Feb. 20, 1919.
6   Quoted in Henry Pringle, *The Life and Times of William Howard Taft*, 2 vols. (New York, 1939), 2: 943; "Borah, The Fable-maker," *New Republic* 18 (Mar. 1, 1919):129-32; and ibid. 18 (Mar. 8, 1919):162-63. See also ibid. 18 (Mar. 22, 1919):229; and *New York Times*, Apr. 2, 1919.
7   John A. Garraty, *Henry Cabot Lodge* (New York, 1953), p. 363; W. Stull Holt, *Treaties Defeated by the Senate* (Baltimore, 1933), pp. 277-78; and R. Stone, *The Irreconcilables*, pp. 90-99.
8   R. Stone, *The Irreconcilables*, pp. 1 and 183-88.
9   Ibid., pp. 128-70; and W. S. Holt, *Treaties Defeated by the Senate*, pp. 292-302. On the Lodge (Republican) resolution to ratify the treaty, there were three votes in November, 1919; Poindexter voted nay on all three. On the Underwood (Democratic) resolution, there was one vote; again Poindexter voted nay. U.S. Congress, Senate, *Congressional Record* 58, 66th Cong., 1st sess., 1919, 8786, 8802, 8803. On the motion to ratify the treaty in March 1920, Poindexter did not vote. U.S. Congress, Senate, *Congressional Record* 59, 66th Cong., 2d sess., 1919, 4599.
10 MP to C. Glass, Sept. 4, 1919.
11 *Congressional Record* 57:3746-56. David A. Shannon, *The Socialist Party of America* (New York, 1955), pp. 143-49; Melvyn Dubofsky, *We Shall Be All* (Chicago, 1969), pp. 349-468. See also B. Noggle, *Into the Twenties*, pp. 84-121; and Robert K. Murray, *Red Scare* (Minneapolis, 1955).
12 Robert L. Friedheim, *The Seattle General Strike* (Seattle, 1964), especially 123-45; and Robert and Robin Friedheim, "The Seattle Labor Movement," *Pacific Northwest Quarterly* 55 (Oct. 1964):146-56.
13 MP to W. Carlisle, Jan. 26, 1919; and *Congressional Record* 57:2654 and 2730.
14 A. Polson to MP, Feb. 1, 1919; MP to A. Polson, Jan. 7, 1919; and Allen M. Wakstein, "The Origins of the Open Shop Movement, 1919-1920," *Journal of American*

15 MP to E. Constantine, Feb. 8, 1919.
16 Stanley Coben, *A. Mitchell Palmer: Politician* (New York, 1963), pp. 155-70.
17 *Congressional Record* 58:331-32. Because Poindexter made so much of Wilson's speech of January 8, it should be pointed out that only with a considerable stretch of imagination could one find "Bolshevistic" sentiments in it. Wilson spoke in general terms about the "Russian people." Referring to them and to the Russian delegates (who were Bolshevists) at Brest-Litovsk, he said, "Their conception of what is right, of what is humane and honorable for them to accept, has been stated with a frankness, a largeness of view, a generosity of spirit, and a universal human sympathy which must challenge the admiration of every friend of mankind." *Congressional Record* 56:680.
18 MP to F. W. Strong, Sept. 26, 1919.
19 *Congressional Record* 58:6865-69.
20 *New York Times*, Oct. 15 and Oct. 18, 1919; and *Congressional Record* 58:7063.
21 MP to J. N. Donovan, Nov. 11, 1919; S. Coben, *A. Mitchell Palmer*, pp. 219-21; and D. C. Johnson, *The Challenge to American Freedoms* (Lexington, 1963), pp. 136-38.
22 *New York Times*, Nov. 16 and Nov. 23, 1919; and *Congressional Record* 58:8616-17.
23 S. Coben, *A. Mitchell Palmer*, pp. 196-214; and R. K. Murray, *Red Scare*, pp. 190-92. The *New York Times Index*, 1919, no. 3, 265-66 and no. 4, 280-81 cited Palmer's name during July, August, and September seventy-one times, but only one of those described in the *Index* was related to radicals or aliens.
24 *New York Times*, Apr. 1, Apr. 12, June 4, and June 18, 1919; *New Republic* 18 (Apr. 5, 1919):289; *Nation* 108 (Apr. 5, 1919):487 and (June 14, 1919):927. Palmer was not quite as moderate as the *Nation* believed, however, for on June 14 Josephus Daniels, Secretary of the Navy, recorded in his diary that in a cabinet meeting Palmer indicated a need for a new alien and sedition act to "make it possible to reach radical socialists who did not resort to force." Josephus Daniels, Diary, June 10, 1919, Library of Congress, Washington, D.C. See also Palmer's defense against charges that he was slow to act against radicals, "The Case Against the Reds," *Forum* 63 (Feb. 1920):173-85.
25 K. Austin Kerr, *American Railroad Politics, 1914-1920, Rates, Wages, and Efficiency* (Pittsburgh, 1968), pp. 128-231 and B. Noggle, *Into the Twenties*,

pp. 76-83. The total number of votes cast in the Sixty-sixth Congress was 406, and the average Republican voted with his party majority 86 percent of the time. The scores of the prewar progressives ranged from slightly above average to the lowest Republican loyalty scores:

Fall, N.M.	89%	Nelson, Minn.	81%
Curtis, Kan.	89%	Johnson, Calif.	80%
Jones, Wash.	87%	Kenyon, Iowa	77%
Poindexter, Wash.	85%	McCumber, N.D.	73%
Cummins, Iowa	85%	Gronna, N.D.	72%
Townsend, Mich.	85%	Norris, Neb.	67%
Sherman, Ill.	84%	Borah, Idaho	67%
Sterling. S.D.	82%	LaFollette, Wis.	67%

For comparison, Lodge voted with the party majority on 95 percent of the votes he cast and Warren G. Harding of Ohio, 94 percent. For a general discussion of party loyalty in this Congress see Charles M. Cannon, "A Statistical Analysis of Senate Roll Calls by Party Loyalty for the Sixty-sixth Congress and the Sixty-seventh Congress" (Master's thesis, Southern Illinois University, 1972).

26 H. Johnson to C. K. McClatchy, Apr. 15 and May 20, 1919, Johnson MSS. See David P. Thelen, *Robert M. LaFollette and the Insurgent Spirit* (Boston, 1976), pp. 158-60.

27 MP to A. W. Bond, Jan. 10, 1919; and MP to I. S. Good, Oct. 22, 1919. See also Poindexter's endorsement of continued postwar federal operation of the railroads in his remarks in 1918 during Senate consideration of the Railroad Control Act, *Congressional Record* 56:2386-90.

28 *New York Times*, Oct. 19, Oct. 26, Oct. 29, and Nov. 1, 1919; MP to J. C. Kinsler, Nov. 11, 1919; B. J. Simon to MP, Oct. 21, 1919; MP to J. Simon, Nov. 3, 1919; and K. A. Kerr, *American Railroad Politics*, pp. 147-49.

29 *Congressional Record* 59:569, and 641-60, 741-42; and MP to J. Ford, Dec. 31, 1919.

30 *Congressional Record* 59:816-17.

31 Ibid., pp. 741, 754, 755, 811, 821, 866, 890, 896, 898, 902, 951, 952 and 3349-50. Cummins did not vote twice, pages 900 and 901. He was paired with La-Follette in the vote on page 821; this vote has been included. The prewar progressive Republicans who voted with Senator Cummins and against him were (the first number indicates the number of votes cast with Cummins, the second is the number of votes cast against him):

308   Notes to pages 216-220

With Cummins		Against Cummins	
Cummins	13-0	Borah	2-5
Curtis	7-5	Gronna	1-6
Jones	7-1	LaFollette	1-9
Kenyon	6-2	Norris	2-9
Nelson	6-0		
Poindexter	10-1		
Sterling	11-2		
Sherman	4-3		
Townsend	6-1		

32 *New York Times*, Feb. 5, Feb. 24, and Feb. 29, 1920; and *Congressional Record* 59:952, 3349-50.
33 Wesley M. Bagby, *The Road to Normalcy: The Presidential Campaign and Election of 1920* (Baltimore, 1962), pp. 25-53; William T. Hutchinson, *Lowden of Illinois: The Life of Frank O. Lowden*, 2 vols. (Chicago, 1957), 2:385, 424-25; and George E. Mowry, *California Progressives* (Berkeley, 1951), pp. 285-86.
34 H. Johnson to M. Lissner, Feb. 18, 1919, H. Johnson to C. K. McClatchy, Apr. 24, 1919, and H. Johnson to J. F. Neylan, July 2, 1919, Johnson MSS.
35 W. H. Cowles to MP, Feb. 5, 1919; and MP to W. H. Cowles, Feb. 10, 1919.
36 D. T. Ham to MP, Aug. 11, 1919; R. L. Rutter to MP, June 23, 1919; J. Ford to MP, Sept. 10, 1919; H. Kimball to MP, Sept. 10, 1919.
37 J. Bourne to I. M. Arneson, Nov. 13, Nov. 21, Dec. 6, 1919, and Mar. 5, 1920; J. Bourne to T. McCusker, Nov. 13, 1919 and Mar. 5, 1920; and J. Bourne to R. Hawkins, Nov. 14, 1919, Bourne MSS; *Who's Who In America, 1920-1921* (Chicago, 1920), p. 130; and U.S. Congress, Senate Committee on Privileges and Elections, *Presidential Campaign Expenses, Hearing Before the Subcommittee Pursuant to Senate Resolution 357 Directing the Committee on Privileges and Elections to Investigate the Campaign Expenses of Various Presidential Candidates In All Political Parties*, 66th Cong., 2d sess., 2 vols., 1921, 1:77.
38 *New York Times*, Oct. 27 and Nov. 1, 1919.
39 "Senator Poindexter Who Wants To Be President," *Literary Digest* 63 (Dec. 6, 1919):74-80; and Mark Sullivan, "For Rent, A White House," *Collier's* 65 (Jan. 24, 1920):5-7, and 18. Also see William deWagsaffe, "What Poindexter Stands For," *Forum* 63 (Feb., 1920):197-204; and Jonathan Bourne, "The Times and the Man," Poindexter MSS.
40 *New York Times*, Dec. 3, 1919.
41 *Seattle Union-Record*, Apr. 22, 1920.
42 H. Rice to W. P. Edris, May 22, 1920; *New York Times*, Nov. 27, Nov. 28, Dec. 2 and Dec. 9, 1919.

43 *New York Times*, Mar. 26, 1920; and H. Rice to J. A. Desmond, Mar. 26, 1920.
44 *New York Times*, Apr. 6, and Apr. 7, 1920; and *Seattle Union-Record*, Apr. 7, 1920.
45 *P-I*, Apr. 28, 1920; MP to J. A. Desmond, Apr. 7, 1920; and see statement issued by Poindexter's headquarters, *P-I*, Apr. 22, 1920.
46 *Literary Digest* 65 (May 30, 1920):16 and 65 (June 5, 1920):24-25.
47 *P-I*, June 5, 1920.
48 Ibid., June 12, 1920; and *New York Times*, June 12, 1920. For a general discussion of the convention see Robert K. Murray, *The Harding Era. Warren G. Harding and His Administration* (Minneapolis, 1969), pp. 3-42, and W. M. Bagby, *The Road to Normalcy*, pp. 79-101.
49 Senator Calder had arranged a dinner in New York in December 1919, for Poindexter to meet and speak to a group of businessmen. See Calder to MP, Dec. 4, 1919. W. T. Hutchinson, *Lowden of Illinois* 2:461-63; and R. K. Murray, *The Harding Era*, pp. 36-44.
50 *New York Times*, June 13, 1920; and MP to J. Ford, June 22, 1920.
51 MP to H. Kimball, Jan. 29, 1920; and *New York Times*, July 14, July 20, Aug. 27 and Sept. 5, 1920; and MP to J. W. Bryan, Sept. 6, 1920.
52 Congressional Quarterly, *Guide to U. S. Elections*, p. 286; and Secretary of State, "Abstract of Votes Polled in the State of Washington at the General Election Held November 2, 1920," Olympia, Wash. See also Hamilton Cravens, "The Emergence of the Farmer-Labor Party in Washington Politics, 1919-20," *Pacific Northwest Quarterly* 57 (Oct. 1966):148-157; and James Weinstein, "Radicalism in the Midst of Normalcy," *Journal of American History* 52 (Mar. 1966): 773-90.
53 H. Cravens, "Emergence of the Farmer-Labor Party in Washington," pp. 148-57.

10. A Harding Republican

1 U.S. Congress, *Congressional Directory*, 67th Cong., 1st sess., 1921, 182-86. Poindexter voted with the majority of his party 91 percent of the time in the Sixty-seventh Congress. In this Congress Poindexter was more loyal in terms of his voting record than the average Republican senator (the average for Republican senators in this Congress was 86 percent), but actually more than half of the Senate Republicans had similar or higher party loyalty scores and only

a few Republicans had lower scores. Lodge, by comparison, voted with the Republican majority 95 percent of the time, but LaFollette only 32 percent. For aggregate statistics on this Congress see Charles M. Cannon, "A Statistical Analysis of Senate Roll Calls by Party Loyalty for the Sixty-sixth Congress and the Sixty-seventh Congress" (Master's thesis, Southern Illinois University, 1972), p. 105.

2   Robert E. Osgood, *Ideals and Self-Interest in American Foreign Relations* (Chicago, 1953), pp. 333-35; and Harold and Margaret Sprout, *Toward a New Order of Sea Power* (Princeton, 1940), pp. 85-99.
3   J. C. Vinson, *The Parchment Peace: The United States Senate and the Washington Conference, 1921-1922* (Athens, 1955), pp. 45-63; and Thomas H. Buckley, *The United States and the Washington Conference, 1921-1922* (Knoxville, 1970), pp. 3-17.
4   U.S. Congress, Senate, *Congressional Record* 60, 66th Cong., 3rd sess., 1921, 2825-28.
5   Ibid., p. 2991; and MP to H. L. Day, Feb. 14, 1921.
6   Quoted in J. C. Vinson, *Parchment Peace*, pp. 76-77. See also Robert K. Murray, *The Harding Era: Warren G. Harding and His Administration* (Minneapolis, 1969), pp. 140-66.
7   *New York Times*, May 4, 1921.
8   W. G. Harding to MP, May 14, 1921; and *New York Times*, May 5, 1921.
9   U.S. Congress, Senate, *Congressional Record* 61, 67th Cong., 1st sess., 1921, 1507; *New York Times*, May 18, 1921.
10 A breakdown of the votes of the prewar progressive Republicans on the naval appropriation bill is as follows (the first number indicates the votes cast with, the second the votes cast in opposition to, Poindexter):

With Poindexter		Against Poindexter	
Curtis	10-0	Borah	3-9
Jones	9-3	Cummins	5-5
Nelson	10-3	Kenyon	2-9
Poindexter	13-0	LaFollette	2-11
Sterling	10-0	Norris	3-8
		Townsend	4-7

Congressional Record 61:1520, 1521, 1522, 1527, 1529, 1625, 1682, 1846, 1912, 1961, 1971, and 3374. The vote on the Borah resolution, page 1758, and on the Walsh amendment which related to cooperation with the League of Nations, page 1850, are not included. The vote on the Borah resolution was unanimous and the Walsh amendment seemed unrelated to the naval disarmament issue.

11 *Congressional Record* 61:1758 and 1841-47; and *New York Times*, May 31, 1921.
12 J. C. Vinson, *Parchment Peace*, pp. 78-84 and 118-19.
13 MP to A. H. Curtis, Aug. 20, 1921; MP to R. D. Bowen, Oct. 5, 1921; and MP to W. H. Little, Nov. 2, 1921.
14 *New York Times*, Nov. 13, 1921.
15 Ibid., Nov. 20, 1921.
16 Ibid; see R. E. Osgood's perceptive discussion of disarmament attitudes in *Ideals and Self-Interest*, pp. 333-46.
17 H. Johnson to C. K. McClatchy, Oct. 5, 1921, Johnson MSS.
18 MP to J. W. Bryan, Jan. 21, 1922; and *New York Times*, Jan. 22, 1922.
19 U.S. Congress, Senate, *Congressional Record* 62, 67th Cong., 2d sess., 1921, 4172-80, 236-37; R. E. Osgood, *Ideals and Self-Interest*, pp. 343-45.
20 MP to J. W. Bryan, Jan. 21, 1922; and *Congressional Record* 62:4074.
21 H. Johnson to C. K. McClatchy, Jan. 15 and Mar. 4, 1922, Johnson MSS.
22 *Congressional Record* 62:4497.
23 *New York Times*, Mar. 5, 1922; and *Congressional Record* 62:4718.
24 W. Stull Holt, *Treaties Defeated by the Senate* (Baltimore, 1933), pp. 245-46; and Robert K. Murray, *The Harding Era* (Minneapolis, 1969), pp. 340-41.
25 *Congressional Record* 61:387-91; W. E. Borah to J. H. Gipson, Mar. 15, 1921, Borah MSS; and H. Johnson to H. L. Ickes, Mar. 12, 1921, Johnson MSS.
26 *Congressional Record* 61:483, 484, 485, 486, and 487. The progressive Republicans who voted with Poindexter were: Borah, Jones, Kenyon, LaFollette, Nelson, Norris, and Townsend.
27 John D. Hicks, *Republican Ascendancy, 1921-1933* (New York, 1960), pp. 50-78.
28 Harriet A. Crawford, *The Washington State Grange* (Portland, 1940), pp. 233-87.
29 MP to J. C. Rainey, Oct. 22, 1921.
30 *Congressional Record* 60:1959, 1960, and 1962; and ibid., 61:2662, 2673, 2675, 2676, 2680, 2704, 2708, 2712(a), 2712(b), and 2713. The prewar progressive Republicans divided on the Packers and Stockyards Act as follows (the first number indicates the number of votes cast with Poindexter, the second the number of votes cast against him):

Notes to pages 240-242

With Poindexter		Against Poindexter			
Curtis	7-3	Borah	1-8	Kenyon	1-9
Poindexter	10-0	Cummins	3-7	Nelson	1-7
		Johnson	1-9	Norris	1-9
		Jones	2-8	Sterling	1-9

31 MP to H. B. Creel, Feb. 1, 1921.
32 H. Johnson to C. K. McClatchy. Mar. 9, 1921; and H. Johnson to H. L. Ickes, Sept. 26, 1921, Johnson MSS.
33 MP to G. Albern, June 23, 1919; MP to A. Lewisohn, Feb. 19, 1920; and MP to A. M. Curtis, Aug. 20, 1921.
34 The figures include the vote on final passage and on the conference report. *Congressional Record* 61: 6229, 6260, 6488, 6548, 6569, 6646, 6647-48, 6669, 6684, 6685, 6725, 6743, 6800, 6801, 6865, 6867, 6918, 6920, 6921, 6929, 6939, 6941, 7032, 7036, 7040, 7045, 7047, 7051(a), 7051(b), 7076(a), 7076(b), 7082, 7086, 7088, 7089, 7097, 7108, 7254, 7298, 7305, 7312, 7315, 7338, 7365, 7374, 7380, 7421, 7474, 7477, 7482, 7483(a), 7483(b), 7484, 7486, 7498, 7500, 7509, 7512, 7517-18, 7519(a), 7519(b), 7520, 7521, 7523, 7524, 8175. The prewar progressive Republicans divided on the tax bill as follows (the first number is the total of votes cast with Poindexter, the second the number of votes cast against him):

With Poindexter		Against Poindexter	
Poindexter	63-0	LaFollette	8-54
Curtis	54-9	Kenyon	12-35
Townsend	45-16	Norris	3-24
Nelson	37-9	Borah	10-22
Sterling	14-4	Johnson	5-18
Cummins	17-15		
Jones	21-20		

35 MP to A. Morrison, Dec. 20, 1920; the generalization is based upon the first roll-call vote taken on each commodity. *Congressional Record* 60:2552, 2560, 2921, 3193, 3200, 3201, 3238, 3257, 3260, and 4041.
36 *Congressional Record* 60:3260 and 4498; and ibid., 61:1308 and 3084.
37 J. D. Hicks, *Republican Ascendancy*, pp. 55-59; and *Congressional Record* 62:7863-75, 9902, 10028-31, and 10040.
38 This generalization and the votes cited in table 6 refer in each instance to the first vote taken on each commodity. *Congressional Record* 62:9390, 9543, 9558, 9560, 9565, 9670, 9897, 10667, 11131, 11430.
39 This generalization and the votes cited in table 7 refer in each instance to the first vote taken on

each commodity. *Congressional Record* 62:7480, 7710, 7783, 7925, 7962, 8261, 8326, 8393, 8413, 8471, 10229, 11451, 11558, 11563, 11612.

40 *Congressional Record* 62:11626-27, 12907. The total number of votes cast on the Fordney-McCumber tariff was 321, and on these 321 votes the average Republican senator voted with the Republican majority 87 percent of the time. The party loyalty scores of the prewar progressives varied considerably as follows:

Curtis, Kan.	96%	Jones, Wash.	82%
Townsend, Mich.	91%	Cummins, Iowa	67%
Johnson, Calif.	88%	Norris, Neb.	41%
Poindexter, Wash.	88%	Borah, Idaho	40%
Sterling, S.Dak.	87%	LaFollette, Wis.	27%
Nelson, Minn.	84%		

41 MP to C. E. Roberts, Jan. 3, 1920. See also MP to A. A. Elmore, Jan. 15, 1920.
42 *Congressional Record* 60:878; and MP to L. Hodgeon, Dec. 13, 1920. See also MP to G. F. Messer, Dec. 13, 1920; and *Congressional Record* 60:551-54.
43 *Congressional Record* 60:377; ibid., 62:2282; and MP to A. Morrison, Dec. 20, 1920.
44 Spencer Ervin, *Henry Ford vs. Truman H. Newberry* (New York, 1935), pp. 1-39; and Thomas A. Bailey, *Woodrow Wilson and the Lost Peace* (New York, 1944), p. 61.
45 *Congressional Record* 62:1115-16 and 2100.
46 MP to R. L. Rutter, Feb. 25, 1922.
47 J. N. Colver to "Dear Friend Reba"[?], undated.
48 Ibid.
49 R. Woods to MP, Feb. 10, 1922.
50 Statements by W. H. Paulhamus dated Jan. 12 and Jan. 26, 1922.
51 MP to J. Ford, Jan. 25, 1922; MP to T. Murphine, Feb. 4, 1922; H. Kimball to MP, Feb. 1, 1922.
52 B. Poe to MP, Dec. 8, 1921; W. A. Todd to M. Davis, Dec. 13, 1921; W. A. Todd to MP, Dec. 13, 1921.
53 R. Woods to W. H. Paulhamus, Feb. 10, 1922.
54 *New York Times*, Aug. 27, 1922; Austin E. Griffiths, "Great Faith, an Autobiography of an English Immigrant Boy in America, 1863-1950." Typed manuscript. Seattle, Wash.; University of Washington. Clarence B. Bagley, *History of King County, Washington*, 2 vols. (Chicago, 1929), 2:235; and *P-I*, Aug. 5, Aug. 7, Aug. 9, Aug. 19, and Sept. 3, 1922.
55 *Union-Record*, Sept. 1, Sept. 7, and Sept. 8, 1922.
56 *S-R*, Sept. 1 and Sept. 2, 1922; *Argus*, Aug. 5, Aug. 19, and Aug. 26, 1922; and *Seattle Times*, Aug. 30 and Sept. 3, 1922.

57 Secretary of State, "Abstract of Votes Polled in the State of Washington at the Primary Election Held September 12, 1922." Olympia, Wash.; *P-I*, Sept. 13, 1922; and *Union-Record*, Sept. 13, 1922.
58 *S-R*, Oct. 13, Oct. 14, Oct. 28, Nov. 4, Nov. 5, and Nov. 7, 1922.
59 *P-I*, Nov. 2, Nov. 4, and Nov. 5, 1922.
60 *Union-Record*, Nov. 7, 1922.
61 Secretary of State, "Abstract of Votes Polled in the State of Washington at the General Election Held November 7, 1922." Olympia, Wash.; and Congressional Quarterly, *Guide to U.S. Elections*, p. 507.
62 *P-I*, Nov. 9, 1922; and *Union-Record*, Nov. 10, 1922. The county vote for Dill in 1922 correlated with the vote for Poindexter in the 1910 Republican primary election at .60.
63 *New York Times*, Nov. 29, 1922; J. D. Hicks, *Republican Ascendancy*, pp. 88-89; and Congressional Quarterly, *Guide to the Congress of the United States: Origins, History and Procedure* (Washington, D.C., 1971), pp. 68-69.
64 J. Bourne to MP, Nov. 26, 1922; MP to J. Bourne, Nov. 29, 1922; and W. Harding to J. Bourne, Nov. 21, 1922.
65 MP to W. A. Anderson, Jan. 29, 1923; and MP to R. Woods, Feb. 5, 1923.

11. The Final Years

1 *New York Times*, Jan. 9, Feb. 1, and Feb. 20, 1923; W. Sulzer to MP, Jan. 17, 1923; and MP to C. E. Allison, Jan. 29, 1923.
2 MP to H. S. Garvin, Mar. 6, 1923.
3 William J. Dennis, *Tacna and Arica. An Account of the Chile-Peru Boundary Dispute and of the Arbitrations by the United States* (New Haven, 1931), pp. 1-226.
4 MP to W. H. Ellis, June 28, 1924.
5 F. B. Kellogg to MP, Jan. 24, 1926, *Papers Relating to the Foreign Relations of the United States: 1926* (Washington, D.C., 1941), 1:260-62. MP to F. B. Kellogg, Jan. 9, 1926, *Papers*, 1:269-73. Another indication of Poindexter's sympathy for Peru may be seen in MP to F. B. Kellogg, Oct. 27, 1925, *Papers: 1925*, 1:404. The historian of the Tacna-Arica controversy shared Poindexter's assessment. See W. J. Dennis, *Tacna-Arica*, p. 271.
6 F. B. Kellogg to MP, Feb. 3, 1926, *Papers Relating to the Foreign Relations of the United States: 1926*,

1:284-85; and MP to F. B. Kellogg, Feb. 15, 1926, *Papers*, 1:296-97; and Gary Brown, "Miles Poindexter in Peru: An Attitudinal Study," seminar paper, Department of History, Southern Illinois University, Carbondale, 1977.
7. W. J. Dennis, *Tacna-Arica*, pp. 227-89.
8. *S-R*, Aug. 24, 1927, and Aug. 19, 1928; Peru, Biblioteca Nacional, "Miles Poindexter," *Anuario Bibliogratico Peruano de 1946*, pp. 236-37.
9. Miles Poindexter, *The Ayar-Incas*, 2 vols. (New York, 1930); and Miles Poindexter, *Peruvian Pharaohs* (Boston, 1938).
10. Poindexter, *The Ayar-Incas*, 1:xi.
11. Ibid., pp. xi, xvii, and *Ayar-Incas*, 2:258.
12. *Outlook* 155 (July 9, 1930):387; and *S-R*, June 19, 1938.
13. *New York Herald-Tribune, Books* (Aug. 17, 1930), p. 12; and *Saturday Review of Literature* 7 (Nov. 1, 1930):296.
14. *New York Times*, Aug. 24 and Nov. 8, 1927; and *S-R*, Sept. 21 and Oct. 24, 1927, and Feb. 19, Mar. 12, Mar. 16, Apr. 10, and Apr. 18, 1928.
15. *S-R*, Apr. 21, 1928; and Secretary of State, "Abstract of Votes Polled at the Primary Election Held September 11, 1928." Olympia, Wash.
16. *New York Times*, Dec. 21, 1929; *S-R*, Dec. 2, 1929 and Sept. 22, 1946; and interview with Gale Poindexter.
17. MP to H. Kimball, Aug. 26, 1919.
18. MP to G. M. Cheney, Apr. 26, 1921.

Index

Addams, Jane, 152, 201
Agricultural depression in 1920s, 242-43
Alaska: and Ballinger-Pinchot controversy, 43; coal deposits in, 73; and MP's bill to develop, 102-5; mentioned, 165, 263
Alaskan Railroad bill, 103-4, 160, 167
Aldrich, Nelson B., 36, 40-43, 59, 93
Aldrich plan, 93
Alliman, M. T., 98
American Federation of Labor, 22, 97, 212, 213, 230, 253
"Americanism," 156, 162
Anderson, Francis T. (MP's grandfather), 2, 3, 260
Anderson, Gen. Joseph Reid (MP's great-uncle), 3
Anderson, Mary A. (MP's grandmother), 2
Anderson, William A. (MP's uncle), 3-4, 20
Anglo-Japanese Alliance of 1902, 232, 233
Ankeny, Levi, 16, 25
Argentine, 127
Armaments: reduction of, 230
Army bill of 1916, 138
Article 10, 200
Aryan race, 258-59

Ayar-Incas, The, 257, 258-59
Axtell, Mrs. Frances C., 250

Bache, Jules S., 218, 221, 248, 249
Bacon, Augustus O., 68
Bacon-Bartlett bill, 97, 98
Bailey, Joseph W., 68
Baker, John D., 47-48
Baker, Newton D., 187
Ballinger, Richard A.: and the Ballinger-Pinchot controversy, 43-44; endorsed by Washington State Republican convention, 53
Banker's Commercial League, 17
Belgium, 132, 193
Benedict, Ruth, 259
Berger, Victor, 250
Bernstein, Barton J., 60, 127, 283 n.3
Beveridge, Albert J.: as opponent of William Jennings Bryan in 1896, 32; endorsed MP in election of 1910, 55; and Progressive National Convention, 80; and enthusiasm for Progressive party, 109; nominated for U.S. Senate, 111; and Progressive party, 112; defeated in 1914, 118; and foreign policy views, 119; as "nationalist," 127; and

Theodore Roosevelt's behavior in 1916, 156; foreign policy views compared to MP's, 168; as irreconcilable, 202; and Treaty of Versailles, 205; mentioned, 108, 110-11
Billings, Warren K., 180
Blackstone Hotel, 222
Bogue, Allan G., 283 n.3
Bolsheviki, 183, 200, 207, 219, 264
Bolshevism, 186, 200, 266
Bolshevist revolution: MP's reaction to, 177-78; mentioned, 202, 206, 265
Bone, Scott C., 112, 118
Borah, William E.: on Canadian reciprocity, 65; and Progressive party in 1912, 78; defended high tariff rates on western products, 88; criticized Federal Reserve Act, 95; refused to join Progressive party, 111; as leader of anti-imperialism, 127; opposed ship-purchase bill, 133-34; opposed preparedness, 137, 139; and Philippine Islands, 145; favored Hughes in 1916, 155; compared to MP, 165; and Espionage Act, 175; and inconsistent support of war, 185; and Woodrow Wilson's war aims, 192; and breakup of progressive coalition, 197-99; as irreconcilable, 203, 204; as isolationist, 205; and Esch-Cummins Transportation Act, 213; and Cummins Railway bill, 215; and attitude toward MP, 223; and disarmament resolution, 227-30; and Washington Conference, 230-33; and naval disarmament, 232; and Four Power pact, 234-35; and Treaty with Colombia, 236; and Farm bloc, 238, 242; and Fordney-McCumber Tariff, 242; and T. Newberry case, 246; mentioned, 108, 264, 265, 266
Borah disarmament resolution, 227-30

Borah-Johnson group, 220
Boston police strike, 209, 219
Bouck, William, 238
Bourne, Jonathan: on Robert M. LaFollette's candidacy in 1912, 73; and Progressive party in 1912, 78; and MP's presidential campaign, 218; and MP's defeat in 1922, 254; as supporter of progressivism, 266
Brandegee, Frank B., 130, 223
Brandeis, Louis, 67, 68
Brazil, 127
Bremerton Naval Yard, 160, 251
Brest-Litovsk, Treaty of, 209
Bridges, Robert, 247
Bristow, Joseph: and Progressive party in 1912, 78; blocked Taft appointments, 86; refused to join Progressive party, 111
British Admiralty, 227
British Empire, 122
Brown, Norris: and Progressive party in 1912, 78
Bryan, E. A.: and the election of 1916, 153
Bryan, J. W., 83
Bryan, William Jennings: and election of 1896 in Washington, 8; MP's aversion to, in 1896, 10; in Washington elections, 21; opposed by Republican progressives in 1896, 32; and Washington election patterns, 56; resignation of, 135; and voting patterns in Washington, 163, 164; and election of 1922 in Washington, 253
Bunker Hill: battle of, 173
Burke, Thomas, 50, 54, 56
Burleson, Albert B., 191
Business, regulation of: and New Freedom, 96; and New Nationalism, 96; MP's opposition to, in 1920s, 239; mentioned, 20, 34, 57

Calder, William M., 195, 222, 309 n.49
California, 154, 158

Index 319

Camp Lewis, Washington, 207
Canadian reciprocity: in U.S. Congress, 61-66; MP's voting record on, 62; voting on, 284-85 n.12; mentioned, 71, 242
Cannon, Joseph G.: as opponent of progressive reform, 21; as issue in Washington State election of 1908, 29-30; reelected speaker, 33-35; and opposition to tariff reform, 33-36; embarrassed Insurgents on tariff voting, 37; and House rules reform, 45; defeated for reelection, 56; immigration policy criticized by MP, 146
Capper-Volstead bill, 245
Carnegie Endowment for International Peace, 146
Carnegie Hall, 183
Cary, William J., 38
Case, C. R., 79
Chamberlain, George E., 103, 130, 187
Chicago Tribune, 93, 131, 203
Child Labor Act of 1916, 69
Chile, 127, 255, 256
Clark, Champ, 35, 78
Clarke amendment, 143-45
Clapp, Moses E., 61, 78, 110-11, 168
Clayton Anti-Trust Act: considered by Senate, 96-100; and farm-labor exemptions, 97-100
Cleveland, Grover, 145
Closed shop, 208
Colby, Bainbridge, 113, 118
Collier's Weekly, 93, 219
Colombia, treaty with, 235-37
Columbia River Basin project, 252, 260
Columbia River Gold, Silver and Lead Mining Company, 17
Colville Indian reservation, 162
Commerce and Labor, Department of, 67
Commerce Court, 45-46
Communist Labor party, 206
Communist party, 206
Congress: Sixty-first, 35, 37, 46-49, 62; Sixty-second, 59, 60, 62, 66, 86-87; Sixty-third, 85-85, 87; Sixty-fourth, 143, 152, 170; Sixty-fifth, 170; Sixty-sixth, 228, 241; Sixty-seventh, 226, 228, 241, 309 n.1
Coolidge, Calvin, 224, 256
Cooper, Henry A., 34
Cooper, John Milton, Jr., 127
Cory, Arthur, 64
Cotterill, George F., 56
Cowles, W. H.: and Businessmen's Bimetallic Club for Bryan, 11; as editor of *Spokane Spokesman-Review*, 11; early career and views of, 14-15; and election of 1910, 50; as Taft supporter in 1912, 73; and election of 1912, 74; and MP's presidential campaign, 217, 218; mentioned, 24
Crawford, Coe I., 78
Creed, George, 174
Cummins, Albert B.: and Mann-Elkins Act, 45; endorsed MP in election of 1910, 55; and Canadian reciprocity, 65; and LaFollette's candidacy in 1912, 73; and Progressive party in 1912, 78; proposed farm-labor antitrust exemption, 99; and amendment to Clayton Anti-Trust Act, 100; refused to join Progressive party, 110-11; and immigration restriction, 148; and Espionage Act, 175; and support of war, 185; and Esch-Cummins Transportation Act, 213, 307-8 n.31; and Cummins Railway bill, 215-16; mentioned, 266
Cummins Railway bill: and progressive Republicans, 215-16; voting on, 215-16. *See also* Esch-Cummins Transportation Act
Curtis, Charles, 237, 266
Cushman, Francis W., 15

Dague, R. A., 101
Daniels, Josephus, 306 n.24

320   Index

Davis, James J., 251
Debs, Eugene V.: and election results in Washington in 1912, 83
Democratic Convention: in 1912, 78
Democratic party: and party cohesion on Underwood Tariff, 87
Democratic party platform: and protective tariff, 36
Democrats: Senate party cohesion of, 86; and significance of support for progressive legislation in Senate, 165; and breakup of progressive coalition, 197-98
Dill, Clarence C.: elected to House of Representatives, 118; and election of 1922, 247-48, 251-53; and issues in 1922 campaign, 252; attacked by Republican press in campaign of 1922, 252; charged MP had abandoned progressive principles, 252; elected U.S. Senator in 1922, 252; captured reform vote in 1922 election, 253; and election of 1928, 259; mentioned, 162, 255
Dilling, George, 157
Direct Primary League, 22
Dixon, Joseph M.: and Progressive party in 1912, 78; as national chairman of Progressive party in 1912, 80; mentioned, 115
Doland, A. W., 113, 116
Dow, Lorenzo, 74
Duncan, James A.: and Thomas Mooney, 180-81; attack by MP, 181; responded to MP's position on Mooney case, 182; and election of 1922, 252-53

Eastern "colonialism": as cause of progressivism in Senate, 166
Edris, W. P.: and election of 1910, 50
Election of 1896: in Washington, 8
Election of 1900: in Washington, 14

Election of 1904: in Washington, 16
Election of 1908: primary election, 25-27; MP endorsed policies of Theodore Roosevelt, 27; and MP's campaign for the House of Representatives, 27-31; and reelection of Cannon as Speaker, 29-30
Election of 1910: discussed, 49-57; and voting patterns in Washington, 56
Election of 1912: discussed, 72-84; and voting patterns in Washington, 83
Election of 1914: results of, 117-18; and impact on MP, 150
Election of 1916: discussed, 150-164; and voting patterns in Washington primary and general election, 163-64
Election of 1918: and Wilson's call for Democratic Congress, 194-95; as a repudiation of Wilson's leadership, 196; results in Washington, 196; and Wilson's peace program 200; mentioned, 188
Election of 1920, 224-25
Election of 1922: discussed, 247-55; and voting patterns in Washington primary, 251; MP defeated, 252-53; and voting patterns in Washington, 252-53
Election of 1928, 259-60
Ellis Island, 211
Emergency Agricultural Tariff bill, 241
Emergency Fleet Corporation, 207
"Empire of the Amazon," 257
Employers' Association of Washington, 98
Esch-Cummins Transportation Act, 213, 252
Espionage Act of 1917, 174-76, 178, 180
Everett, Washington, 176
Excess profits tax, 240

Index

Falconer, J. A., 83
Fall, Albert B.: praised by Theodore Roosevelt, 141; as irreconcilable, 204; mentioned, 236, 266
Fancy Hill Academy, 5
Farm bloc: and prewar progressives, 238; and regulation of business, 238-39; and Mellon tax bill of 1921, 240; and agricultural depression, 242; an issue in 1922 campaign in Washington, 252; mentioned, 199, 216
Farmer-Labor party: and election of 1920, 225; mentioned, 238, 252, 254
Federal Farm Loan bill: passed, 149; mentioned, 165-66
Federal Livestock Commission bill, 239
Federal Railway Control Act, 212
Federal Reserve Act: considered by Senate, 93-96; and rural credit, 148-49
Federal Reserve Board, 245
Federal Trade Commission, 238
Federal Trade Commission Act, 97
Five Power pact, 233, 235
Foch, Gen. Ferdinand, 188
Ford, Henry, 239, 245-46
Fordney-McCumber Tariff, 241-44, 313 n.40
Foreign Relations, Committee on, 60, 121
Forestry Bureau, 43
Foster, Addison G., 15
Four Power Treaty: praised by MP, 233; ratified by Senate, 235; mentioned, 250
Fourteen Points, 183, 192, 193, 200
France, 122, 132, 193, 200, 227, 233
France, Joseph I., 179
France Amendment, 179
Free coinage of silver, 8, 11

Gable, John A., 286 n.37; and 291 n.51
Gale, Joseph: ancestor of Elizabeth Page Poindexter, 6
Gallinger, Jacob H., 59, 67, 195
Gardner, Augustus P., 155
Gary steel strike, 209, 210
Geographical Society of Peru, 257
Germany: MP's suspicions of, 125, 140; invaded France and Belgium, 132; and submarine policy, 135; threat of war with, 137; mentioned, 192, 193, 195, 202, 227
Glavis, Louis R., 43, 67
"Glenwood," 2
Goldman, Eric, 166
Gompers, Samuel: endorsed MP in election of 1910, 55; and the Clayton Anti-Trust Act, 97; and antistrike provision of Esch-Cummins Transportation Act, 213; mentioned, 182, 219
Goodyear, William, 30
Gore, Thomas P., 136, 179
Gore resolution, 136, 295 n.36
Graham, Otis, Jr., 196
Grandview District Fruit Growers Association, 64
Great Britain, 122, 128, 227, 228, 231, 233, 235
Gregory, Thomas W., 183, 207, 208
Griffiths, Austin E., 250
Gronna, Asle J.: voting record in Sixty-second Congress, 61; and Progressive party, 78; and preparedness, 139; foreign policy views compared to MP's, 168; as opponent of war, 185; and breakup of progressive coalition, 197-99; as irreconcilable, 204; and Esch-Cummins Transportation Act, 213; and Cummins Railway bill, 215; and attitude toward MP, 223; mentioned, 266
Guam, 234
Guttman Scale Analysis, 60

Hale, Frederick, 228
Hale, Nathan, 173

322   Index

Ham, D. T.: opposed MP in election of 1910, 50-51; endorsed W. E. Humphrey in 1916, 160; mentioned, 218
Hanson, Ole: as Progressive candidate in 1914, 117; and Seattle general strike, 207; mentioned, 266
Harrison, Benjamin, 8
Harding Administration: and Treaty with Colombia, 235-37; and economic policies of, 237-39; aided MP's 1922 reelection campaign, 251; mentioned, 226, 256
Harding, Warren G.: and Republican convention of 1920, 223; elected in 1920, 224; inauguration of, 228; and naval disarmament, 228-29; revised position on naval disarmament resolution, 229; signed Emergency Agricultural Tariff bill, 241; and MP's defeat in 1922, 254; and party loyalty, 306-7 n.25; mentioned, 230, 237
Hartson, M. T.: opposed MP in election of 1910, 51; and prospects of MP's victory in 1916, 157; on Wilson's popularity in Washington, 159
Hay, M. E., 84
Hay-Pauncefote Treaty, 128
Hays, Samuel P., 58, 61
Hays, Will H., 195
Hearst syndicate, 247
Hearst, William Randolph, 247, 248, 250
Hepburn Act, 20, 24
Hepburn, William P., 34
Hinman, Harvey D., 112
Hodge, Robert T., 84
Hofstadter, Richard, 31, 58, 166, 278 n.48, 290 n.42
Hoover, Herbert, 221, 257
House, Edward M., 135
Huerta, Victoriano, 124
Hughes, Charles Evans: favored for president in 1916 by W. H. Taft, 155; and election of 1916, 155-64; and presidential campaign in Washington, 158; compared to W. H. Taft and T. Roosevelt, 159; and Wilson's foreign policy, 162; as delegate to Washington Conference, 230-33; and treaty with Colombia, 236; and Tacna-Arica controversy, 256; and campaign of 1916 in California, 299 n.38; and 1916 campaign in Washington, 299 n.37
Humphrey, William E.: and election of 1916, 153-54; and prospects of victory in 1916, 157; launched 1916 campaign, 160

Illinois Manufacturers Association, 131
Immigration: MP's support of, 142; as popular West Coast issue, 145; and League of Nations, 202; voting on, by progressive Republicans, 263, 297 n.12
Inca civilization, 257, 258-59
Income tax: considered in Senate, 91-92; war-time rates supported by MP, 184
Industrial army bill: proposed by MP, 101, 168-69, 263
Industrial Workers of the World: and Lawrence strike, 66-67; debate in Senate on, 66-68; treatment in Spokane of, 68; and opposition to World War I, 176-77; and Seattle general strike, 207; and Gary steel strike, 210; mentioned, 169, 186, 200, 202, 262, 264,
Inland Empire Implement and Hardware Association, 28
Inland Empire Retail Dealers Association, 55, 69-70
Insurgent Republicans: and reelection of J. Cannon, 34; and reforms of House rules, 34-35; and position on Payne-Aldrich Tariff, 37-41; and William Howard Taft, 42-43; and the Mann-Elkins Act, 45-46;

Index   323

and record in Sixty-first Congress, 46-49; as a western voting bloc, 61; and voting record on Canadian reciprocity bill, 62-65; and tariff reform, 66; and Progressive party, 78. *See also* Progressive Republicans
International Court of Justice, 123
Interstate Commerce Commission, 20, 45-46, 214
Irreconcilables: and Treaty of Versailles, 200-206; and MP, 201; and progressive Republicans, 204-5; and naval disarmament, 232-33
Italy, 233

Japan, 227, 231, 232, 233, 235
Johnson, Hiram: endorsed MP in election of 1910, 55; withdrew from Republican party, 109; reelected in 1914, 118; and Theodore Roosevelt's behavior in 1916, 156; and Hughes's 1916 campaign in California, 158; and Espionage Act, 175; and Sedition Act, 180; and war profits tax, 185; and breakup of progressive coalition, 197; as irreconcilable, 204; and Esch-Cummins Transportation Act, 213; as presidential candidate in 1920, 217; and MP's presidential aspirations in 1920, 217; and election of 1920, 223; on naval disarmament, 232-33; and Four Power pact, 234-35; and Treaty with Colombia, 236; and Mellon Tax bill, 240; mentioned, 110, 115, 194, 220, 221, 266, 299 n.38
Johnson, Lee, 27
Johnson, Tom, 32
Jones, John Paul, 173
Jones, Wesley L.: as candidate for Senate in 1908, 25; criticized MP's position on Payne-Aldrich Tariff, 38; threatened by MP's candidacy for Senate, 49; opposed MP in election of 1910, 51; attended Republican rally, 53; and voting in Sixty-second Congress, 61; and Progressive party, 112; reelected in 1914, 117-18; and immigration restriction, 148; and committee assignments, 153; and election of 1916, 153-54; and prospects of MP's victory in 1916, 157; reelected in 1920, 225; and Fordney-McCumber Tariff, 242; and Newberry case, 246; mentioned, 131, 255
Jones Act, 143
Justice, Department of, 210, 211
Juvenile court, 23

Kahn, Julius, 194
Kegley, C. B.: endorsed MP in election of 1910, 55; praised MP's stand on Canadian reciprocity, 63; and Canadian reciprocity, 65; on parcel post law, 70; on Robert M. LaFollette's candidacy in 1912, 73; and election of 1912, 74, 79; supported MP in 1916, 157; death of, 238
Kellogg, Frank B.: and Tacna-Arica controversy, 256; mentioned, 195, 257
Kenyon, William: and voting record in Sixty-second Congress, 61; and Progressive party in 1912, 78; and support of war, 185; and naval disarmament, 230; and Farm bloc, 238; and T. Newberry case, 246; mentioned, 111
Kimball, Horace: career of, 13-14; candidate for Spokane County prosecutor in 1900, 14; supported MP for Republican nomination for House of Representatives, 26; and election of 1910, 50; and election of 1912, 75, 76, 79, 81; elected Spokane County Chairman of

324   Index

Progressive party in 1912, 82; and MP's presidential ambitions, 116-17; supported MP in 1916, 157; and Hughes's 1916 campaign in Washington, 158; and MP's presidential campaign in 1920, 218; and MP's 1920 campaign for reelection, 248-49; mentioned, 111, 266
Kolko, Gabriel, 289 n.18

LaFollette, Robert M.: spoke to Spokane 150,000 Club, 24; and Mann-Elkins Act, 45-46; spoke in Washington for MP, 50; visited with Theodore Roosevelt, 52; endorsed MP in election of 1910, 55; refused to attend Republican caucus, 59; and voting record in Sixty-second Congress, 60; and Canadian reciprocity, 65; as candidate for president in 1912, 73; and election of 1912, 74-75; and Progressive party in 1912, 78; blocked Taft appointments, 86; defended high tariff rates on wool, 88; and amendment to resolution on Mexico, 126; as anti-imperialist, 127; opposed preparedness, 137, 139; and Federal Farm Loan Act, 149; and foreign policy differences with Roosevelt, 152; compared to MP, 165, 168, 264-66; and armed ship bill, 171; as opponent of war, 185; and breakup of progressive coalition, 197-99; as irreconcilable, 204; as isolationist, 205; and Plumb plan, 212; and Esch-Cummins Transportation Act, 213; and Cummins Railway bill, 215; and attitude toward MP, 223; and naval disarmament, 230; and Four Power pact, 234-35; and Farm bloc, 238; and Fordney-McCumber Tariff, 242; and Newberry case, 246; reelected in 1922, 253; filibuster, 304 n.57; and party loyalty, 309-

10 n.1; mentioned, 108, 169, 220
LaFollette, William L., 105-6
LaFollette Seamen's Act, 69
LaFollette's Weekly: endorsed MP in election of 1910, 55
Lamping, George B., 250, 251
Lane, Harry, 130, 138-39
Latin America, 140
Laurier government, 65
Lawrence, Massachusetts: IWW strike in, 66, 167, 169, 176, 262
League of Nations, 183, 195, 200-206, 207, 209, 222, 233-34, 235, 265
Leehey, M. D., 103, 104
Leguía, Augusto, 257
Leib, Franklin A., 60, 127, 283 n.3
Leuchtenburg, William E., 168, 293 n.18
Lindbergh, Charles A., 34
Lindsey, Ben, 23, 25
Link, Arthur, 132
Listor, Ernest, 84
Literary Digest, 219, 221
Livermore, Seward, 173
Lodge, Henry Cabot: Lawrence strike, investigation of, 67; on IWW in Spokane, 68; and A. T. Mahan, 121; opposed Taft's arbitration treaties, 122; demanded intervention in Mexico, 125; compared with MP on foreign policy views, 127; opposed Ship Purchase bill, 133-34; compared with Roosevelt on foreign policy views, 152; and MP's committee assignments, 152-53, 170; and election of 1916, 155; endorsed for president in 1916 by Roosevelt, 155; as critic of Wilson's foreign policy, 156; compared with MP on conduct of war, 186; attacked Wilson's conduct of war, 188; and war aims, 192; and armistice negotiations, 193-94; as supporter of the war, 197; and Treaty of

Index   325

Versailles, 202-5; and attitude toward MP, 223; and naval disarmament, 230; and Washington Conference, 231; and Treaty with Colombia, 236; and Mellon tax bill, 241; and party loyalty, 306-7 n.25, 309-10 n.1; mentioned, 189, 226
Lodge "round robin," 203-4
Lowden, Frank, 217, 220, 221, 223
Lund, C. P., 162
Lusitania, 135, 137

McAdoo, William G., 133
McClatchy, C. K., 180
McCormick, Medill: criticized leadership of Progressive party, 113; as irreconcilable, 204
McCumber, Porter J., 66
McKinley, William J., 8, 14, 32, 36
Mackintosh, Kenneth, 260
McLemore, Atkins, 136
McNary, Charles L., 251
McNary-Haugen bill, 260
Madero, Francisco, 123-24
Mahan, Alfred T., 121
Mann-Elkins Act, 45-47
Mead, Albert, 22
Mellon, Andrew, 240
Mellon tax bill, 240-41, 312 n.34
Mexican revolution, 123-28, 140, 142-43, 162
Mexico: MP's resolution to declare war against, 125-26; and effect of Pershing expedition in, 155
Michigan primary election of 1920, 221
Monroe Doctrine, defended by MP, 121, 123; as MP's justification to intervene in Mexico, 124-26; and Panama Canal tolls exemption, 129; and MP's view of foreign affairs, 140; and Treaty of Versailles, 201, 204; and Peru, 256; mentioned, 234, 264
Mooney, Thomas, 180-81, 182, 183, 207, 208, 252
Moore, J. Z., Judge, 12, 13, 26

Moore, O. C.: and election of 1908, 26; and election of 1910, 50; and election of 1912, 75; and organization of Progressive party in 1912, 82; left Progressive party, 113; as Republican candidate for the House of Representatives in 1914, 116; supported MP in 1916, 157; mentioned, 44, 156
Morgan-Guggenheim Syndicate, 43
Mowry, George W., 32, 299 n.38
Munsey, Frank, 109
Murdock, Victor: as insurgent Republican, 34; and Payne-Aldrich Tariff, 38; and election of 1910, 55; defeated in 1914, 118; mentioned, 111
Murphine, Tom: and election of 1912, 76, 77, 79, 80; mentioned, 248-49
Muscle Shoals controversy, 239-40
Muzzey, David A., 173

Nation, 189, 190
National Association of Manufacturers, 208
National Monetary Commission, 93
Naval appropriation bill of 1921: and voting of progressive Republicans, 229-30, 310 n.10; mentioned, 227-28
Naval armaments race, 226-27
Naval War College, 121
Navy, Department of, 226
Navy bill of 1916, 138
Navy League, 136
Nelson, Knute, 148, 266
New, Harry S., 195
Newberry case, 254
Newberry, Truman H., 245-46, 248, 250, 252
New Freedom: and business regulation, 96; and MP's contributions, 108
New Nationalism: and business regulation, 96
New Republic, 182
New Seattle Chamber of Commerce: opposed farm-labor antitrust

exemption, 98; and development of Alaska, 103; and Panama Canal tolls exemption, 129
New York Sun, 40
New York Times: and Ship Purchase bill, 133; and MP's amendment to Espionage Act, 174-75; and MP's amendment to Sedition bill, 178; and MP's position on Treaty of Versailles, 203; and MP's resolution on Wilson's leniency with radicals, 210, 211; and MP article on lenient treatment of radicals in, 211-12; and MP's 1920 presidential campaign, 219-21; and naval disarmament, 228-29; and MP's reversal on Borah naval disarmament resolution, 229; and naval disarmament, 230; and MP's article on disarmament, 231-32; and MP's article on Washington Conference, 233; and MP's article on need for strong navy, 235; mentioned, 130
Non-Partisan League, 225, 250, 254
Norris, George W.: as insurgent Republican, 34; on Payne-Aldrich Tariff, 38; and House rules reform, 45; and Canadian reciprocity, 62; refused to join Progressive party, 111; and preparedness, 137, 139; and immigration restriction, 148; and foreign policy differences with Roosevelt, 152; compared to MP, 165, 168, 264-66; and Espionage Act, 175; as opponent of war, 185; and breakup of progressive coalition, 197-99; as irreconcilable, 204; as isolationist, 205; and Esch-Cummins Transportation Act, 213; and Cummins Railway bill, 215; and attitude toward MP, 223; and Farm bloc, 238; and Newberry case, 246; mentioned, 169
Northern Securities Company, 20

O'Gorman, James A., 136
150,000 Club, 24
Open shop, 208, 219
Order El Sol del Peru, 257
Osgood, Robert E., 119, 311 n.16
Overman, Lee S., 187

Packers and Stockyards Act, 239, 311-12 n.30
Page, Thomas: father of Elizabeth Page Poindexter, 7
Palmer, A. Mitchell: attacked by MP for leniency with radicals, 208, 210; and Red Scare, 211-12; impact of MP's resolution on, 212; mentioned, 266, 306 n.24
Panama, 235
Panama Canal, 236, 259-60
Panama Canal tolls, 128-31, 165, 167
Parcel post: as issue in election of 1908, 28-29; debated in U.S. Congress, 69-71
Parental school, 25
Parker, Alton B., 22
Parry, W. H.: and national leadership of Progressive party, 113-14; and problems of Washington Progressive party, 115
Paulhamus, W. H., 248
Payne, Sereno E., 37
Payne-Aldrich Tariff: discussed, 36-42; voting on, compared to Underwood Tariff, 88; condemned by MP, 92; mentioned, 61, 165
People's Party: in eastern Washington, 7-8; and protective tariff, 36. *See also* Populism
Perkins, George C., 130, 148
Perkins, George W., 77, 114-15, 151
Perkins, S. A., 112, 158, 162, 218
Pershing, Gen. John J., 143, 155, 221
Peru, 255, 257, 259
Peruvian Pharaohs, 257, 259

Philippine independence: voting of progressive Republicans on, 296 n.5
Philippine Islands: independence and self-government debated, 143-45; mentioned, 142, 234
Piles, Samuel, 16, 49, 53
Pinchot, Amos, 115, 152, 156
Pinchot, Gifford: and the Ballinger-Pinchot controversy, 43-44; and visit with Theodore Roosevelt, 52; and parcel post law, 70; on Robert M. LaFollette's candidacy in 1912, 73; visited Alaska with MP, 73, 102; and election of 1912, 76; defeated, 1914, 118; mentioned, 67
Plumb, Glenn, 212
Plumb plan, 212, 214
Poindexter, Elizabeth Page (MP's wife), 6, 18, 74, 255, 260
Poindexter, Ernest (MP's brother), 2, 10, 15, 17, 19, 105
Poindexter, Fielding (MP's brother), 2, 3, 4, 15, 19, 105
Poindexter, Frances Hubbard Bowyer (MP's grandmother), 1
Poindexter, Gale Aylette (son), 7, 74, 86, 105-6
Poindexter, George (MP's first ancestor in America), 1
Poindexter, George B. (MP's grandfather), 1
Poindexter, George Fauntleroy (MP's brother), 2
Poindexter, Josephine Anderson (MP's mother), 2, 3
Poindexter, Mary (MP's sister), 2
Poindexter, Miles
—early life: and family history, 1-5; personality of, 5; attended Washington and Lee University, 5-6; political career in Walla Walla, 6; married Elizabeth Page, 6; move to Spokane, 9
—as lawyer in Spokane: converted to Republican party, 9-11; as candidate for political office, 14-16; business activities of, 16-17; personality of, 18-19; assistance to father's family, 19-20; as superior court judge, 22-25; and election of 1908, 25-31; as middle-class progressive reformer, 1908, 28; and views on parcel post, 28-29; and views of J. Cannon as Speaker, 29-30; and nature of his progressivism, 31-32
—in House of Representatives: opposed Cannon's reelection as Speaker, 34-35; and Payne-Aldrich Tariff, 36-41; and corruption in eastern cities, 41-42; praised by *Collier's Weekly*, 42; and Taft administration, 43-44; and record in Sixty-first Congress, 46-49; and 1910 campaign for Senate, 49-53; and reform views of, 54-55; and influence of Populism on, 57-58
—in U.S. Senate 1911-17: and record in Sixty-second Congress, 59-61; Canadian reciprocity, 62; and IWW in Lawrence strike, 66-69; on IWW in Spokane, 68; and parcel post, 69-71; and popular election of Senators, 71; and conflicting interests of constituents, 71-72; and election of 1912, 73-82; and committee assignments, 87; and Underwood Tariff, 87-93; proposed higher income taxes, 92; and Federal Reserve Act, 93-96; praised Wilson's early achievements, 96; endorsed women's rights, 96; and Clayton Anti-Trust Act, 96-100; and Federal Trade Commission Act, 97; and Industrial Army bill, 101-2; and bill to develop Alaska, 102-5; and fear of social revolution, 105; and social views, 105-8; person-

ality of, 108; and contributions to New Freedom, 108; and Progressive party, 109-14; and presidential ambitions, 116-17; and foreign policy views, 119-21, 123, 168-69; influenced by Social Darwinism, 120, 140, 168; influenced by A. T. Mahan, 121; and need for Pacific fleet, 122; praised Roosevelt's naval policy, 122; opposed Taft's arbitration treaties, 122-23; and Mexican revolution, 123-28, 142-43; and Roosevelt Corollary, 124; and suspicions of Germany, 125-32; as advocate of Roosevelt's foreign policy, 127-28; and Panama Canal tolls, 128-31; and ship-purchase bill, 132-35; on Bryan's resignation, 135; and Gore resolution, 136; and preparedness, 136-37, 139-40; and intervention in World War I, 137-38; on preparedness, compared to progressive Republicans, 138-39; on Latin America, as American sphere of influence, 140; compared to Theodore Roosevelt, 141; on value of war, 143; and Philippine Islands, 143-45; and immigration restriction, 145-48; and Burnett Immigration bill, 145-48; and Federal Farm Loan Act, 148-49; and election of 1914, 150; and election of 1916, 150-64, 299 n.37; and presidential ambitions, 151; and meeting with Roosevelt, 152; humiliated by committee assignments, 152-53; progressive career analyzed, 165-69
—in U.S. Senate 1917-23: and armed ship bill, 171; and American entry into World War I, 171-72; and Roosevelt's effort to take volunteer unit to France, 172; and World War I as test of national will, 172; and the impact of World War I on progressivism, 173; and Selective Service Act, 173; and German-Americans, 173; and disloyal residents, 174; and amendment to Espionage Act, 174; and opponents of war, 174-75; defended Espionage Act, 175; and change in attitude toward IWW, 176-77; and Bolshevist revolution, 176; introduced loyalty bill, 178; and Sedition Act, 178-80; and T. Mooney case, 180-82; and Bolshevist conspiracy in Seattle, 181-82; and organized labor, 182; criticized by J. Duncan, 182; accused Wilson of being pro-German, 183-84; and wartime income tax, 184; and war profits tax, 184-85; and change in political associations, 185-86; and Wilson's conduct of war, 186-92; defended patriotic criticism of Wilson administration, 190, 191-92; and his relationship with Roosevelt, 191; and Wilson's war aims, 192-93; and armistice negotiations, 193-94; praised by Roosevelt, 193-94; and election of 1918, 195-97; and shift to the right, 196-97; and fight against Treaty of Versailles, 200-206, 305 n.9; and presidential ambitions in 1920, 206; and Red Scare, 206-12, 306 n.17; as regular Republican, 212; opposed Plumb plan, 213, 214; and Esch-Cummins Transportation Act, 213-16; and bolshevism in labor unions, 214; and presidential campaign in 1920, 216-24; as chairman 1920 Republican Senatorial

Campaign Committee, 224; and naval expansion, 226-27; and naval disarmament, 227-30; and Four Power pact, 233-34; and Five Power pact, 235; on need to maintain navy, 235; and treaty with Colombia, 235-37; hostility to radicalism in 1920s, 238; and domestic legislation in 1920s, 238; and criticism of Federal Trade Commission, 238-39; defended Standard Oil Company, 239; as opponent of regulation of business in 1920s; and federal livestock commission bill, 239; and Packers and Stockyards Act, 239; and Muscle Shoals controversy, 239-40; and Mellon tax bill of 1921, 240-41; and Emergency Agricultural Tariff bill, 241; and Fordney-McCumber Tariff, 242; and agricultural depression in Washington, 242-43; supported bill for farm relief, 245; and Capper-Volstead bill, 245; and Newberry case, 245-46, 254; and progressive principles, 246-47; and election of 1922, 247-54; and rumors of appointment to Harding cabinet, 255
— as ambassador to Peru: appointed, 255; and Tacna-Arica controversy, 255-57; and Augusto Leguía, 256; as advocate of Peruvian point of view, 256-57; and the strenuous life in Peru, 257; fascinated by Inca civilization, 257; named honorary member of Geographical Society of Lima, 257; named member of Order El Sol del Peru, 257; and *Ayar-Incas*, 257-59; and *Peruvian Pharaohs*, 257-59; and "Empire of the Amazon," 257-58
—final years: and election of 1928, 259-60; death of, 261; and significance of career, 261-67; mentioned, 6, 73, 86, 87, 146, 155, 156, 170, 301 n.1

Poindexter, William A. (MP's brother), 2, 19, 105-6
Poindexter, William B. (MP's father), 1, 2-3
Poli's Theater, 207
Polson, Alex, 208
Polson Logging Company, 208
Pomerene, Atlee, 230
Populism: and influence on politics in Washington, 57; and rural credit, 148. *See also* People's party
Preparedness: debated, 136-39; Senate voting on, 138-39, 304 n.57; endorsed by Progressive party in 1916, 155; endorsed by Democratic platform in 1916, 156; mentioned, 162
Pringle, Henry, 169
Progressive era, 20, 21, 237
Progressive National Committee, 1912, 80
Progressive party: formation of, 77-82; and MP's enthusiasm for, 109; and convention of 1916, 155; and nomination of Theodore Roosevelt in 1916, 155-56
Progressive reform: in Spokane, Washington, 15; nature of in U.S. Senate, 69
Progressive Republicans: and Underwood Tariff, 87-93; and Federal Reserve Act, 93-96; and intervention in Mexico, 126; and disagreement on foreign policy issues, 126-27; and preparedness, 139; and Philippine Islands, 145; and immigration restriction, 147-48; and role in Progressive era, 165; and imperialism, 168; and Espionage Act, 175-76; and Sedition Act, 180; and war-time income tax, 184; and war profits tax, 184-85; as opponents of World War I, 185-86; and breakup of pro-

gressive coalition, 197-99; as irreconcilables, 204-5; and Esch-Cummins Transportation Act, 213-14; and railway rate discrimination, 214; and Cummins Railway bill, 216; and naval disarmament, 230; and Washington Conference, 232-35; and Hughes's disarmament proposals, 233; and Four Power pact, 233-35; and Treaty with Colombia, 236-37; and Farm bloc, 238; and regulation of business in 1920s, 239; and Mellon Tax bill of 1921, 240-41; and protective tariff, 241; and Fordney-McCumber Tariff, 242; and T. Newberry case, 245-46; and MP's career in Congress, 261-67; and foreign policy, 264-65; and party loyalty, 287 n.2, 306-7 n.25; and imperialism, 293 n.18; and foreign policy, 295 n.36; and voting on Philippine independence, 296 n.5; and voting on immigration restriction, 297 n.12; and problems of blacks and minorities, 297 n.13; and voting on war profits tax, 303 n.31; and voting on preparedness, 304 n.57; and voting on LaFollette filibuster, 304 n.57; and voting on Esch-Cummins Transportation Act, 307-8 n.31; and voting on naval appropriations, 310 n.10; and voting on Packers and Stockyards Act, 311-12 n.30; and voting on Mellon tax bill, 312 n.34; and voting on Fordney-McCumber Tariff, 313 n.40. See also Insurgent Republicans

Progressivism: influence of Populism on, in Washington, 57-58

Protective tariff: endorsed by Progressive party in 1916, 155; as issue in 1916 election, 160; and Harding administration, 237

Proto-Aryan race, 258-59

Public Information, Committee on, 174

Puget Sound: economic growth of, 7

Pujo Committee, 93, 167

Railroad Brotherhoods, 212, 213, 214

Railroad rate discrimination: and Esch-Cummins Transportation Act, 213-14

Railroad regulation: support for in Spokane, 11-12; mentioned, 165, 261, 262

Railroads: and dissatisfaction with in Washington, 8, 11

Railroad Workman's Compensation bill, 71

Ransdell, Joseph E., 130

Raymond (Wash.) Commerce Club, 129

Red Scare: origins of, 182; MP and, 206-12; and voters attitudes in Washington, 225; mentioned, 172, 211, 266

Reed, James A., 131, 203

Republican Club (Cambridge, Mass.), 209

Republican National Convention: in 1912, 77-78; in 1916, 155-56; in 1920, 221-23

Republican Party Platform, 1908: endorsed tariff revision, 36

Republican Progressive League: organized, 50

Republicans: and Senate party cohesion, 86

Robinson, Joseph T., 138, 209

Rogers, John R.: elected governor of Washington, 8

Roosevelt, Theodore: and election of 1904 in Washington, 16, 22; as leader of progressive reform, 20; as opponent of Bryan in 1896, 32; and Cannon's reelection as Speaker, 34; and protective tariff, 36; visited by MP, 52; and Osowatomie speech, 72-73; and election of 1912, 74-84; formed Progressive party in 1912, 77; and Progressive National Convention, 80; and Seattle speech, 82; carried Washington in 1912, 83; and Progressive party, 108, 112; defended G. Perkins, 115; and foreign policy views, 119; and A. T. Mahan, 121; and U.S. Navy, 122; opposed Taft's arbitration treaties, 122; and suspicions of Germany, 125; and intervention in Mexico, 125; "nationalism" of, 127; attacked Wilson's Mexican policy, 128; denounced Wilson's neutrality, 132; and ship-purchase bill, 134-35; attacked Wilson's leadership, 134; and preparedness, 139; foreign policy views compared to MP, 140, 141, 168; and interpretation of Monroe Doctrine, 140; praised MP, 141; praised Albert B. Fall, 141; ended segregation of Oriental students, 145; and MP's decision to run as a Republican in 1916, 152; endorsed Lodge for president in 1916, 155-56; as critic of Wilson's foreign policy, 156; and popularity among Washington Progressives, 157; compared to C. E. Hughes, 159; and fear of social violence, 169; and effort to lead volunteer unit to France, 172; on Wilson and bolshevism, 184; and war profits tax, 185; and Wilson's conduct of the war, 186-92; supported War Cabinet, 187; attacked Postmaster General Burleson, 190-91; and war aims, 192; and armistice negotiations, 193-94; and shift to the Right, 196; death of, 202, 216; and Treaty of Versailles, 202, 205; and treaty with Colombia, 236-37; and election of 1922 in Washington, 253; and influence on MP's career, 264; and conservative trend after 1917, 266; career of, 290 n.42; mentioned, 108, 188, 189, 223

Roosevelt corollary: influence on MP, 124
Root, Elihu: on Cannon's re-election as Speaker, 34; and Lawrence strike, 67; and ship-purchase bill, 133-34; and foreign policy views, 152; and Washington Conference, 230; mentioned, 68, 222
Rowell, Chester, 110, 115
Russia, 206, 207
Russian Bolshevists, 209
Russian revolution, 169, 177, 265
Rutter, Isabel Page: married Robert Lewis Rutter, 9
Rutter, Robert Lewis: career of, 9-10; member of Spokane Businessmen's Bimetallic Club for Bryan, 11; and MP's conversion to Republican party, 11; as promoter of MP's law practice, 16; and 150,000 Club, 24; and MP's campaign for House, 26; and election of 1910, 50; opposed farm-labor antitrust exemption, 98-99; opposed Federal Farm Loan Act, 149; and election of 1916, 150, 157

San Francisco school board, 145
Saturday Review of Literature, 259
Seattle Argus: supported MP in 1922, 251
Seattle Central Labor Council: and farm-labor antitrust exemption, 98; and general strike, 180; as part of international Bolshevist conspiracy, 181; mentioned, 182, 207
Seattle Chamber of Commerce, 215
Seattle general strike: discussed, 206-8; and voter attitudes in Washington, 225; mentioned, 211
Seattle Post-Intelligencer: and MP's bill to develop Alaska, 104; praised MP on Alaska Railroad bill, 104; and per-

sonal attack on MP, 105-8; and Panama Canal tolls exemption, 129; attacked MP, 154, 160-61; charged MP had deserted progressivism, 250; and results of election of 1922, 253; mentioned, 162, 251

Seattle Times: supported MP for reelection in 1922, 251

Seattle Union-Record: and MP's 1920 presidential campaign, 220, 221; charged MP betrayed progressive citizens, 250; supported J. A. Duncan in 1922 election, 252; and results of election of 1922, 253; mentioned, 251

Sedition Act, 178-80, 190, 191

Selective Service Act, 173

Shafroth, John F., 157

Sherman, Lawrence Y., 185, 204

Sherman Anti-Trust Act, 45-46, 97

Shipp, Thomas R., 73

Ship-purchase bill: discussed, 132-35; mentioned, 137, 140

Short, William M., 250

Siracusa, Joseph M., 293 n.18, 295 n.36

16th Amendment (income tax), 91

Slater, L. Roy: on weakness of Progressive party, 113; and election of 1916, 157, 158; mentioned, 218

Smith, Edward, 147

Smoot, Reed, 195

Social Darwinism: and influence on MP, 120, 146, 263; and foreign policy views of MP, 140; and MP's views of League of Nations, 201; mentioned, 265

South Dakota primary election of 1920, 220-21, 223

Spokane (Washington): early history, 9; and MP's move to, 9; and economic interests of, 215

Spokane and Eastern Trust Co.: and R. L. Rutter, 9; hired MP's legal services, 16; opposed Federal Farm Loan Act, 149

Spokane Businessmen's Bimetallic Club for Bryan, 11

Spokane Chamber of Commerce, 23, 98

Spokane Fruit Growers Company, 98

Spokane 150,000 Club, 23

Spokane Poindexter Club, 1916, 159

Spokane Spokesman-Review: and MP's reception in Spokane in 1916, 158; and results of primary election of 1916, 161; supported MP for reelection in 1922, 251; attacked C. C. Dill's war record, 252

Standard Oil Company, 239

Sterling, Thomas, 148, 237, 266

Stone, William J., 190

Sullivan, Mark, 55, 219

Tacna-Arica question, 255-56

Tacoma Chamber of Commerce, 129

Taft, William A.: supported Cannon's reelection as Speaker, 34; favored tariff reduction, 36, 37; and Payne-Aldrich Tariff, 41; and Insurgent Republicans, 42-43; and friendship with N. Aldrich, 43; and speech in Winona, Minnesota, 43; and Ballinger-Pinchot controversy, 43-44; and dislike for MP, 49; and election of 1910 in Washington, 50-56; criticized Roosevelt for receiving MP, 52; endorsed by Washington Republican Convention, 53; and efforts to defeat MP in election, 54; rebuked by results of election of 1910, 56; and Canadian reciprocity, 61-62; and election of 1912, 74-83; and election results in Washington in 1912, 83; and arbitration, 122, 123; vetoed immigration bill, 145; compared to C. E. Hughes, 159; and voting patterns in Washington, 164; criticized MP's position on Treaty of Versailles, 203; and attitude toward MP, 223;

mentioned, 72, 73, 154, 158
Taft Republicans: agreed with MP on foreign policy, 152; and hatred for MP, 154; supported MP in 1916 election, 162, mentioned, 170
Taft's Arbitration Treaties: with France and Great Britain, 122-23
Tampico, Mexico, 125, 128, 142
Tariff: Payne-Aldrich Tariff, 36-42; see Canadian reciprocity, 61-66; Underwood Tariff, 87-88, 91-93; Fordney-McCumber Tariff, 241-44
Tariff reform: and Insurgent Republicans, 66
Thelen, David P., 288 n.8
Third International, 206
Thomas, Charles S., 143
Todd, William H., 218, 248-49, 250
Townsend, Charles E., 149-266
Turner, George: candidate for governor in 1904, 22; and voting patterns in Washington, 56; and election of 1916, 162-64

Underwood, Oscar W., 78, 231
Underwood Tariff: discussed, 87-93; voting on, compared to Payne-Aldrich Tariff, 88; and election of 1916 in Washington, 159; mentioned, 129, 165, 242
Union of Russian Workers, 211
United Mine Workers, 209

Vardaman, James K., 130, 138
Veracruz, Mexico, 125, 127, 128
Versailles, Treaty of: discussed, 200-206; voting on, 205, 305 n.9; related by MP to bolshevism, 206
Villa, Pancho, 143

Wadsworth, James W., Jr., 195
Walker, George H., 222
Walker, Sam, 218
Walla Walla Union, 150
War Cabinet, 187

War Finance Corporation, 245
War of the Pacific, 256
War profits tax: discussed, 184-85; voting of progressive Republicans on, 303 n.31
War Revenue Act, 184
Washington (State): and agricultural depression of 1920s, 238
Washington Conference: discussed, 230-35; mentioned, 226, 237
Washington Manufacturing Company, 64
Washington State Federation of Labor, 225, 250
Washington State Grange: supported reform measures, 22; on parcel post issue, 28, 70; and Canadian reciprocity, 65; and election of 1920, 225; mentioned, 261
Washington State Progressive Party, 80
Washington State Republican Convention: in 1912, 76; in 1920, 221
Washington State Republican Executive Committee, 157
Watson, James E., 222
Watson, Tom, 234
Weaver, James B., 8
Weeks, John W., 155
Western hemisphere, 192
White, William Allen: as opponent of William Jennings Bryan in 1896, 32; and enthusiasm for Progressive party, 109; and Roosevelt's behavior in 1916, 156
"White" race, 258-59
William Sumner Silk Importers Company, 63
Wilson (Woodrow) Administration: and development of Alaska, 103; and ship-purchase bill, 135; and Gentlemen's Agreement, 147; accused of being pro-German, 183, 189; and Mooney case, 208; charged by MP with sympathy for bolshe-

vism, 208-9; attacked by MP as lenient with radicals, 219; and Treaty with Colombia, 235; and farm relief, 245
Wilson, John L., 50, 54, 103
Wilson, Rufus Rockwell, 50
Wilson, Woodrow: opposed Bryan in 1896, 32; and election of 1912, 78; and voting patterns in Washington in 1912, 83; elected president, 84; and Underwood Tariff, 87, 92; praised MP's vote for Underwood Tariff, 93; and Federal Reserve Act, 93-96; praised by MP, 96; and Federal Trade Commission bill, 97; and policy toward Huertan government, 125; and intervention in Mexico, 125-27; accepted mediation of American withdrawal from Mexico, 127; and Panama Canal tolls, 128-31; and neutrality in World War I, 132; and sinking of *Lusitania*, 135; and preparedness, 137; Mexican policy attacked by MP, 142-43; and Philippine Islands, 143; vetoed immigration bills, 145, 148; and Democratic platform in 1916, 156; and popularity in Washington, 157, 159; and voting patterns in Washington in 1916, 163; and peace objectives, 170; and Everett, Washington, incident, 176; and Thomas Mooney case, 181, 183; conduct of the war attacked by MP, 183-84; accused of weakness by MP, 187; criticized for ignoring Senate by MP, 188; and conduct of the war, 189-92; and armistice negotiations, 193-94; called for election of Democratic Congress in 1918, 194-95; and Treaty of Versailles, 200-206; and peace program, 200; and meeting with congressmen on Treaty of Versailles, 203; and concessions to critics of League of Nations, 204; and MP's resolution on leniency with radicals, 210; vetoed Emergency Agricultural Tariff bill, 241; vetoed bill for farm relief, 245; and voting patterns in Washington in 1922, 253; and the Gore resolution, 295 n.36; mentioned, 154, 155, 161, 171, 172, 174, 190, 207, 262, 306 n.17

Winona, Minnesota: Taft speech at, 43

Woman suffrage, 71, 96

Wood, Gen. Leonard, 155, 217, 218, 219, 221

Woods, Rufus: supported MP for House, 26; and election of 1910, 50; and Wenatchee (Wash.) postmastership, 51; and MP's presidential ambitions, 116-17; and MP's prospects for reelection in 1922, 248; defended MP, 249; mentioned, 150

Works, John D.: and the Progressive party, 78, 110; voting record on Underwood Tariff, 88; criticized Federal Reserve Act, 95; and preparedness, 137; on immigration restriction, 148; and Hughes's 1916 campaign in California, 158

World War I: and MP's views on intervention, 142; and breakup of progressive coalition, 197-99; mentioned, 132, 169, 237

"Yellow Peril," 146